WITH WALKER PERCY AT THE TUPPERWARE PARTY

Other titles of interest from St. Augustine's Press

Marion Montgomery, *Romancing Reality:* Homo Viator *and the Scandal Called Beauty*

Marion Montgomery, *Making: The Proper Habit of Our Being*

John Poinsot, *Tractatus de Signis: The Semiotic of John Poinsot*

John Deely, *The Impact on Philosophy of Semiotics*

Josef Pieper, *In Tune with the World: A Theory of Festivity*

Josef Pieper, *Happiness and Contemplation*

Josef Pieper, *The Silence of Goethe*

C.S. Lewis, *The Latin Letters of C.S. Lewis*

René Girard, *A Theater of Envy: William Shakespeare*

Edward Feser: *The Last Superstition: A Refutation of the New Atheism*

Roger Scruton, *On Hunting*

Roger Scruton, *An Intelligent Person's Guide to Modern Culture*

Roger Scruton, *The Meaning of Conservatism*

Otto Bird and Katharine Bird, *From Witchery to Sanctity: The Religious Vicissitudes of the Hawthornes*

Peter Kreeft, *The Philosophy of Jesus*

Peter Kreeft, *Jesus-Shock*

James V. Schall, *The Regensburg Lecture*

Seth Benardete, *Achilles and Hector: The Homeric Hero*

Seth Benardete, *Sacred Transgressions: A Reading of Sophocles'* Antigone

Friedrich Nietzsche, *On the Future of Our Educational Institutions*

Friedrich Nietzsche, *Prefaces to Unwritten Works*

Jacques Maritain, *Natural Law: Reflections on Theory and Practice*

Fulvio di Blasi, *God and the Natural Law*

Peter Augustine Lawler, *Homeless and at Home in America*

Gabriel Marcel, *The Mystery of Being* (in two volumes)

Gabriel Marcel, *Man against Mass Society*

Leszek Kolakowski, *My Correct Views on Everything*

John Paul II, *The John Paul II LifeGuide*™

St. Augustine, *The St. Augustine LifeGuide*™

Dietrich von Hildebrand, *The Heart: An Analysis of Human and Divine Affectivity*

Ralph McInerny, *Some Catholic Writers*

Michael Davis, *Wonderlust: Ruminations on Liberal Education*

WITH WALKER PERCY AT THE TUPPERWARE PARTY

In Company with Flannery O'Connor, T. S. Eliot, and Others

Marion Montgomery

ST. AUGUSTINE'S PRESS
South Bend, Indiana
2009

Manufactured in the United States of America.

1 2 3 4 5 15 14 13 12 11 10 09

Library of Congress Cataloging in Publication Data
Montgomery, Marion.
With Walker Percy at the tupperware party: in company with Flannery O'Connor, T.S. Eliot, and others / Marion Montgomery.
p. cm.
ISBN-13: 978-1-58731-928-0 (hardbound: alk. paper)
ISBN-10: 1-58731-928-4 (hardbound: alk. paper)
1. Percy, Walker, 1916-1990 – Criticism and interpretation. 2. Percy, Walker, 1916–1990 – Philosophy. 3. O'Connor, Flannery – Criticism and interpretation. 4. Eliot, T. S. (Thomas Stearns), 1888-1965 – Criticism and interpretation. 5. Christianity and literature – Southern States – History – 20th century. 6. Southern States – Intellectual life – 1865– 7. Philosophy in literature. 8. Christian ethics in literature. 9. Intersubjectivity in literature. I. Title.

PS3566.E6912Z785 2008
813'.54 – dc20 2007040607

∞ The paper used in this publication meets the minimum requirements of the American National Standard for Information Sciences – Permanence of Paper for Printed Materials, ANSI Z39.48-1984.

St. Augustine's Press
www.staugustine.net

This book is for a Diaspora of the Spiritually Restless, at the beginning of the new millennium.

– Ascension 2000

“Catholic or Protestant, the believing writer is equally unhappy. He feels like Lancelot in search of the Holy Grail who finds himself at the end of his quest at a Tupperware party.”

– Walker Percy, “How to be an American Novelist in Spite of Being Southern and Catholic,” 1984

“When Rome was devastated as a result of the invasion of the Goths under the leadership of Aleric, the worshippers of the many false gods, whom we are accustomed to call pagan, began, in their attempt to blame this devastation on the Christian religion, to blaspheme the true God with more bitterness and sharpness than usual. Wherefore, fired with a zeal for God’s house, I determined to write my book, *The City of god,* against their blasphemies and errors.”

– St. Augustine, *Retractions* 2.43.2

Introduction

Flannery O'Connor, in her "Some Aspects of the Grotesque in Southern Fiction," to an audience at Wesleyan College for Women in Macon, Georgia (Fall of 1960), speaks of herself as a Southern writer, remarking that "The presence alone of Faulkner in our midst makes a great difference in what the writer can and cannot permit himself to do. Nobody wants his mule and wagon stalled on the same track the Dixie Limited is roaring down." It is a remark made two years before Walker Percy published his *The Moviegoer*. Twenty-five years later Percy delivers to a Louisiana audience in Lafayette his own "How to be an American Novelist in Spite of Being Southern and Catholic," addressing those personal circumstances to him as writer, his being Southern and Catholic, which he shared with Flannery O'Connor. One might, I think, argue that both Percy's and O'Connor's mule and wagon – their own fictions – do not so much stall on the tracks as much as they are pushed across them, moved beyond that seemingly inevitable collision, through a locomotion supplied only in part by their limited sharing of a "Southernness" with Faulkner. More important to Percy's and O'Connor's added power are their Catholic commitments. Certainly both believed so.

They differ from Faulkner, then, in a commitment to formal, orthodox Romanism, while nevertheless finding themselves in the midst of a dominantly Protestant South, a tensional point of importance to their art. But Flannery O'Connor, born Roman Catholic – cradle Catholic, as it is said – is from the beginning more comfortable in her position than Percy could be. Indeed, the position which she cultivates, with the help of St. Thomas Aquinas, allows her a perspective highly sympathetic to the evangelical tendency in Southern Protestantism, the effect of which in the history of Southern religion has been that multitude of "Churches," splintered and splintering, for which the South is notorious in the eyes of a secular society. It will lead O'Connor to observe that, while the South is not Christ-centered it is very deeply Christ-haunted, a remark Percy summons on several occasions to his own concerns with his "Southernness." That haunted disquiet she sees all about her is sympathetic fuel to the fire of her own art. What was at first overlooked by her baffled critics, many of them at first (and still by some of them), is her abiding sympathy for the Christ-haunted. Old Tarwater is her fierce version of Elder Zosima – to borrow a parallel from Dostoevsky's *Brothers Karamazov*. (And Dostoevsky is, in respect to man as Christ-haunted, very much a "Southern" writer, in both O'Connor's and Percy's readings of that prophetic Russian.)

Even O'Connor's Haze Motes, who founds his Church of Christ without Christ, is her hero, and she will have high hopes for her Misfit in "A Good Man is Hard to Find" as potential prophet. What appeals to her in the Southerner as Christ-haunted is his intuitive reaction to those invasive attempts by Modernist philosophy and religion to exorcise Christ from our spiritual concern in order that a new orthodoxy called Modernism may make the well-adjusted citizen better suited to a civil order through his first denying the transcendent. (I have explored this concept of Modernism in "Modern, Modernism, and Modernist," *The Truth of Things,* 1999.) But given our intuitive nature, Modernism must find a substitute god, and that god in our century has been the state, served by pseudo-sciences as a substitute for scholastic philosophy. We note, then, that both Percy and O'Connor pay tribute to Thomas Aquinas, even as both make excoriating critiques of sociology as a superadded science to biology, rationalized into a compound science through psychology. It is a science which F. O. Wilson proposes as the only acceptable gospel to Modernist orthodoxy, "Sociobiology." In their common concern counter to Modernism, then, one finds Dostoevsky more companionable to Percy and O'Connor than Tolstoy, a point worth suggesting, given their awareness of that Dixie Limited Faulkner, whose range and sweep bears comparison to Tolstoy's. (Napoleon's invasion of Russia bears parallels to the Yankee invasion of the South in their work.)

Not, of course, that there is not also a certain Dostoevskian dimension in Faulkner. It is evident if we counterpose *War and Peace* to *Absalom, Absalom!* In that greatest of Faulkner's novels, Faulkner is more Dostoevskian. Even so, Miss O'Connor's figure of the train on what for Faulkner is largely a linear track through history is apt to a point: Faulkner himself intends to come to terms with history, with "tradition" in its descent into a secularization under the impact of Modernism. But he cannot come to any comfort through a faith in history only. Nor can he, as O'Connor and Percy do, find comfort in *being* as transcendently rescued by the Incarnation. He will engage Christian themes metaphorically along the way, and even attempt – almost half-heartedly – a "fable," an allegory, dependent upon the Crucifixion as James Joyce's *Ulysses* is dependent upon the *Odyssey*. But that can be for Faulkner (as finally for Joyce) only a historical dependence through literary tradition, or a literary dependence within historical closures. With a difference here of course: Faulkner in his *Fable* appears to be in quest of poetic correspondences through allegory. Joyce, with a deeper sense of myth, allows Homeric myth to shadow his structure, whereby that structure – as shadowly formed – helps make convincingly incarnated the actualities of persons in a place, Irishmen in Dublin, as his fictional agents. Faulkner cannot manage the same for his *A Fable*. He will then be more persuasive in his Joe Christmas of *Light in August* than in his corporal and twelve disciples in the World War I trenches of France.

And so Percy and O'Connor differ in a fundamental way from Faulkner, though all are at one level very Southern writers. But as important to our present concerns, these two also differ from each other as well. If O'Connor is "cradle-Catholic," Percy is a late convert. That imposes a level of spectacle (history) to his presence to us as a person. He is not indifferent to the final things – the final possibility of salvation – but the labor of his concern as person is distinctive from O'Connor's certainty. There is a signal here of a difference, in that for Percy a comfort in his faith seems always most difficult for him. Indeed, the fascinating Modernist world draws him in ways O'Connor is not drawn. At times his personal risk seems even problematic to him, his seemingly late devotion to the Incarnation in contrast to O'Connor's long comfortableness. In this respect, Percy as person appears at times suspended between the pull to a companionship with Flannery O'Connor, on the one hand, and to his long-time skeptical friend Shelby Foote on the other. At least we may thus pose this tension in him metaphorically. Early in their correspondence, Foote reacts to this counter attraction of Flannery O'Connor to Percy, himself given to a skepticism which is more comfortably accommodated for him by Stoicism. He seems irritated that his friend Percy has gone running off to Rome, seeming to have abandoned a dependable Stoicism under the influence of that brash upstart from Milledgeville, Georgia, Flannery O'Connor. In those letters between Percy and Foote, one will find an excoriating dismissal of O'Connor as writer, though subsequent letters suggest that at the point of his dismissal of her, Foote had not actually read her.

My own suggestion, which we are about to explore, is that Walker Percy is very much inclined to waver intellectually, though he desires not to do so. And that wavering I suggest has a significant cause in his initial education, in his early commitment to science. Science seemed at first a dependable rescue from uncertainty, especially as it might be buttressed by a "Southern" Stoicism whose primary justification for Percy is Marcus Aurelius. Aurelius as Stoic appeals to the aristocratic intellect, whether that intellect is like Thomas Jefferson's or Robert E. Lee's. Stoicism also allows a certain validity as well, out of Epicurius, to the pursuit of the "good things" of this world. Along that way, Percy will engage playfully and satirically in his essays as well as in his novels some of those "good things," especially our age's growing obsession with sex, a primary theme in his *Lost in the Cosmos*. (Among those good things valued is that favorite Southern potable Percy celebrates in an essay, "Bourbon.") In *Lost in the Cosmos,* written in the middle of his literary life, his playful concern is that the orientation of sex to community's fabric has long since been rejected by Modernist gnosticism. The effects on the *hoi polloi* prove sordid grist for Percy's artistic mill, his very playfulness making the sordid entertaining as witty satire.

From an initial inclination as a "Southern" Stoical scientist, then, Percy subsequently becomes fascinated with European Existentialism, which like the old Stoicism develops in disparate schools, as diverse as those of Jean-Paul Sartre and Gabriel Marcel. The flood of arguments from European intellectuals lost in the cosmos fascinates Percy, as if promising him an intellectual reorienting to his own world, he having escaped the peril of tuberculosis but not yet escaped the perils of intellectual Cartesian entrapment as a resident of the ambiguous South. His initial interest in this recent continental thought evolves for him, he tells us, out of Søren Kierkegaard. But he also reads Thomas Aquinas as well, and will often allude to Aquinas in relation to that continental thought, though perhaps not always sufficiently recognizing a radical antipathy to Thomas in some of them.

Out of this amalgam of ideas, out of his reading as he is recuperating and turning South towards home, he concentrates his attention upon the "self," the Modernist term supplanting "soul" out of the amalgamated thought of 19th-century Phenomenology and Psychology. Percy pursues the difficulties of the self in an increasingly unsettling cosmos which seems to resist science's theories as sufficiently dominant over the cosmos itself. Here, in this context, he also discovers Charles Peirce and settles upon Peirce's argument for the "Delta" factor as the key he has needed to unlock a metaphysics out of science, one suited to the dilemma of the "self" trapped in the problematic cosmos. He is drawn to Peirce intellectually by a recognition in himself of the circumstances to his own intellect that make him very much a child of Modernist dislocations from Thomistic metaphysics, a dislocation inherited by the intellectual community out of Occam through Descartes and Locke and Kant, down to the Phenomenologists and the Existentialists. And he will even attempt to reconcile Peirce and Aquinas. This is a tendency deep in his own intellectual actions which will make a distinction necessary between Percy as Catholic and O'Connor as Catholic. We must observe as well that he is himself acutely aware of this intrusive "historical" dimension upon his own speculative thought about man's nature, engaged under the rubric of *semiotics*. That is the burden of his essay, not long before his death, "The Fateful Rift: The San Andreas Fault in the Modern Mind" (1989). His last attempt at a reconciliation of his own Modernism and Roman Orthodoxy comes in the year of his death (1990), a setting aside of uncertainty as best he may in answering that old and persistent question put to him: "Why Are You a Catholic?"

Our concern in the pages ahead is with Percy's uncertainty in this tensional ground between Modernist science and Christian orthodoxy, becoming increasingly and disturbingly ideological ground – or rather ungrounding – in an age of theory. For theory comes to triumph over orthodox metaphysics under the growing authority of science as superseding philosophy no less than theology. The orthodoxy of Thomistic realism must have seemed to Percy at first a forlorn answer to any rescue of those "good things" of life, though he was much drawn by that realism in reading Thomas. How difficult to rescue intellect through its recovery of attention to the holiness of the ordinary, given the pervasively gluttonous consumption of the world's body encouraged by technologies out of science. The general presumption of Modernism that man is but a socio-biological entity might perhaps leave one with a lonely survival for a time through Stoicism. Percy will, at last, nevertheless declare emphatically beyond Stoical resignation the "Holiness of the Ordinary," we know. Meanwhile, before that late witness, he will with an irony somewhat sustained by Stoicism turn attention particularly to one of those tensional poles holding the intellectual self in its suspension over the abyss opened within it by Cartesian thought. He is amused, if somewhat disturbingly so, by the spectacles of "looniness" let loose by consumer appetite. These tensional poles to the self – a drawing toward loony excess against an intuitively recognized holiness of things not yet exorcised from consciousness – provide a context for dramatic actions to be explored as diagnostic novelist. And that circumstance to the dislocated self, perhaps the last surviving universal commonness to selves, will also supply spectacles suited to such speculative occasions as his "Last Self-Help Book."

We shall, then, take as a primary center for thematic speculation Percy's popular tour de force, *Lost in the Cosmos: The Last Self-Help Book* (1983), returning to that work in counterpointing it by observations about his other work and the work of others. *Lost in the Cosmos* is especially well-suited to our own concerns in that it is ambiguous in form – in part a philosophical questioning, in part a fictional exposition, often with shameless exaggerations of fictional characters he puts in absurd circumstances. Underlying always: Percy's fundamental questions about the nature of man. Of special interest to us, those questions about human nature seem often to turn specific, turning back upon Walker Percy himself, for whom – though not the last of his attempts – this work is rather surely a "self-help" engagement of signs to Percy himself. Before we engage this gift to us of this last self-help work which presumes its reader lost and disoriented, first we will use a speculative strategy borrowed from *Lost in the Cosmos*, a juxtaposing of two passages raising fundamental questions.

The first is from a fiction by Faulkner, the second from Percy. From them rises the tensional question he puts to himself directly in assays of his position, in talks and essays but more persuasively by the indirection of his fiction. What is the relation between one's being a Southerner and a Catholic when drawn into the larger "American" arena? He reminds us on more than one occasion of his early intellectual inclinations to accommodate his Southernness, a Southernness which seems inescapable, through the influence of Marcus Aurelius. It would be natural enough, given his cultural origins, to see that dignified figure out of an old Pagan world antecedent to Western Christendom as a continuing influence upon Christian history, from King Richard down to Robert E. Lee. But as Faulkner's expatriate to the American East, Quentin Compson, would suggest, it would not have been a likely climate for reflection to those New York "Yankees" among whom Percy found himself during his internship. (Quentin was perhaps more fortunate, having a Canadian interlocutor, to whom he insists that he, Quentin, doesn't "hate the South." He could be more open with a Canadian than with a Yankee interlocutor.)

The quiet, almost secret support of Marcus Aurelius on Percy's New York pilgrimage came to him very probably through the earlier scholarly presence to Percy of his Uncle Will, a considerable intellectual influence on his Mississippi adolescence. This would make that hidden support even doubly appealing, given his affectionate regard for his kinsman mentor and surrogate father. Like Quentin Compson in exile at Harvard, remembering the South that he insistently doesn't hate, Percy might well in his New York residency look homeward, summoning memories of Uncle Will from an uneasy distance. He might even thus be somewhat reassured by a Stoical detachment, despite any sense he might already have of a spiritual inadequacy of Stoicism. That weakness will begin to be inescapable for him subsequently, once he begins to put it to the test by the Christian philosophy of St. Thomas. Percy puts those weaknesses before us as he begins his slow recovery in his "Stoicism in the South" in 1956, an act of intellectual exorcism attempted while deporting himself with piety toward Uncle Will's species of "Southern" intellectualism.

Stoicism in its purer classical form, as found in the *Meditations* of Aurelius, is intellectually attractive, especially to a "self" coming to itself in a trying age – at a point when intellect is in retreat from social and political responsibilities associated with the Southern milieu. Percy's generation of intellectuals, especially those not handicapped by "Southernness," seemed to find acceptable refuge through scientific theory feeding appetitive desire. But that was not an easy circumstance to an intellectual such as Percy, though he is by no means inclined to asceticism. He feels a responsibility wider than to himself, an inclination to charity toward a world in which he finds himself almost confounded by this age which is increasingly skeptical of the validity of *caritas*. An age, indeed, growing increasingly cynical almost as a necessity if it is to justify the selfishness of the "self." After World War II, he finds himself at last forced home from the liberated North by illness and denied a sense of "place" in that "foreign" community of service he had known in his internship at Bellevue in New York; those acts of charity through science which he might have made at Cook County Hospital seem now futile. But how may he recover *place* in a new strange world, his own South? It is a world made more strange by his having sojourned out of it. The "South" had been his native land, but now he has been forced to return because of a microscopic creature, the *tubercle bacillus*, and with a baggage of thought erosive to any possible comfort. That small creature, as he must have been aware, had for over a hundred years been a steady literary presence, seemingly even a cause of great works of art – operas, novels, poems in Russian, German, French, English, and Italian. A haunting sign in his thought itself, challenging reconciliation.

In such uncertain circumstances, heroism is required at a personal level at least. It is in that quiet, personal, withdrawn disciple of courage, the Roman Emperor Aurelius, that one might find sustaining encouragement to a deportment which, though steeped in pathos, may yet allow the courage of personal endurance – an endurance not likely to be either known or appreciated beyond a private self-knowledge, the self-appreciation of the enduring self. History reveals, and especially the more local "Southern" history, a Stoicism which allows intellectual endurance through hard social and political times – but only as a lonely endurance of history. Remember Robert E. Lee. Remember also William

Alexander Percy, "Uncle Will." Such remembrances are important as one attempts to deal with current local confusions. In that small parenthesis of history between the end of World War II and the Vietnam War, and more especially as that history must be addressed within the parentheses of geography called the "American South," Percy sees causes antipathetic to each other, increasingly magnified in spectacular eruptions. These causes are championed by ambiguous actions in an ebb and flow of social and political washes that are both philosophically and theologically confused. A confusion of causes could but make very problematic anyone's devotions to any cause, especially to a problematic "Southern Cause." That was a vague cause, concerning which one might have grown up holding blind sympathy bred of cultural and historical traditions that more and more seemed untenable.

Percy's homecoming, his slow recuperation of body and of mind, corresponds to very troubling eruptions in that home country, his South. And so the virtue of endurance requires a rescue beyond superficial appeals to "traditions," especially when those appeals rest in even more superficial and so confused supports out of "history" in an untenable selectivity. That history, alas, increasingly seemed to reach back and largely stop at Appomattox in the spring of 1865. Who now could remember, beyond Lee, a King Richard or a Thomas More, let alone Marcus Aurelius? Whatever one might sense as valid in that old tradition was being denigrated by violent, sometimes comic, spectacle, regardless of any hidden depths in that tradition. One signpost pointing nowhere: those Confederate battle flags pasted on bumpers by rowdy elements of the local community. These social elements seemed largely ignorant of the history of itself as a people, not only ignorant of that history before 1865 but as well of the complexities of history between 1865 and 1954, events still existing as residual presences in the moment's chaos in a local spirit though unrecognized, like that hidden bacillus discovered in his blood in New York City. Shibboleths as signposts in the desert seemed increasingly unrelated to political and social desires for a just order based in reality – an order conforming to the truth of things, including history's truths. For an intellectual at once concerned for valid elements of that tradition and witnessing their rapid exclusions in rejections of *all* that tradition, a trying time. Passionate contentions for vague justice and retribution in the 1960s, lacking the order of reason itself, made it even more necessary to the person who might find himself alienated from causes, politically left or right. It might prove precisely those Stoic virtues of courage, perseverance, endurance that enabled survival short of suicide. But that there were indeed valid virtues to be found in the old tradition, in a traditional Southern Stoicism, seemed only to isolate one increasingly in a dependence on merely personal virtue. And that personal practice could only the more isolate the enduring self. Uncle Will, the Last Gentleman no doubt, stood a communicant through memory. But he was now himself dead.

The virtues one inherits from Uncle Will and from Lee and from Aurelius justify the "self" to itself perhaps, but they do so through what intellect must at last confess a rather arbitrary commitment to *noblesse oblige*, the responsibility of the aristocrat, whether social or intellectual aristocrat. One is drawn to honor that public obligation, and if one's actions in that responsibility are those of a novelist, he might well see encouragement in Faulkner. Faulkner dramatizes such responsibility in his Stoic heroes. It is a deportment Quentin Compson wonders about in his father. It is conspicuous in the lawyer Gavin Stevens – perhaps Faulkner's "last gentleman." But the arbitrariness of the position, its dependence upon personal character as isolated from the *body* of a viable community, casts a shadow of pathos across such deportment. Quentin can't survive it, can't endure it, the sacrifice of endurance alone insufficient to his sensitive intellect. And so he at last kills himself in "Yankee" country. "Southern Stoicism," though commanding a sympathetic allegiance in the midst of social and political turmoil, seems only to lend itself to the sadness of an ultimate defeat of the increasingly isolated "self." That becomes a theme Percy will explore in his *The Last Gentleman*, with a pathos counterpointed by its comic version in *Lost in the Cosmos*.

The final discovery of arbitrariness in the old classical deportment of the Stoic to the world will, to the acute intellect, reveal itself as disappointingly arbitrary. And it will be especially disappointing if examined for its validity from the perspective of Thomistic metaphysics – a position informing the Christian Church with which Percy associates himself. Perhaps with a sadness, since that means he must distance himself from the Uncle Will he remembers with love. There will appear in Percy a similar deference to Faulkner, but with a recognition as well that for all Faulkner's power as artist, there can result only the pathos of loss, despite the Stoical defenses made so appealing by such an artist of humor and wit as Faulkner, or Uncle Will. Sadness, no doubt, for one need not deny that a Stoic devotion may produce in the advocate himself, given points of severe circumstantial stress, a mode whereby he may maintain a private honor in serving what he believes to be the common good, a good which his surrounding community seems to have abandoned.

If that tubercle bacillus, seemingly a curse but in the course of Percy's life increasingly accepted by him as a gift of grace, had turned him to art and away from medicine, a further complication to that turning also proved inescapable. The turning could but exacerbate the seeming conflict between his sympathetic inclinations to the "South" and antipathies to a species of his own "Southernness" consequent upon his commitment to Rome. It is the Emperor Aurelius as "Southerner" whom he admires, but we must examine that inclination from the position of Christian orthodoxy. We shall attempt to do so from a more severe Thomistic perspective than perhaps Percy himself made. Thus we turn to the passage from Aurelius, quoted sympathetically by Percy in his essay on Southern Stoicism. The words reveal an intellectual position which leaves the Stoic as hero on a very lonely pinnacle, like that of Lee as defeated warrior, isolated as President of Washington College after April 1865. Aurelius's advice might be helpful, but only for the moment: "Every moment think steadily, as a Roman and a man, to do what thou hast in hand with perfect and simple dignity, and a feeling of affection, and freedom and justice." It is a doctrine evident in the character of Percy's hero Robert E. Lee. And Donald Davidson will capture that deportment of Lee's character in a moving poem, "Lee in the Mountains." Davidson's poem catches the poignant moment in which Stoicism reveals its committed hero maintaining honor even in defeat. Whether it is an honor sufficient to recover community as a viable presence, supporting the dignity of man under the pressures of unfolding history after 1865, becomes the issue. It will leave a somewhat isolated Uncle Will, for instance, perhaps honored locally, yet leaving him as well isolated within his local circumstances, isolated from the body of community.

The tensional grounds intellectually engaged, as Percy engages them, contribute significantly to the tensional drama of his fiction. It is a drama especially evident in his treatment of Will Barrett as Will struggles to understand his father's Stoicism. The theme is first engaged by Percy in *The Last Gentleman* and then in *The Second Coming*. But we discover that it is also tensionally present in Percy's essays, suggesting a personal dilemma, from which tension he is relieved at times by a witty, satirical manner underlining outrageous actions of his contemporaries who seem hardly to be recovered to sanity from "looniness." For the Stoical deportment of *noblesse oblige* is very far gone from Percy's South. It is his circumstance in the present moment of history as a private person, who by his calling as novelist finds himself forced upon a public stage. His dilemma must first be accepted as a personal one, though all about him is evidence of its being all too common in the post-World War II South. As person he is on his way nevertheless. He is *homo viator*. And so he assumes quite deliberately the role of diagnostic novelist, a role which allows him a certain detachment by his "scientific" perspective, a modern means to that old detachment of the Stoic Aurelius.

As undeniably a Southern writer, however, and having to deal steadily with "Southern" particularities (often hilariously counterpointed by "Yankee" or "California" absurdities), he remains acutely aware of the presence of that Dixie Limited, William Faulkner as Southern writer, as Flannery O'Connor dubbed him.. Percy recognizes that the world available to Faulkner, out of his circumstances and his own "private" inclinations, is quite different from his own. Indeed, the circumstances to any "Southern" writer, given that brief interval between Faulkner's day and Percy's, must deal with the current history of the South as in rapid change. Or is it only that his perspective compared to Faulkner's differs? Several times Percy will remind us that he himself was born in a new house on a new golf course in Birmingham, Alabama, a personal circumstance introduced dramatically into *The Last Gentleman*. Will Barrett is old family Mississippian, put in the position of attempting to accommodate to his condition as a deracinated Southerner who encounters other "expatriates" in New York. He follows these rambling "Southerners" South into Alabama, thence to Mississippi, and then on to New Mexico. We might, given Will's sense of dislocation, be reminded of Faulkner's Gavin Stevens as we hear Will remember his own father in a Mississippi moment, though from Will's judgment his father took too easy an exit with a shotgun – an exit Gavin Stevens as Southern Stoic will not accept, though Quentin Compson as failed Stoic in Connecticut takes that way.

If Will in *The Last Gentleman* feels denied the comfort of history's support, in the light of his father's defeat, his is a feeling familiar to Percy in a very personal way. Or such is our speculative suggestion. Certainly Percy's family history doesn't seem a sure support to his art, as it could be for Faulkner's. And therefore not history but science becomes art's demeanor. But is that a choice or a necessity? Or is it at last but a complex working out in him of the gifts of grace? As we read his essays and interviews, we find that it will seem to him first one then the other, this conflict between history and science. But there also continues in such tensional fermentation of the spirit what he will at last accept as a presence of grace to him. Not Doctor Percy, after his New York training in science, nor a resident Stoic Southerner responding to the local community as did Uncle Will in historical circumstances that establish William Alexander Percy on a Mississippi plantation. But a Roman Southerner closer to Thomas More.

There is a once famous, but now little valued, passage in Faulkner's *Intruder in the Dust*: a meditation upon history and event which, given the recent vicissitudes of history itself in the 1990s, is not likely to be recalled with any of that passion which the idea held for Faulkner. Of course Faulkner, nevertheless, himself saw (as Percy would see) a problematic dimension to that idea: the mystery of the *past* as a *present*, brought into the present as history remembered. But if it is a remembered history unrescued beyond time, it may very likely mean, in the personal history of the person remembering it, only an arrest of action, the person himself thus becoming delayed or disoriented as *homo viator*. An old problem, which one might find analogy to in St. Augustine's *Confessions*, or in an analogous moment much closer to us in those opening lines of T. S. Eliot's *Burnt Norton*: "Time present and time past/ Are both perhaps present in time future,/ And time future contained in time past." For Eliot, that entangled thought to a present consciousness as not yet rescued beyond time realizes that if "all time is unredeemable," consciousness itself is confounded. Less abstract than this beginning by Eliot (which becomes increasingly concrete, we might remember, in the subsequent lines of his poem) is that passage from Faulkner we have anticipated, concerned also with an almost timeless moment, but an arrest of history rather than a rescue of history. Pathos settles heavily upon it:

> It's all *now* you see. Yesterday won't be over until tomorrow and tomorrow began ten thousand years ago. For every Southern boy fourteen years old, not once but whenever he wants it, there is the instant when it's still not two o'clock on that July afternoon in 1863, the brigades are in position behind the rail fence, the guns are laid and ready in the woods and

> the furled flags are already loosened to break out and Pickett himself with his long oiled ringlets and his hat in one hand probably and his sword in the other looking up the hill waiting for Longstreet to give the word and it's all in the balance, it hasn't happened yet, it hasn't even begun yet, it not only hasn't begun yet but there is still time for it not to begin against that position and those circumstances. . . . *This time. Maybe this time* with all this much to lose and all this much to gain.

These are words remembered by Faulkner's protagonist in *Intruder in the Dust* as spoken to him by his Uncle Gavin Stevens, the Stoic of Stoics in Faulkner. And young Charles Mallison remembers more of those words as posed against this suspension of history's event by a Stoical imagination serving desire. Gavin also spoke of a "sound sensitive lady poet of the time of my youth" for whom "*the scattered tea* goes *with the leaves and every day a sunset dies.*" This sentimental nostalgia, out of Fitzgerald's *Rubaiyat of Omar Khayyam*, Gavin rejects out of hand. For if the "poet's extravagance" often "mirrors the truth," it may well be the truth "upside down and backward." Yesterday's sun and tea, he says, become "inextricable uninfusable grounds blown through the endless corridors of tomorrow, into the shoes we will have to walk in and even the sheets we will have (or try) to sleep between." But on either hand, whether as seen by the lady poet or by the Stoic Gavin Stevens, there is the tone of lament, a sense of being trapped in history beyond Stoicism's powers of rescue, an entrapment Faulkner cannot himself avoid.

Now Faulkner is a powerful presence to the "Southern" writer, his being a gift with which he himself struggles toward redeeming the time through history. He cannot do so, though moving us with the power of his attempt so much that other Southern writers feel intimidated. Thus Flannery O'Connor will set aside attempts to juxtapose her as "Southern" writer to Faulkner. Hence, she doesn't want her paltry mule and shabby wagon stalled on the tracks, she says, when that *Dixie Limited* is due. But there is, perhaps not intentionally, an implied difference reflected in her metaphor of likeness to Faulkner as the famous *Dixie Limited.* About those old trains now gone, country and blues singers spin out a "Southern" sense of loss and melancholy. History, as addressed by either Gavin Stevens (and by Faulkner or by the last country singing engineer) or by his lady poet, is limited, certainly from the perspective of Flannery O'Connor. With Eliot she believes history alone incapable of redeeming time. To recognize history as "inextricable uninfusable grounds blown through the endless corridors of tomorrow" is a first step beyond historical entrapment. It is that first step toward an escape of history's "many cunning passages, contrived corridors/ And issues," in which history unredeemed deceives us "with whispering ambitions,/ Guides us by vanities." That is a recognition which Eliot's Gerontion comes to, he being himself unable to die comfortably between history's sand-blown sheets in his final moment of history.

And so, how uncertain history is as a rescue of consciousness, especially should one be born on a new golf course in a new house, into a cultural ambiance whose only monument in history seems likely to be "the asphalt road/ And a thousand lost golf balls." Thus Eliot on a theme troubling to Percy: the coming to terms with place and time – coming to terms especially with those irritating grains of sand out of his "Southernness." We see him reflecting on that difficulty, turning back in history to the heroic figure of Lee – Robert E. Lee as the last knight of Christendom, more Stoic than Christian. That hero of Southern history is a large one in Faulkner's fiction, played out in the history of his Mississippi postage stamp place called Yoknapatawpha. But for Percy as a later son of the South, not even the Lone Ranger as hero has survived in a common nostalgia suitable to a novelist engaging Southern culture. Not a Southern nor Western myth, but myth out of H. G. Wells for that country club boy. His nostalgia is for a future in which worlds are in war beyond yesterday's sunset. A fourteen-year-old in such a cultural circumstance has his manipulable robot-spaceship made in Japan or South Korea, a toy which by manipulation as if it were a Rubik's cube becomes many things in the spectacles of form. That "Southern boy fourteen years old" has as hero, then, Luke Skywalker as his Huck Finn. He becomes a space explorer capable of gaining eternal youth only through extrapolations of Einstein.

Such is the cultural and historical Southern milieu as the background of *Lost in the Cosmos*. Percy engages time's entrapment of the self through the fancy of science fiction. With mischief he creates our last "self-help," a choice between dealing with the Fall of man from Lost Cove, Tennessee, or dealing with it by colonizing a New Ionia beyond our galaxy. He posits a pre-lapsarian world, though necessarily out of our own fallen world, since art's *possible* or *probable* depends on *nature* and its *history*. In the fictional dimension to his argument, it is a world not only fallen but almost extinguished. Percy is "playing" with us as readers, though his is a serious play. Underlying the choice between Lost Cove and New Ionia (Either/Or, Kierkegaard might put it) is no prospect of a Paradise Regained, at least according to the Modernist dreams that make it seem possible that we can reconstitute future history before it happens – by a gnostic transformation of the world's actual present being. That is the way of Modernist *angelism*, an illusion of transcendence through power over being which proves as Romantically nostalgic to us as Gavin Stevens's version of history's tea and sunsets to Gavin, though we think of ourselves as "realistic" in extrapolating the promises of the latest science.

What is to be regained is reality itself, and Will Barrett almost accomplishes that recovery. Percy chooses a passage from *The Last Gentleman* to make this point in closing his "Diagnosing the Modern Malaise" (1985), pointing us beyond the limited concerns of diagnosis toward a recovery. In the passage which Percy borrows from his own novel, Will Barrett is standing in the shadows, having reached his old Mississippi home, the point from which he began his journey that led him all the way to Eastern schools and then to New York City, before his turning home again to Mississippi as Quentin Compson cannot do. Along the way, much talk with others about that War which is central to Faulkner's historical fiction: much talk of lingering effects from a hundred years ago into mid-century Modern America, a civilization Percy will call "the age of theory and consumption." That old Southern world is a prelude which Will Barrett sees in Mississippi shadows as the "time of fake beauty and fake victory" following the Second World War.

In using this passage from *The Last Gentleman* to draw to a close his essay "Diagnosing the Modern Malaise," Percy says "in fact, it was written as a kind of counterstatement" to a scene in Sartre's *Nausea,* in which Sartre's protagonist Roquentin sits in a park, looking at the roots and bark of a chestnut tree. Sartre, also, he says, means this to be a scene giving a glimpse "into the very nature of the being of things," which nature Sartre describes "by such adjectives as obscene, bloated, viscous, naked, de trop, and so on." An apt counterpointing of his and Sartre's readings of the nature of things, of course. But there also hovers in Percy's words presences other than Sartre as authoritative diagnostician of the evilness of being, as Percy must be aware. To uncover those presences, then, we counterpoint Faulkner's passage from *Intruder in the Dust* to Percy's chosen passage, in order to look more closely at his own qualifying words and phrases as counter to the nauseous ones he quotes from Sartre to characterize being itself as evil.

It has taken Will a considerable journeying to stand in this darkness, aware of his aging aunts on the porch and in the house, playing canasta and watching "Strike It Rich." They are a "tough hearty crew, . . . hearty as muzhiks, . . . good haters, yet not ill-natured," a residue of that Southern past. They are "Christian ladies every one," at the edge of this world in a Mississippi darkness "ecumenized," for they are Protestant, Presbyterian, Catholic, Scotch-Irish, Creole aunts. There is something more underneath this moment, however, teasing Will to an epiphany never fully realized. He has labored to get here, believing all along that this wayside stop on his journey to the New Mexico desert is unpromising of a delivery for him. It is a necessary stopover to confirm a memory, a sad act of historical piety, nevertheless. Later when he arrives in the desert, looking back, he will declare from his isolation in the Southwestern wasteland near Albuquerque, that he thinks that there he has found "the locus of pure possibility," an escape of his personal past as mired in Southern history. In the desert, each "passing second" is muffled in silence, with "no antecedents" in contrast to the Mississippi he has just escaped. Back in Mississippi "it is always Wednesday afternoon, or perhaps Thursday," where "*déjà vu* fly up like a shower of sparks" from the turning wheel of history as history sharpens the moment to an arrest. The phrase, as Percy puts it in his novel, echoes Gavin Stevens's arrest of history for the Southern boy entering teenage mysteries. Now, however, it is "always . . . afternoon" and, "not two o'clock on that July afternoon in 1863."

Will Barrett has missed something crucial in that moment in which he listened to his gay aunts at their frivolous entertainments on the edge of death. And Percy in "diagnosing" the scene in his essay calls our attention to it by his lengthy quotation. In that passage, as if the novelist had intentionally echoed Gavin Stevens, Will looks at his own past moment as a Southern boy, another evening in this place where he now stands. His father, given to Brahms and sentimental poetry (which inclination Gavin has attributed to nostalgic women poets), had missed something, even as Will does now, though he is very near discovery. He now realizes that the secret to recovery "was not in Brahms . . . and not in the old sad poetry . . . but here under your nose, here in the very curiousness and drollness and extraness of the iron and bark that . . . that. . . ." Will is fingering an old horsehead hitching post now almost consumed over time by the tree trunk's bark. The oak has grown almost completely around it. Will stands with his "fingertips [touching] the warm finny whispering bark."

In his late, reflective revisiting of his novel, closing his speculation on the novelist (himself) as diagnostician, Percy calls attention to the terms cropping up in this passage, terms that suggest Will almost out of time: that *curiousness, drollness, extraness* of the iron, the bark whispering to him through his fingertips as he listens to the old ladies and remembers the night of his father's suicide in this very house. His father had missed something by his too heavy attendance upon Brahms and old Romantic poetry. His father had rejected history's entrapment in the only way the Stoic can at last depend upon, suicide, when he has failed to move beyond that intellectual arrest which is possible through an "extraness" in the world. It is signaled at times by so insignificant an experience as the warm whispering of bark closing over arrogant iron, the horsehead of the hitching post.

Or perhaps it is encountered in rose moles in stipple on a trout's back or fresh falls of chestnuts; that is, if he is Gerard Manley Hopkins, upon whom Percy depends as a poet enlightening him about such moments. (Flannery O'Connor does so as well, and one might see a parallel in Will's recovered memory of himself as boy touching the iron and bark to O'Connor's dwelling upon a similar moment with another hitching post central to an epiphany – her "The Artificial Nigger.") Here, in this Mississippi moment, however, Will Barrett fails to remove obstacles to the moment of grace pending. He sees, or almost sees, not something bad, Percy advises us, but something good, having caught "a glimpse of the goodness and gratuitousness of created being." Not often does Percy sound so clear a Thomistic position as here, which he will underline more heavily in that last of his essays, "The Holiness of the Ordinary." And, as we shall be suggesting along the way of the pages to follow, not always is he himself (let alone his fictional Will) firm in holding that position, though he recognizes it as crucial to the faith he would hold. Indeed, the very difficulty of maintaining that faith – an uncertainty common to us all – will lead him once more to engage Will Barrett, in *The Second Coming*, and with an audacious spectacle of theological implication. Will falls through a greenhouse roof, into the lap of his Beloved. He falls (Percy remarks in his *Paris Review* interview) "out of his nutty Gnostic quest into sacramental reality." That is the second fall he *almost* makes in *The Last Gentleman* (the first being Adam's) when the oak bark whispers warmly to him through his fingers.

This, then, is the recovery necessary, which Percy understands with an immediacy through Gerard Manley Hopkins, rather than through the *Summa Theologica*. It is a vision into and beyond the thing engaged by the senses, a recognition of the *instress,* the *beingness* of things, which speaks the meaning of existence as beyond science's measure. It is a message in the thing – in the bottle of the Cosmos in which alienated man at century's close takes himself to be entrapped. But most often Percy will, having pursued that journey which is so immediate and personal to him to the threshold of a conclusion, demur from naming it, though his argument in "The Fateful Rift: The San Andreas Fault in the Modern Mind," his Jefferson lecture at the very end of his life, has concentrated upon the mystery of naming. It is a concentration upon the uses of science in a pursuit of valid signs. On that threshold of naming, having invoked Charles Peirce and Martin Heidegger and Gabriel Marcel, almost coyly he demurs from a final naming. His last words: "But that's a different story." That different story begins with "once upon a time," or in St. John's words, "In the beginning was the Word."

This different story – different from the stories possible to him to present comfortably to a secular audience – is that of the Incarnation, through which revelation history is Divinely transformed, Divinely redeemed. It is a story Percy believes, embraces, but it is not one easily talked about to a secular world. Especially difficult for one like Percy, who in considering the question endlessly posed to him, "Why Are You a Catholic?" (1990), writes that last essay to forewarn us that "novelists are a devious lot to begin with," since their "stock-in-trade" is the use of the word by "indirection, if not by guile." When tempted to direct use of words, as in essays, the habit of indirection carries over, though he may be sometimes open: "I have not the least desire to convert anyone or engage in an apologetic or polemic or a 'defense of the Faith.'" From his position as a devious user of signs, however, he is nevertheless guided largely by his intuitive recognition of the Sign within the sign, or as Eliot phrases it, "the Word within the word." So, he will on occasion mention the "mystery of art."

It is a mystery Flannery O'Connor speaks of as art's "incarnational" responsibility to the thing made, the poem or story. And that responsibility is one fraught with a terror for the artist if taken in the way she takes it. As a creature created in the image of God, her gift is to make in celebration, requiring a surrender to the good of the thing she makes. There is, thereby, in the act of making a story, a sense of resonance, an abiding echo of necessity. For her, not only is that making dependent upon the actualities of creation, whereby she imitates in an incarnational act through signs, depending as art, out of the possible or probable in relation to the actual – depending in the reality of creation itself. There is in her awareness as well a sense of responsibility to the proportionate correspondence between herself as maker and that ultimate reality, the Artist as Creator God. That is a relation implied in the rubric of faith that man is created "in the image of God." Thus (in Eliot's phrase), that Word – the Creator – is evidenced by his gifts to the maker of the art word, his created word, by which naming we acknowledge the complex of both the creation – Percy's Cosmos – and that walking word as it were, *homo viator* as maker and steward to the created word, the Cosmos. The Creator's action (the continuous sustaining act of the Word) is from St. Thomas's perspective a double one. It is the act whereby the diverse Cosmos *is* (despite Cartesian Idealism's doubt) and the maker himself is in a peculiar office of responsibility as maker. (This is the mystery of our nature as created "in God's image" which I have explored in *Making: The Proper Habit of Our Being.*)

The decisive reality to this complex of circumstance to the continuing existence of the person as intellectual soul incarnate? That is for the Christian the Intercession in history itself, whereby the Word in an act of love surrenders in submission to creation in expiation of our fallen nature. It is remembered as event in actual history, celebrated as the act of Incarnation, Crucifixion, and Resurrection – a drama revealing an actuality possible to the intellectual soul incarnate through its own answering love, a love proportionate in stewardship to its gifts of being from the Word. That sacrificial act of Love was a sacrifice in submission to creation. And out of that sacrifice a continuous Sacrifice redeems the time – redeems the First Adam man – in the moment on the Cross. The good news of that redemption is the empty tomb. That is Percy's "other story." But it is a story any good poet as novelist, will echo – intentionally by a consent to or a rejection of it; or ignorantly, since he cannot avoid it insofar as he engages truthfully the "ordinary," those created things and their actions in history as necessities to his incarnational making. He cannot avoid that reality in which a holiness is resident, whether he recognize it "personally" or not. But insofar as he knows this participation in being as a steward to the word, the poet discovers that he stands in a holy ground, stands within the contextual support of Divine things themselves. His art is dependent upon existential reality as *creaturely* because Divinely created. (And for Thomas, let us remember, this is a knowing vouchsafed intellect as *natural law.*)

Thus in his address to the actual, the poet unfolds the possible or probable as dependent upon the actual. But his is a making, not a creating, since he depends, both in his own person and in the substance of preexisting reality to his making, upon the actual. He depends upon *givens*, upon a preexisting reality, which since it is preexisting as actual reality bears an aspect of history. In this sense, "history" is involved as a perspective upon man in nature. That is the mystery which fascinates Faulkner's Gavin Stevens, who would in response impose the possible or probable upon the moment, in an arrest. It is by the use of memory that it is always "still not two o'clock on that July afternoon in 1863" at Gettysburg. What if? Suppose that? A speculative act of detachment, despite the concession that history sands the sheets of such withdrawal as if toward a sleep freed of history.

The perspective upon art, upon man's gifts as maker, involves him in an incarnational act, an embodiment of form, whose witness as good in itself rests with the artist through that act. It is a sufficient responsibility, requiring of the poet, for instance, no necessity to "defend the Faith" directly by his art – to engage in apologetic or polemic. Indeed, St. Thomas argues that such would be a violation of art itself. Percy also observes this in passing, while Flannery O'Connor dwells insistently on the point. Quite enough to surrender to the making in a risk of "transparency," a self-forgetfulness through an act of love toward the thing made. That is a possibility to the poet which Percy recognizes, then, and at times defends. It is also, or so I suspect, at times an accomplishment he ascribes to O'Connor with a touch of envy of her success. He also sees this "transparency" as overwhelming any angry political reaction in Dante as he sets out in exile as *homo viator* from Florence, becoming a wanderer within the company of Divine things. St. Augustine will find it especially testified to even in made works from the pagan Greeks, as well as by the created works of the world. It is this aspect of Dante's history which makes him – at least metaphorically – a "Southerner" in exile.

But here's the rub: Percy takes his own gifts to be somehow lesser. His perspective, early and late, he understands primarily to be more those of the scientist than poet. He is fearful of scientism, of course. Thus in attempting to dramatize "The Coming Crisis in Psychiatry" (1957), and with a sense of responsibility as diagnostic novelist in "Diagnosing the Modern Malaise" (1985), he deprecates his own contribution as artist. Enough to make him both rueful and wry when engaged intrusively by interviewers who are "nosey" about his art, and doubly so when they engage him (usually themselves as skeptical secularists) about his religion as artist, about why he is a "Catholic." That "other story," which he hints at knowing and believing, and sometimes overtly subscribes to, haunts him as novelist, as maker. It will lead him, not to a disclaimer of his work or a rejection of it, but to a sharper awareness of his tensional role as maker in service to an abiding Presence reflected in a continuousness of creation, from the Big Bang to the fancifully imaged lesser terminal Bang in his "Space Odyssey," a future projection enabling reflection upon the present "self" marooned in the Cosmos. For how is one to affirm that Presence in art to a secular age?

In a very real way, one may speculate, Percy often seems like his Will Barrett: suspended on the threshold of revelation, praying with St. Paul and St. Augustine, "I believe; help thou my unbelief." A tendency to an unbelief makes its intrusion into the faithful deportment of this maker – or so I suggest – through his fascination with science. Concerning that fascination he tells us an anecdote, in "Physician as Novelist" (1989). Growing up, he says, "I was a reluctant attendant at Sunday school and a secret devotee of science, or what I took for science. My favorite writer was H. G. Wells." That anecdote perhaps reflects not only a childhood moment, but a continuing tensional moment to Percy. It is a moment in which he is often disturbed by the inadequacy of science to the mystery of existence, despite the most arresting diagnoses. And because disturbed, it is the moment in which he is drawn into the holiness of a thing and through it into that other – that different – story from the one told by physicist or biologist or evolutionist or psychiatrist.

In his "Questions They Never Asked Me," a self-interview approximately midway in his writing career (1977), Percy brings this self-examination to conclusion by speculating upon a portrait of himself, hanging on the wall where he is writing questions and answering them. He sees a "cold-eyed and sardonic" figure – a "mean . . . yard dog," and suggests the painting a "portrait of a kind of composite of the protagonists of my novels." If "cold-eyed," his is the cold eye of the scientist looking beneath the tanned skin of *homo viator* who is comfortable with bourbon and a summer sunset – the consumer at a moment of satiation and oblivious to any possible apocalypse in the world or in his own soul. If he as writer suggests a pending explosion in terms of the dreaded "Bomb," that is a manner of indirection as novelist, his way of speaking about a reality of the soul itself – the "self" – which is on the brink, yet placid and seemingly content when seen reflected by a flatulent consumerism not yet exploded and collapsed.

As for the "sardonic," that is the species of irony which turns back upon the user of irony, in this instance that mean "yard dog" we are indirectly introduced to through the portrait. (It is, incidentally, an actual portrait.) Not himself the figure of the consumer – though he partakes of the "good things" of life – but rather the theorist, who comes to a dead end of theory in his last novel and last essays. He begins his "Physician as Novelist" (1989) with that childhood memory of growing up a "reluctant attendant at Sunday School and a secret devotee of science, or what I took for science." The recollection, in a late moment of tranquility at the end of his life, suggests an innocence which lingered beyond childhood, insofar as Percy is long lured by the authority of science, though he takes it as quite other than it is taken by many of our scientists at the end of our century. In his last understanding of it, explored in the late essays and in *Thanatos Syndrome,* its virtues are undeniable, but its inclination to raise theory to absolute truth about things is destructive of the spirit, as it proves also encouraging to the appetitive dimension of man whereby we are persuaded to consumerism as the only acceptable heaven for the Modernist religion. Thus science may serve man by withering soul itself.

It is a temptation in science which Percy recognizes himself vulnerable to. He becomes far less tolerant of the presumptions of science – of theory – than of the "loony" indulgences of the flesh. For things in themselves are good, being created. That we are drawn to them implies a drawing proper to our natures as ourselves created – as intellectual souls *incarnate*. It is a subversion of intellect by theory, disorienting us from the truth of things, that is destructive through an intention to a usurpation of Providence itself. Perhaps he too succumbs to theory? Perhaps his sense of having broken the code of sign through hints heard out of Charles Peirce's arguments may have distorted a more simple language to intellect, a language spoken to Will Barrett, for instance through the bark of that tree.

Will's fingers hear what he cannot yet translate, though the signs are spoken with surety to the sense of touch. Like Blake's figure of God touching with his finger the made world (Adam) in the very act of making. Will however is a reverse image. Though created in the image of God, he stands in darkness, touching the "elephant lip" of the bark as it closes with slow-chapped power over the severe iron hitching post. Will is almost touching a Something beyond both the senses and intellect. That idea of order, theory of order, of which the hitching post is a lingering reminder, is vaguely echoed in the chatter of the aunts at their childhood moment on death's edge, but in words Will cannot translate to spiritual hunger in himself. Paths of theory lead but to the grave – unless we hear an "extraness" speaking through creation itself. "I believe, help thou my unbelief." Thus St. Paul, even earlier than St. Augustine. Thus also Walker Percy as diagnostic novelist.

I

The year Percy published his *Lost in the Cosmos*, purportedly "The Last Self-Help Book" (1983), he also published a brief essay on Herman Melville, in which it is evident that he feels an affinity with Melville which he describes as common among "Southern" writers of our century, especially those principal writers of the "Southern Renaissance." His position needs some qualification in order that we may see the affinity as shared in a more limited way by those Southern writers he has in mind. For not Melville, but Hawthorne is more conspicuously a sympathetic presence to many of them. A notable instance, Flannery O'Connor, to whom Percy is also drawn, though he sees significant differences between himself and O'Connor. His fascination with her is evident along the way, but in many of his comments in his essays, as distinguished from his fiction, he marks that difference carefully, given that they both are Roman Catholic and Southern.

In his fiction, he will come closer to her position late rather than early. In *Thanatos Syndrome*, for instance, it is Flannery O'Connor he echoes in a stirring sermon by his Father Smith, whose concern for sentimentality toward the common good as unfolded in our century leads to horrors difficult to summarize. In her "Memoir of Mary Ann" (1960, included in *Mystery and Manners*), she asserts other ages as more perceptive than ours, though we may accuse them of seeing "with the blind, prophetical, unsentimental eye of acceptance" of the unacceptable. Theirs was a faith we have lost, and with that loss comes the rational sentimentality she sees dramatized in Dostoevsky's Ivan Karamazov. It is the Ivans, or Hawthorne's Alymers, as well-intentioned scientists who are "making headway . . . on the raw material of good" in an attempt through science and philosophy to cut down "human imperfection." As for the philosophical reductionism, akin to and precedent to scientific reductionism, Ivan Karamazov "cannot believe, as long as one child is in torment; Camus' hero cannot accept the divinity of Christ, because of the massacre of the innocents. That has become a "popular piety," through which "we mark our gain in sensibility and our loss in vision." And where does it lead us?

It leads us, O'Connor says, to govern by tenderness in the absence of faith. It is a tenderness which, long since cut off from the person of Christ, is wrapped in theory. "When tenderness is detached from the source of tenderness, its logical outcome is terror. It ends in forced-labor camps and in the fumes of the gas chamber." We recognize here her anticipation of the theme upon which Percy will rest his case against our age, an argument made most openly near the end of his life. In his last essay, published in the year he dies (on May 10, 1990), he will observe that "We live in a post-modern as well as a post-Christian age which as yet has no name." One might put it that, presuming ourselves a civilization, we are isolated, lost in the cosmos, on the brink of the historical abyss. For the term "post-Christian age" names historical dislocation consequent upon that loss of faith which is Flannery O'Connor's concern. But the term "post-modern age" also suggests a further dislocation, in which the Modernist promises have proved ashes to our appetitive nature. One might remark here that, if one hold the Christian belief, a belief in an ultimate reality to the human condition beyond the merely appetitive, there is no room in that belief for definitive terms, for a decisive *ante* or *post*. It is a timeless condition at last, and so always a present, even in a present disquieting perspective upon mankind as now seemingly lost in the cosmos. As for that condition of dislocation, of deracination from reality including a separation from the Cosmos itself, what one might conclude, from the Christian perspective to which Percy would hold, is that our quest for the "Modern" has proved a quest for an illusion.

But then the temptation to Modernist illusion is itself timeless, located as it is not in *nature* and so limited to *history*. It lies in the *given* nature of man. It is as ancient as the Garden of Eden of the old myth, which for the Christian bears an abiding truth about human nature. That is, the "modern" aspect of our dislocation is itself timeless and placeless, in that it is inherent to human fallen will. There we locate the illusion of self-sufficiency, self-autonomy, which Percy will present to us in its "lost" stage to the forlorn soul in his *Lost in the Cosmos* under the rubric of an ambiguous term, *transcendence.* The presumption of transcendence through willed autonomy is that heresy in Christian dogma characterized as *angelism*. And in his recognition of our failure as "Moderns," Percy will characterize this present age at last. As does Flannery O'Connor, Percy too sees "the Age of Enlightenment" as leading to "the catastrophes of the twentieth century. The present age is demented. . . . It is the most scientifically advanced, savage, democratic, inhuman, sentimental, murderous century in human history." That is a severe indictment, in which is included not only the sentimentality of the "democratic" spirit as it consents in a "popular pity" (O'Connor's phrase) to "govern by tenderness." Here Percy includes in his indictment as well the hero of our moment, the scientist, whom he has tended at first to exonerate, though he cannot at last, despite his attempts to do so along his way.

Up to this point – and we are taking reference to that last of his essays – he has often distinguished between *science* and *scientism*, himself given to science as the dependable way of knowing. The distinction seems less tenable to him at the end, so that he now suggests that we call our age, which has no name, "the age of the theorist-consumer." Again, there is a foreshadowing in Flannery O'Connor's 1960 essay, her introduction to a "Memoir of Mary Ann" written and published by the Sisters of Our Lady of Perpetual Help Free Cancer Home, in

Atlanta, founded by Nathaniel Hawthorne's daughter. It is science as dictated by theory that Percy now calls into question: not because such an approach is not proper to science, but that it fails to recognize its limits and transgresses thereby. He will have associated himself along the way, for instance, with evolution against the fundamentalist's arguments for Creationism. But on this late reflection about our unnamed age, he will call science itself to order because of its presumptions, self-justified by what is now to be seen as a most ambiguous "progress" of humanity since the Enlightenment. He addresses Newton, Freud, Darwin as theorists who "pursued truth more or less successfully by theory – from which, however, they themselves were exempt. You will look in vain in Darwin's *Origin of the Species* for an explanation of Darwin's behavior in writing *Origin of the Species.*" It is a point made by C. S. Lewis concerning the "abolition of man" as engineered by Freud as theorist, whose theory (Lewis observed) seems to account for everything but Freud. What theory fails to account for is *person* – a term we shall relate to Percy's "self" in *Lost in the Cosmos* along our way. He remarks of such Enlightenment and post-Enlightenment lights as Newton, Freud, Darwin: "One's self is always a leftover from one's theories."

In the light of this juxtaposition of early Flannery O'Connor to late Walker Percy, we note that more than once Percy alludes to a remark made by "someone" that the South is "Christ-haunted." That someone is of course Flannery O'Connor, who says that, though the South is certainly not "Christ-centered" it is undeniably "Christ-haunted." That is the spiritual climate of the South which she concentrates upon, seeing it as significant of an abiding human condition hardly peculiar to the South, though by caricatures of the "Southerner" as backward, the abiding human hunger for spiritual rescue may be denied as anything more than a local residue of history. It is a condition of spiritual hunger which for Flannery O'Connor was actively evident in the popular spirit of the South, providing her art with valid spectacles of that hunger. Her own "loonies," then, are her heroes. Here we may make a difference between her and Percy, as he will do himself though in terms somewhat different from our present ones. Percy as diagnostic novelist, as opposed to O'Connor, addresses this Southern aspect of the "Christ-haunted" at the level of psychology, in his assumed role of the diagnostician as novelist. Both writers are very much attuned to the symptoms of our age's dislocation as evidenced through the media reports of "loonies." But there is a difference requiring comment.

Flannery O'Connor in her reading of newspaper events reporting the local is rather like Dostoevsky in his interests in that "bad" news as counter to the "good" news, the Gospel. (Dostoevsky's fiction is rich with borrowings of scandalous events from newspapers.) She will, for instance, discover a beginning for her Misfit of "A Good Man Is Hard to Find" in a buried newspaper story. But in exploring the possible or probable truth about human nature suggested by such a story, she will at last, after writing the story, declare her Misfit himself a prophet gone wrong. He may at last even recover to his proper calling through the mystery of grace to her thinking. For the old grandmother's gesture toward him, just before he shoots her, may "like the mustard-seed . . . grow to be a great crow-filled tree in the Misfit's heart, and will be enough of a pain to him there to turn him into the prophet he was meant to become."

Much of the initial misreading of O'Connor's fiction (some of which continues three decades after her death) followed from the failure of her critics to recognize or understand her uses of the "fundamentalist" inclination in the Southerner as Christ-haunted. Not surprising, since the South had so long been caricatured by the popular national media, often in sit-coms, in an emulation of H. L. Mencken's vendetta against Christianity he associated with the "Bible Belt" in order to promote his own prophet, Nietzsche. (The Scopes Trial was an event in which Mencken could take devilish delight, exploiting it to his ends.) Just how problematic that trial, in relation to the truth of things, however, is subjected to incisive analysis in an essay now largely forgotten. Richard M. Weaver in his "Dialectic and Rhetoric at Dayton, Tennessee," in his *The Ethics of Rhetoric,* 1953, offers a devastating view hardly acceptable yet to the Modernist intellectual. Southern "backwardness," then, has been a staple in media reports of the progressive "American" spirit for a long time. So much so that Percy will engage this as a disadvantage to him as "American Novelist" having to struggle "Being Southern" but the more confounded in that disadvantage because also a "Catholic."

For Flannery O'Connor, the backward South, much remarked in its political and social circumstances, was a considerable challenge to her art, given her Southern sympathies. She will describe her Old Tarwater in *The Violent Bear It Away* as a "natural Catholic," akin to her in both his understanding of man's nature and his commitment to God, though it is difficult for him to articulate his vision save through a violence learned of the Old Testament's prophetic rhetoric in actual acts of violence. (Old Tarwater shoots the Modernist nephew Rayber, for instance). If Old Tarwater is a "natural Catholic," she describes herself as a "hillbilly Thomist." (She read some of Thomas each night.) And from her Thomistic perspective, she saw a necessity to her art to deploy the seemingly grotesque to dramatic ends, given that her audience is confused as to what is truly grotesque. What is truly grotesque in her view (as it becomes for Percy) is a reductionism whereby the person is atrophied into what Percy calls the "theorist-consumer." She remarks that "for the hard of hearing you shout and for the almost blind you draw large and startling pictures." It is a bold strategy as "maker" of fiction, in that she makes use of the "looniness" of our time (as Percy might call it) as symptom to an ancient disease.

But a difference here is that Percy tends to focus upon symptom. As diagnostician-novelist, he is reluctant to prescribe remedy, declaring (with a good Thomistic authority in doing so) that remedy is an improper concern to art. Flannery O'Connor will insist the same. But she will also insist upon probing symptom to discover and perhaps reveal the actual disease. Her fiction is rich with symptoms large and startling, and her unfolding actions shout rather loudly. But for her, those symptoms blossom evilly in our world out of the deepest malady to human kind, alluded to as the Fall of Man. Now these "symptoms" used by both writers need here a quite different term, insofar as we are concerned with art and not medicine. What Percy treats diagnostically as *symptom* by his art, we shall call *spectacle* in the Aristotelian sense. Percy differs in his concern from Hawthorne's use of spectacle, remarking the dangers of allegory to art, allegory being Hawthorne's tendency in treating the symptomatic surfaces of his principle theme, namely man's sinfulness associated with the Fall. (Henry James will complain about Hawthorne's concern for sin in his book on Hawthorne, as if the concern and not Hawthorne's art is to be faulted.)

Flannery O'Connor is herself wary of the allegorical, but she is even more wary of resting her vision of our condition in this nameless age at the level of symptom – spectacle. One may, then, contrast her address to Southern "fundamentalism" to Percy's. Both derive their perceptions of it largely from the media. Or, at least, I know of no record that either attended tent-meetings, evangelical gatherings. They know primarily the newspaper and radio and television accounts, though they would surely in occasional social encounters have met specific "fundamentalists." Their sure ear for language as spoken is a symptom of such encounter. Encounter for Percy speaks spectacle to a malady which he tends not to probe, however. Thus it is that he will distinguish his own deportment as novelist from Flannery O'Connor's. Her concern, he observes, is for the world as largely the territory of the devil, requiring by that perspective a concern for evil as a mystery. He instead (he will add) is concerned for human looniness, the goofy spectacle of man in a context largely circumscribed by the present state of symptomology, available to him not through philosophy nor theology, but through psychology and psychiatry.

Consider, then, his allusions to the fundamentalist, a response to symptoms expressed satirically. The goofiness of the California guru is rather like the goofiness of the TV evangelist. But, as we have already observed, in the end, his responses (in *Thanatos Syndrome* and in the last of his essays) seem to reflect a perspective somewhat changed. It is with a very real difference of concern for "fundamentalism" that he treats his Fr. Smith in that last novel as very much a fundamentalist. Fr. Smith is by analogy closer to Flannery O'Connor's Old Tarwater in *The Violent Bear It Away* than Percy could have managed earlier on his way. Nor could he have made his Fr. Smith so persuasive earlier, we may suggest, because earlier he was less certain in his belief himself. There lingers in Percy almost to the end this uncertainty, out of a skepticism, even when he has declared himself Christian. It is a point we shall touch upon again. But here we first observe a skepticism as it affects his playfulness. We may see it reflected in his being drawn to that dark figure in our literature, Melville, with a recognition of kinship. In this respect, Percy's friendly disposition to O'Connor may find echo in Melville's to Hawthorne.

In this light, Percy's sense of kinship to Melville is shared as well by another Southern writer of considerable literary stature, one who is skeptical from beginning to end, a writer whose work is also ironic, often sardonic, and especially so in respect to his own concern to come to terms with his own Southernness. I refer to Robert Penn Warren, who writes revealingly of Melville, his own themes as poet and novelist often relevant to Percy's smaller engagement of their mutual kinsman Herman Melville, in arguments we shall presently introduce. But first Percy. In the year he published *Lost in the Cosmos*, Percy writes a brief meditation on Herman Melville which begins, "What does a present-day Southern writer make of Melville?" That "Southern writer" is Percy himself, of course, still wrestling with the problem of his Southernness as writer, a concern related to other concerns, but especially to his having been more scientist than Christian philosopher in respect to the problem of the sign-as-sign locating the "self" in history. And so he will say in this brief piece, "It may be that the South, which has been called a Christ-haunted place, is something like New England a hundred years ago" as experienced by Melville. The South *now*, as Percy himself must respond to it and come to some accommodation of it as an impinging cultural place upon his restless sensibilities as writer. (It is, once more, Flannery O'Connor who remarked the South as "Christ-haunted.") One of our own thematic concerns in reading Percy is the question of whether he himself is more Christ-haunted than Christ-centered, at least in this period of his journey. We may be sure he intends to be so centered. But we are less sure that he is as firmly so as Flannery O'Connor. Hence very evidently, given his meditative reflection on Melville, he recognizes an affinity with that restless New England skeptic whose restlessness was a continuing concern to Hawthorne.

As for his interest in Melville, Percy from his Southern perspective wonders why there is not a "single Melville . . . in the entire antebellum South?" The answer is not so simple in its cause as a destructiveness to the imagination out of the dark shadow of slavery, as Percy recognizes. After all, Percy remarks, both Aeschylus and Sophocles owned slaves. If one should see the South as Stoic in its intellectual inclinations (as Percy does) and recall that Roman Stoicism seems to portend a decline from a Golden to a Silver Age in Roman literature, why should Stoicism in the South seem in retrospect rather to portend a Golden Age in Southern literature, a "Southern Renaissance"? Did the South lack a community of writers such as New England had, centering about Concord? But then (we might pose an answer) Melville is in radical defiance of the community which existed there – as was Hawthorne. Hawthorne reacts to the "Transcendentalists," though not with the defiant deportment of Melville. Percy himself will react in Melvillian manner to the "mind-set" of the Modernist intellectual community at last, those theorists who – as one might argue – are descended rather directly from the New England "Transcendentalists" through a transmogrification of Puritanism to Pragmatism, on the way to a Positivism justifying intellectual autonomy.

And so Melville reacts to the New England intellectual community, on Hawthorne's side of the issue, in holding that "mind-set" under suspicion. But Hawthorne will hold fast to the Puritan concept of sin, though addressing it in reaction to the Puritan perspective which tends to Manichaeanism, whereby Nature must be held as evil and to be subdued. (See his "Maypole at Merry Mount.") That separation of grace and nature in Puritan Manichaeanism, Hawthorne anticipates intuitively, can but distort reality. A present evidence to him is Emerson, who treats "nature" as a thing to be used, though sentimentally used, in order to set aside sin itself. It is a reduction in the understanding of human nature, indeed, which will serve Pragmatism and Positivism most helpfully. (It is no accident that Emerson becomes the intellectual hero to President Charles W. Eliot of Harvard after 1865. The theme here touched upon I have pursued at some length in my *Why Hawthorne Was Melancholy*.) But if Hawthorne is in reaction to what proves a secularized adaptation of Puritanism, his own more dogged inclination to an orthodoxy differs from Melville's own address to sin. It is a difference to be contemplated, especially in relation to Percy's interest in Melville at this early point of his own intellectual and spiritual journey as an American writer who is also both a Catholic and a Southerner, willy-nilly he suspects on both counts.

In his meditation, Percy juxtaposes not Hawthorne but Dostoevsky to Melville, aware of course that Melville always seems to write as if Hawthorne were looking over his shoulder. Melville is drawn to Hawthorne through a recognition that both writers feel obligated to engage, not history, but the mystery of man himself. Both see that nature unfolding as history in distortions of the abiding realities of human nature. There is rapidly underway the growing secular sense to the popular spirit of a predestination, but it is an imperial predestination by man's will bent on a conquest of "nature" through impositions of intentional order. That would seem to be a violation of the inherent order of nature itself, including human nature. Indeed, this is precisely one of the concerns of the early writers of the Southern Renaissance. Theirs is an opposition to "Yankee" intentions to reconstitute nature itself. But if they respond to that intention as a growing danger to the South, they do so through appeals to traditions older than those associated with that shibboleth of rebuke, the "Old South." That pejorative epithet (given that our political history since the mid-19th century has effected confusions) was a charge against the Fugitive Agrarians. In *I'll Take My Stand*, their adversaries tended to shout rhetorically that these Vanderbilt youth wanted "to turn back the clock." Even in our day their deeper concern to recover known but forgotten things about the nature of man as social creature (in order to recover a viable community) is largely ignored through rhetorical strategies obscuring what they actually said in their symposium. Percy finds himself divided in response to that controversy, drawn to Southern writers such as Allen Tate and Caroline Gordon and Cleanth Brooks, and certainly to that rather insistent "Southerner," Flannery O'Connor. But nevertheless he is not at ease in his tensional circumstance as a "Southern" writer with being associated with the Fugitive Agrarians. That is a disquiet he addresses, soon after *Lost in the Cosmos*, in "How to Be an American Novelist in Spite of Being Southern and Catholic" (1984).

And so, perhaps there is more to be gained by juxtaposing Dostoevsky rather than Hawthorne to Melville. In his reflection on his New England counterpart, Percy says that "Melville is Dostoevsky turned inside out. Both men saw the depravity of man. One saw it as the occasion of his salvation; the other blamed it on God. . . . [I]n the end both are perhaps incoherent." Or they are likely to appear so from the triumphant position of the secular intellect, rising to an "American" status out of Emerson. Thus, says Percy, "It is hard to say who would be more certifiable at Yale or Harvard now – Melville, who believed in the depravity of man and blamed God for it, or Dostoevsky, who believed in the depravity of man and looked to God to save him from it." Either/Or. There is a suspense of judgment between the two visions of man's depravity, and it is in suspense in Percy himself at times. But in that suspended judgment Percy (unlike "Yale or Harvard") is prepared to accept man as depraved, certainly on the general evidence of man's destructions by mid-century, by the end of World War II. Depravity unresolved, the "American" intellectual at mid-century appeared to be in an increasing revolt against his older inheritance, Western culture.

That growing tendency to reject both history and its relation to transcendence underlined for Percy his problem of suspension between being a scientist or a Christian. It is a circumstance of suspension which Eliot addresses in his *After Strange Gods: A Primer of Modern Heresy* at the University of Virginia in the 1930s, in which Eliot argues the necessity of Orthodoxy (Christian) beyond mere Tradition – Eliot conspicuously addressing those Southern Agrarians who have just published *I'll Take My Stand*. Those "Twelve Southerners," Eliot seems to fear, have not sufficiently recognized the importance to their position of Christian orthodoxy in justifying their concerns for a tradition which for them is, or seems to be, a blood inheritance. Eliot is not yet forgiven that argument, though the attack of it is by a rhetorical indirection. Thus, he argues in those Virginia lectures the dangers to viable communities in which there is "any large number of free-thinking Jews" plus the increasingly evident influence of "*Protestant* agnosticism." In order to discount the argument Eliot makes, he is declared "anti-Semitic" by ignoring the key terms in such phrases, *free thinking* and *Protestant agnostics,* which intellectual deportments in combination effect a sentimentality in the popular spirit. In a recent review of *The Liberal Education of Charles Eliot Norton* (James Turner), Richard Poirier associates Eliot and the Southern Agrarians, rejecting both. The Agrarians are consumed by "nostalgia," while Eliot's *After Strange Gods* is "notoriously reactionary and anti-Semitic" (*New Republic,* May 8, 2000). One could make an argument that the Neoconservatives of *Commentary* in the 1990s call advance arguments ironically parallel to Eliot's, in respect to the uncertain community of Israel as it is embroiled increasingly in secular versus religious controversy. The intellectual bias in such arguments as

Poirier's have long since become, not out of agnosticism, but more baldly atheistic, and as such require their rejecting Percy and O'Connor for their "nostalgia" no less than Allen Tate or John Crowe Ransom or Robert Penn Warren.

For Percy, nearly half a century after these engagements of Modernism by the Agrarians and Eliot, what is to be made of this depravity in man? Especially as addressed with such a radical difference by Dostoevsky and Melville? Percy, having just completed his *Lost in the Cosmos* with a playful fiction, a science fiction positing man in the future as if before his Fall ("A Space Odyssey, I and II") – or rather a drama of man as having experienced an almost total annihilation after that old Fall of Adam has reached Hegel's "End of History" – writes his essay on Melville. "Billy Budd is," he argues, "man before the Fall, man exempted from the Fall, a creature dragged in from some loony planet invented by Melville and Rousseau, who neither understands evil nor needs salvation from it. Dostoevsky would have laughed out loud. Billy Budd, in Dostoevsky's hands, would have turned out to be a child molester. And thereby a good deal more believable. But Melville was not afraid to address such matters, and that's why he means so much to us." Us: the "Southern" writer. It is the risk of questions addressed as if never dared, addressed seriously in fiction, which appeals to Percy, as it would not to Flannery O'Connor insofar as such questions may tend to indict God or God's creation. As it would not to Allen Tate. But as it certainly does so appeal to Robert Penn Warren. Percy is more hesitant in that risk than Warren, since he is a Southern *Catholic* novelist by conversion. There is, then, a discordant intrusion upon his meditation on Melville, a turning to himself as a Southern writer who is also a Catholic writer.

It leads Percy to these curious words about Melville: "The freedom and happiness of the artist is attested by his playfulness, his tricks, his malice, his underhandedness, his naughtiness, his hoodwinking the reader." So happy is the metaphorical distance between the novelist and his narrative that he is free to cover his tracks at will. Not only do I not have to strive to mean such-and-such, he seems to say, but I deny that I mean it. I might mean the opposite. Hardly a description of Melville as writer. Percy's position, cast as if speculative reflections by the artist on his freedom and happiness, is hardly applicable to Dostoevsky either. Nor to Percy himself, except that, as the "ex-suicide" proclaimed in *Lost in the Cosmos,* he can now take satiric pleasure in a pursuit of "freedom and happiness" as diagnostic novelist. Not a Billy Budd before the Fall but a Binx or a Will Barrett or the like, drawn up by the imagination into a fictional agency out of this "loony" world we now inhabit. Not pure innocence sacrificed, but characters displaying spectacles of depravity sufficiently diversified as spectacle for a satiric echoing of man in this moment, through current events witnessed by the daily press and television.

It is dangerous to the point of risking one's own soul to delve too deeply into man's depravity, if one lack certitude about the good. One might, after all, be destroyed by dark discoveries. For as writer, he may not pretend himself innocent, as is Melville's Billy Budd. He may even discover himself potentially a child molester. Dostoevsky rather certainly feared as much about his own potentiality as person, suffering a spiritual agony with Ivan Karamazov and with his Raskolnikov of *Crime and Punishment.* But then, what if one should discover himself through this fear reduced to nothingness, not surviving at all and so becoming, not an "ex-suicide" but an actual suicide? To be a diagnostic-novelist is dangerous, requiring the safety of playfulness, tricks, malice, underhandedness, naughtiness, and perhaps most of all a necessity by art to that strategy of hoodwinking the reader, lest the reader discern that more than spectacle made comical lies in words underway as art. Should he risk a reader's suicide, in the interest of a chance that the reader might instead survive as "ex-suicide"? Even so, what is most deeply underway is an engagement of the writer's self, his own prospects as a self, in a world less than propitious to his freedom and happiness.

That other Southern writer who discovers kinship to Melville – Robert Penn Warren – has given us a rich poetry and fiction out of the ironies of history, as well as in his devotions to the truth of the natural world responded to in its beauty. But Warren does not take the refuge Percy finds necessary. Warren's own indirections are in a primary service to art, so that one might consider his indirections art's necessities rather than a means of protecting the artist from the danger of the abyss yawning under the Modernist intellectual. In contrast to Percy, then, Warren is steadily skeptical. He sees and admits man as inclined to depravity, but he is never accepting of it. Yet neither is he able to reach a comforting perspective upon it at the metaphysical level. Rather late in life we have what one might speak of through analogy as his severely restrained reflection on his being still lost in the Cosmos, his poems in *You, Emperor and Others*, in which the irony turns sardonic – turns noticeably back upon the poet as if he finds himself still in a suspension, unable to break through and continue the journey. And there is a poignant biographical dimension here, if one reflects on that long friendship between Warren and Cleanth Brooks, the one a skeptic, the other steadily orthodox in his Christian belief.

It is not Warren's fiction or poetry with which we are most directly concerned here, however, but with his response to Melville, revealed in an extended essay in which it becomes evident that the piece is a species of literary analysis as intellectual autobiography – a popular species of criticism this century whose most celebrated instance is Eliot's *Selected Essays.* The essay is a prelude to a selection of Melville's fiction and poetry in an anthology, *American Literature: The Makers and the Making – Book B – 1826 to 1861*, which Warren participates in publishing with Cleanth Brooks and R. W. N. Lewis in 1972.* It is a rich essay to

* Since I wrote these paragraphs, there have appeared the letters between Cleanth Brooks and Allen Tate, edited by Alphonse Vinh. Tate writes Brooks (July 16, 1973) about the Warren-Lewis-Brooks anthology, asking "how could three men, individually and collectively, know so much?" Brooks responds at length (July 21, 1973), remarking in the course of his recollection of their joint labor, that "Red [Warren] did

our concerns which argues that Melville (and by our extension Warren) struggles for a metaphysical position whereby to reconcile Percy's version of the "self" to the contradictory impingement of the Cosmos upon human nature. The conflict out of which drama arises is caused by willful impositions of human nature itself upon the Cosmos. Thus the essay speaks of Melville as suspended in "the unending and extraordinary creative struggle between fierce and irresolvable contradictions" which have as focal nexus man's consciousness itself. The words are reminiscent of Eric Voegelin's description of consciousness as the nexus of the *metaxy*, the In-Between. The essay names the unending and contradictory impingement: "the contrary realities of good and evil, freedom and fate, knowledge and the unknowable, belief and unbelief, the life of safety and common sense and the life of dangerous, perhaps catastrophic pursuit of ultimate truth."

The resolution of this seeming impasse for Melville seems echoed in words from *White-Jacket*: "Sailor or landsman, there is some sort of Cape Horn for all," whether "boy" or "greybeard." Remembering Percy's suggestion of Billy Budd as Melville's prelapsarian innocent, we find this recognition also in W. H. Auden's tribute to Melville, quoted in the essay, about Melville's driving terror. (Percy remarks in praising Melville that he does not shy away from that terror, being "not afraid to address such matters.") Melville chooses the risk of the gale, Auden says, which blows him "past the Cape Horn of sensible success." The gale cries against that Cape Horn refuge: "'This rock is Eden. Shipwreck here.'" Defiant courage is Melville's stance, in company with that gale, recognizing it as well as a doomed courage since he is not himself one of those innocent "boys" whose courage proves but the bravado of youth innocent of inevitable doom.

But defiant courage isn't reserved to actual boys. Greybeards themselves are also capable of it. Thus Ahab in a middle way defies the St. Elmo's fire in the rigging: "Thou art my fiery father. . . . I now know that thy right worship is defiance. To neither love nor reverence wilt thou be kind." It is the gale's shout out of the breast of Ahab, a defiance out of that permanent strain in Melville's thought which our essay attributes to Melville's Calvinistic origins, against which he is in futile revolt. (And here, perhaps another thread relating Percy and Melville, if we remember the importance of Pascal to Percy, and that always hovering question of Pascal's relation to Jansenist associates, for any strictly orthodox mind skeptical about Pascal's own orthodoxy.) Melville, out of that Calvinist tradition, believes in Original Sin, but with a qualified adoption. Thus Melville, praising Hawthorne, speaks in praise of the "power of darkness" in Hawthorne which is derived "from its appeal to that Calvinistic sense, from whose visitations in some shape or other, no deeply thinking mind is always and wholly free. For, in certain moods, no man

Melville's poetry" but that Lewis did Melville's fiction. The essay would nevertheless have been done "collectively" for consistency. In addition, Warren's concerns with Melville elsewhere are consistent with the essay's argument, so that this essay, though a joint undertaking by Warren and Lewis, provides insight to Warren's reading of man in creation, especially in relation to what is said in this text of Melville as poet.

can weigh this world without throwing in something, somehow like Original Sin, to strike the uneven balance." Whatever that thrown weight, it effects an "uneven balance," but ironically it does so always against the thinking mind. It is a theme in Melville which we discover as well in some of Warren's work: in *Brother to Dragons*, or more explicitly perhaps in *All the King's Men*.

In the novel, Jack Burden stands as thinking mind against the force of Willie Stark's earthy defense of Original Sin as justifying his own lust for power. But as intellectual, Jack can so stand only through that almost destroying conclusion that he must be antagonist to nature itself, at whose heart is that mystery of evil which he calls "The Great Twitch." It is a conclusion which would seem to force Jack into the position Melville holds from time to time, seeing a "Natural Depravity" pervasive of nature – beyond any attribution to man as Fallen, but attributable to God, if there is a God. Of that depravity, Melville will add, that "though savoring of Calvinism," it "by no means involves Calvin's dogma as to total mankind." Thus he gives a more decidedly Manichaean bent to his own residual Calvinism. Depravity is suspected as a property of nature itself, not an effect of violence upon the person consequent in the person's own will as a weakening consequent to the Fall. In those circumstances to his "thinking mind," defiance seems the only acceptable position.

It is a position which, insofar as thought sustains him in a deportment of action he might discover to be best supported, not by that orthodox Christianity toward which his friend Hawthorne seems to struggle out of his own Puritan heritage, or as Eliot will similarly struggle to achieve a hundred years later out of his own Puritan heritage which has become "*Protestant* agnosticism." Perhaps, then, Stoicism may serve irresolution? There is, it would seem, a dogged endurance in Melville out of a jealousy to preserve his dignity against whatever the dark force permeating nature, resident even in his own mind. Such is the San Andreas Fault with which he must contend. And this reminds us thereby of a similar intent to an endurance in Percy as a "self." We see him characterize it in *Lost in the Cosmos* as the Depressed Self, attempting to transcend depression as an "ex-suicide." It is Stoicism then that is a first defense against whatever dark force threatens consciousness from within its troubled *metaxy*. As a Southern writer, affected by Southern history more deeply than he might wish to be, Percy discovers Stoicism endemic to the South, especially residual in its recent history – that is, a history reaching back only a hundred years to that decisive moment at Appomattox in the spring of the year 1865.

II

In an essay published in the year of his death, 1990, Percy enlarges upon his initial answer to the question serving as his title: "Why Are You a Catholic?" He has on occasion answered, "What else is there." Now, after a rather careful turning of the question in several perspectives, he gives a summary answer and then explicates it. His reasons, "this side of grace," can be enumerated: "Roman, Arthurian, Semitic, and semiotic." Here, to continue our reflections on his affinity to Melville, it is the "Roman" and the "Arthurian" that are of interest. By *Roman* he is not alluding to his Catholicism, but to the Romanism of Marcus Aurelius. By Arthurian he would recall Richard I of Scott's *Ivanhoe*, the "hero of the South for a hundred years" and his own "first hero." And he sees the two drawn together: "If one wished to depict the beau ideal of the South, it would not be the crucified Christ [though with Flannery O'Connor he agrees the South is Christ-haunted] but rather the stoic knight at parade rest, both hands folded on the hilt of his broadsword, his face grave and impassive as the Emperor's. In the South, of course, he came to be, not the Emperor or Richard, but R. E. Lee, the two in one."

Not the Emperor, who as supreme in power can afford the grave, impassive demeanor of the Stoic. Nor Richard I, leaning in triumph upon his broadsword, having overcome the infidel. But Lee, both in one, with an ambient poignancy in his person in that he is the defeated knight. It is in this defeat in large part, one might suggest, that Lee resonates for the Southerner after 1865, in his noble deportment as the defeated knight. Meanwhile, Percy does not abandon his first hero in consequence of his having become Christian. "After all, the pagans converted by St. Paul did not cease to be what they were. One does not cease to be Roman, Arthurian, Alabamian" by becoming Catholic. It is this sense in Percy of a continuing community with his first heroes out of history that interests us, but in respect to the history of the South it interests us primarily under the rubric of Roman Stoicism. Percy sees from Marcus Aurelius a significant intellectual inheritance to the Southerner. In our present context, it is an inheritance we might also detect Melville gravitating toward, especially evident in his little known but highly revealing book published the year after Lee's surrender at Appomattox. The poems of *Battle-Pieces and Aspects of the War: Civil War Poems* (1866) are written in response to current events during that war, in response largely to daily accounts from the war front. In reading them, we discover Melville's growing uncertainty about the justness of the "Northern" cause.

And well he might, not only given the climactic arrest of his sympathies in the political aftermath of the war, the radical Reconstruction period beginning at once at the war's end. There are as well conspicuous spectacles from the war itself as it moves to its end. Sherman's March to the Sea, following the burning of Atlanta, leads Melville to write two poems. The first, "The March to the Sea (December, 1864)" builds on a refrain increasingly ironic: "It was glorious glad marching,/ That marching to the sea." For "columns grooved their channels" (a figure out of Melville, the sailor) in a scorched-earth destruction in the name of victory. That was a progress in which "Fighting was but frolic," though that frolic left the countryside and its people devastated. At the poem's end Melville, that Northern patriot, raises a disturbing question: "Was it Treason's retribution – / necessity the plea?" Hawthorne a little earlier had raised much the same doubt in 1862, in an essay in the *Atlantic* called "Chiefly about War Matters," which piece made him notorious in the North, especially so since he called into question aspects of the Northern cause and exhibited his own irreverence for Lincoln.

The editor of the *Atlantic* suppressed his less than sympathetic portrait of Lincoln, Hawthorne's recollection of meeting Lincoln in Washington. Nor is he particularly kind in treating General McClellan and his staff. Lincoln as a Western man and Kentuckian by birth "is the essential representative of all Yankees," "honest at heart, and thoroughly so, and yet, in some sort sly, – at least endowed with a sort of tact and wisdom that are akin to craft, and would compel him, I think, to take an antagonist in flank, rather than make a bull-run at him right in front." How shocked Hawthorne might have been had he known this sly and crafty American hero in one of his machinations at about the time he met him. The week before the Battle of Gettysburg, Secretary of War Edwin Stanton, with Lincoln's approval, promised Medal of Honor awards to any member of the 27th Maine Regiment who would reenlist, lest they return home. And 864 medals were awarded, awards revoked in 1917 by the Adverse Action Medal of Honor Board.

Necessity, Milton had cried out, is the tyrant's plea, echoed by Melville in his "March to the Sea." Melville then writes of that swath of destruction from the Southerner's perspective in "The Frenzy in the Wake," dealing with Sherman's subsequent burnings in South Carolina. It is in this poem that one detects Melville's recognition of a Stoic necessity, forced first upon the South in order that it survive destruction. It is determined to endure since it has failed to prevail in its position. But to do so, it must be "Strong to suffer . . . and break/ The sinews of the Oppressor's knee/ That grinds upon the neck." The poem, Melville tells us, was written as reports reached the North of Sherman's progress from Savannah into South Carolina, laying general waste as a deliberate act of war against a civilian population. (The tactic had worked for Sherman as a young lieutenant sent against the Seminoles in Florida.) The destruction, therefore, (Melville observes in a note) "Undoubtedly [was] not in contravention of orders," and so must have been officially sanctioned. Melville then compares the strategy to Plutarch's account of the war between Pompey and Julius Caesar. But it is the residual suffering of the populace that troubles the poet. It is suffering doubled, since the populace is first sacrificed by their Southern leaders, a theme stronger in the earlier poems. But neither is it a noble cause on the part of the North, the cause betrayed through an intent to power by the victors. How could it fail to ingrain hate in the Southerner's heart, a hate deeper than despair in the suffering Southerner? That is Melville's late witness on behalf of the South.

An ironic conclusion by the poet, his final irony aimed at God, is engaged when Richmond falls: how "deter/ The helmed dilated Lucifer" now? Still, "God is in Heaven, and Grant in the Town,/ And Right through might is Law – *God's way adore*." Thus Melville speaks in the ironic mode Warren is attuned to, with allusion to Robert Browning's Pippa. It is a mode already present in the first of the poems, "Misgivings," dated 1860, long before the March to the Sea. In "Misgivings" Melville muses "on my country's ills" as a storm off the ocean rages outside his house. Here is "Nature's dark side" at work in a storm "formed behind the storm we feel" because we worry about our country's fate. Dark prospect of war, in which ignorant youth glories in exploits whose issue will very suddenly be the red wound blossoming but turning to dust as its only fruit. With such a dark view, Stoicism seems the only steadying possibility – a Stoicism which (lacking authority beyond the sense of survival) pits itself against the dark storm of the moment. For there is a difficulty with Stoicism which reveals itself at last, as it was to do to Percy.

There is an irony to our seeing Melville and Percy akin, as Percy does. Melville, too, sees Robert E. Lee as the last knight of Europe. In a long poem appended to his *Battle-Pieces*, "Lee in the Capitol," Melville imagines Robert E. Lee called before Congress after Appomattox. He imagines the event occurring in April of 1866, Lee called away from that "quiet seminary" in Virginia to defend himself before the victors. "Who looks at Lee must think of Washington," Melville writes, before Lee's name is associated with that quiet Virginia seminary. And that means we must look at both our founding father and first president, but also at the politically corrupt environment we call Washington, D.C., in April of 1866, a year after Appomattox. To his antagonistic interrogators, Melville's Lee says, "My word is given – it ties my sword;/ Even were banners still abroad, never could I strive in arms again/ While you . . . that pledge retain." A knight whose word is bond. But the South is a devastated land, and the victors must respond, not as they currently intend to do through a Radical Reconstruction. "Push not your triumph," Lee admonishes. "[D]o not urge submissiveness beyond the verge" in such a "broad anathema" which can but be more destructive than Sherman's marches.

Thus Melville, with Lee his spokesman, lessons the revengeful radical Congress, telling a fable of the Moorish girl, whose seducers would have her abandon her "sire" – a Christian – surrendering allegiance to the now powerful and triumphant Moors. She refuses, and the lesson is drawn. Every subversive plea to her has been vain because they are made against "Nature's strong fidelity," which is that fidelity of the local sustaining community. The Northern imposition upon the South, then, is a transgression against nature itself. For the Southerner is "True to the home and to the heart,/ Throngs cast their lot with kith and kin,/ Foreboding, cleaved to the natural part – Was this the unforgivable sin?" The poem continues briefly with a passionate plea from Lee for an honoring of these natural virtues, though without success.

Melville's final line in ironic summary: "Heaven shall the end ordained fulfill,/ We march with Providence cheery still." Melville, as does his Lee, reacts to that distortion of *human* nature as sustained in nature. Were he Thomas Aquinas rather than the disoriented son of Calvinist Puritanism, he might well decry a violation of natural law by the radicalized political sector, exercised through a positive law divorced from nature but advertised as proclaimed in the name of God. Its manner is that of the revengeful Moor. The manner of power thus decrees a positive law divorced from natural law. It is thus, in Lee's words, that the victors seem determined to "copy Europe in her worst estate," becoming Napoleonic in the name of democracy. Stark oppression then must be justified in the name of "God's will," when it is rather man usurping providence in the interest of power over the world's body. The inevitable economic, political, and social destructions are witnessed by Melville's Southern speaker in "The Frenzy in the Wake": the Northern invader is "an awful host," and "They move like a roaring wind." They are a present storm, behind which lies that other and more terrible one, the darker storm which shakes the hemlock in the rafter of the house, and even the oak in the driving keel of the ship at sea, to recall Melville's initial "Misgivings" in 1860.

Melville's portrait of Lee bears in it correspondences to a later and better poem, in which Lee speaks the whole: Donald Davidson's monologue "Lee in the Mountains." Lee here, as in Melville's poem, is no longer a Rebel but President at Washington seminary. Davidson's is a portrait of heroic endurance of defeat, under the necessities of that defeat in which Lee also remembers the world changed. "Those people came," he says, and after Appomattox the rest is an uncertain history for Western civilization. For if some poets measure a turning point into uncertainty as following World War I, centering perhaps in the Battle of the Somme (as does David Jones), to the Southerner as intellectual after 1865, the center becomes Appomattox in April 1865. Percy sees it so, and does not fully abandon that recognition, though he modifies it as he turns "Semitic" and explores semiotics. He will himself declare the turning point represented on the world stage in that bloody disintegration of souls in the trenches of World War I.

It is perhaps as much through the "Roman" influence on Walker Percy's thought (the Aurelian) as through the "Semitic" influence (the Christian) that he enlarges his perspective upon the Southern Stoic, discovering in doing so a complication requiring that Semitic rescue to the position. From his new perspective he can better hold the old and as yet not abandoned heroes as still dear to him. He may thereby come to some reconciliation with his own Southernness and so more comfortably settle in the vicinity of the Louisiana bayou near that increasingly

Modernist city, New Orleans. In his reflections on this enlargement of historical vision, he will remember old Southern heroes, especially Lee. But he does so in honoring as well that house in Greenville, Mississippi, where he spent twelve years of his youth. It is the house of Uncle Will, in which he witnessed from his thirteenth year "all manner of people who were trying to 'understand the South,' that perennial American avocation." They came to talk with Uncle Will, his "bachelor-poet-lawyer-planter" uncle: "other poets, politicians, psychiatrists, sociologists, black preachers, folk singers, itinerant harmonica players."

These are phrases from Walker Percy's introduction to a new edition of Uncle Will's famous *Lanterns on the Levee: Recollections of a Planter's Son* reissued in 1973, to which there will be added a brief note on "Uncle Will's House" in 1984. It is *Lanterns on the Levee* that has drawn that mixed collection of passengers through the South, and many of them stopped over at that "sort of bastard Greek Revival . . . gabled pile with a portico and two-story Ionic columns." Three years before his coming to stay with Uncle Will, the levee at Greenville had broken, flooding the town and for "four months the house rose from a fetid brown sea ten-feet deep. Dead mules floated into the front gallery." Interesting details to recall the year after *Lost in the Cosmos*, for the *Architectural Digest* (October 1984). But the details are more interesting in the light of his attempt three decades earlier to come to terms with Uncle Will's South in his essay on "Stoicism in the South" (1956), published a few years after Uncle Will's death. Out of his teenage experiences with Uncle Will as Southern Stoic, the piece suggests a self-exorcism, though it does not get Stoicism out of his system entirely.

The same year in which he recalls for the *Architectural Digest* the flood-ravaged house with mules floating in the front gallery, he speaks to a gathering at the University of Southwestern Louisiana, concerned with "How to Be an American Novelist in Spite of Being Southern and Catholic." Earlier, in 1956, addressing the topic of the intellectual Southerner as Stoic (and surely with Uncle Will very much in mind), he had suggested that the South "had always a stronger Greek flavor than it ever had a Christian," its "nobility and graciousness" being that of "the Old Stoic." For that intellectual Southerner, how like him "to go into Chancellorsville or the Argonne with Epictetus in his pocket; how unlike him to have had the Psalms." Thus an early beginning of an exorcism of the Stoic in himself, which had been absorbed through cultural osmosis in living with Uncle Will. But it is a judgment without a sufficient recognition of the variousness of Stoic influence in the South.

A reflection on Southern intellectual training, beginning from the signing of the Declaration of Independence well into the 19th century, would find as more influential on the Southern intellectual ambiance the presence of another Roman Stoic, Cicero. Cicero stood in opposition to the "Yankees" of his day, the centralizing power executed through the sword which brought the Caesars to triumph, costing Cicero his head. Cicero is primary in the South, though Aurelius is important to the more reflective Southern intellectual. Epictetus, however, may well be a later presence to the Southern intellectual in defeat – to an Uncle Will. To reduce the variousness of Stoical influences may thus tend to suggest that the Southern intellectual is of "a" mind when there is a variousness of influence. Donald Davidson examined this inclination to a reductionism in order to explain *the* "Southern mind" in an essay showing the inadequacy of such an attempt, in his *Attack on Leviathan* (1938). More directly he does so in his "Mr. Cash and the Proto-Dorian South" in *The Southern Review*, in which Cash's *The Mind of the South* undergoes a historically-learned examination of Cash's attributed singularity to the ambiguous "South."

When Walker Percy contributes his "Uncle Will" as an "Introduction" to *Lanterns on the Levee: Recollections of a Planter's Son*, he observes it is published the same year as Cash's book, and by the same publisher. (That same year Cash commits suicide, an irony Percy would not miss.) Cash's book, he suggests, treats the "Southern" class structure (aristocrats, poor whites, blacks) with better understanding than possible to Uncle Will in his position as the last Stoic. As for Uncle Will as Stoic, though not directly advanced as exemplum to Walker's early "Stoicism in the South," how "immediately we recognize the best in the South in the words of the Emperor [Aurelius]." Percy then quotes from him, not from Epictetus whom he has introduced earlier. The words for the Southern aristocrat who is not yet seduced to becoming a "Yankee of the mind," in Allen Tate's phrase, are an apt recollection of Robert E. Lee – Lee as a figure combining Aurelius and Richard I leaning on his sword at parade rest. Not "Marse" Robert, beloved of the predominantly non-aristocratic and non-slave holding Southerners who fought under him. Thus Aurelius in his own words: "Every moment think steadily, as a Roman and a man [for which, substitute as *Virginian* and a *gentleman*], to do what thou hast in hand with perfect and simple dignity, and a feeling of affection, and freedom, and justice."

We remember Herman Melville's dramatizing of Lee before a Congressional Committee. And we remember that poignant monologue by Donald Davidson as well, "Lee in the Mountains," which begins with Lee greeted on the steps as he goes up to his office as president of the Washington Seminary. Davidson's Lee sees himself "Walking into the shadows, walking alone/ Where the sun falls through the ruined boughs of locusts/ Up to the president's office. . . ./ Hearing voices/ Whisper, Hush, it is General Lee!" But not General Lee, this exile in his own land who "still must face,/ Day after day, the courier with his summons/ Once more to surrender, now to surrender all." And so let us remember Lee himself, in his own words rather than in these imagined circumstances of Melville or Davidson. Lee writes Markie Williams a year after Appomattox (April 7, 1866): "I am now considered such a monster, that I hesitate to darken with my shadow the doors of those I love best, lest I should bring upon them misfortune."

Again, Lee to Charles Marshall after Appomattox: "My experiences of men have neither disposed me to think worse of them nor indisposed me to serve them; nor in spite of failures which I lament, of errors which I now see and acknowledge, or of the present aspect of affairs do I despair of the future. The truth is this: The march of Providence is so slow and our desire so impatient; the work of progress so long, that of the individual so brief, that we often see only the ebb of the advancing wave and are thus discouraged. It is history that teaches us to hope." But for Walker Percy, these teachings of art and history, our remembering Lee, hardly promise recovery of hope, given the century he lives in. Lee is not Epictetus, but an Aurelius in defeat, with perhaps some faint recognition of Cicero in support of a slow progress of history under the vague influence of Providence. Meanwhile, observing the radical Reconstruction directed by Congress, under the banner of justice – actions against the defeated South which are increasingly disposed to revenge as justice's mode (as Melville objected) – how is one in exile to deport himself? As Virginia gentleman, even if the last one?

And so an added poignancy, reflected in a scrap of paper discovered in Lee's military valise after his death:

> The forebearing use of power does not only form a touchstone, but the manner in which an individual enjoys certain advantages over others is a test of a *true gentleman*.
>
> The power which the strong have over the weak, the magistrate over the citizen, the employer over the employed, the educated over the unlettered, the experienced over the confiding, even the clever over the silly – the forebearing or inoffensive use of all this power or authority, or a total abstinence from it when the case admits it, will show the gentleman in a plain light. The gentleman does not needlessly and unnecessarily remind an offender of a wrong he may have committed against him. He cannot only forgive, he can forget; and he strives for that nobleness of self and mildness of character which impart sufficient strength to let the past be but the past. *A true man of honor feels humbled himself when he cannot help humbling others.*

These are the words of a true gentleman in defeat, whose dignity lies in his enduring the disregard for him by a power no longer administered by a true gentleman devoted to the common good. They are words that Percy's Will Barrett has been denied, though he sees or senses the gist of them echoed in the life of his father. But his father, in a moment of despair, abandons the calm dignity of Lee's endurance of defeat. And perhaps Will hears something stirring toward a possible recovery in the murmuring voices of his old aunts as he listens to their evening talk. He stands in the dark, fingering the hitching post which is being slowly but inexorably encompassed by the oak. He cannot articulate as signs the sounds he hears, nevertheless intuitively responding to them. On the verge of a revelation, of a life-altering epiphany, he is unable to rationalize in words the disquiet he experiences, and so he strikes out for the Southwest desert.

Stoicism, then, is at last insufficient to the necessities of a "self," always in some respect in defeat, in that any self waits the "courier with his summons . . . to surrender all." It will be a reflection Walker Percy makes, though whether or not he was actually familiar with this final word from Lee about the "true man of honor," perhaps through his friend Shelby Foote, I do not know. Percy will declare that we in the South "can no longer afford the luxury of maintaining the Stoa beside the Christian edifice. In the past we managed the remarkable feat of keeping both, one for living in, the other for dying in." This is a remark whose roots may well lie in Tate's "Ode to the Confederate Dead," a point to reflect upon. And in that reflection we recall a letter Percy wrote Allen Tate (February 17, 1963), having read Tate's essay "Narcissus as Narcissus," quoted by Patrick Samway in his biography of Percy. "Through a falling out of events which escape me, I find myself ridden by two incubuses who appear to have no necessary connection with each other beyond the fact that there they are together: 'the formal ebullience of the human spirit' of the Confederacy and the solipsism-narcissism of the modern intellectual. Indeed your pairing of these two in the 'Ode' has always struck me, until now, as a shotgun wedding." Tate's essay, in relation to the poem which Percy knows well, reveals the voice in that poem to be a presence within his own consciousness, he distracted by the two incubuses: that of historical "Southerness" and of historical "Modernism."

Tate's is a poem whose concern is with the inadequacy of mere history to the person and ultimately to community, the insufficiency of a tradition unsupported by orthodoxy. As such, it registers a recognition in at least one of those Agrarians of the danger Eliot feared for them – a commitment resting final authority in history, in tradition unrescued by orthodoxy. It is a conviction Eliot is already insistent upon, shocking many of his erstwhile advocates who had celebrated *The Waste Land* as an epic certifying the end of history, so that orthodoxy having been routed, history itself might be set aside. Actually, Tate writes his poem some years before Eliot addresses, somewhat indirectly, his fear that the Agrarians may be unmindful of the depths of orthodoxy as a rescue of tradition. Indeed, Tate's poem appears the same year Eliot's "Ash-Wednesday" does, two years before *I'll Take My Stand* and five years before Eliot's *After Strange Gods*. At that earlier point, Tate is aware that tradition alone becomes an easy idol, leading intellect through nostalgia to set up the "ravenous grave" in the house of memory. That can but burden community tradition by an unwanted duality: history held in the amber of intellect by nostalgia – on set holidays – as counter to a present moment of consciousness divorced from history and ravenous for progress. The Stoa had thus been set "beside the Christian edifice," as Percy sees the old but continuing dualism in the South. It was a strategy doomed to failure. Now we have Hegelian reductions of history in the interest of progress, with brief time-outs – holidays as moveable secular feasts on our calendar, oriented to the future in concessions to a convenience of a busy world. Fourth of July or Memorial Day (and even for awhile a Confederate Memorial Day) made to coincide with memorial holidays on which postal service is suspended. Reflecting on his own poem in "Narcissus as Narcissus," Tate observes this division as antecedent to Appomattox. It is reflected in "Pascal's war between heart and head, between *finesse* and *geometrie*."

In turning from Cartesian temptations, Percy will also recall Pascal, coming to a recognition very like Tate's. It is this reflection which will lead him at last to suggest an epithet (which might even prove an epitaph) for our age: the Age of the "Theorist-Consumer." One notes a common "Southernness" between Percy and Tate, then. For both of them it reaches further back in history than to Appomattox and deeper into history than tradition without orthodoxy can explain. The speaker of Tate's poem, indeed, is the theorist in the process of becoming or serving the consumer. He turns from a moment of arrest in the Confederate graveyard, unable to see the graves as signs of anything but time's futile markers, demarcations of a dead past from a restless present, disturbed by that conclusion. He possesses a "knowledge/ Carried to the heart" but a knowledge which the head cannot riddle. Head says that man must at last carry his acts, but only to the grave – into history's abyss. A disturbing conclusion when honestly confronted by the uneasy Modernist mind. But what alternative? To set up the grave in the house? This has been a futile inclination by various communities as this Modernist speaker of Tate's poem considers it, needing only a counting of local and state and national museums, official graves set up in our community houses. Or there is that active sterilizing of history, "historical preservation" practiced on old school houses or court houses which are no longer even haunted by the ghosts of a community past.

Donald Davidson's Lee, from a position removed by time past from Tate's speaker – whom we suggest as a figure of the Modernist as history's victim – lingers on the steps of history, reflecting as he slowly climbs them. It is a dramatic circumstance one might find counterpointed with comic irony by Binx on the library steps in Percy's *The Moviegoer*. Binx, fresh from having read arguments left and right in the library's periodicals, stands arrested, in an equal agreement with both sides. And General Lee, on his way up the steps to his office on the quiet campus (in Davidson's poem) is moved by the boys' responses to him as their commander-in-chief in a cause now lost. He himself knows as they cannot a poignancy in that loss as he waits the "courier's" final call. And in those words of Lee himself as imaginatively provided by Davidson, there is a reflection upon man in defeat under an inscrutable Providence. Lee deports himself to those young gentlemen as kindly as he may. His darker thoughts on recent history, out of which rise foreboding thoughts on an uncertain future, are held close and unspoken, as if this were the last action of a "true man of honor" in protecting the boys at his feet. It is this aspect of Lee as the "last gentleman" that holds Walker Percy's loyalty. His is the Stoic's demeanor, even in Davidson's poem – Davidson burdened himself with an obligation of surviving against Modernism's spectacular erosions of his own beloved South.

Stoicism will not answer the necessity. Percy says in concluding his "Stoicism in the South," "the good pagan's [Aurelius'] answer is no longer good enough for the South." And yet . . . and yet. . . . One does not "cease to be Roman, Arthurian, Alabamian" through conversion, through entering that temple. One nevertheless will recognize that "the European knight with his broadsword at Mont-St.-Michel" will "make [no] sense without the crucified Jew above him." So Percy in "Why Are You a Catholic?" the year he died. That Stoic hero only becomes fulfilled upon entering that great Cathedral. Percy has come back to a position he speculates about many years earlier, in a letter to Caroline Gordon written four years before he speaks publicly on "Stoicism in the South." In April of 1952 he writes her:

> I agree with you about St. Thomas More. He is, for us, the Road Back. For our countrymen, I mean, for southerners. For More is the spiritual ancestor of Lee. He is the man to pray to for the conversion of the South. One of the stumbling blocks to the Southerner (or the American) who is drawn to the Church is that he sees not the Church of More, not the English church which is his spiritual home, but the Church of St. Alphonsus Liguori by way of the Irish Jesuits. If he does go in, he must go in with his face averted and his nose held against the odor of Italian-Irish pietism and all the bad statues and architecture. Of course this is somewhat exaggerated and prideful, because it is a salutary lesson in obedience and humility to take St. Alphonsus (Hell, he was a great saint!) But if Allen is forming a St. Thomas More Society I want in.

This, the year after *The Moviegoer* was published and his tribute to St. Thomas More still ahead of him, especially that of *The Thanatos Syndrome*. How to rescue the Southern Stoic to the Church, if not by the novelist's indirection in a pathological exploration of the Modernist malady of spirit? That is a task undertaken soon after Tate's and Davidson's engagements of the dilemma, to which Tate's own novel *The Fathers* (1938) is also relevant. It is a rescue more formally engaged by a German lawyer turned scholar by necessity, in recovering an orthodox understanding of *natural law* in resistance to the rise of Hitler. Percy, in the 1930s, had witnessed in Germany that disturbing presence, though whether along his subsequent way he became familiar with Heinrich A. Rommen's *Natural Law: A Study in Legal and Social History and Philosophy* is uncertain. In that work Cicero as Stoic proves a pivotal point of turning in respect to natural law, from a Classical concept toward the Orthodox concept later explicated by St. Thomas. Rommen's work published in German gained him imprisonment by the Nazis, after which he fled West in 1938. Eric Voegelin also fled in that year, and Percy will certainly encounter in Voegelin those stirrings toward a recovery of natural law as relevant to social community, though Voegelin is long in associating his concerns for that recovery with the arguments of Thomas Aquinas. In the concluding posthumous volume of his *Order and History, In Search of Order* (1987), and in a late recovery called "Quod Deus Dicitur" published in December 1985 and taking its title from Saint Thomas, we see Voegelin as having moved a considerable way toward an orthodox conclusion in respect to natural law.

III

Heinrich A. Rommen's *The Natural Law: A Study in Legal and Social History and Philosophy*, appeared in Germany in 1936, our present text reissued by Liberty Fund in 1998. It is a response to his recognition that bad ideas were beginning to reach consequential crises, though the Great Depression's heavy presence in the West allowed a delay in dealing with those ideas at a public level of action. The spectacle of general poverty prolonged the life of those bad ideas which were based on theory divorced from the truth of things. In Germany, however, Rommen's prophetic warnings gained for them a sufficient attention to lead to his arrest. That same year, 1936, Allen Tate and Herbert Agar published a symposium, *Who Owns America?*, with the intention of drawing together Thomists, Chestertonian Distributists, Humanists such as Irving Babbitt and George Santayana, and the Southern Agrarians in opposition to the Modernist intellectual establishment and its systematic erosion of community. This was not long after Eliot's Virginia lectures, *After Strange Gods: A Primer of Modern Heresy*, which had come just after the Agrarians' *I'll Take My Stand*. Presently John Crowe Ransom would publish his Kantian resistance to Modernism (though Kant is very much at the heart of that dominant secular religion), his *The World's Body*. Presently, too, Donald Davidson would publish his *Attack on Leviathan*, engaging current Hobbesean political philosophy. Intellectual waters long stagnant were being stirred.

With hindsight, we may regret that Rommen's little book was not more widely known this side of the English Channel at that time, especially by those contributors to *Who Owns America?*, since in it he reveals deeper, more ancient, causes of the ascendancy of power over any prospects of a "gentlemanly" administration of power. The causes are more ancient than the Battle of the Somme or the surrender at Appomattox. Rommen centers upon the necessity of our recovering an understanding of the reality of the natural law as necessary if we are to find our way through Modernism and into that Christian edifice Walker Percy is to speak of much later. In an irony of historical coincidence, then, as Rommen is putting himself in jeopardy, the young Percy on tour floats down the Rhine or hikes in the German hinterlands, encountering in the Black Forest enthusiastic young Nazis with their backpacks, singing toward a terrible history which much much later Percy will have his Fr. Smith anathematize as defiant of nature and of nature's God. The dark icon of that new Paganism will become the gas chambers.

What was necessary to recovery, Rommen argues, is an orthodox philosophy which might make viable the Western tradition everywhere in rapid decay. It was a decay whose effect was Rommen's own personal exile, he spending his subsequent years, from 1938, in America, building a career in political philosophy at Georgetown University. Thus he, along with Eric Voegelin and Leo Strauss, were early attuned to the cultural decay incipient to philosophical dislocations from Classical natural laws, the current aspect of which decay is the triumph of intellectual carpetbaggers in the Western academy under the authority of the "politically correct."

In what now seems to us a consummation of intellectual decay, a melding of totalitarian gnosticism is such that we seem baffled (as we need not be) by the coincidence of a new "liberal" autocratic tolerance dictating compassion in the name of abstract *culture*. Our current species of tenderness is also divorced from the source of tenderness and "wrapped in theory," as Flannery O'Connor remarked in her "Memoir of Mary Ann" at the beginning of the now notorious 1960s. Such theory divorced from the reality of human nature, she says, leads logically to terror, to the "forced-labor camps" and to "the fumes of the gas chamber." It is a warning not lost to Percy, who in his last novel meets the denizens of the gnostic wasteland that is our century. He insists with no uncertainty that abortion is but a logical extension of the gas chamber solution to universal tenderness. His is a position, indeed, that some of his admirers yet have difficulty forgiving him. What Percy was coming to recognize, long after his Rhine expedition but as well long before his *Thanatos Syndrome*, is the fundamental weakness of secular Modernism, whatever the species of its "transcendental" disguise. A considerable beginning was that early essay, his "Stoicism in the South" (1956). It is the same inadequacy he will engage by the novelist's indirection in what one is tempted to call his pseudo-novel – or at least a novel in the manner of St. Augustine's *Confessions*, his frustratingly engaging *Lost in the Cosmos*. We have remarked that, where St. Augustine must address confessionally his own recent radical Manichaeanism, Percy more subtly engages a species of that heresy under the motif of the Cartesian "self" in its variety of "loony" attempts to escape increasing entrapments of the self in a seemingly random Cosmos. Only in illusions of the "self" as autonomous does the self seem capable of a "transcendental" escape, but then it finds itself alienated in the end from reality. What a friendly approach, Percy's playful drama of the self at the end of its tether in his "self-help" book, hiding as it does an arresting tether which might well prove a reality called "natural law."

What Percy engages in his first-person narrative essay is a philosophical impasse which Rommen in his *Natural Law: A Study in Legal and Social History and Philosophy* understands and argues persuasively as not simply an impasse. It is rather a desperate strategy suited to the moment of denial by a gnostic power attempting to justify our general consent to an illusional impasse. That is the manipulative strategy requiring first of all a rejection of the doctrine of natural law in both its Classical and its Christian philosophical aspects. And here we should observe that Rommen did not run afoul of Nazi gnosticism because he addresses an unreal philosophical abstract concept, the *natural law*. His subtitle signals the grounds of his pursuit, with ominous implication for Nazi gnosticism. The argument is concerned with radical consequences to legal and social circumstances of community consequent upon the philosophical dislocations of natural law from reality itself – consequences become disruptively actual in social and political disorder of the 1930s. His adversaries could recognize at once the dangers of such an address to their own credentials as advocates of a new order intent upon totalitarian uses of power in the Germany of the 1930s. It is a totalitarianism rather engagingly presented through spectacle initially, evident not only in huge rallies with flags, but as well in the social byways of those enthusiastic youths marching toward their future destruction with knapsacks on their backs and songs anticipating triumph on their lips. (Melville might well have written a poem about it.)

Percy as tourist in Germany in the 1930s observed these high-spirited young Germans, no doubt with a disquiet akin to Will Barrett's experiences of deracination, to judge from Percy's later recollections of his experiences. Will and his maker Percy in New York City both set out for home, for Alabama and Mississippi, only to find themselves yet in exile in the place of their cultural origins. In a fiction, Will sets out for that Western desert, we observed, where lies "the locus of pure possibility" as an escape from that Mississippi cultural arrest where "it is always Wednesday afternoon, or perhaps Thursday." Percy was himself fond of that arid West, though made the more comfortable with it in knowing he could return to the Louisiana swamp land to which he had become accustomed. He had perhaps as person a sufficient experience of the dangers of any "locus of pure possibility," after those disquieting encounters with German youth in Bavarian forests in the distant 1930s, a youth intoxicated by a deracination in that locus which may be so easily misunderstood as promising untrammeled freedom. At least metaphorically, that old personal experience could be played in relation to Will in a Western desert, a vacuum of history to Will. There are disparities in the spectacles of Bavarian forest and Western desert, of course, but either lends itself to thought, supplying to that thought "objective correlatives" speaking an inherent common danger to a person's wandering desire. Dislocation through illusions of freedom, this is to say, may feed that danger to the self in which it desires of place – of "locus" – that in it there never be a "Wednesday afternoon" so to speak. And so there is a haunting familiarity between the *Wandervögel* clubs on Bavarian holiday and Will's encounter of accidental friends in a Southwestern desert.

It will be through a Will transmogrified from consciousness deracinated as it were in Tom More of *Thanatos Syndrome* that the dark mystery of spiritual deracination is resolved. And it is resolved dramatically for Tom More through that refugee from Germany, Fr. Smith, withdrawn to his Louisiana firetower. On one occasion of his own tour of Germany (Percy later recalled) he himself had even been bullied into rendering the Nazi's salute. But after all, he was soon to return to the more comfortable and safer environs of Chapel Hill – that intellectual center in the 1930s (some of the Agrarians might wish us to remember) which had already set itself against the Agrarian concerns voiced in *I'll Take My Stand*. There was a set of mind at North Carolina against those dangerous young "radicals" at Vanderbilt, a rejection made largely (as some of the Agrarians argued) in the name of an abstract tenderness requiring state programs poured into the local community by centralized authority from the top, in the name of progress. It will only become evident much later that the Liberal political agenda, beginning then to be ascendant at the North Carolina academy, is but another species in its intellectual origins of that "conservative" agenda (as it will be characterized by the political Left) of the Nazi regime. A shocking assertion! That is why Solzhenitsyn at Harvard in 1978 proved so shocking when he made his challenge to the American intelligentsia. His shocking words, yoking Western "democracy" and Stalin's species of totalitarianism:

> The mistake must be at the root, at the very basis of human thinking in the past centuries. It is the prevailing Western view of the world which was born during the Renaissance and found its political expression starting in . . . the Enlightenment. It became the basis for government and social sciences and could be defined as rationalistic humanism or humanistic autonomy: the proclaimed and enforced autonomy of man from any higher force above him. (June 8, 1978)

These words continue to be a challenge to the intellectual Left, which is still attempting to come to terms with the revolt of its own children in the 1960s. It is a challenge which will be seconded much later, with an equally alarmed response from the aging Liberal community (many of them associated with the Neoconservatives) in response to a now famous symposium in Richard John Neuhaus's *First Things* in the mid-1990s: "The End of Democracy? The Judicial Usurpation of Politics." Especially offensive, even to some patrons of *First Things* who quickly dissociated themselves from that periodical, was the argument by the contributors in which they speak of our judicial "regime." The symposium and its aftermath may be suitably considered in relation to a spectrum of work subsequent to *I'll Take My Stand*, principle among them Bertrand de Jouvenel's *On Power: The Natural History of Its Growth*; C. S. Lewis's *Abolition of Man*; Richard Weaver's *Ideas Have Consequences*; Eric Voegelin's *Science, Politics & Gnosticism* and his *From Enlightenment to Revolution*. And of course, here central to our own and to Percy's concerns, Rommen's *Natural Law*.

Rommen in his address to Classical Stoicism is more kindly inclined to that concept than a strict Thomistic address might warrant. For Stoicism must at last be seen as a species itself of a gnostic exercise of power, distinct from Christian understandings of the doctrine of natural law. Percy is becoming attuned to a parallel to, not an amalgam of, the two doctrines, and he will find them incompatible. Hence he will remark in his early essay Faulkner's Stoic, Colonel Sartoris, as bearing "the nobility of the natural perfection of the Stoics, the stern inner summons to man's full estate, to duty, to honor, to generosity toward his fellow men and above all to his inferiors." But Percy then remarks the nature of the Stoic's devotion to virtues, the limited grounds to this species of a holy cause. For the Stoic is not a subscriber to the doctrine of *noblesse oblige* "because they [his fellow man] were made in the image of god and were therefore lovable in themselves, but because to do them an injustice would be to defile the inner fortress which was oneself." It is this parallel of coincidence between Classical Stoicism and Christian love which has allowed a luxury no longer viable in the South, no longer tolerable, the "maintaining of the Stoa beside the Christian edifice."

Stoicism founded on Classical natural law had allowed a public deportment to a defeated people – the South – which in a small span in Western history seemed capable of sustaining the self in honor and courage, even under the burden of a pervasive defeat and of radical dislocations of local community through that defeat under the absolute dictation of central government. In our own moment, in which there is such a general cynicism about the risks of public service, given the daily reminders of corrupt public servants in high and low station, it is difficult to appreciate as salvific – if but *temporally* salvific – any virtue in this Stoical self-justification. It is nevertheless a deportment remembered as heroic out of the residue of the generally destructive wash of recent history, which wash proved vital to much of the literature now categorized as that of the "Southern Renaissance," beginning with the Fugitive poets in the 1920s. (At the time Percy received the National Book Award for *The Moviegoer*, responding to the question of why there had occurred such a flowering of letters in the South, Percy responded that, a principal cause was: "Because we lost the War.") Faulkner recognized this as at least something we must hold on to, dramatizing heroic futility in his Colonel Sartoris, who would not (in Percy's words) "defile the inner fortress which was oneself."

That is the unifying theme of one of Faulkner's more popular "adventure" stories – or series of stories – about the "late unpleasantness," his *The Unvanquished*. The ironic complexity of the title itself points toward Percy's own concern for the inadequacy of the Stoa as fortress to the self, a central reason for public obligations to heroic public service in the name of social and political order. What a poignant confederacy then of the young Bayard Sartoris and his black companion Ringo and that Southern lady, Drusilla, who turns willfully masculine (compare Clytemnestra) to defy the Yankees. (Drusilla is a more complex figure than the ever-popular Scarlett O'Hara). Bayard, Ringo, Drusilla view the late Colonel lying in state, much smaller than any of them can remember him in life. The Colonel leaves them each with the riddle of how public office may be maintained against the growing social and political disorder most various in its erosions. Hero or traitor? Unvanquished or vanquished? The question rises out of the disparity Bayard Sartoris recognizes between his memory of his father, Colonel Sartoris alive, and his present repose in death. Bayard knows, as those around him don't, that his father occasioned his own death – a self-execution at the hands of an honorable enemy. Bayard, recognizing this, makes his way to his father's bier through those others, a "chorus" who watch him as he has now become the central protagonist. Those others "stood with the unctuous formality which the Southern man shows in the presence of death – that Roman holiday engendered by mist-born Protestantism grafted onto this land of violent sun." And then he sees his father lying as he had anticipated, "saber, plumes, and all." He sees that familiar face "in repose for the first time . . . the empty hands still now beneath the invisible stain of what had been . . . needless blood," a recognition which had led Colonel Sartoris himself to accept death at the hands of Redmond whom he had wronged rather than kill Redmond. Bayard looks at that presence that so recently seemed larger than life itself to him as a boy. But his father (as Bayard knows) had wronged Redmond and because of his father's Stoic code has seen as the only righting possible a sacrificing of his life – not for Redmond but for the code itself. Colonel Sartoris now lies small and cold in all the trappings of that code. He can hardly seem to Bayard the Stoic knight as if leaning on his sword at parade rest. Now he is only man reduced to the compass of a worldly death.

That is a scene from Faulkner warranting a considerable explication not here possible, an explication suited nevertheless to our reflective contemplation, especially perhaps by a reflective juxtaposition of that other scene from Percy's *Last Gentleman* in which Will stands alone in that Mississippi darkness, hearing the inane chatter of those old aunts as he touches that hitching-post which is slowly being consumed by the sheltering oak, remembering his own father as a suicide. That is a dramatic moment verging on a mystical recovery of the reality of natural law as understood by Thomas Aquinas, such a moment as that dramatized in its reality by Gerard Manley Hopkins in quest of his own understanding of the pied, imperfect, beauty of creation itself through man's abandoning responsibility of stewardship, revealed to rational intellect through natural law. But it is at a remove from Faulkner's fictional moment when Ringo and Drusilla are obsessed by death, expecting Bayard to avenge his father as a resolution of that ambiguous mystery of justice as always complicated by good and evil in the actions of man. They are incapable of understanding that Bayard, in refusing to kill Redmond, as they charge him to do, emerges unvanquished.

For Percy himself, though still drawn to the honor and courage of the hero as Stoic, he must as Christian begin to acknowledge the Stoic's deportment possible only on the presumption that honor and courage are at last to be reckoned only at a private level. Even the Emperor Aurelius, undefeated Stoic, must answer that summons of the last courier demanding all in the midst of an unraveling Rome. And so the conclusion forced by the logic of the Stoic is that his noble doctrine proves dependent upon the will of the self to its own self-rescue. The courage of the heroic act in the moment of self-sacrifice can at last but prove an uncertain legacy to community, insofar as its vital continuity is at issue. Thus the Stoic hero is isolated as hostage to history and to the poignancy of dramatic art. As a doctrine, it lacks any guiding authority other than that of the isolated Stoic himself, evidenced as in isolation by the diversity of manifestations, even in old Classical Rome as that formidable state turns toward decay. Epictetus, Cicero, Aurelius – a complex company of disciples who share no ultimate end beyond the possible pleasure of self-esteem, save perhaps the poignancy of monuments in decay. No mean end, but not an end capable of a community become vital, become embodied under the transcendent authority of Love.

This recognition by Percy, made within the grounds of his own Southernness, is not limited to the local history and geography of the defeated South. For if it were, it could only be "historical" memory. Eliot, after "Ash-Wednesday," will engage a larger prospect of our Western decline from abiding truth. In his "Choruses" from *The Rock* (1934), contemporary to Percy's sojourn into Nazi Germany, Eliot's prophetic voice enjoins us to "Make perfect your will," a necessity quite contrary to that sense that perfection lies through Modernist willfulness. Eliot's voice insists that "There is no life that is not in community." The theme of this "Pageant Play" is community, in that sense of community spoken to by St. Paul, whereby tradition is accommodated to the Incarnation as the rescuing act to community by Love. Eliot will there touch themes Percy will come to, as when Eliot observes that in our century something has happened which has never happened before in our history. For now men "both deny gods and worship gods, professing first Reason,/ And then Money, and Power, and what they call Life, or Race, or Dialectic." Thus will we have earned our epitaph as an age, the age Percy dubs that of "theory and consumption." Eliot's phrasing: "Here were decent godless people: Their only monument the asphalt road/ And a thousand lost golf balls." Epitaph suited in its ironies to an age which Flannery O'Connor describes as governed by tenderness wrapped in theory. This decent godless people, since Eliot's words and O'Connor's, yet struggles burdened by that icon to its godlessness: the gas chambers first, then ethnic cleansing loosed as a new "universal" at the lag end of this Modernist age of history which has been devoted to an intellectual abandonment of natural law. With those dislocations, the self is now left suspended in terror over the San Andreas Fault of Cartesian isolation of that self from both nature and community.

And so for the restless self, Stoicism proves a dead end – given history's inevitable triumph over the self, since even memorial tombs decay. But Stoicism as doctrine had begun to erode under the assault of the Skeptics even before the empirical triumph of Rome, as Rommen argues. The eroding path to the abyss has been mined by the deceit of philosophical signs buried in our way by the Sophists. For the Sophists themselves depended upon that ancient heresy which our world thinks it discovered, the presumption of intellectual autonomy, with man the ultimate measure of truth. Given that presumption, man measures by power – the power of any idea sufficient to any current activist's power over community. We see it in history, on display in the Age of the Caesars at Rome, from whom Aurelius is a descendent. As for an early victim of that usurpation of man's Stoic role in his sacrifice to the common good, standing Stoically against usurpation of power: it is Cicero who loses his head in the shower of spectacle accompanying the defeat of Pompey by Julius Caesar. The principle of that doctrine which Aurelius will pronounce, quoted by Percy, will only serve courage and honor as virtues of the self self-recognized.

IV

"Democratic" Rome is no more, though Cicero proves to have cast a long shadow as Stoic, one not sufficiently acknowledged perhaps in our concerns for Southern Stoicism. It is Cicero who is a principal figure much revered in the South up to 1861 and beyond. His great speeches, along with Caesar's *Gallic Wars* of course, were a mainstay at places like Washington seminary in Virginia. Cicero is important also to the intellectual training of the "European knight" whom Percy sees as residual in Robert E. Lee. Rommen in his study of the natural law will hold that Stoicism "prepared the way for the Christian natural law," a school of thought in its Classical roots reaching back to Zeno and "flowering in Rome in the imperial age." One of its great figures in this flowering was Seneca, an early interest of T. S. Eliot, we note. Especially there was that "emancipated slave Epictetus," whose appetitive Stoicism was to erode aristocracy's responsibility of *noblesse oblige*. But most important to the European knight as Romantic hero, especially in Percy's estimate, was the Emperor Marcus Aurelius. In Aurelius, self-sacrifice is persuasively articulated to an intellectually elite. Yet it is Cicero, Rommen says, who was Stoicism's "great popularizer," through whom "the wealth of Stoic thought was handed down to the medieval world" by his writings. And it is that "wealth" which we must appreciate (as Rommen had had little occasion to observe before his exile) in the political and social history of the South. Cicero was the dominant presence through his writings, taught in the widespread Southern academies.

Here we may observe a presence always in opposition to Stoicism from its beginnings, that of the Skeptic. Skepticism as a philosophy is formally derived from the Sophists, those notorious antagonists to Socrates. Our own perspective speaks its derivation as much older, of course, reaching back to the garden in Genesis. The ruthless varieties of that revolt, littering our century with uncounted casualties sacrificed in the name of intellectual autonomy, we would associate with the Fall in Christian doctrine. And it is that Christian perspective upon Stoicism which becomes of increasing concern to Walker Percy, who as a skeptic (but not in any formal sense belonging to a "school") begins to make his way toward the steps of that Christian edifice. Along that way he plays in words, with an ironic effectiveness, upon a certain skeptical suspension that he knows well. It is in that scene in which Binx Bolling stands on the library steps in a decayed city in a Louisiana swamp country, himself amusingly and cheerfully lost in the swamps of thought's despond, agreeing on the one hand with the "Liberals," and yet agreeing as well on the other hand with the "Conservatives."

Rommen summons as a principal figure out of that old Skeptical School, one Carneades (2nd and 3rd centuries B.C.), who is a fierce evangelist for Skepticism, attacking the natural-law doctrine of the Stoics such as one finds in Cicero. That Stoic law as propounded by Cicero in "For Milo" is cited by Rommen and quoted: "This . . . is the law, O judges, not written, but born with us, which we have not learnt, or received by tradition, or read, but which we have taken and sucked in and imbibed from nature herself, a law which we were not taught, but to which we were made, which we were not trained in, but which is ingrained in us, namely, that if our life be in danger from plots or from open violence or from the weapons of robbers or enemies, every means of securing our safety is honorable." That is the *lex nata*, which in its Stoic formulation is not merely an animal survival, but animal survival on *honorable* terms. The extremities of violence are justified by the dishonorableness of the enemies to our survival: those enemies exercising plots, or robbers and the like. Very well, argues Carneades, but what if. . . ?

And so to the honor-bound Stoic, Carneades proposes what is remembered as "the plank of Carneades," with the intent to ridicule the Stoic's sense of justice through his reductionism. Suppose, he says, two survivors of a shipwreck, happening upon a board from the wrecked ship at the same time, a "plank" sufficient to buoy only one of them? Where then lies any prospect of a "justice" sufficient to the situation? Seventeen centuries later, Rommen suggests, there is given a sufficient answer, by Suarez in the 16th century A.D. That is a juncture in our history just before Descartes and Pascal and the growing agonies of the self as alienated from fellow selves through the emerging doctrine of self-sufficiency. Even as the Cosmos begins to haunt the Western intellectual community with its increasing fascination as scientifically solvable, the self becomes increasingly remote unto itself. In that circumstance, Suarez argues, the order of justice gives way to the order of charity, the action of openness to the creation through love, exercised in response to particularities.

Rommen concludes his anecdote by suggesting that "Positivism in ethics and law reached its climax with Carneades . . . in connection with the repudiation of objective knowledge of reality and essences and with the denial of metaphysics." And we remark once more the dilemma: in the absence of metaphysics, intellectual action proves only *ad hoc*, in service to some radical version of Positivism in defense of the autonomous self. That Positivist mind is a presence not only alive at the time of Suarez. It is latent from the beginning in the intentionality whose rubric is *non serviam.* And it will survive and prosper after sound refutation of it on the Christian principle of charity, of love. For this is not a love which prevails in the political and social arena where there is nevertheless always much talk of the common good. A Positivist force regardless of love comes to prevail, persuasive to us through a sentimentality stirred in the name of the common good. That is the infection in Western thought, to the horror of Dostoevsky as he sees it beginning to flourish in his beloved Russia at the middle of the 19th century, first engaged by him emphatically in *Notes from Underground*. It bursts out in sores on the body politic East and West, recognized belatedly by some of us, with the promptings of Rommen or Solzhenitsyn or Voegelin.

In the interest of a just tribute to Stoical intentions, Rommen finds the core of its ethics as preparing a way for fulfillment through the Christian understanding of the natural law. For the Stoic, knowledge and a unity of knowledge issuing in conduct for the common good is the ideal, the configuration represented in the "sage." The sage is an ideal intellectual hero at least, and as Stoicism begins to decline, the sage is rescued in that "grander representative of Christianity, the saint." It is the saint, then, who is capable of refuting Carneades, as Cicero cannot. And so it is in praise of the Stoic as foreshadowing the saint that Rommen gives us his moving tribute to the sage, revealing at once why Percy is drawn to such a figure but showing us as well why that is a position not at last sufficient. Its inadequacy will lead Percy to pronounce against the residual Southern Stoicism, saying that "the good pagan's answer is no longer good enough for the South."

Rommen's tribute then:

> The sage is the man who carries his happiness within himself, who in inner self-sufficiency remains undisturbed by external events. Knowledge and conduct are not dependent on the irregular influences of the world: the sage is calm, unmoved by passion. It is owing to the passions and their excesses that clearness of perception and judgment becomes impossible. For this reason man does not attain to a clear knowledge and judgment of what is truly worth striving for. This consists essentially in conformableness to the rational nature of the sage. Virtue consists in the positive determination of conduct through will power in accordance with rational insight into man's essential nature. Virtue is right reason. Nature and reason are one. Right reason and the universal law of nature, which holds undisputed sway throughout the universe, are also one. Obedience to the eternal world law in a life lived according to reason: such, embraced with religious fervor, is the ethical principle of Stoicism. It thus means to live in harmony with oneself, to live in accordance with one's rational nature; for the latter manifests the world law.

The problem is that, after encounter with Revelation, the "world law" is not enough as St. Paul cries out again and again. Indeed, even to the Classical Stoic it isn't, as witnessed by an intrusive pathos, hinting at melancholy, at those points of reflection when the self as Stoic finds self-awareness removed from action in the world. The knight leaning on his broadsword, if oblivious to that crucified Jew under whose authority alone he can be true knight, is subject to melancholy, perhaps even unto death. It will require "rationally" as contemplative idea, one fears, the final solution to be not death on the battlefield, but suicide.

At that point where the Stoic seems to have reached a harmony with himself in living in "accordance with [his] rational nature," he will have come to the threshold of an inevitable indifference to natures separate from his own increasingly isolating self-ideal. His specific rational nature turns more and more to a service of his will, serving as a rational virtue "the positive determination of conduct through will power." That is one of the origins of Positivistic deportment to creation itself. How easily, as experience teaches each of us when thoughtfully engaged, does a "right reason" become sufficient authority as its own universal law of nature. Thus a subversion of reality at large is justified. But more destructively, that reality of the givenness of the person as a "self" is distorted by his deporting himself through right reason as the ultimate authority. It is a subversion of intellect underway, whereby at last – the Stoic reduced to Positivistic solution of his own alienation – the rational Stoic is transformed to authoritative Positivist, "universalizes" his own specific existence as person and arrives at a sovereignty of the self.

It is a deportment, let us observe, which has been at the expense of that complex reality which impinges circumstantially upon the increasingly isolated self, making most uncertain any possibility that it may maintain self-harmony. Here speaks the danger of a final spiritual failure through indifference to givenness, first that of creation at large, but at last an indifference to that "self's" own existence. There, a final threshold – which to cross is spiritual suicide. For Percy, that leaves one in that Modernist distortion of contingencies, leaves him astride what he calls (in a late reflection) "The San Andreas Fault in the Modern Mind," a "Fateful Rift." The yawning abyss occurs as the ultimate terror. For then "Mind" finds itself self-betrayed through illusional manipulations of Cartesian Idealism. It is self-betrayed beyond an excuse that, as history's victim, history is the predetermining force resulting in the self sacrificed to nothingness. That is the failed excuse of Eliot's Gerontion. For history with its "cunning passages" and "contrived corridors" and "issues" proves such a subtle enemy only through our "ambitions" stirred out of our "vanities." Thus has occurred a journey of the self in collusion with history which Percy recognizes as evident "historically." In our Modernist philosophy and science it commands a servitude of autonomous intellect. But Percy sees as well that the journey of the lonely self may yet allow a recovery. It is the recovery possible which he advocates as that of the "ex-suicide" in *Lost in the Cosmos.*

The *lex nata* of a Cicero, dictating a heroism of the Stoic which is internal to him as a "self," will itself lead to a sense of isolation, then, so that in that "honorable" deportment to the general good as celebrated in either Cicero or Aurelius, Stoicism proves a deportment hardly approaching the action of love, which Christianity will declare the overriding commandment. Only love can solve the dilemma between justice and mercy ultimately – even solving that dilemma of the "plank of Carneades." In this solution as seen from the Christian perspective (we are reminded) lies the opening upon a transcendence far other than that species of Stoical "transcendence" which proves to be but a withdrawal of the self from the world. The Stoic's way is not a surrender to creation in that "way" of transcendence which is spoken of when we are reminded that he who would save his life must lose it. For the saint, then, the Witness – the Word – speaks abidingly: "I am the way, the truth, and the life." One is therefore called to sacrifices in an open surrender to life itself through love.

Suarez, this is to say, suggests a solution to the impossible dilemma to which Carneades submits the intellectual Stoic: the order of justice when challenged by an impossible dilemma gives way to a new dimension of intellectual vision: the order of charity – of love. In that order, as opposed to the order of justice, death is the summoning courier but he is met with an ultimate self-surrender that denies death itself its dominion. The pagan world, Percy argues, is no longer sufficient to his South, for it is a world peopled by a variety of survivors of that old inadequate address to life which proved at last to be actually an opposition to life in the futile attempt of self-salvation. The hidden antagonist death must still be met, when all attempts at self "transcendence" have failed. Thus the commandment to the order of charity challenges us beyond logic's reductionisms. That is why the traditionalist must sort tradition in the light of orthodoxy. Certainly that proved necessary for Eliot and at last for Percy. Both of them struggled with complications out of Occam and Descartes and Kant, and their kindred intellects recognized and unrecognized. Percy will turn to persons struggling to overcome reductions of life, often in bizarre ways, providing him a comic dimension to his art. Not that many of these likenesses in real life would recognize their intellectual origins in such "ancient" philosophies as those of the Sophists or Skeptics or Stoics, whether those actual persons giving rise to fictional agents in his novels were inhabitants of the geographical South or of the wider world. But, given the natural law in St. Thomas's sense, at some level of self-awareness, whatever the place or time, the person is always Christ-haunted.

Our deracinated selves, on the threshold of a new millennium, are survivors of an old paganism resurgent and ascendant in the latest history – self-justified at least in part out of a cynicism bequeathed by the Sophists and by a skepticism about life distantly echoed in the old formal Skeptics, with both of whom Socrates did battle. In this course of our argument, we might consider that Plato anticipates St. Augustine, with Socrates as a confessor lacking an awareness of the historical event, the Advent, that rescued Augustine. It is a suggestion related as well to Eric Voegelin's own monumental engagement of the dilemma of reason in contention with faith in his own spiritual and intellectual autobiography which we know as his five-volume *Order and History,* the early volumes of which both Percy and O'Connor welcomed to their concerns. For all of them (Voegelin, Percy, O'Connor) the necessity is to recover an order beyond the byways of history, requiring Revelation's transcendent dimension to that longed-for order. In this respect, Voegelin's *Israel and Revelation* and his *Plato and Aristotle* are of particular relevance, and in a more immediate aid to this speculative concern we might turn also to Josef Pieper's essay *"Divine Madness": Plato's Case against*

Secular Humanism. In these lectures, Pieper explores correspondences between Plato's quest and St. Thomas's metaphysical vision. In such reflections, then, we find Percy's attempts as diagnostician of the Modernist malaise in his fictions and in his speculative essays enriched for us. For it is with his own comic resistance that Percy engages a naive, residual Stoicism, now reduced to sentimentality in Percy's and our world. In the public arena of psychological and social and political concerns this sentimentality has become ubiquitous, among random "selves" who, variously self-justified, take refuge in selfishness in the name of the "common good." With an Enlightenment fillip heavily present out of Voltaire, Percy turns a residual Enlightenment thought back upon itself, that being his mischief through signs, one aspect of his "indirection" as analytic novelist.

Flannery O'Connor addresses the same contagion of spirit, though remarking the malady in terms somewhat differing from Percy's. She is excoriating in her address to Modernist sentimentality in her letters and her talks, as well as devastating to them in her fictional treatments. What concerns her is the loss of *person*, though she sees as well that there always lingers at least a cause of hope in the reduced person, who can't be poorer than dead. Not yet dead, the person tends to be Christ-haunted in spite of himself. Her first novel *Wise Blood* is devoted to this condition in her protagonist, Haze Motes. Meanwhile and contrary to her vision, the loss of spiritual life is celebrated as a gain by a dominating science and philosophy built on the presumption that intellect is independent, capable of seizing its own absolute freedom. That presumption, assimilating support through popular sentimentality, leads to a simplified ethical address to the common good. Thus O'Connor's remark that we wish to "govern by tenderness" though we have abandoned the source of tenderness, Christ. That tenderness has been "wrapped in theory" to such a clever extent that it proves palatable to any intellect considering itself sophisticated – proud to have advanced itself beyond traditions outworn. Its "present" is for such an intellect the first moment of any world – until it encounters a terror buried deep in tenderness as deracinated from its source, a floating idea, ending in "the fumes of the gas chamber." A shocking spectacle, but shocking to a "self" for reasons difficult to name with the current shibboleths of a pervasive sentimentality excusing any self of participation in its own destruction. For such false theory is the spring of intellectual action independent of truth itself, and while it may seem to justify the actor, it can do so only so long as the will obfuscates the true nature of its origin of action: self-love.

By such self-disorientation, a turning in upon the self and away from the truth of things, what wonder that we discover ourselves "lost in the cosmos"? We flounder in what has become a civil and political and social swamp of random ideas. Yet we cry out for a rescue by a light drawing us, fitfully called upon as the "common good." Poor, foolish – or as Percy has it, "loony" – man. Governed by spectacle, reduced in a service to theory seldom pursued to its bubbling center (self-love), we as random community implode the age into this "Age of the Theorist-Consumer." Is this the last stage upon which intellect as pagan is to have its last dance? That is the contingent possibility Percy unfolds with mischief in his "Last Self-Help Book." And with that contingency in mind, we remark the relation of spectacle to theory, a theme to be pursued *passim*, since it is a concern very centrally relevant to our own intellectual wanderings and so to any prospect of a recovery that might reorient us in our journey as *homo viator* through the cosmos and beyond, if we are to escape a circling randomness. For randomness is the intellectual vortex of the self which leads downward to despair. It is by this summary statement that we underscore the common theme shared by Percy and O'Connor.

In a panic moment, sensing the self caught in a downdraft to nothingness, we most probably seize upon *spectacle*. But since spectacle is largely accidental to substance, it sloughs off in fragments, dragged down by the self clinging to it in the descent. In a last desperation, that self may rid itself of spectacle clung to as if it were reality's essence, through becoming "ex-suicide" Percy suggests. The most pressing ghost of spectacle? The consciousness, become itself insubstantial. Edgar Allan Poe foretold it: "All that I am or all I seem/ Is but a dream within a dream." Thus the temptation to suicide as solution, a temptation, incidentally, which Percy speculates about all along his way, coming to affirm that speculation a prelude to rescue of the self in *Lost in the Cosmos*. That is, the self as "ex-suicide" comes to survive more fundamentally than allowed by the spectacles of selfhood. He who would lose his life to solve the terror of this grave descent into the abyss must, with the Stoic's resolve, embrace that descent to oblivion in a surrender to the absurdity of existence. It is a lesson Percy learned in part from Jean-Paul Sartre, one ventures. It threatened to cost him dearly, in that by an Existential adaptation of Aurelius to Modernist circumstances one risks actual oblivion, only (as Percy will say often) escaping that oblivion through grace. There will continue with Percy to the end a shocked recognition of how near he came to oblivion, perhaps somewhat prevented by his labor in removing obstacles to grace – including the labor of his comic response to absurdity as novelist. In that comic "role" we discover in him an almost forgiving stance toward creation itself, creation – the cosmos – being the context to his intellectual dilemma.

One might imagine (as a diagnostic novelist certainly) a character in similar intellectual dilemma whose response might be to seek revenge against existence by a literal suicide. It is a theme developed with psychological finesse in *The Last Gentleman*, in that retreat by Will into the desert Westward. (In that Western desert there had also been a confrontation of what Robert Penn Warren's Jack Burden calls "The Great Twitch" in *All the King's Men.*) What we seem to notice in Percy, as reflected subsequently in *Lost in the Cosmos,* is his own escape from that confrontation, for he as a "self" become ex-suicide eschews the literal response taken by Will's father and by Percy's own father. Actual suicide is a futile revenge against or rejection of existence. Instead, there is Pascal's wager. In his last year, in "Why Are You a Catholic?", Percy is still aware of having survived as such an "ex-suicide." But in accounting for the "Why" of his having chosen

Roman Catholicism, he defers his own answer to grace, grace being a mystery of rescue "which leaves one unclear about who does the choosing." In such uncertainty as to whether one chooses to be rescued or is rescued despite either choice (an old Jansenist problem bordering on a heresy which Pascal is sometimes charged with entertaining), little surprise that such a person might surrender to existence itself through spectacle. If one is diagnostic novelist and understands that to be his gift and limit as artist, he might very likely dwell upon the symptomatic – upon spectacle. Otherwise he might risk the hubris of a pretense to being theologian or philosopher. Better a minor scientist whose instrument is art than to pretend to a major understanding as if having penetrated to the core of reality as *sage*, even Rommen's Stoical *sage*. Saint? That is out of the range of speculation.

We seem, as intellectual community at this pass of our history, rather cursed as persons entrapped in the symptomatic conditions of "Modern" man, revealed in spectacle. Increasingly we seek solution through theory as speculatively imposed upon symptoms. By theory, this is to say, we dream of making spectacle substantial. Especially in the genres of art and history we attempt to riddle mystery at the level of spectacle as if by the riddling spectacle were made substantial. As if spectacle were thus transmogrified to essence in full bloom in intellect only. It is an inevitable confusion, following the rejection of a belief about the human condition in nature which once held man a fallen creature struggling to recover as *intellectual soul incarnate*. Under the common community of thought held by that old faith, the theological circumstance to man of Original Sin was a reality and not a myth. Or, as Tolkien might put it, it was myth as the most profound reality. We have heard Herman Melville engaging Original Sin out of his Calvinistic conditioning, associating his own concern with the dark undercurrent he detects in Hawthorne's fiction. There must be something loose in existence "like" Original Sin, though Melville tends toward believing it a Manichaean evil which by universal osmosis infests all of nature. In this respect, one might measure a dissociation of that old reality of Original Sin as held by St. Augustine and St. Thomas into a *myth*, speaking only with uncertain metaphor: something *like*. And in doing so, one might also take a measure of a dissociation from Milton's *Paradise Lost*, in which that poet fights a last battle to defend *myth* as true, that dissociation reaching a final triumph whereby myth is to be dismissed as but fiction in Melville's own great epic, *Moby Dick*.

In this respect, the Renaissance reductions of myth toward "fiction" emerges triumphant, though we are still left puzzled by the relation of good and evil, about which there is much ado in our art. Disarmed of our old faith but supplied only an insufficient faith in science as empowered by autonomous intellect, how are we to solve that riddle of good and evil? We might note, then, our lingering wishful thinking in pursuit of a myth suited to the continuing dilemma. That is, one might, to borrow Walker Percy's playfulness, suggest that we have a sense of a momentary stay of spiritual confusion insofar as we can substitute Cholesterol for the old Original Sin. For we seem by nature born to pursue myth as drawing us toward truth, requiring that myth be supplied to science itself. That was the troublesome Modernist distortion as seen by J. R. R. Tolkien, whose friend C. S. Lewis observed (before Percy does) that science as myth appears to account for all save the most elementary concern of the seeker: the mystery of this particular *person,* the "scientist." (Thus Freudianism can account for all save Freud, Lewis observes.) It is the point Percy will come to make as he is gradually weaned from a comfort in science, and particularly from psychology and psychiatry, though lingering effects in his thought and words from old scientific allegiances are not obliterated.

Certainly, Tolkien would be adamant about the insufficiency of Percy's address to myth as we find him expressing it in that late engagement of the Modernist predicament, his reflection on those "two signs in the post-modern age which cannot be encompassed by theory" as he puts it in "Why Are You a Catholic?" (1990). One of those signs is the *self*, always a "leftover" in any theory. The other is the Jews, "a stumbling block to theory." But in his insistence upon the Jews as a sign making possible a recovery from the cosmos as desert, he will say that "whatever else the Jews are, they are not mythical. Myths are stories which did not happen." For Percy in "this desert, that of theory and consumption, there remains only one sign, the Jews." The sign of the "self" differs in that it is interior, away from that desert called the Cosmos. It is the self's response to the sign of the Jew that orients the self in the desert, making the self a wayfarer, "which is to say, open to signs."

Confronted by such an argument, Tolkien (or Lewis or Eliot, for that matter) would say *yes* and *no*. For they would insist that myth is more complex than the reduced use Percy makes of it: "stories which did not happen." The Jews are indeed the chosen people, in whom yet survives to us as sign that mythical dimension of the true. And when Percy in this same essay emphasizes the antipathy of the scientific "set of mind" because it is the mind most offended by Judeo-Christianity despite science's origins in that history of the Judeo-Christian West, what he is touching upon (as Tolkien would insist) is science's rejection of myth as true. Science can tolerate myth as fiction, and even welcome science fiction. Science fiction can be an entertainment by the fancy in an escape from disturbing implications of myth as truth on the one hand, or from the deadening effects of "true" science on the intellect, in a "R and R," relieving physical and psychological tensions. There is also an advantage of science fiction as pseudo-myth in that it is suited to the popular mind in a projection of current scientific "truth" into a future – though it finds itself discomforted by even that tolerance of fiction when it must deal with works like Huxley's *Brave New World* or Orwell's *Animal Farm* or *1984*.

This scientific set of mind is likely, however, only to be baffled by Tolkien's *Lord of the Rings.* And indeed, given the popular spirit in its confused state subsequent upon a faith rested in science, through which faith man becomes dominantly a "consumer," even that popular spirit will find itself confused by Tolkien.

We need only observe that the very wide popularity of Tolkien's *Lord of the Rings* includes within its membership an almost cult-like following of what Percy (or Tolkien) would describe as "New Age" types. The stricter scientific mindset Percy comes to oppose would consider these fringe freaks. In his own scientific parable, *Lost in the Cosmos*, Percy shows as much of these fringe folk, not only in his concluding pages of "science fiction" pitting Deep Cove against New Ionia, but initially in that gathering of specimens of random mindsets gathered around the spectacle of a corn dance in a Southwest scenario, in the shadow of Los Alamos – out there in Will Barrett's desert.

Tolkien himself argues that myth is far other than mere fantasy, that is, fantasy as a story about what did not happen. A close reading not only of his fiction but especially of his letters in which he attempts to engage the Modernist distortions of myth will show this emphatically. The importance of Tolkien's position perhaps sheds a light upon what we might take as lingering scars on Percy's own reflections about fiction, effects from his initially setting forth as a wanderer out of his first commitment to Modernist science. Their difference in this respect suggests a juxtaposition of Tolkien and Percy in contrast to clarify the point. In his *Letters* (edited by his beloved son Christopher), many of Tolkien's letters are to Christopher as World War II is underway. Tolkien is writing, fearful that Christopher may become victim, not as an actual casualty in the war, but a victim seduced to the more subtle subversion of humanity through science as represented by the machine. When Christopher solos, his father writes, noting a distinction between the "skimming martins" Christopher has written him of observing in South Africa and which he remembers seeing over their home in England. The difference between the flight of martins and fighter planes speaks "the tragedy and despair of all machinery laid bare," as ancient as with Icarus, but more ominous now in the "Giant Bomber." Later, as the "first War of the Machines" is drawing to a close, the only triumphant survivor apparent to Tolkien is the Machine, raising the question "What's their next move?"

Later, the war some years behind him, the war's effects upon community in relation to the Machine is still troubling. He writes Milton Waldman (c. 1951) that his work is concerned with "Fall, Mortality, and the Machine." His contemporary context, within which he must struggle through art to recover myth, is viable because in its depths it is true to reality. But the contemporary intellectual world values the Machine as it does not myth. As sub-creator, man through machines becomes possessive of the world but proves thereby to be in fundamental rebellion against the world's Creator. For he is in pursuit of a self-made immortality through "power," the means whereby to make "the will more quickly effective" through the Machine as Magic. It is through the Machine that Power sets about "bulldozing the real world, or coercing other wills. The Machine is our more obvious modern form" of conquest, "though more closely related to Magic than is usually recognized." But if because of such arguments in Tolkien some of our New Age "environmentalists" embrace him as their advocate, they can do so only by ignoring his real center. That is a center which is in an accord with Gerard Manley Hopkins rather than with the pagan worshipers of Gaia. Tolkien's prophetic stance is counter to the Modernist world, which he sees as dark, though himself rescued by the recognitions of a mystery, visions actual for him on more than one occasion. One instance of visionary experience he shares with Christopher in hope of counteracting those enchantments of the Machine through Magic which might seduce Christopher with the thrill of flight as Icarus was seduced. It is a vision we might, without too much liberty, see in relation to Percy's Will Barrett, his hand on the hitching post and the swallowing oak bark in a Mississippi darkness.

It is in the interest of a recovery of himself, and as a fatherly act of protection of Christopher, that Tolkien writes his son (November 7–8, 1944). Christopher is in training at an RAF base in South Africa. His father has experienced what Eliot would call a "still point" or Wordsworth "a spot of time," a visionary moment "in St. Gregory's before the Blessed Sacrament." It was "a sudden vision. I perceived or thought of the Light of God and in it suspended one small mote (or millions of motes to only one of which was my small mind directed), glittering white because of the individual ray from the Light which both held and lit it." One might be reminded here as well of a much earlier moment, that in which Dame Julian of Norwich held a similar "mote," a hazel-nut, on her open palm, wondering that it did not fall to naught for its very littleness. Tolkien continues to Christopher: "And the ray was the Guardian Angel of the mote: not a thing interposed between God and the creature, but God's very attention itself, personalized."

Tolkien, citing other instances of similar still points to the "self," says, "They are intrusions (as we say, erring) into real or ordinary life." That is, they are "miracles." The effect upon him was "quite unlike any other sensation. And all of a sudden I realized what it was: the very thing that I have been trying to write about and explain in that fairy-story essay. . . . For [in the essay] I coined the word 'eucatastrophe': the sudden happy turn in a story which pierces you with a joy and brings tears (which I argued it is the highest function of fairy-stories to produce)." Now fairy-tales are not for Tolkien fancy's impositions upon actual experience, fancy imposed on reality, or what we have heard Percy call "stories which did not happen." In that essay on fairy-tales, now famous but in 1944 not yet even read by his beloved Christopher, Tolkien adds "I concluded by saying that the Resurrection was the greatest 'eucatastrophe' possible in the greatest Fairy Story – and produces that essential emotion: Christian joy which produces tears because it is qualitatively so like sorrow, because it comes from those places where Joy and Sorrow are at one, reconciled, as selfishness and altruism are lost in Love."

Then he speaks of the relevance of the reality of the Incarnation to reconciliation as the greatest fairy-tale – greatest because true in joining history to the transcendent and the unhistorical, that "which Is" but which doesn't "happen" as man's stories are said to happen imaginatively. The Gospels, he says, tell the greatest fairy-story of all. "Man the story-teller would have to be redeemed in a manner consonant with his nature: by a moving story. *But* since the author of it is the supreme Artist and the Author of Reality, this one was also made to Be, to be true on the Primary Plane. So that in the Primary Miracle [the Resurrection] and the lesser Christian miracles too though less, you have not only that sudden glimpse of the truth behind the apparent *Anankê* [necessity, restraint] of our world, but a glimpse that is actually a ray of light through the very chinks of the universe about us."

It is this enveloping of the isolated mote of the self in its limits as mote and thereby its rescue through Love centering in the Incarnation which is the greatest fairy-story, the greatest myth. It is so, because it is true. That is the theme Tolkien will advance to his baffled publisher, Sir Stanley Unwin, in distinguishing allegory from story, allegory becoming a "literary" imposition upon reality, externally imposed, as opposed to story (myth, fairy-story) which is an uncovering of – a recovery of – the reality of our transcendent possibility as story teller, in which telling we participated in that greatest story ever told through the Mass. We similarly participate as well through our devotions in art, in *making*, when those devotions are undertaken with a consent to the mystery abiding in reality. It is a devotion to making which, perhaps, John Keats might recognize as like his own intuition of "negative capability." Eliot will enlarge this recognition as a consent through Love to reality in the making of a thing, a poem or a story.

There is a considerable argument underway in the letters, then, which counters what Tolkien would see in Percy as a consent to art as itself a science closely allied to science in its Modern manifestations, focusing upon the spectacle which obscures reality. Indeed, Tolkien might describe such a version of art as closer to magic than to mystery, art especially endangered by the sciences of psychology and psychiatry disjoined from mystery. As himself the "Physician as Novelist" (1989) concerned with "Diagnosing the Modern Malaise" (1985), especially as occasioned to him by "The Fateful Rift: The San Andreas Fault in the Modern Mind" (1989), Percy as novelist engages the spectacle of the self as mote, but from Tolkien's perspective his art tends to the pathological to a considerable degree, in which respect Percy may be said to depend upon the comic – upon an attention to "looniness," as the physician-pathologist might well be forced to do when his attention as diagnostic novelist explores the dead and dying "self" in the Modernist world. That Percy at last runs deeper as intellectual soul incarnate than pathological artist is witnessed finally, however, in his setting science aside as inadequate to "The Holiness of the Ordinary," no doubt including an ordinary moment at the Mass, seeing motes suspended in light as more profound than physics can account, or than psychology can account for in our visionary response to such small things. And that is why "In the end, ten boring Hail Marys are worth more to the novelist than ten hours of Joseph Campbell on TV."

V

One of the delights of Walker Percy's work, especially evident in *Lost in the Cosmos*, is his playfulness, an aspect of his art which does not hide the seriousness of it, and indeed is a consequence of that seriousness, confronted as he finds himself by man's "looniness." His is in part one might suspect a playfulness out of a continuing skeptical response to our world by Percy as a "self" very much immersed in that world. Being such a self, his skepticism emerges from uncertainty about knowing. In this respect, his intense concern for semiotics as possibly opening toward some certainty touches upon both his fictional and essay explorations of the "self" as circumscribed by trying entrapments. He is looking for sign-posts in the impinging desert. And so along this way, in quest of some certainty, he enjoys a playfulness with sign no less than a serious concern for the sign as sustaining of his journey.

Given such a sophisticated intellect engaging the looniness of his time, this playfulness with sign carries in it for the reader the delight we also experience in those "metaphysical" poets who attracted Eliot's attention in conjunction with the appeal to Eliot of those poets of French Symbolism. For, before Percy, Eliot had found himself also besieged by uncertainty, responding with a skepticism deliberately cultivated intellectually in playing a role – projecting a "self" in defense of the more deeply besieged self. For the reader, a considerable sophisticated response is called for in reading either Eliot or Percy, considering their deliberate indirection as poets, as makers of signs under the authority of art's uses of signs, but the task was especially notable in Eliot, making him for a time good subject for academic courses.

No easy address for the poet, given a skeptical age in which there is no acceptable common ontological orientation of the self. The difficulty will lead Eliot in his salad years as poet to cultivate the role of intellectual dandy, taking some delight in shocking his peers. Some thirty years after Eliot has abandoned that defense, Percy finds himself (in the 1950s) challenged in much the same way. His response will be, not to take on the role of dandy, but more nearly that of a "good old boy" of a Southern provenance, especially so when his playful eye turns to those intellectuals scornful of that "South" with which Percy is attempting to come to terms. It is through such a role that one detects in Percy's mischievous indirection, in his signs, an exuberance suggestive of the clever adolescent. We might observe as well that one detects the adolescent in the dandy. In Eliot and his "Bloomsbury friends" especially this role-playing irritated D. H. Lawrence almost beyond endurance. (One might conjecture that Eliot, after "Ash-Wednesday," makes some amends in his praise of Lawrence in his Charles Eliot Norton Lectures, 1932–33.)

If the "dandy" as poet tends to be self-exclusive, sometimes irritating in that deportment (a deportment Eliot will caustically remark as his own irritating adolescent manner long after), there is something more endearing in the good-natured deportment we encounter in Percy, though that very deportment may obscure something of the agony of the recovery he attempts, leading to his late position as an "ex-suicide." Shelby Foote is attuned to this dilemma to his friend Percy, especially in that decade of the 1950s when Percy returned to the South. In a very long letter (and the letters of this period are largely those of Foote, few of Percy's surviving), he picks up what has apparently been a comment by Percy on the difficulty of writing. It requires a dogged perversity in the engagement of signs, Foote says, to overcome [Percy's?] "break through the shell of indifference and pessimism every time he takes up the pen." Not, it appears, the indifference and pessimism of any audience or any editor, but of the writer himself. Foote in his attempt to encourage Percy quotes from Eliot's *East Coker.* In the "break through," one discovers that he has only learned (Eliot says) "to get the better of words for the thing one no longer has to say." The battle all along is "a raid on the inarticulate with shabby equipment always deteriorating. . . ." Eliot's is an apt figure, given Foote's current wrestling with that history of the old war that haunts any Southerner, but particularly haunts Foote and Percy at that moment.

In remarking, then, an "adolescent" kinship of these poets, Eliot and Percy, at their outset as poets, we might speak figuratively of them by allusion to that American writer whom Foote keeps insisting to Percy is our first important American writer, Mark Twain. That is, we might suggest that Percy seems closer to Huck Finn, Eliot to Tom Sawyer – though both are sophisticated intellectuals. What one might suggest out of this allusion as well is that Twain too is a poet of the self, one often comically given to an adolescence in his own person, even late into life – until that darkness settles upon him as a self near his end. In this respect Hemingway finds Twain his own literary father in his pursuit of the self, energizing Hemingway as poet. He remarks that American literature grows out of *Adventures of Huckleberry Finn.* No mention of Hawthorne here of course. And if Foote in this early decade of Percy's engagement makes constant peons to James and Joyce, to be "studied" by Percy in his pursuit of his new career as poet, we might also remember that James, in respect to this dilemma of the "self," is more nearly a brother of Twain than he is a son of Hawthorne. Joyce too is of that lineage in his own concerns. What is emerging in the late 1800s and early 1900s is the dominance in letters of the poet's self as protagonist, alienated from nature and community, and that requires a hiding of the poet by his artfulness. There grows a species of romanticism, however much an accomplished fiction by a James or Joyce may be celebrated as social and psychological "realism." That is a recognition we already remarked in Flannery O'Connor, who learned much from James and Joyce, but recognized in Hawthorne the visionary poet struggling to break beyond the self's entrapment within the condensing Modernist malaise.

In this tradition of the poet as protagonist in poems and fictions since Twain and James, what is the American poet to do when there is no longer a West to "lite out" to, as Huck muses still possible to him. (That "liting out" of the adolescent culminates in our literature in *Catcher in the Rye* and *On the Road,* as in the social and cultural community it erupts in the 1960s.) What is that poet to make of the "American Experience" when laws protecting endangered species prevents an African safari? (We might try to imagine a Hemingway with camera rather than gun.) Dislocations of the self, attributed to a very long time-bound history, and in a geography shrinking under the constrictions upon it of technological science, may well force a Jack Burden (of *All the King's Men*) to lite out for the West, only there to encounter, as bourne with him on that long trail, the presence of "The Great Twitch," more terrifying than Ivan Karamazov's Grand Inquisitor. That is the fate which seems to lie in store for Percy's Williston Bibb Barrett as the "last gentleman" not provided a "last self-help book," though *The Second Coming* speaks more directly of a rescue possible.

As for Will's progenitor, Percy seems to have been forced to confront this dark prospect as well, having been arrested by that tubercle bacillus. He does so (with a little help from his close friend Shelby Foote) through combining the virtues of a playful and a serious concern for the sign itself. That is a manner which seems best suited to overcoming the always threatening indifference and pessimism within the poet that endangers his arrest as *homo viator.* As poet, then, Percy proves highly entertaining to a reader, even when that reader may himself be an indirect target of the mischief underway. In this respect, we might suggest that Percy's humor is a combination of gallows and morgue humor – the humor of the physician as pathologist.

As physician deploying a diagnostic instrument of signs and seriously concerned to diagnose the "modern malaise," Percy finds humor a necessary relief to him from internal pressures upon him as the skeptical self as novelist, pressure agitating the novelist as person. It is as well a relief from a hovering sense of responsibility as diagnostician to an ambiguous audience. We saw him exploring his kinship with Melville, very seriously. But then at the end of his exploration, having observed in a backhanded reference to Eliot's famous concern for signs as "objective correlatives," he pays tribute to Melville's art. For Melville, given his extensive experience as sailor, "Objective correlatives are easy pickings, lying around like Sutter's gold nuggets." Thus one describes "the try-pots, the hellish fire, and the head amidships of the *Pequod* at full sail through the night, and it [the ship] becomes one's very soul, both damned and freed." Objective correlatives, easily come by, serve art's illusions in hoodwinking art's audience – though that audience in the event should prove Melville himself.

But the next words set a difference between Melville and Percy, in a surprising intrusion. Melville is intense in his concern to free his damned soul, one might say. But that was in another world which was still able to use such a term as *soul*. Now the diagnostic physician, riddling the flatulent spirit of the *self* a hundred years later, must find relief otherwise, by cunning and comic indirection in a combination of gallows and morgue humor. Percy as diagnostic novelist, in contrast to Melville as the tortured soul as novelist, examines the self-hanged self to discover the source of those winds of change which hardly leave the self heroic in its confrontation of Cape Horn, even if it escape the satirical scalpel. "The freedom and happiness of the artist [the diagnostic novelist] is attested by his playfulness, his tricks, his malice, his underhandedness, his naughtiness, his hoodwinking the reader." Hardly a description of the artist suited to Melville, these words in the midst of his praise of Melville. Percy chose a comic intensity about his own damned and perhaps thereby (as ex-suicide) freed soul as it skeptically skims the dark waters of our world, far removed from Melville's *Pequod*.

On occasion such an attempt to claim happiness and freedom as diagnostic artist will, indeed, lead Percy perilously close to slapstick. It does so near the end of that last novel, *Thanatos Syndrome*, when we discover that "Van Dorn and His Staff were not convicted of child abuse" – shades of Dostoevsky treating Melville's Billy Budd. They are instead committed to the State Forensic Hospital, suffering "bizarre symptoms and behavior, which once abated" allows their being given into the custody of an old redneck sheriff, Sheriff Vernon "Cooter" Sharp, to do community service. We are given a tour, then, of the Tulane Primate Center, with Van Dorn recalled to our memory as recently roaring and thumping, knuckling across his cage and hiding behind the toilet. On that tour we also hear an excited prospect: primates might be taught to speak, a parody of the current "zoo-semiotics" whom Percy considered absurd. Very near slapstick, this satiric diversion.

In a letter responding to his first reading of *Thanatos Syndrome*, in high praise of it, Percy's friend Jan Gretlund demurs from this scene, though it is not only funny but hilarious. It is "too much of a movie-script," in which Gretlund confesses having lost any sense that the characters are "human beings, whereas only some of them have been reduced to primates." (Gretlund's and Percy's correspondence is in Gretlund's *Frames of Southern Mind*, 1998.) In response (June 13, 1987), Percy comments on his "Marx-Brothers moviescript" as "simply a self indulgence. I enjoyed it, mainly as satirical fun with certain semioticists, primatologists, and post-structuralist critics." He also remarks that he is surprised to find his novel on "*Times* best-seller list for 9 weeks – me and Louis L'Amour and Stephen King!" But he himself is "fed up with it" and wants to get back to semiotics. He is "contemplating a book elucidating Peirce's 'triadic theory' (which I consider probably as important as Quantum Theory) toward end of reconciling it with people like Wittgenstein, John Poinsot (John of St. Thomas) a 17th Century Dominican – All best, Walker." A letter in haste, as he turns to quieter reflections on this quantum leap concerning the mystery of signs.

An old concern, this with the mystery of signs, and one addressed by indirection in the manner of the diagnostic novelist in his *Lost in the Cosmos*. But addressed there seriously only after another slap-stick hilarity, the presentation of "The Last Donahue Show" featuring "Dr. Joyce Friday" confronted by Bill, "a homosexual and habitué of Buena Vista Park in San Francisco." Upon this encounter group as entertainment for bored housewives there intrude three strangers: a "John Calvin," then a Confederate officer "for all the world like Colonel John Pelham," and then, apparently, an extraterrestrial creature in the form of a man bearing news of our world's end. The question put to the reader, when that reader has recovered from the hilarity of the movie-script of the last Donahue Show: "If you heard this Donahue Show, would you head for Lost Cove, Tennessee?" to a cave where might be found "corn, grits, collard greens, and smoked sausage in abundance"? Percy himself rather certainly would.

Between the "Last Donahue Show" and the concluding "A Space Odyssey (I)" and "A Space Odyssey (II)" occurs an "Intermezzo" which very much concerns us, though our author-guide encourages us just to skip it. There are in the central text eighty-plus pages of a playful engagement of the semiotic game afoot in the intellectual community at that time (1970s), a game rising to excited attention in the American academy in imitation especially of what has occurred among the French intelligentsia. But in addition to the playful pages, there is also an initial and by no means playful footnote appended – in small type occupying the bottom of the opening pages. In the text itself the playfulness is evident, but in the note lies a quieter and a very serious and central concern to our analyst-guide himself about his exploration of the uncertain self. It is a concern centering deeply at a personal level for Percy, we are suggesting. We are encouraged to skip the whole section, since there will be no "fatal consequences" to our doing so, given its boring subject, semiotics. A strategy of deception, like that of the Chaucer teacher who urges his students to skip certain of the "Tales" as perhaps too salacious for their tender appetites. That this is the deliberate strategy, Percy will confess in his *Paris Review* (Summer 1987) interview much later. There he remarks that "*Lost in the Cosmos* was a sly, perhaps devious, attempt to approach a semiotics of the self." What "was underhanded" about the book was the insertion of the forty-page "'primer of semiotics' in the middle of the book, with a note of reassurance to the reader that he could skip it if he wanted to. Of course I was hoping he, or more likely she [another devious bit], would be sufficiently intrigued to take the dare and read it, since it is of course the keystone of the book." And in it the key to be drawn out of that keystone is in the submerged footnote, we here add.

Percy's concern is to discover the nature of the *self* in relation to its own history, the perennial mystery to consciousness as it becomes a self-consciousness. For in an initial moment of self-consciousness rises an awareness of some "before," some sense of the necessity of an anterior state of consciousness, antedating this point of self-recognition. In his "Intermezzo," then, but especially in the appended footnote to it, we find ourselves close to intellectual autobiography. Not of course one spelled out in linear terms by allusion to what Percy has read, or when or under what immediate intellectual circumstances. The note itself is summary, centering in semiotics as the science promising a resolution to persistent questions about the "self," but not of a "self" so generalized as science inclines to make it by abstractionism. The concern is for *this particular self*, Walker Percy, though it is a concern disguised by an authorial "underhandedness" which fluctuates between ironic distancing from the reader to a closer presence as a good-old-boy, humorously entertaining. There is also sometimes a self-deprecation, lest our guide seem too presumptuously the "philosopher." He is not, in his note especially, addressing "texts and other coded sign utterances but the self which produces texts or hears sign utterances" – those most immediate selves being (1) the speaker of these signs called *Lost in the Cosmos* and (2) the "hearer" of them, the present reader.

The note itself puts aside playful underhandedness. In reduced type and crowded at the bottom of three pages, it (more than the main text) might be skipped, though in it is the record of Percy's pause at a way station of his journey, here witnessing a current state of himself as very self-conscious in reading his own existence. It is tonally counter to the general text, and one might even suspect that Percy's editor played a role in reducing it to an aside, given its serious engagement of old questions he addressed nearly a decade earlier in a collection of essays. The title of those old essays is teasingly playful, but it is not at all the title he first proposed. We know the work as *The Message in the Bottle: How Queer Man Is, How Queer Language Is, and What One Has to Do with the Other*. Among the included pieces are "Toward a Triadic Theory of Meaning," "The Symbolic Structure of Interpersonal Process," "Culture: The Antinomy of the Scientific Method," "Symbol as Hermeneutic in Existentialism," hardly playful titles.

As with the general title of this collection there are nevertheless pieces so titled as to hint at the Percy popularly known for his playfulness: "Notes for a Novel About the End of the World" and perhaps "Metaphor as Mistake." But the contents page suggests formidable concerns (which they are), not likely to draw a sufficient readership to hear those concerns. Even his own first choice of a general title could but have further estranged him, at least as his editor argued. Percy wanted to call it *Contra Gentiles*. This he recalls in an oral interview broadcast on "New Letters on the Air" (April 1989). That title, *Contra Gentiles*, he says is "a title I stole from St. Thomas Aquinas." But there was a problem. His editor responds: "Yeah, Walker, that's fine. But do you know how people are going to read it? They're going to read it, first, 'contra' – that means the people that are fighting in Nicaragua. And they're going to read 'gentiles' as gentiles – they're going to think you're talking about gentile contras in Nicaragua." But Percy concludes his anecdote by saying he had "borrowed" his own title from St. Thomas because "there are certain resemblances between what St. Thomas was doing in the 13th century and what I'm doing." (From *More Conversations with Walker Percy*, 222.)

Such the autobiographical context to this "Semiotic Primer of the Self" midway into his *Lost in the Cosmos*, written under the guise of playfulness but deadly serious: deadly serious in relation to the seeming imminent death of the self according to this diagnosis of the end of Western history as revealed in the death of its cultural signs. So dire the circumstances that he sets aside as frivolous the current fascination with "zoo-semiotics" as a sort of tabloid level of scientific concern for signs. And so pronounced is this tonal difference, speaking the personal, that in his buried note to the forty-page primer on semiotics he will acknowledge allies and remark as well enemies to the seriousness of his concern.

Although Percy often appeared as speaker on campuses, he was hardly sympathetic to the academic climate of his day, for he saw that the academy was eroding the seriousness of his concern for the self. One nevertheless observes that those listed as friends to his cause in the note were, through their own texts, a growing presence of authority to the increasingly dissolving intellectual community on many campuses, where by our century's end there now appears such an intellectual bankruptcy. Especially some of his named friends were present in "Modern Literary Criticism" courses in English or Comparative Literature programs. Ernst Cassirer is his ally, he says, in that Cassirer argues symbols as necessary means to "articulating reality." Also especially important is Ferdinand de Saussure and his "analysis of the human sign as the union of the signifier (*significant*) and the signified (*signifié*)." Friendly also, Hans Werner, "who systematically explored the process in which the signified is articulated within the form of the signifier" (though just what is meant by "*within* the form of the signifier" here is uncertain – if by signifier we mean the *person* using signs as well as the signs themselves – for signs carry the sign-maker in a personal way). There is one other ally of considerable importance, as she proved of considerable influence to academic literary criticism itself: Susanne K. Langer, who "from the posture of behavioral science, . . . clearly set forth the qualitative difference between animals' signals and man's use of symbols," that clear distinction progressively eroded by a subsequent "zoo-semiotics" which Percy will treat with slap-stick satire in *The Thanatos Syndrome*.

But of a very special importance as allies in his own struggle to recover the sign have been German thinkers such as Heidegger and Eccles, who distinguish between *Welt* and *Umwelt*. It is Heidegger's *Welt* "into which the *Dasein* or self finds itself 'thrown,'" or Eccles' "World 3," which is the "public domain of signs and language within which man . . . lives." That *Umwelt* of von Uexküll is, "roughly, the significant environment within which an organism lives." In terms deployed in *Lost in the Cosmos* and elsewhere by Percy, the *Welt* is that "world" *imposed* by the self upon the *Umwelt*, a *world* imposed upon the *cosmos* by an act of will using signs for the imposition, in a response by the self as itself "thrown." The self by *enacting* a world upon the cosmos seeks a reconciliation with its own "thrown-ness." And the instrument of the quest for reconciliation is the sign.

These German thinkers, we may conclude, are devoted to a rescue of consciousness itself beyond the seeming "thrown-ness" recognized by a moment of self-awareness, the "thrown-ness" having occurred in some vague past of consciousness. What they would rescue this "thrown-ness" *from* is, at last, its submission through behavioral science (*pace* Susanne Langer) to the limits of a merely evolutionary biology. To oppose a *world* to the *unworld*, a *self* to the *cosmos* as the arena of "thrown-ness" in which we find the self lost, is nevertheless to subscribe implicitly to a primal necessity of self-rescue, which Percy will treat as a "transcendence" in his cataloguing of a variety of "transcendences" to the lost self in his playful book. But this is an approach which will return questions of the self to the province of intellectual autonomy, a most dangerous inclination. And indeed, Percy's interest in the trail of existential thought from Kierkegaard leads him to Husserl's "phenomenological" concepts which seem suited to the imposing of a world upon the cosmos by Husserl's logical persuasiveness. This will in turn lead to Heidegger and from him to – a dead-end in Jean-Paul Sartre.

That trail which Percy chooses to follow has from its beginning a double dislocation of the self: that one which is consequent upon the rise of Nominalism as ready instrument to Positivism, and then the added accompanying doubt out of Descartes whose dead-end becomes the question whether the self even exists. Thus the self along that way, the self as intellectual man, finds himself suspended within intellect over that San Andreas Fault which Percy declares at last so troublesomely unresolved. This is to suggest that, despite Percy's guarded skepticism about these originating thinkers in their concern for the self's dislocation in the cosmos, he does not himself escape a continuing presence of their thought in him. He can say, in "Diagnosing the Modern Malaise," that "Christendom began to crumble, perhaps most noticeably under the onslaught of a Christian, Soren Kierkegaard, in the last century." Initially that is the onslaught which wakens Percy, and in response to a fading call of the self to itself he pursues it in quest of a *science* of the self, a science of the self derived from the behavioral sciences (given his training as physician). It brings him to those subsequent sciences that so attracted him, psychology and psychiatry. But this is the context in Western thought in which has occurred a dislocation of signs from an older scholastic (Thomistic) understanding of the sign, the initial dislocation begun within scholasticism itself by the putative author of that erosive concept of Nominalism, William of Occam. Thus the most powerful signs of all, convenient to the establishing of a "world" upon the cosmos, are at last but abstract and general ones, signs suited to *scientific* reduction of the cosmos to a manageable world.

One does not suppose that such "universals" as those of science can fully represent objectively any existing particular thing, as Percy in his last days insistently declares. They become as signs rather a sufficient fencing-in of many like things by abstractions. But what they fence things *from* – that is the issue. What is denied to things actual by such isolation in signs is their distinctly "Divine" aspect as created things. Thus Nominalism provides an instrument suited to an intentional autonomy of intellect, which will progressively reveal "empirically" the effectiveness of an application of intellectual intent through abstract signs, a *process* as *form*, impressively imposed as *worlds* upon the *cosmos*. (Consider for instance the at once vexing and fascinating worlds promised by abstract genetic science in our moment.) It is an inclination rising through Francis Bacon and his successors in an empiricism tending to pragmatism, whose symptomatic effect is to convert community to a new religion in the end, that of consumerism. Thus Nominalism will also prove the acceptable ground in the 19th century to the increasing triumph of Logical Positivism, whose authority will be based on the popular consent consequent upon the pragmatic conveniences out of those sciences, supplied to the consumer in mesmerizing him to materialistic limits as person. Logical Positivism, through Pragmatism as popular philosophy, will effectively build those worlds, enslaving things. But they can do so only by destroying any Divine dimension to things. It is an accomplishment by intentional denials of any divinity save that of autonomous intellect itself. That is, the Logical Positivist will not likely bear a legitimate charitable dimension toward the consumer society, upon whose consent his position depends for the logistics of Positivist actions. For to be so inclined would create within the mind of that Logical Positivist a San Andreas Fault hardly acceptable: his own suspension over an abyss created by the polar rifts in thought between *power* and *love*.

At the end of our century there is much concern for the "ending of history," a considerable library available with titles speaking an end, whether of cosmology or biology or history. But here the most significant end might well be, not a fulfillment of Hegel as prophet, but a fulfillment of that initial Fall in the old garden itself, in which the "self" chose separation from the cosmos which had been given to it as created. The role of Nominalism in this aspect of the gradual abolition of man, then, requires our reflection upon its gradual appearance and steady progress in its occupation of and dislocation of intellect. General, abstract universals, representing no actually existing things (the position holds) are uttered. They are merely *flatus vocis*, vocal utterances empty of human gestures embracing actual things. Indeed, even as that troubled Stoic Boethius says of them, they exist *post res*, consequent to the things of the cosmos, perhaps a sort of intellectual whistling in the dark in response to consciousness discovering itself alienated from the cosmos.

When the Nominalist movement comes to a focus, in those early Scholastic confrontations, how significant that it should have been over the reality of the Sacrament of the Eucharist (by Berengar in the 11th century). It is that troublesome question which the "Romantic" Abelard, now remembered largely in relation to Eloise, struggled to reconcile: the relation of Nominalism and Realism. He would recover a unity of body and soul which he reflects upon as radically divided in himself, exposed as he was to the polar attractions of soul and body as we romanticize it subsequently in the "love story" of Abelard and Eloise. (See Helen Wadell's famous novel.) It was Occam who seemed to provide a reconciliation, by opposing Aquinas: Occam would distinguish the real from the *grammatical*. The grammatical, nevertheless (he suggests), may be said to represent a "real" status of universals *within the mind*, thus providing that growing breach between the subjective and objective upon which Descartes will flounder in seeking his own reconciliation of the science of mathematics as "real" within the mind and therefore sufficient to an authority of imposition upon the cosmos to "create" thereby an intentional world through mathematical signs. A faint after-echo of this old battle, but one signifying Western intellect's general submission to Nominalism (especially that intellect as resident in our emerging nation) was observed by that good Thomist storyteller, Flannery O'Connor. Ralph Waldo Emerson, she reminds us, in 1832 "decided . . . that he could no longer celebrate the Lord's Supper unless the bread and wine were removed," thus beginning "the vaporization of religion in America."

It is in this novelist believer, Flannery O'Connor, that some recovery of the sign may begin to emerge, but also as important we may find it in those philosopher believers such as Eric Voegelin, who resist the gnostic intent to a Modernist dislocation of being in the interest of power. That intent is to an imposition of worlds upon the cosmos through systems in order to suit at least portions of it to the appetites and conveniences of autonomous intellect. Percy, too, recognizes and opposes this dislocation, reading Voegelin as an ally in his opposition. And yet he is also affected by the Modern gnostic stance in his arguments against it in respect to semiotics (as who among us has not been in some degree). There are recently, of course, philosopher believers especially relevant to an opposition to this strain of Nominalist-Cartesian dislocations of intellect, this infection of intellect which Voegelin through his diagnosis labels modern gnosticism. And a principle one, most particularly relevant to the science of semiotics as engaged by Percy, is Etienne Gilson.

An irony attaches to the circumstances of Gilson's lectures at Harvard in 1936, the William James Lectures, published in 1937 as *The Unity of Philosophical Experience.* For in them Gilson will observe (near the end) that James's work proves an elaboration of "a pragmatic conception of knowledge, where ideas were not true, but became true in proportion to their practical verification," making James "a victim of philosophy gone astray" for want of a rational metaphysics. That is, James has been intellectually seduced from recognizing that need of metaphysics by the thought of Kant and Hume. But the lectures nevertheless defend the philosophical attempt, though it fail, with Gilson's exploration of "The Medieval Experiment" in his opening lectures as also revealing philosophy already going astray through "logicism" misapplied, as by Abelard and Occam. The course of these lectures, from Abelard to Descartes and down to Bertrand Russell, concludes that philosophy in the 1930s has reached a dead-end. It "is either collective mental slavery or skepticism," from which we must recover lest ours become the concluding dark age of intellect itself.

These are lectures in exploration worthy of an attention not yet given them, a complex and kindly attention to serious philosophical intent gone astray since the late Middle Ages. More economical to our present purposes, however, is a series of small essays Gilson published in periodicals at that time, in the 1930s, now conveniently available as *Methodical Realism.* Both these works, let us remember, are published in that decade when Percy encounters the exuberant German youth in Bavarian nature, just before World War II. Out of that dead-end of philosophy, alas, Percy's Fr. Smith makes his way to the firetower in Louisiana swampland. In *Methodical Realism,* Gilson effectively engages in Descartes' thought which ends in the Modernist mind suspended over the San Andreas fault. Additionally we should remember, given Percy's footnote concerning semiotics, Gilson's *Linguistics and Philosophy: An Essay on the Philosophical Constants of Language*. The French edition of this work appeared in that troublesome decade of the 1960s, though its English translation appears only in 1988, contemporary to Percy's "The Fateful Rift: The San Andreas Fault in the Modern Mind" (1989). Gilson's concern is with confusions by the semioticists of philosophy with science, a limited science of the sign argued as if philosophy. And he especially addresses a concern with Saussure, one of Percy's allies, on this confusion. (The chapter "Word and Meaning," pages 25–29, directly relevant to Percy as artist semiotist.)

What Gilson observes is that in the strain of semiotics as a science is to be detected the hidden presence of Nominalism, so that in further engaging Saussure he brings Aquinas (pages 46–47) to oppose Saussure with a stricter philosophical concern for the *significant-signifié*, demurring from Saussure's argument and coming to his own concerns as philosopher with the sign-symbol. (See especially Note 20, pages 174–75.) We do not intend to introduce extensively the passages here cited, though those passages cited are succinct and easily available. We may refer to them as supportive of our own address to problems with Percy's belief that he has been intellectually rescued through his cited "allies" such as Saussure. Of more special concern is Percy's faith in Peirce's theory of the "Delta Factor," the triadic rescue of intellect beyond its biological dyadic entrapments. That is a concern which requires our fuller address, for in that theory there are philosophical difficulties not to be ignored. But in order to engage those difficulties in the intellectual context of semiotics, we may first remark others to whom Percy assigns the role of "foes" to his own emerging semiotic position in that long footnote to the "Semiotic Primer of the Self."

VI

There are secondary foes whom Percy dismisses at once, the French structuralists and their "whimsical stepchild 'deconstruction.'" He cites Levi-Strauss and Michel Foucault, who at the time were considered rather primary and impressive intellectuals by the academy. But one need not "feel obliged to speak of the deconstructionists," so untenable their position – though at the time they seemed to have taken command of academic criticism, especially through the ready welcome of that growing academic fad by Yale and Harvard and therefore by provincial universities and university presses across the country. It is to a more worthy foe that Percy addresses himself, "the honorable tradition of American behaviorism," represented for instance by Charles Morris. They are honorable in that they attempt "to deal only with observables and so to bypass the ancient pitfalls of mind, soul, consciousness, and self which have bogged down psychologists for centuries. I start from the same place, looking at signs and creatures which use them."

Percy starts, then, from Langer's posture *vis-à-vis* behavioral science, but he adds a demurer to that position insofar as these thinkers declare a closed position. "My difficulty with the behaviorists is that they rule out mind, self, and consciousness as inaccessible either on the doctrinal grounds that they do not exist or on methodological grounds that they are beyond the reach of behavioral science." It is Peirce who, from a similar address, convinces Percy that this "is not necessarily so." To be content with the behaviorist's position is to deny in advance the "Delta Factor," that experience Percy insists upon as a triadic complex to consciousness in its relation to the sign. One does not rule out mind, self, soul, consciousness by a behaviorist dogma, nor by an admission of defeat which declares these to be nonrealities because they allow no demonstrable relation (through science) to this limited biological creature, man.

Percy as does any intellectual, but especially one at our juncture with the cosmos as we bear a cumulative intellectual history, has difficulties in attempting to articulate the nature of the *self*. The self is a reality we recognize as actual but it eludes any firm identification. That is what leads Percy to a conclusion that the self is the unidentifiable residue left after all else has been identified, an unnamable "I." What is most exacerbating to this attempt to name the self *significantly* in the face of empiricist dogma is an inadequacy of language itself. This is challenging, we may observe, not simply because the names we have seem inadequate to the thing we would name, but as well because the names we have in such great profusion are inherited and so bear historical baggage. They are therefore encumbered by old settlings into our signs out of the history of the self's intellectual pursuit of itself, made through such names as *mind, soul, consciousness, self.* That is a complication the further encumbered by our age's explosions of signs out of the explosion of specializations to intellect which demand peculiar sets of signs to the specialties – peculiar signs jealously guarded.

Chaucer on an occasion of playful poetry makes a parable about this problem with signs. Through fancy he imagines an empyrean into which our signs when uttered ascend. Words never die, only float collectively in that stratosphere overarching earthbound mind. That is, signs loosed from the tongue as *flatus vocis* lose the gravity of signification and rise beyond our confident reach, save through such fanciful ordering of them as the poet may conjure. Or, at Chaucer's juncture with history, by Nominalistic fancy under the eventual rubric of "universals," increasingly commanded to earthly power. In that suggestion lies some purchase perhaps upon the subsequent issue of signs in the desert. It is spoken to by G. K. Chesterton in a figurative description of *homo viator* in this desert into which intellect enters after Occam. Chesterton in his little book on Chaucer observes that up to Chaucer's time, life is understood as a dance – after which it becomes a race. From our point of reflection, we suggest that for *homo viator* it becomes more and more a frantic race through the desert. Thus man finds himself confused by signposts along the way that appear increasingly illegible to his intellect and blurred by his rapid gait. Signs increasingly appear merely *flatus vocis*, balloons only tenuously anchored in reality by the will and diversely bloated by rhetorical flatulence, as reality is reduced to a cosmos declared to be an accidental desert. Those swaying signs emit a cacophony of encounter as if inflated tin balloons. Or in an alternate figure, they gradually emit a prohibitive ozone which seems to seal any transcendent neuosphere from the wandering *homo viator* who must nevertheless scan the horizon seeking some guiding star. Signs are thus denied any rescuing to a transcendent cause of either the seeming desert or of the uncertain signs. And so the self, *homo viator,* is reduced to circular wanderings of the cosmos. The self thus tends to discover itself increasingly subservient to the God of chaos. (One might, again with Percy's playfulness, suggest the temporal outposts of this reigning god – Old Chaos come to intellect – to be our current academic conclaves, for reasons I have elsewhere engaged in *The Truth of Things: Liberal Arts and the Recovery of Reality*.)

In our world, such is our supposed sophistication with our sign machines as summed under the rubric of *computer*, we easily conjure the residue of signs afloat in that empyrean called history, anticipating a riddling through Descartes' mathematics, that faith in number as name which yet haunts intellect. Our material world becomes increasingly littered by abandoned signs which do not yield meaning, given that our faith lies in a technology suited only to material existence. Meanwhile, a "recycling" of signs is but an uncertain science, hardly sufficient to expunge the stains of history. Even at a material level, as if a rebuke of the presumptuous self, nature's stratosphere is increasingly strewn with the debris of actual satellites – all of them "communication" satellites of one sort or another. That debris may prompt bad dreams. For we fear we may yet experience falling objects (coded of course) upon our heads if we go unprotected by hard hats of common sense.

And so we may wonder whether any *significant* order of signs is possible to intellectual speculation about the nature of reality. That is a growing problem to science itself, which seems increasingly to exacerbate the difficulty by turning science into a pseudo-philosophical address to signs and their uses. What wonder then if there is an even greater problematic worry about signs as they are used to make the art thing, the poem or novel. Percy (or any poet) might well feel threatened by the difficulty of breaking "through the shell of indifference and pessimism every time he takes up the pen," given such uncertainty of sign. Scientist, philosopher, poet find themselves floundering in a slough of signs always deflating, becoming themselves the more entangled in the wash of reality. For signs seem more and more but those improbable inflated balloons, unable to lift consciousness in a rescue beyond taunting reality. What is most threatening in this intrusiveness upon the self is the insufficiency of whatever Nominalistic system one might summon as a defense against the *givenness* implicit in a complex and seemingly threatening reality, including the givenness of the very self which desires its freedom from all gift lest freedom be compromised. That is why, of course, one might well summon Thomas Aquinas to cast a line to us that might reanchor us to reality. He reminds us that the purpose of our explorations of philosophy – and we add, of science and art as well – is not so simple as to learn merely "what others have thought," as if thereby we might counter by an originality effecting autonomous freedom. It is rather "to learn how the truth of things stands" – stands in a proportionate measure and anchor of what men have thought and said about their actual experiences of reality.

This is to insist, toward recovering from the swamp of despair into which we have lured ourselves by our own projected signs, that the truth of things measures knowing, not knowing truth, a distinction exacerbated by the dominating "thought" of a Modernist world whose central dogma is that intellect is autonomous. The "malady" of mind which concerns Percy has origin in this presumption of intellectual autonomy, whereby intent alone is posited as sufficient to a pseudo-transcendence. It is an action which proves at last but a species of angelism such as Percy playfully unfolds in the specimens of the "self" seeking "transcendence" in his last self-help book. *Playfully* unfolds, lest one be misled into despair by the futility of decayed sign in the forced use of them as if thereby we might command sign to *comprehend* reality. Playful in part as forewarning of the inevitable despair in failure, the suicide of intellect. For in the issue, that despair is in response to the actual cosmos as confronting the self as reduced by its deracination to the conclusion that both the cosmos and the self are but illusions. Such despair, alas, proves the threshold to that "literal" refusal of the cosmos, the ticket which Ivan Karamazov would return to the Conductor of the cosmos only to discover that he has already declared that Conductor not to exist. The only rescue left is an "actual" suicide. But it is a suicide consequent upon a forced conclusion of the will, based in illusion. Having denied the transcendent, intellect by that denial seems destined to deny the immanent as well, through its inversion of that ancient Manichaeanism which would deny the immanent except as an evil. That actual refusal through biological death "self"-induced is a theme undulating through Percy's signs early and late: a recognition of his *being* (as a self) teetering on the edge of the abyss of nonexistence. It is to recover balance, in a gravity of consciousness oriented to the cosmos, that in large part leads Percy to such a playful underhandedness with signs.

Meanwhile, as he recognizes, our disquiet over being lost in the cosmos is such that we no longer trust our own "self" to recover from its uneasy consciousness through the immediacy of experience, progressively fearing as the only certainty to such an attempt a centripetal drawing inward into self-entrapment: consciousness turned inward upon itself. We cry for the scientist, but less loudly for the philosopher, to rescue us. We seldom call for the poet. But is there any faint hope yet residual in consciousness? Perhaps a recognition that we need a guide through our desert which we may tentatively concede as "theoretically" the only "real world." Though there is perhaps not a great outcry for poet as guide, Walker Percy hears the cry as of a sufficient loudness within himself that he responds, cultivating what he understands as an acceptable indirection of the poet. That cultivation seems at points to amount almost to a denial that he responds to *our* cry at all – as of course he does, since it is first of all his own cry to which he responds and since we share in a connaturality as persons. We see as much not only in the argument of his text but in his playful titles. And that playful manner reflects something of a very "personal" aspect to his concern as himself *this particular person*. Or so we contend. And that recognition can at last but lead to a recognition of connaturality.

There is a complication: as if inherent accident to his specific nature, he finds himself, both by that personal nature and by his willed preference, a very *private* person. When he begins to publish essays in the early 1950s he attracts a few other concerned selves. When he publishes *The Moviegoer* (1961) the crowd gathering about him swells almost to intimidation. He is amazed to realize that *Thanatos Syndrome* has been on the *New York Times* bestseller list for nine weeks, "me and Louis L'Amour and Stephen King!" By his own words he finds himself to have been increasingly forced upon a public stage, and the pressure is such that he cannot sufficiently resist it. His only protection, as becomes increasingly apparent to him, is to appear in public in the role of the comic, or at least witty, physician-analyst-novelist, warning us repeatedly that in that role he is much given to tricks, malice, underhandedness, naughtiness. He is not, he warns, a doctor of the soul, a philosopher or theologian. As novelist, his primary intent is to "hoodwink" the reader, surprise the reader out of intellectual indolence. It is this role, suited to the hoodwinking of the reader, which may serve the private, personal, serious concern in him as himself a person, a hidden presence – a self caught up in a forced march in the desert as *homo viator*. At that depth, the polarities may yet seem to suspend him over his own San Andreas Fault, between *life* and *death*.

The polarity of life and death is a theme of fundamental concern to Percy, then, more than any political or social or even literary concern he may argue in whatever intellectual arena of the moment he inhabits. By philosophical and theological concerns, cried out to him from lost selves within that common arena of the Modernist world, echoing himself to himself, he becomes so intensely drawn inward to confront his own polarity that theology or philosophy as intellectual disciplines seem hardly relevant at last. Sufficient to that moment are the evils thereof. The signs of those disciplines prove at last inadequate in themselves to rescue his self from the suspension over "The Fateful Rift: The San Andreas Fault in the Modern Mind." His becomes a concentration of concern at a personal level beyond or beneath any formal address possible through philosophy or theology, though those pressures of intellectual discipline upon him seem demanded of him by a growing public audience. It is an audience intent upon forcing him toward intellectual formalities. ("*Why* are you a Catholic?") He resists that pressure at every turn, usually by metaphorical references to himself not only as diagnostician of the modern situation of the self, as if he were a scientist but pretending no remedy for maladies of the self since he is but a forensic diagnostician. Among the ironies of his "place" in community, occasioning a sometimes sardonic humor (he is a mean "yard dog" guarding the deeply private), he finds himself drawn repeatedly into the academy as "sage," out of that place he comes increasingly to love, his Louisiana bayou as a place *to be*. But if the university podium is not necessarily within a territory governed largely by the devil for Percy (as Flannery O'Connor was rather inclined to believe), it proved nevertheless a territory whose intellectual denizens Percy recognized as largely and increasingly antipathetic to his concerns. Before such audiences he conducts himself in a mannerly way. That mannerly way, of course, involved an indirection of necessity, evident in talks and essays given in academic territory – until a new directness begins to emerge in those essays he leaves us in the last two years of his life.

We know how unhelpful novelists are, insofar as they serve to unravel the Gordian tangle of society in its civil and political disarray. And Percy adapts that general suspicion to his own deportment, advising us (*soto voce* at times) that the novelist is undependable. In this respect, we find him not only akin to Melville but to Hawthorne, though Hawthorne is rather more explicit in addressing the generally unsympathetic attitude toward the poet or novelist which he suspects to be residual in his readers, given their Puritan origins. And Hawthorne also recognized this attitude as having become more largely an "American" suspicion by mid-19th century, but with less bitterness in him than one finds in Melville. That is a theme Faulkner, too, will touch upon, as in the passage we quoted from *The Unvanquished.* In relation to civil manifestations of the effects upon the defeated South after 1865, in that continuing civil war known to history as The Reconstruction, Faulkner speaks (through Bayard Sartoris) of that "mist-born Protestantism grafted onto this land of violent sun," the South. It is a graft made in a desperation to survive, or in a favorite Faulkner term, to "endure," even against nature itself. Faulkner like Hawthorne experienced one aspect of this Protestant – Puritan – graft, which we have argued transmogrified to a pragmatically driven Positivism whose public shibboleth becomes "The New South," a Southern version of the Puritan dream of building a city upon a hill, but with a modification of that Puritan dream to technological means to economic ends quieting the public spirit – or burying spirit – by the dominance of the appetitive appetites. For the "New South" doctrine that grows out of the turmoil of Reconstruction becomes secularized. A hundred years later, it is glorified as a new frontier, that of a "Sunbelt Economy," whose "money grubbers (as he termed them) set Percy's teeth on edge. The State of Georgia will declare itself the "Empire State of the South," in an imitative rivalry of New York. Faulkner's response to this increasing perversion is to dramatize the effects of pragmatic exploitation upon community and nature, not only through such homegrown scalawags as the Snopes clan, but in the poignant effects on Ike McCaslin in *Go Down, Moses!* (Perhaps Faulkner's own distancing from a nostalgically romanticized South, on the one hand, and the attempt to transmogrify the South into a "New South," on the other, tempt him to role-playing at home as a dandy, as Count Noaccount.)

There is, then, an "American" suspicion of art, a suspicion that art may even be antipathetic to the "American" spirit unless carefully modulated by ideological concerns. Meanwhile, in Percy's South there occurs a triumph of this new "American" spirit under the promotional epithet of the "New South," in imitation of the 19th-century's "Golden Age" success in monetary economics, sanctioned by centralized power in what will become, from a regional perspective, a devil term: "Washington, D.C." The shifting lies in replacing "agrarian" based communities with industrialized communities, though in respect to "farm" seen at an abstract level, the formalized structures of industrial community still echo by degree the agrarian community, though progressively losing a grounding in created nature. The "City on the Hill" becomes New York City, to be imitated by Atlanta through the shibboleths of "New South" economics as the religion of the future to community. And by Dallas and Denver, and Charlotte and Nashville.

The citizenry, become centralized, bears in it yet some cultural habits born in the blood though now transported to the city. In our day, those cities are sometimes spoken of as "asphalt jungles," prompting reactions seeking a recovery of civilization vaguely understood. Thus a residual cultural memory (held on to very often by "ethnic" loyalties) are involved in urban problematics to civilized life. In reaction, the "flight to the suburbs," in which there begins to emerge cultural modifications of urban nightmares, pursued in the suburbs with Edenic dreams of lost "good old days." Thus enclaves exist, shorn of cultural sustenance by and to community. Such, Percy recalls with his mischief in *Lost in the Cosmos*. Oh, to regain life in "Lost Cove" Tennessee, there to grow "wild maize, collards, and trap rabbits, wild pigs, and quail, eat grits and sausage and side meat." (Just where this Romantic vision to the person lost in the cosmos leads us is disturbingly suggested by Robert D. Kaplan, in his recent *An Empire Wilderness: Travels into America's Future* (1998), a political and sociological vision worth reading alongside Percy's "Last Self-Help Book.")

Those young poets at Vanderbilt just after World War I began to discover the consequences of an "American" ideology serving concentrated power, reacting to it in that symposium published subsequent to their poetry periodical the *Fugitive,* called *I'll Take My Stand.* Against the triumph of centralized and centralizing ideology – the "American" spirit parading on the local scene under banners of a "New South" – they were dawning to the dislocating effects upon community of that ideology. They began to confront secular pragmatism as devoted to economic, abstract ends (the notorious ultimate ideal of the "bottom line"), realizing first of all the sterilizing effects of ideology on art in local community. Davidson, in reaction, will write his "folk" opera *Singin' Billy,* with libretto by Charles F. Bryan, performed in Nashville, then largely forgotten. But before that attempt, Davidson had argued that community art had become vaporized in its local provenance by nationalistic ideology. What he, and his fellow "Agrarians," were confronting was the secular pragmatism devoted to concentrations of power, under the magic of money as the fuel of the machine of state. If we remember from Dante's *Divine Comedy* that for Dante "money" is an effect of art engaging nature, and hence always manifestly local in its origins, we may the better see the limited relation of an Ezra Pound to the Agrarian's concerns. For both, money as fuel speaks to a destruction of both art and nature. Pound departs from them in pursuit of the poet as tyrannical king, in the interest of the general good. Davidson to the contrary observes the growing poverty of art in the home as museums proliferate.

With the triumph of the "American" spirit, then, there occurs an obfuscation of appetite for power by a pragmatic sentimentalizing of the public spirit through terms like *democracy* and *common good* and *individual rights.* Such terms relegate *sin* and *grace* and *God* to the attic of memory, as Percy observes. Art becomes increasingly an afterthought in a new regimen, as community itself becomes collectively concentrated in Atlanta and Charlotte and Dallas and Chicago and Los Angeles. With this growing progress of "Americanism," however, there begins to appear in the public spirit as well what one is tempted to call a residual sense of guilt over the abandonment of art. For at least intuitively we recognize that art provides a visionary perspective upon nature, upon creation. The acceleration of consumerism as the new way of life delays reckoning with that guilt, though it erupts symptomatically in community life itself, leading for instance to embattlement over the relation of pornography to art.

The cause of what we are calling a collective guilt in the public spirit, as that spirit has been seduced to nationalistic ideology, may be sufficiently remote in public consciousness that to make a concentrated point of analysis is difficult. For, as Percy became increasingly aware, the pathology of spirit raised to nationalistic level makes him as Southerner and Catholic a problematic "American" novelist. Ezra Pound as a young revolutionary poet reacted against this same "American" spirit, as did those Nashville Fugitives, and as did Eliot, as we have observed. But Pound would attempt to centralize power in the poet – not "power to the people," except insofar as the poet attained a dominant vocal authority through his signs – Confucius being Pound's adopted father in consequence. But Pound recognized as well that art is necessarily local, a point he repeatedly argues. What he opposed was a concentration of power at the level of "stupidity" as he termed it, at the national level where the local was reduced to subordinate service. Thus (in his perspective and in that of the Fugitives turned Agrarians) the power of community became "purified" by a central authority through process, the increasingly triumphant process being Marxism. In consequence, art becomes but a manner, though the alienated poet might well turn revolutionary against it, intuitively if not rationally. What he would reject is art purified by psychological process in the interest of centralized political power, which power by appropriating authority over art would unify public spirit in a consent to feed centralized power. (One searches long on Capitol Hill to find a politician "against" art.)

The uses of the poet as engineered out of Marxist doctrine has at last become notorious, though defended on "democratic" principles in the West for decades. What is still less recognized, though Solzhenitsyn sounded a clarion call in the halls of Harvard, is the kindred uses of art by centralized power under that ancient shibboleth of political power, *democracy*. If one wonders at the destructive uses of "opinion polls" on the political level in our day, he might well explore the appropriations politically made of the techniques of advertising, a coincident merging of *theory* with *consumerist philosophy* reflected in our political scene to such a degree as to turn the "American" spirit increasingly cynical. What has been let loose upon that spirit is gnostic process such as those Vanderbilt poets engaged as a manifestation of the old dragon. And in doing so, they gradually clarified to themselves, by their active opposition to abstract nationalism, the intellectual and spiritual principles put at risk in community. It is through that clarification that they part ways with Pound as ally – as they would do also in opposition to Neoconservatism at a later date, a movement beginning in the 1960s as disaffected Liberals move to the right in the political spectrum. What bothers the so-called "Paleoconservatives" (an epithet attributed to the traditionalists by this new "conservative" movement) is that the Neoconservative opposition to current nationalistic power still holds semi-sacred the centralized power itself, though in doing so its arguments become vulnerable in its humanistic aspects. The argument becomes less over centralized power than over who is to control it. Thus the "politically correct" agenda becomes difficult for these semi-reformed centralists to counter, to say nothing of its difficulty in coming to terms with a growing spiritual reawakening in the public spirit. For in that reawakening political power centered in the individual is required to recover recognition that the individual is a person, not an integer of power. (Indeed, Eliot anticipates this as the possible danger to those Agrarian poets on his reading of *I'll Take My Stand,* arguing (in *After Strange Gods*) that necessity of Orthodoxy in support of Tradition lest tradition become merely reactionary and the community succumb to what he called "free-thinking Jews" and "*Protestant* agnosticism." Hence the current irony alluded to, the political turmoil in Israel between the theistic and the free-thinking Jews, an emerging political battle unsettling to the Neoconservatives, some of whom (in *Commentary*) sound increasingly like Eliot in his *After Strange Gods* we have suggested.

The "Agrarian" disposition (a complicated epithet, especially given the "agrarian" concerns of Marxist ideology) could find no advantage in opposing centralized power by an alternate version of centralized power. Their concern is rather (in respect to politics) for a proportionality of power suited to *membership* in union. In a world rejecting Christ as the "head" of community as a body, the substitution of the centralized "state" as head of the political body appears fraught with difficulties to the orderliness of – to the very life of – community, especially community as experienced at the local level. That is the level proper to art as supportive of the intellectual and spiritual aspects of the specific person in community. And this is to say that the "Agrarian" spirit was incipiently a spiritual concern for the person in community, though Eliot might fear it isolated to merely historical tradition. Hence the poet, such as Tate or Davidson or Lytle or Warren, discerns no solution in the opposition of one species of centralized power rejecting another. On this point, one is well advised to read Bertrand de Jouvenel's *On Power: The Natural History of Its Growth,* published at the end of World War II and counter to the euphoria of the "American" spirit in that moment, a moment when Percy is about to confront such issues. It is a work well read comparatively alongside Gilson's *The Unity of Philosophical Experience.* For *On Power* unfolds the historical evidence of the increasing power of centralization from Medieval kingship down to our day, as Gilson unfolds evidence of philosophical aberrations of thought that complement that process to centralization.

As for that continuing sense of guilt over the fate of art in community, whereby community becomes anemic in the absence of the feeding properties of art to that community, we observe that (since Gilson and de Jouvenel and Voegelin and others, including Walker Percy), we become increasingly concerned to establish symphony orchestras and theaters and museums at the local level. Where there erupts some controversy over these attempts, the arguments tend to concentrate upon the role of centralized power to such establishments. Federal "grants" become a decisive concern. Very seldom does argument engage the desirability to community of symphonies or theaters or museums. And so, on occasion, community health appears at risk out of the random sovereignty of individual poets and artists sustained at "public" expense to the embarrassment of centralized largesse. The "freedom" of the artist when embraced by the auspices of centralized justifications appears to risk, not local control but the very life of community. What appears in consequence, nevertheless, and increasingly often, is a mimicking of centralized power at the local level, in the name of an abstract nationalism of the self paraded under the banner of free speech. It is such fare that one meets very regularly in the daily media, and opposition to any destructive ideology paraded as art gains for its opposition the epithet of *benighted.*

Donald Davidson will remark this mimicking in a less than scandalous but nevertheless a pretentious art, a public monument in Nashville. He reflects on a Disney-land version of our cultural heritage in his "On a Replica of the Parthenon," a cement edifice raised in local ground in imitation of those ancient ruins of Greece. Caustically, he raises question, since this monstrosity (in the 1990s now become a public expense since in rapid decay) can only speak a "blind motion," a "dim last/ Regret of men who slew their past" and out of a sense of guilt have now "Raised up this bribe against their fate." Davidson in his "A Mirror for Artists," his essay in *I'll Take My Stand,* sees little hope of art's rescue, though, in his view, "the industrial Maecenas" (an allusion to Virgil's patron), the directors of the machines of industry, seem intent upon "the separation of our lives into two distinct parts, of which one is all labor . . . and the other all play, undertaken as a nervous relief. . . ." (Freud's address to art as a species of "nervous relief" has served only to second this general suspicion of art – art thus justified primarily as therapy, not as an aspect of the deportment of a harmonious life of person or community within existential reality.) What Davidson fears is the growing dominance of an "art gallery or art museum theory of art" which removes art from the home. His fear seems justified in the emergence of art isolated to centralized concerns, as by the National Endowment of Art, long after this essay in 1930. Since Davidson's day (i.e., in our day) the evidence of ideological intrusions upon art at the local level advances apace. But consider a "grass roots" reaction: as if a natural response to dislocations of persons from community, folk art reemerges after World War II, a phenomenon unrestricted by geography or cultural variances incidentally. And it does so largely regardless of nationalistic ideology, save when media technology concentrates ideology upon it. At millennium's end, that phenomenon "folk art" in the local community has become occasion to a new struggle to gain power over community nevertheless. The ideological cover for that new appropriation of art as a political process suited to ideology is notorious, advanced under its current banner of the "politically correct." Thus system as intrusive upon the local evolves, commanding art to a generalized and generalizing service to ideological power – contrary to the proportionate relevance of art to community in art's responsibility to immediacy. In response, at the local level there develops suspicion of art, a suspicion often dislocated in the local "popular spirit" when the community most proximate rejects art itself rather than to ideological intrusions that have become dominant in it. No wonder a Walker Percy finds himself engaging the problem of how to be an "American" novelist, while also a Catholic and a Southerner. No wonder, as well, that, in the interest of recovering an immediacy of metaphysical vision of the local, Flannery O'Connor calls herself a "hillbilly Thomist."

This latent suspicion of art in the "American" mind, becoming local to the South, increasingly, save as rescued in its "grass-roots" immediacy, is accompanied by an uneasy guilt in the generalized American mind, prompting the establishment of national recognitions of the artist, including our recent office of national poet laureate on a rotating schedule to touch all the "cultural" bases. It will lead Percy to wonder in reflecting on the history of the poet in the South. Why, he muses, was there no Melville in the 19th-century South? And how curious that absence in our "local" history, as we observe the social and political trauma of Reconstruction after 1865 and then the extensions and intensifications of social and political trauma of World War I. But suddenly art blossoms in the South, in that so-called "Southern Renaissance." That phenomenon (Percy suggests with mischief) might be explained by a fact of history: the South lost the war. There may be a relation between the historical fact that the South lost The War (O'Connor and Percy both agree) and the flowering of letters after World War I. And in much of that literature one may find embedded some aspect of that sad image of Lee at Appomattox, Lee continuing as residual icon through which to appeal for endurance through vicissitude.

That icon might even begin to stir to a recovery following World War I, insofar as there may have begun to emerge a suspicion that we had not quite won that "World" war though declared victorious in newspaper headlines. The "Southern Renaissance" of letters gets underway in the 1920s, but already English soldiers had reacted in somber disappointments over the war to end all wars. When Johnny came marching home to our own South and North and West and East, most passing in view of the Statue of Liberty on their way, all seemed less than well to him, increasingly. He was, in this respect, a small private soldier in the ranks, loosed now into the uncertainties of his homecoming after that parenthesis in his life called a World War. (There will occur later the march on Washington, ex-soldiers routed by Douglas MacArthur.) In American places, at last back home, he was not greeted as an Odysseus returned, as were many ragged Southerners after 1865, nor as King Richard or General Lee. He did not return to any encompassing, mollifying myth reassuring of his heroic sacrifice, despite Woodrow Wilson's high sentences. Our own generation (at century's end) is attuned more to the absence of any reassuring welcome to Vietnam veterans on their return from Asia than to that ancient general neglect of those returning from France in 1918. That old neglect might well set the poet in quest of a myth to rescue at least the "self" to some order after the war's intrusions of chaos upon community. Especially so, perhaps, if one were a poet stirred by dreams of the heroic, though isolated in a suburb of Chicago. That is, if one were an Ernest Hemingway. Hemingway catches the pathos of warrior neglect in his early "Soldier's Home." And he goes from there in quest of a personal heroism, through the warrior as alienated Stoic, enduring to the point of a resolving death as revenge against a wicked world. For there is much to be said in Hemingway's view for the solution he presents in "The Short Happy Life of Francis Macomber." Hemingway tells us in his "Preface" to his gathered *Short Stories* (1955) that this is one of "the last ones I have written," a signal of his position on heroism as it permeates his work. In it Macomber, on an African safari seeking trophy animals, is shot in the back of the head by his wife as a wounded buffalo charges him. His "short happy life" spans the brief moment of his courage in facing the charging animal. In the light of this story, then, we might suggest that Hemingway shares with Melville that old suspicion of an inherent perverseness, which he will not call sin, of course, but rather cowardice in not confronting a world threatening and so allowing occasion for the happiness of courage as the only happiness possible to man. In this perspective, Hemingway is more nearly descendent of Melville than of Twain, whom he celebrates as the father of "American" literature. How apt, then, a juxtaposition of "The Short Happy Life of Francis Macomber" to Melville's "Bartleby the Scrivener," as at once a rebuke of Bartleby's tedious courage in a long unhappy life, and as well a consent to Melville's own dark view of man's circumstances in the world.

In a quest for recovery after 1918, the Southern poet (a Faulkner or Davidson or Tate) might well see the Battle of the Somme as an ending consequent to that temporary arrest at Appomattox, seeing Lee's surrender at a waystation to Modernism's triumph – a pause in history capturing intimations of Lee as somehow akin to King Richard leaning on his sword, and perhaps akin, as well, to Thomas More committed to a bravery of spirit beyond Hemingway's comprehension. Such is Percy's intimation. It is quite noticeable that, in their correspondence, Shelby Foote is a persistent advocate of Hemingway, to which persistence Percy seldom seems to respond. For the alienated warrior as Stoic is somehow insufficient to his concerns. (Walker and his wife, on one occasion, see Hemingway in a Cuban bar, apparently keeping a distance, more out of manners than awe one suspects.) But it is not only our Southern poet who is disquieted by the anomalous circumstance to the late anonymous hero in the French trenches of 1914–1918. We see in retrospect a range of poets beginning to raise questions about that interrupting moment of history between 1914 and 1918, questions that had already been raised by Wilfred Owen, killed in France a week before the Armistice. In a preliminary "Preface" for his poems, his "elegies" as he called them, which he was not to see in print, he remarks a "Strange Meeting" in the trenches with imminent death. That encounter was "not about heroes," for all a poet "can do to-day is warn. That is why the true Poets must be truthful." Such warnings may be said to reach a culmination for the English soldier with the publication in 1937 of David Jones' *In Parenthesis* (through the auspices of T. S.

Eliot). In his "Preface," Jones remarks war "itself a parenthesis," so that "how glad we thought we were to step outside its brackets at the end of '18." But that was only to discover, for Jones, a "curious type of existence here [in England]," which increasingly appears to leave us "altogether in parenthesis." The poem, recovering an agony of spirit and body in the trenches at the Battle of the Somme, engages a new isolation of the self other than that experienced in the trenches, an anticipation of a larger separation. For Jones, the Battle of the Somme spoke an ending much larger even than the wholesale slaughter of anonymous soldiers in a cause they could not understand. It is a recognition the poet struggles to articulate – not only a Wilfred Owen and David Jones, but those young "Fugitives" gathered at Vanderbilt, who begin to explore causes buried in their regional history, effecting an increasingly present disquiet in their slumbering communities.

After the poets come the speculative critics, in works like *I'll Take My Stand* and Eliot's *After Strange Gods.* In John Crowe Ransom's *The World's Body* and Donald Davidson's *Attack on Leviathan.* There is an intellectual stir exacerbated by World War II, leading to signal small books: C. S. Lewis's *The Abolition of Man,* which engages the destruction through signs decayed, and Richard Weaver's *Ideas Have Consequences,* arguing a perversion of intellect by ideas in signs since Occam, isolating the self from community. Richard Weaver had already written his dissertation at Louisiana State University, under the direction of Robert Penn Warren and Cleanth Brooks, to be published posthumously as *The Southern Tradition at Bay: A History of Postbellum Thought,* with a "Foreward" by Donald Davidson. (It appeared late in that now notorious decade of the 1960s.)

Our principal point here in iterating these titles is that out of such remembrance of war there begin to stir intellectual concerns, leading to a literary and critical Renaissance. The theme of art's relation to society is increasingly a disquieting presence in the "American" mind, even as there occurs such a pronounced "progress" commanding the natural world – creation – to social conveniences. And it becomes manifest in the literature of the "Southern Renaissance." Davidson, Tate, Faulkner, O'Connor, Percy, and (by now) a host of persons begin to set themselves against that Modernist progress, out of a recognition that such changes prove sorely dislocating to selves and to community. And these poets and critics, many of them certainly, begin to discover in Hawthorne a direct antecedent poet, one who a hundred years earlier already recognized the tendency of those progressive ideas. Hawthorne sees our dislocation grown out of religious origins, a recognition which will increasingly become a central concern for those writers of the Southern Renaissance in particular. Even Warren's Willie Stark believes in Hawthorne's "sin," using sinful nature itself to establish his political power over parishes and cities in Louisiana swamps. He is especially adept at deploying upland citizens as agents to that power against the "lowlanders" in whom European cultural elements survive.

Those religious origins are touched upon in terms like *puritan* and *protestant* as variously associated with historical persons and movements since the

Renaissance as we explore our spiritual antecedents. In the phenomenon to society pointed to by "Protestant Puritanism" there hover difficulties to the artist more complex to understand than when merely caricatured by spectacle, as in current alarms over pornography for instance. But many of the counter alarms by the poet, usually appealing to the First Amendment, obscures a certain likeness in unlike things: the recent secularized Puritan as father to the Modernist poet. It is a recognition of this likeness between religious ideology and aesthetic ideology which attracts the attention of such writers as O'Connor and Percy – and Faulkner as well. It is the most central complication confronting that intentional skeptic T. S. Eliot, before his spiritual crisis that leads to his conversion. That is the origin in him as poet which lies at the heart of what he calls his "personal grouse," his *Waste Land.* What Percy or O'Connor may see, and perhaps more fully than Faulkner is prepared to see, is the origin of their antipathy to Modernism, common to them. Percy speaks of it as our loss of ontological certainties about being itself.

The mutual suspicion of Puritan and Poet come to focus in the mystery of the sign, but with a disquiet in the poet over whether the one or the other is dependent upon the devil in his own ink pot. Of course very anciently there is this fear of a dark presence always hidden in celebratory joy, raising questions of whether even King David is justified by music and song in praise of God. It is a fear leading to suspicions of the ceremonial, of festivity in nature as but "pagan." For some there rises a violent suspicion of the high festivals of sacramental worship. In this respect, how closely akin are Governor Endicott, that old Puritan whom Hawthorne summons to his tale of festival at Merry Mount, and Ralph Waldo Emerson, that secular Puritan who rejects bread and wine as unsuited to his version of worship in an intellectual violence whose spectacle appears serene. Especially in the modern world a suspicion of sacramental festival is raised in consequence of Modernist dislocations, abandonments of metaphysical harmony, whether in respect to the Puritan, the Poet, or the Scientist. And so we observe that there is a dark aspect to the fiddle or tambourine, to song or story, all anciently fascinating to us in part in that they tempt us to discovery of hidden dimensions in the sign, suiting sign itself to a conjuring of power through rhetorical manipulations. For surely there is a rhetorical dimension to music, one which Hitler would command through Wagner, for instance. How quickly the gnostic totalitarian recognizes this susceptibility in the human heart and mind. And how quickly he evolves a science of signs devoted to reducing persons to units of force, to be collectively deployed as power. (Orwell continues famous for his exposé of "double-speak.") Lenin and Hitler are currently our notorious instances, though already removed by time to a dark mythical past. Their signs, derived from theory to serve a perverse political consumerism, linger in residual ways disturbing to our recognitions. How cleverly entertaining becomes our own science of advertising, for instance, which we once associated with Fifth Avenue but now find endemic by an internet cast over us as wayward fishes, serving a consuming of things and services as perversely a spiritual self-consumption, in pretense that thereby persons are enabled to a sovereignty justifying appetitive desire. As if promising new miracle of loaves to fishes genetically perfected, we turn cannibalistic, as "consumers" feeding upon our own substantial nature.

To the poet's old concern for his possible alliance with the devil in his ink well, to speak metaphorically of a possible actuality, we risk a few signs here. Insubstantial form, simulacrum, summoned into a presence through signs by the poet hints at some devil in his ink pot, as he is often uncomfortably aware. Indeed, that is the suggestion of magic which St. Augustine detects in Manichaeanism, though philosophically the difficulty lies in that ancient heresy's Nominalistic presumption of sign's conjuring power – a sense of power to be accomplished through an alchemy of signs divorced even from the realities of actual ink and pen. Hardly the same perspective upon sign as understood by Flannery O'Connor when she speaks of fiction's incarnational aspect to which she is responsible as maker. For, in her perspective, the mystery of being itself makes art subservient to the Cause of being, even as St. Augustine and St. Thomas hold. For art's "form" in respect to the sign, in respect to image for instance, tends *toward* an insubstantiality, according to the degree of the artist's attempt to remove form from the governance of creation itself, against which tendency the poet must be alert.

To attempt such removal, forcing it to an extreme severance of form from any dependence on the actualities of substantial existence and thus subverting Aristotle's *possible* or *probable*: that is the artist's temptation when he presumes himself creator and not maker. It is this dependence of art upon creation itself, then, which the artist as alchemist abhors but cannot fully exorcise at last from his signs. Such is that species of "Romantic" rejection of existential reality as governing art which Joyce's Stephen Dedalus rationalizes in *The Portrait of the Artist as a Young Man.* For Stephen attempts to justify himself as artist by conjuring the evil into his ink well as ally, declaring his principle as artist to be *non serviam.* With our own mischief as diagnostic critic (rather than Percyan novelist) we might suggest that the old suspicions of the poet, the continuing Puritan disquiet, makes the audience itself into young Stephen's antagonist as artist. In this respect, there is in Stephen (and in Joyce) an uneasy sense of guilt, residual out of his own historically affected Puritan mind. (To this point, one might think of *Finnegans Wake* as a rejection of audience, save those fit but few audience – those committed to a vision rather the observe of Milton's concern in *Paradise Lost.*)

Stephen (and Joyce) reject the assumptions they suppose to lie in orthodox expectations of the poet (remembering here Joyce's own Jesuit education against which he rebelled by adapting it to art). In that rejection, young Stephen shares common ground with the Reformationist spirit, however caustically condescending Stephen may be to intellectual weakness and cowardice in the "Protestant" submission to authority or of the Catholic Irishman in his submission. Stephen must declare independence at last from Church, State, and Family, on the authority of that devil he has summoned. How difficult to this reduced species of a

Puritan inclination to Manichaeanism (in Stephen), its rejections of the "natural" body. Under Jesuit pressures, young Stephen as adolescent attempts dutifully to embrace responsibility to a self-purification, in an elaborate and systematic scourging of his senses. For to intellect, determined to free itself of a seeming dependence upon its own nature as bodily entrapped, it is difficult to accept the entrapping body as anything other than antagonist. Even Socrates wrestles often with this dilemma, though always confident of a transcendent possibility quite other than that self-transcendence young Stephen would accomplish as artist through his angelistic rejection of the world.

If created in the image of God as intellectual soul *incarnate,* the person may nevertheless desire absolute freedom, a desire which seems to force a reduction of the self to but *intellectual soul.* However, the reality to man as maker out of his givenness (and so necessarily to the poet) is that he himself depends on created reality increasingly through his *embodiment.* He is embodied thereby as *image* of the Supreme Artist, the Creator of the cosmos. One of the metaphysical paradoxes of reality, a continuing conundrum to intellect in its rational deportment, is the mystery of a reversal. For man, in respect to his intellectual deployment of images through signs, deploys an abstraction in some degree. The imaged "thing" is not the thing itself. Thus by his response to the actual – the thing in itself – man as intellectual must always exercise humility in relation to the possible power of his signs. He does so most immediately in that sign to himself: *back to the thing itself,* a concern more ancient than St. Francis of Assisi. That, indeed, is the gist of St. Thomas's observation that our intellectual concern must be, not for what men have said (though we inherit a stewardship of what men have said), but the truth of how things stand in themselves as actual. In respect to that assurance, through remembered signs that man is created "in the image of God," he is created as a substantial embodiment, an explicitly actual thing as body and soul.

How prescient, then, Faulkner's phrase of a "mist-born Protestantism grafted onto this land" by Puritan distortions of man as God's image, a phrase speaking perhaps more deeply of the Southern's ambiguities as intellectual soul incarnate as Christ-haunted, that is, haunted by God become man. The mystery implicit in Faulkner's phrase may be richer in implication than even Faulkner may have known – Old Testament poet that he is. Such, then, an aperçu, opening all the way back to that old garden in which rises a desire to be "as the gods." In the dream of absolute freedom, the protesting intellect would reject a sacramental surrender to creation within the context of creation, refusing thereby the connaturality of the being he shares, his kinship in the creatureliness of created things. Not an *image,* but the real thing, a "real" God. In that intention to autonomy originates actions of a growing presumption that God must at last depend upon man, rather than the other way round – the presumption bequeathed us most recently by Nietzsche in his signs proclaiming man a superman. Nietzsche's signs depend, we might say, upon Descartes thus glorified.

One of the ironies in our intellectual and spiritual confusions in the post-Renaissance, post-Occam world is that the Puritan who is suspicious of art and the artist who is suspicious of the Puritan as a threat to art have common root in a presumption of autonomy. *I will not serve,* save on my own terms. (Hence *private* conscience becomes supreme for John Milton.) Otherwise, I shall return my ticket to existence itself (the threat Ivan Karamazov makes to God which Percy cites in dealing with his ex-suicide). And so we have anomaly: a "Puritan artist" such as Joyce's Stephen Dedalus stands in a fundamental intellectual likeness to a Puritan father like Endicott, whom Hawthorne summons to the drama of his "Maypole at Merrymount." Both reject the goodness of creation, which requires a piety of sacramental stewardship to any making. They reserve by intention the convenience of a manipulation of reality by insubstantial form, to be projected by autonomous intellect upon creation. That is the process of forcing an ideological order, insofar as by a gnostic will the imposed form disregards substance. One finds the dilemma dramatized by Faulkner with moving pathos in Ike McCaslin's last hunt in "Delta Autumn" (*Go Down, Moses!*).

Ike, nearly eighty and camp-bound, is forced to confront the consequences of his having attempted to escape what Faulkner calls "the old furious McCaslin blood." That blood rebukes him now, in the person of a young woman, in her arms the infant son of Roth Edmonds, both the woman and Edmonds bearing strains of that furious blood. The young woman, unnamed, proves to be descended from James Beauchamp (Tennie's Jim). And in the convoluted generational pattern of family complications that so fascinated and delighted Faulkner, she addresses Old Ike as "Uncle Ike." The cowardly refusal of Roth Edmonds as responsible father of the infant is a cowardice from Roth's having been spoiled. "You, and Uncle Lucas and Aunt Mollie. But mostly you." Ike turned from his responsibility, she says, "When you gave to his grandfather that land which didn't belong to him, not even half of it by will or even law."

Ike, that is, refused his inherited Mississippi land and thereby his responsibility as steward. By that refusal he rejects both land and family, though he believes his action quite other. He chose to be ascetic, surviving as a carpenter owning nothing, though nevertheless sheltered by kin. And he is included in those hunts which were originally ordered by responsible rituals, rituals partaking of the sacramental. He must now confront the progressive decay evident in the "traditional" McCaslin hunts. They decline from the old ambiance of responsibility to creation which he had learned of old Carothers McCaslin and the mixed blood mystic, Sam Fathers. A tangle in his own intentionality for Ike. For if he early enough recognized that "We were born lost," meaning by "we" the McCaslins, that lostness must now be seen as enlarging beyond that tribal limit. He must acknowledge that in taking his vow of poverty, surrendering his inheritance, on the assumption that Sam Fathers had "set him free" as citizen of the delta swamp, his freedom proves in retrospect only used to drift through nature as if a spirit. That is less an act of sacrifice and expiation for his McCaslin blood than a refusal of responsibility as steward. Ike, like his beloved swamp, his version of an abiding Eden, has now become constricted and isolated, but those circumstances have causes deeper than the drift of time. In the old days, the November hunt required traveling only a short way in wagons to the old primeval swamp. Now they must drive two hundred miles in automobiles, the swamp contracted by commercial exploitation.

Ike can consent to Providence in the issue, accepting that – as it seems to this old man nearing eighty – he had surrendered his holdings in God's territory, in creation. "God created man and He created the world for him to live in. . . . And maybe He didn't put the desire to hunt and kill game in man but I reckon He knew it was going to be there, that man was going to teach it to himself, since he wasn't quite God himself yet. . . ." But now, with the intrusion of exploiters with machines, reducing the swamp to its last stand, power over nature seems triumphant. The irony of the rebuke Ike must take with him is that his vow of poverty was a refusal of responsibility under Providence, not an act of sacrifice or expiation, however imitative of Christ (who does not enter into Ike's Old Testament reflections of Providence). Now Ike finds himself tolerated, even humored, by his fellow huntsmen on this last expedition to the lost swamp – by his companions, the children and grandchildren of those old companions of fifty or sixty years ago. With the progress of exploitation, where now is that grave of the heroic dog Lion, of Old Sam Fathers, the son of an old Indian chief and a slave. Ike's only consolation is that "The people who have destroyed [the wilderness] will accomplish its revenge." But those people are not simply from the outside, thrusting a railroad line into it and bleeding its life away. Those who might have known better, like Ike, have infected it from within, as these present huntsmen, especially his kinsman Roth Edmunds, suggest. They are content with shooting a doe for camp food but as expediency void of sacramental deportment, offending Ike in keeping – or trying to keep – that act from him.

Cleanth Brooks puts Ike's dilemma arrestingly in his *Yoknapatawpha Country*: ". . . when man loses his awe of nature through a purely efficient utilization of it, or when he ceases to love it and to carry on his contention with it in terms of some sort of code, then he not only risks destroying nature but risks bestializing his own nature." The granddaughter of "Tennie's" Jim remarks caustically both honor and code decayed in the gesture to her of the father of her child: "the envelope of money Ike is charged to give her, since Roth cannot face her." Not just "some sort of code" is necessary, then, as Percy might say. In Percy's comic presentation of man "bestializing his own nature," that is man's fate of those scientific manipulators reduced to literal beasts in *Thanatos Syndrome*. There is a certain code, a "process" even in Modernist code. Faulknerian Stoicism, with its Old Testament ambiance in deference to an ambiguous Providence, yields a code of honor. The rituals of its practices Old Ike remembers now, seeing those rituals decayed. But what he now must acknowledge is that the code and rituals are somehow cut off from that source of a tenderness, a love, whereby ritual and code might prove supportive of sacramental responsibility to creation. As Percy will argue, even the honored figure of King Richard at parade rest, leaning on his sword, is futile emblem, unless over him rises the Church spire with its cross.

Flannery O'Connor, with a firm sentiment eschewing the sentimentality of Ike's vow of poverty (made a sentimentality by its separation from the spring of sentiment, of love), will dramatize man's pretensions as savior. Haze Motes is an instance, a figure of man whom we are to see at last as in some ways rescued from his prideful arrogance as an "innerleckchul." Far less kindly put is the drama of that pseudo-intellectual, Rayber, in *The Violent Bear It Away.* (In this relation, Haze, unlettered, is not pseudo, in that he confronts the abiding questions heroically if presumptuously, in contrast to Rayber, the academically educated sociologist.) Rayber, unlike Ike McCaslin in his surrender to the swamp, is intimidated by the testimony of things in themselves as experienced through his senses. Such an encounter as Ike experiences of the "Old Father," the rattlesnake, in "The Bear," stirs awe in young Ike (under the tutelage of Old Sam Fathers). It would leave Rayber in a quivering collapse. Rayber is incapacitated, indeed, by encounter with a stick or a starling if experienced as the thing it is, for such a still point threatens him with a collapse into mad worship. Rayber's experience of the stirrings of genuine love, then, he can rationalize only as the onset of madness in the machinery of his own brain. How unlike, then, Ike McCaslin and Rayber, or Haze Motes and Rayber as a pseudo-intellectual.

And yet they share in one sense, a sense of some agency independent of the responsibilities of stewardship and an accusing presence to them as responsible agents. For if misdirected, they each "care" about those they encounter, disappointed though they may be in the effects of their caring. As for Rayber, his refuge from the threatening immediacy of things is to see the forest through which he walks with Young Tarwater as so many board feet, destined to yield money to educate Tarwater, saving him from the influence of Old Tarwater. Thus as intellectual (proud of his academic training and of the research practiced on the Tarwaters), Rayber combines the deportment of an exploiter of nature with those of the sentimentalist who dreams of a human nature established by process, through psychological adjustments of such natural creatures as young Tarwater. It is a contradiction of rationalism and sentimentality which is not lost on the Tarwaters, neither upon the boy nor the old man. Nor is that similar confusion lost upon that young girl who accuses Ike most tellingly with the infant in her arms.

VII

Having laid this ground in recent fictions of "Southern" writers who find themselves confronting the consequences on community of Modernist ideology, let us explore somewhat the challenge to them as artists. They discover themselves engaging an audience with whom they share no common vision of community. And we are suggesting this is a loss of a vision which once held members in common bonds, a vision which for all its diversities yet bore the epithet of Western Christendom. We have also suggested that the difficulty of the poet in relation to his audience has become the absence of a common address through "signs" touching the reality of creation itself. It has been a gradually erosive effect upon common signs from a variety of intellectual quarters, though a hidden commonality to this erosion has been the emergence of intellect as autonomously intentional in its power over being. That is the evolving doctrine which Eric Voegelin speaks of as modern gnosticism, out of which doctrine the signs once held in common as an ordering of community have become opaque. It is a loss which can but leave the poet, if he dwell upon the problem too long, struggling to recover terms like *water* to an audience unlettered in its experiences. And it is especially challenging to a Percy or an O'Connor, for whom a term like *water* signifies relief to a thirst deeper than biological necessity.

Percy speaks of this phenomenon, the signs of our "Christian vocabulary." They have become "exhausted, worn slick as poker chips and signifying . . . little." How can one bear witness to the sacrament of Baptism? What were once words comfortably used "within a viable semiotic system," those signs have now been stored in that attic of memory, and few occasions require their being brought down and dusted off – "old words, God, grace, sin, redemption." How such loss occurred at a "national" level has no simple nor singular cause in a limited political or military event, such as the political pursuit of community order under the diverse rubrics of our national Constitution and Bill of Rights, or the Revolutionary War, or that War Between the States, though such rubrics be often scholastically explicated in response to the moment's crisis.

We have been pursuing a general shifting in the public spirit itself occasioned by ideas osmotic upon that spirit. We have suggested that out of theistic Puritanism there emerged a secular Pragmatism, shifting community and its ends from its governance under transcendent auspices (spoken to in terms like *God, grace, sin, redemption*). In consequence, temporal ends of the person in community reduced person to individual by sign eroded. *Society* becomes dominant principle to political and social empowerment, replacing a concept of community as a body of persons diverse in gifts and offices, members one of another. In the defoliation of community, in the dissolution of bonding as members one of another, secular Pragmatism increasingly comes to serve a puritan Positivism as absolutist doctrine – however little perceived in its autocratic presence by the "popular spirit." That is a direction whose culmination arrests Faulkner's old Ike McCaslin on his last hunt. He will say, as if not fully convinced, on that last encampment with companions now foreign to him, that intellect is not "quite God himself yet."

Ike's is an observation provided him by Faulkner, in the early stages of World War II, and within the thematically involved stories of *Go Down, Moses!* (published in 1942). "Delta Autumn" is set in the 1940s. Very soon thereafter, in the history of ideas affecting the academy, a Nietzschean impetus will erase Ike's "yet" through that excitingly new news out of Nietzsche that "God is dead" and to be made risen only in man's own intellect by intentionality. In a triumph of gnostic intellect over being, creation (Faulkner's "swamp" as emblematic of creation in his story) becomes matter suited to an alchemy through the abstract form to be imposed by a gnostic elite. For a successful imposition, however, the popular spirit must be sentimentalized to a service of those intentional manipulations. For only through intellect thus sentimentalized, in respect to ultimate ends as reduced to the immanent world, may the gnostic alchemist effect his ends. He becomes enabled thereby to make persons accept themselves as manipulating machines destined to a vague temporal end designated as for common good in self-manipulation. The "expert" replaces the priest. (This complex manipulation, we have suggested, and shall, is increasingly evident in us, giving rise to our restless concern for the genetic alchemy which promises relief to man as machine by healing all manner of bodily malfunction.)

Flannery O'Connor anticipates this species of intellect which maintains system at lower echelons of a society become sentimentalized. In her Rayber of *The Violent Bear It Away* we see the work-a-day theorist. How comfortable Rayber is, so long as he can avoid his idiot response to things whereby he becomes threatened by a mad worship of the God he denies. Thus that forest through which he and young Tarwater walk (accompanied by the natural idiot Bishop): how reassuring to see it by abstraction to board feet, anticipating the end of any tree as an economic means of fulfilling Tarwater's education to make him a Modernist. And so there has evolved a new religion, one with correspondences to that ancient heretical religion called Manichaeanism in which St. Augustine found himself entrapped. But in this Modernist ideology, society must encompass (or seem to encompass) both the Elect (the intentional Positivist) and the Hearers (the supportive *hoi polloi*). In Percy's terms, there is declared a "political" equality of the *theorist* and the *consumers*. The fundamental shift in this secularized Manichaeanism is that relocation of man's ultimate end from the transcendent to the immanent, with Positivistic intellect self-transcending the immanent. Thus creation in its particularities must be purged of any teleological ends beyond a materialistically founded Eden, built upon trees as board feet and man as biochemical mechanism. Of course, the Positivistic Elect are in their roles as alchemists of being.

This new religion makes common the rubric of "Nature," to be worshiped by the hearer-consumer insofar as "Nature" is made convenient to the self as sovereign – each self promised a Utopian recovery as a new Adam as it were by the clever theorist. From the old theistic Puritan, such as Hawthorne's Endicott in "The Maypole of Merrymount," and from the Positivist ideologue, we inherit a disquiet about the sign's attraction to reality itself, a reality perverse in resisting sign if emptied and then applied by force of intention upon actual things. For signs seem always to haunt, if not actively threaten, rational intellect with hints of some mystery beyond the pragmatic limits of our control of sign by magic uses. (Though initially shocking, the epidemics caused by computer viruses may even stir some hope in us, if we but admit it.) In associating the theistic Puritan as grandfather to the Positivistic theorist, we must not disdain the considerable skills of logic that ordered (and in some instances still order) rhetorical activism through signs, practiced by the theistic Puritan. Otherwise we shall overlook the kinship between an Endicott and a geneticist such as the Englishman Richard Dawkins, who declares persons but "lumbering robots" whose genes create them "body and soul." Or we shall find but an enigma that new purist of biological reality, Professor Singer of Princeton, who sees no moral question in our disposing of handicapped infants within a month of their birth. This is the latest modification from his earlier parameters of a year as acceptable in destroying the defective child. For, he says in a *Princeton Alumni Weekly* interview (January 26, 2000), "babies become persons when they develop some kind of awareness of themselves existing over time." The year's leeway Singer earlier proposed may be too Draconian, if that term may be used, since self-awareness occurs "sometime during the first year of life but not in the first month of life." Do away with the defective quickly, within the first month, for conscience's sake, or then one must test them for self-awareness, scientifically, during the next eleven before executing them – so as not to act in "too arbitrary" a way (Singer as quoted in *First Things,* June/July 2000).

By our term *theistic Puritan,* then, we mean to suggest an ancient kinship with the classical Gnostics, in that they share a common bent to a willed transcendence of creation as itself evil. But we mean as well to designate a transitional intellectual deportment toward creation out of which, under the impetus of empirical science, gnostic ends are diverted from the transcendent to the immanent. We might explore at length the shifting of this sense of ends, as it is implicit for instance in the political prose of John Milton, who as poet and initially as a political philosopher to Puritanism, is remembered as dedicated to the transcendent end of soul as poet, in his *Paradise Lost* and *Paradise Regained.* But under the political pressures of the mid-seventeenth century, finding himself increasingly isolated as polemicist not only from his old "Royalist" adversaries but from his Puritan allies, he becomes especially angered by Parliament's Puritan failures. He comes more and more to certify the personal authority of his own conscience as overriding, but it is a conscience increasingly isolated from any community. In this respect, one should read most carefully Milton's February 1659 "Treatise of Civil Power in Ecclesiastical Causes," in which he excoriates the "forcing protestants" of the Parliament summoned by Cromwell in January of that year. In American Puritanism, there rises similarly a collective intent through signs to build a "City on a Hill," a phrase enjoying a popular rhetorical use in our recent politics, though architects cannot agree on city plans.

In those old American Puritan fathers, thrusting rhetorical thorns into Hawthorne's imaginative art, there is a more sophisticated logic than our increasingly unlettered generations may appreciate, especially if those generations are denied their intellectual progenitors as presences in their inherited nationalistic spirit through "formal" academic training since World War II. From old dreams of God's city on a hill as a stepping place into the absolute, down to visions of forests as board feet (dooming Ike McCaslin's swamp refuge), a theistic Puritanism and atheistic Positivism share in the reduction of "Nature" to a severe service to appetitive nature, though their kinship pass unrecognized. That the old Puritans were themselves given to the appetitive – a pitfall to the Positivist – is ironically engaged by Hawthorne, in his *Scarlet Letter* and "Young Goodman Brown" and other fictions. By intentionalities deployed through the insistent logic of signs, this is to say, Puritan or Positivist may force ideological form upon the popular spirit. The spirit so forced, in the vagueness of its response to such forcing, comes to desire in turn a vague, removed heaven or concrete things as spawned by scientific technology.

The attempted constriction of creation by willed intent appears promising of a comfort to intellect, a comfort beyond its continuing suspension in ambiguity is of the immanent and transcendent in relation to sign. But that very ambiguity, occasioned by the sign's uncertainty, stirs intellect to discomfort precisely because intellect possesses a residual knowledge of *being,* intuitively known. Discomfort is therefore perhaps harbinger of hope. Such disquiet proves always a threat to ideological intentionality, and is therefore subversive antagonist to intentional intellect. It tempts a recovery, then, to the truth of the thing known, a truth which corresponds to the essence of the thing known through encounter, through experience, and therefore that truth as known bears witness to a cause of things other than the intentional intellect. Signs cannot exorcise that knowing through the intentionality of sign reduced to merely formulae of abstract forms. Even so in a desperate reaction to this truth about signs, the intentional will may react the more insistently in its presumptions of authority which is vested in a faith in intellectual autonomy. We speak here, then, of an arena interior to intellect, in which Modernist thought, settled within the particular person, advances itself in the guise of Old Gnostic and New Puritan rejections of the person's dependence in creation, a dependence in the given. This is a rebellion served as well by severe Positivistic Puritanism whose agenda requires the motto *non serviam,* though the public motto is associated with whatever residual sense of that reaction. One must defy dependence in the good of creation in the interest of a "general good," for society reconstituted gnostically

This interior intellectual arena, in which "ideas" are embattled in the person, is burdened as well by a bodily incarnation, which intellect may take to be an incarceration in its gnostic fury, an embodiment which Positivistic theory struggles to reduce to machine. It is in this circumstance to *person* that the Thomistic version of this created entity the person calls man an *intellectual soul incarnate.* Such a naming of the "self" appears, by the very naming, to deploy diverse signs to signify diverse realities. But, from a Thomistic perspective, from a metaphysical view, this is but the necessity to our discursive, finite, limited, and above all fallen intellect. It is an attempt for St. Thomas to recover a vision of that fallen nature of person in a recognition of his potentially unified simplicity, a reality possible to the person beyond the divisiveness of signs as rationally pursued of necessity by intellectual finitude. In our recent intellectual history, as we have observed *passim,* there occurred a usurpation of the rational aspect of the simple intellect in the interest of formulaic sciences of things, an appropriation of philosophical reason to the interest of "science," that philosophical deportment which was once devoted to the metaphysical understanding of the truth of things. Our sense of person subsequently becomes more fragmented, with a concomitant malaise in the self as consequence, its growing sense of alienation, of becoming lost in the cosmos.

Not that there did not also occur a reactionary usurpation in opposition to the rationalistic sciences. It is the usurpation of intuitive intellect in service to imaginative response in opposition to "science." It is the response of the poet which we are accustomed to describe as "Romanticism." And so the poet by excess of the intuitive at the expense of the rational is capable of subverting his own simple nature as intellectual creature, leading to Eliot's "dissociation of sensibilities," a divergence of "thought and feeling." But in elevating "feeling" over "thought" – or in our terms, in elevating intellect's intuitive action over rational action – strangely subversive effects result, confounding the self in its dislocation from impinging reality. It is a confusion more widely abroad than if we put in terms of geography or calendar dates, as if the dissociation occurred simply in relation to theistic Puritanism of a Governor Endicott in reaction to sacramental drama in community. For the dissociation occurs in intellect itself in response to current contingencies. That the confusion is so largely universal might be suggested, then, by taking a recent "foreign" Puritan in evidence, one far removed from the environs of Concord at the period between Endicott and Emerson or the period of embattled Cavaliers and Puritans in Cromwell's day.

I have in mind Leo Tolstoy, a poet sufficiently removed (on the surface of spectacle) from Western embroilments. Tolstoy's struggle to capture the pathos of willful passion is constricted within the human body in his *Anna Karenina.* But after that great novel, Tolstoy turns more and more to writing increasingly Manichaean tracts, whose effect is a preparation of the ground in which Hegelian gnosticism pitches political camp through Lenin. Those tracts proved widely influential in East and West, in respect to the modifications of the popular spirit toward temporal concerns. They prove therefore more influential than Tolstoy's fiction. For in rejecting intellect on the one hand and the body of creation on the other, Tolstoy contributes to an anomalous condition of the popular spirit. Thus his Christ becomes the unlettered and impoverished peasant, convenient to Hegelian-Marxist ideology. As for Tolstoy as person, he turns with bitter fury upon himself, or more specifically, upon the curse of his being incarnate. He struggles to deny his own body as other than an evil impediment to his Manichaean rejections of this world. It is this aspect of Tolstoy's thought which makes him, to speak metaphorically in comparison to Dostoevsky, like Emerson as contrasted to Hawthorne. However cryptically put that metaphorical relation, it suggests why Hawthorne and Dostoevsky prove "Southern" as they are responded to by Southern writers, including Faulkner and Flannery O'Connor and Walker Percy.

In respect to Positivism as a species of the Puritan disdain of creation, the person so inclined intellectually rests his faith in reason, rather than in the "heart," as authority to sovereign conscience. He would set aside the intuitive desire for transcendence, signified by creation for St. Augustine or St. Thomas, lest it enslave reason to that strange desire of the heart. That at least is the Positivist's reading of the theistic Puritan, for from his own "liberated" position as intellect he sees that old Puritan as enslaved to an illusion of a radical transcendence of the soul. For the Positivist, the strictures of logic must distance intellect from creation in the interest of autonomous power. Whether one is the theistic Puritan or atheistic Positivist, then, his becomes a pursuit of desire to a universal or a sovereign transcendence, out of a fear of or disdain of creation itself. Each would deploy reason disjoined from intuition, but especially deploying reason restricted to logic as authority. (Again, one reads New England sermons or Tolstoy's tracts to this point, lest inclined to take either as rejecting logic in intellectual actions.) If we would approach a better understanding of roots common to the Puritanism rising out of the Reformation and Positivism rising out of science as usurper of that tendency in Reformation thought, we may well consider Gilson's exposition of late Medieval "logicism" as it leads to what he explores in his William James Lectures at Harvard, his *Unity of Philosophical Experience,* especially that line of his exploration of Abelard in "The Road to Skepticism" and "The Breakdown of Medieval Philosophy." He follows this line of Western philosophical experience out of logicism, through to a pervasive skepticism, issuing in our moment in which Positivism reigns supreme over intellect. What we may recognize by such an exploration is that Positivistic dogma has become more inclusive of nature than the initial Puritan engagement of nature, since for the theistic Puritan's intent, nature is a means of transcendence *under* God. For the Positivist it is to the contrary: the inclusiveness is accomplished by a reductionism in the interest of intellectual autonomy purified of any *dependence* upon the transcendent, insofar as by that old Gnostic-Puritan theism intellect must be beholden to something beyond itself. (The difficulty to Positivism proves its dependence in mechanistic materialism, a challenge to autonomous freedom.) Positivism's logic requires as its absolute principle a reconstitution of accidental existence, the Positivistic intellect become its own god through rational ceremony of apotheosis. What wonder, then, that T. S. Eliot, emerging as literary critic, cries alarm over the literary effects of such separation of "thought and feeling" in the "dissociation of sensibilities," which he locates as occurring at about the time of Dryden and Milton in English letters, though at that moment he is severely skeptical. That is a crucial turning point, given the concomitant rise of Puritanism and Baconian Empiricism as rivals, each increasingly feeding in the same "ontological" grounds – the primacy of intellectual autonomy. For the Puritan, the justifying presence to consciousness becomes individual conscience. For the Empiricist on his way to scientific transcendence, logic itself replaces conscience. Irving Babbitt and George Santayana at Harvard (teachers of Eliot) fiercely resist the mechanistic "humanism" of President Charles M. Eliot, the process of specializations of intellect as the ideal of an adjustment of intellect and of man himself as machine. By specialization, man is to be energized by the person's immanent will, adjusted in its energies to local ends as a mechanism specifically in service of the state as the only acceptable commonality, ameliorated for any intellectual disquiet over submission to process by arguments for the "common good." Nevertheless, President Eliot's proposed dogmas for a "Religion of the Future" sets the object as anything but "the personal welfare or safety of the individual in this world or the other." Above all, that religion "will not be propitiatory, sacrificial, or expiatory." What wonder, then, that such an intellect as Charles Peirce, at Harvard in this period, should seek an active recovery of intellect from such entanglement. But where Babbitt and Santayana were attempting to recover a high Renaissance culture to academic concerns, Peirce turned further back, to Medieval scholasticism, and particularly to Duns Scotus. By that recovery he would develop his concern that, in respect to epistemology, sign is to be understood as emerging from man's diatic dyadic dimension (properly the purview of evolutionary science). By sign, man makes a triadic escape of entrapment within the horizontal plane of existence. That is the position which becomes fascinating to Walker Percy, his concern for the "Delta" principle to the nature of sign as bearing scientific more than philosophical authority. He writes Jan Gretlund (June 13, 1987) that after all the hoopla over *Thanatos Syndrome* is at last quieting he is "turning to semiotics as usual, contemplating a book elucidating Peirce's 'triadic theory' (which I consider probably as important as Quantum Theory) toward end of reconciling it with people like Wittgenstein, John Poinsot (John of St. Thomas) a 17th Century Dominican."

If Percy becomes intent upon epistemological explorations of the sign to recover the ontological grounding of his intellect, Flannery O'Connor in her engagement of Modernist doctrine is not drawn by such theories of intellect, content with what St. Thomas argues in declaring intellect a simple unity given to modes of action as intuitive and rational. (The theories, she said, are worse than the Furies.) She recognizes nevertheless affinities in Modernist doctrine between Puritan inclinations toward Manichaeanism and Positivism's logical exorcism of the Transcendent from the Puritan thought it adapts to its uses. It is a tensional contention within Modernist doctrine which she dramatizes in its distortions in *The Violent Bear It Away.* Old Tarwater recognizes the same in its destructiveness through his kinsman Rayber, though he cannot articulate it with rhetorical persuasiveness through logic, his difficulty with signs ridiculed by Rayber. What Old Tarwater nevertheless recognizes is Rayber's vested faith in the *name* of science whereby science sees life itself as mechanistic. For Rayber the person is a machine to be analyzed and adjusted as machine by the science of psychology.

How inevitable, then, within the purview of the possible or probable to art as dependent upon the reality of man as person, that Old Tarwater is able to carry his argument against Rayber only through violent acts in his concern to recover the kingdom of Heaven. That old prophet knows intuitively that Rayber is an instrument used against him by his ancient Adversary to the kingdom of Heaven, Satan. Rayber has consented to that service, not in innocence but by naiveté, by his gnostic fascination with the possibility of a formulaic magic through which, using signs, he can adjust "personality." But within the dramatic unfolding of the possible or probable as governed by O'Connor's visionary address to the mystery of man, we see Rayber in spite of his intentions going in terror of that fierce Love advocated by Old Tarwater. It is a Love which threatens him in still moments as he confesses, moments of encounter with "a stick or a stone, . . . the absurd old man's walk of a starling crossing the sidewalk." In such moments there rises in Rayber "a morbid surge of love . . . powerful enough to throw him to the ground in an act of idiot praise. It was completely irrational and abnormal." And so he can interpret it only as the onset of an inherited madness, where St. Thomas (and O'Connor) suggest it an effect of an intuitively visionary response to connaturality. Rayber, this is to say, experiences Eliot's "still point," but his obsession with the rational cannot let him see that or respond to it as a moment occasioned by grace.

Rayber's experience of idiot love is counterpointed by Old Tarwater's intuitive recognition that in Rayber the Devil exercises sovereignty, despite those moments of Rayber's escape into the terror of love. Rayber seems relieved to have escaped such terror, reasserting the existence of man as mechanistic. His experience of love can only be rationally accepted as some glitch in his own operation as a machine. In that recognition he qualifies for O'Connor as one possessed, as opposed to Old Tarwater who is a "natural Catholic." (She affirms her own belief that Satan is actual, a reality for her from which Percy demurs.) Of course, given the violence of the old man's actions, his shooting Rayber with a shotgun (deafening him), the unwary reader may see the old man as but another of those false prophets met on radio and television programs, perhaps a kinsman of Onnie Jay Holy. It is a confusion, a failure of recognition of distinction, which such a reader may share with Haze Motes on his first encounter of Onnie Jay Holy, whose evangelical rhetoric is stolen from Haze. John Holy (Onnie Jay) assumes perversely the role of John Baptist to Haze in preaching the Church of Christ Without Christ in order to fleece his auditors. Recognizing that Onnie Jay is not "true," Haze is forced to confront his own contradictory "truth": if only by attempting blasphemy, as he has insisted, is there any possibility of coming to the truth that God does not exist, such blasphemy signifies at last that God exists.

VIII

By our foray into the intellectual history of Modern gnosticism from Abelard down to Bertrand Russell (as Gilson has it) – down to World War I – we have been attempting to characterize the derivation of an intellectual formula dictating a potion that has proved addictive to the public spirit. The effect is to destabilize community in order to reconstitute it as a society transformed by a magic derived from gnostic power over human nature itself, by consent to the "common good." Such is the disordered reality which a Percy or an O'Connor must engage as poet, attempting to capture vision in art, each recognizing (according to the peculiar gifts to each) that the spectacles revealing community disoriented must be deployed in such a way as to reflect the truth of the disorientation.

This is to say that the possible or probable with which the poet must make (in an accord with the principles of art) depend on, even in that disarray in confusion of the truth of things, our having become lost in the cosmos. Remembering in such a making that art is a virtue of the practical intellect (as Thomas argues), one makes the art thing in response to the truth of things, even the truth of aberrant actions possible to the person. Given the effects upon persons and communities of the Modernist perspective, the aberrant is itself a "truth" involved in art itself. The poet may not be deeply aware of that governance to his making, so that becomes a point Flannery O'Connor makes in declaring that "If a writer is any good, what he makes will have its source in a realm much larger than that which his conscious mind can encompass and will always be a greater surprise to him than it can ever be to his reader."

And so the visionary poet, the prophetic poet, must engage persons in disarray as persons, lost in the cosmos, even as Aeschylus or Dante do. But in the present circumstances to that engagement, in which there is but a residue of a common vision of the "self" since we have lost a metaphysical vision that might once have afforded some common perspective to the poet and his reader – to the reader in at least a philosophical trickle-down effect yet bonding community – how may the poet anneal by his art the disaffected community? Perhaps by devoting himself, as Eliot declares, to a "purification of the dialect of the tribe"? If that poet is Flannery O'Connor, then perhaps a rubric signaling the attempt is the dramatizing of the grotesquerie settled upon personhood. If he is Walker Percy, he may engage man as "loony." Whatever the gambit of the practical intellect as poet, engaging the local circumstances to persons through reason, he does so with some recognition of our lostness. His possible or probable actions of surrogate persons in the art engages the spectacles of disarray. He may recognize in such spectacle that because "grace and nature have been separated," so too have "imagination and reason . . . been separated, and this always means an end to art" (O'Connor). No easy task to the poet, then, a reunification of imagination and reason in recovering a vision of the relation of nature and grace. But this becomes the necessary recovery to be made by the poet in the midst of circumstances hardly propitious to any effectiveness of his art in such recovery insofar as his audience may see.

No wonder then that such a poet may come to himself as does Percy, who as Southern Christian may think of himself as a Lancelot in search of the Holy Grail, only to discover himself at the end of his quest "at a Tupperware party." It is a world that appears projected by a magic which dissolves mystery. Listening at the commercializing pitch of host or hostess at that strange party, the guest must take some time, experience some endurance of the randomness of that party world, in order to discover the cause of that randomness. It is effected, as we have been arguing, by that siphoning of creation itself toward reconstituting creation by intensely limiting formulae imposed upon it. By intellectual abstractionism is derived a magic elixir advertised at the party as allowing a transubstantiation of being. Being thus repackaged may be stored in the freezer, or heated in the microwave oven, depending upon whether the customer as partygoer is ant or grasshopper.

Perhaps this is more than a poet's figurative epithet naming human desire as it has come to be perverted in the interest of an immediate consumption or a storing against the inevitable worldly winter. To Percy's figure suggesting the Tupperware party arranged by Modernist prescription as a shocking recognition of our present circumstances, then, a further figure, turning on the mystery of life itself as reduced to formula. In a recent dialect of the disoriented tribe, life is computerized by abstractionism, laminated as formulaic idol under the pressure and intense heat of that magic power we have called gnostic autonomy. Thus a variety of self icons to be worshipped. The passport to the party: a chargeable Visa card with unlimited purchase of the cosmos as but accidental material to serve appetitive desire. By that card as scientific voucher, the person is credentialed as a Modernist citizen of a random world. And so life itself becomes desubstantiated by the gnostic theorist, graphed as genetic blueprint of life for instance. Process, gnostically controlled, orders an omnipotent power to serve gnostic intentionality.

As we enter a new millennium, what we begin to discover is that through procedural progress, through process governed by ideological dreams of being beyond being itself, we seem to have reached a dead end. Process seems only to have afforded a gradual submission of intellect to an illusional angelism, through its setting aside metaphysical philosophy. Thus an intellect, even that of a

Lancelot, may be left suspended over an abyss, over that San Andreas Fault widening within the Modernist mind itself. In this recognition, Percy will speak of our having lost ontological orientation to creation, an orientation we have recalled as affirmed possible to intellect by Aquinas through connaturality. That is an orientation possible in response to the self-evident out of our actual experiences as intellectual soul incarnate. It is a recognition of shared existence, sustained in that current which Thomas calls being, the ontological ground to specifically existing things, maintaining creation by the grace of Love. A mystic like Dame Julian of Norwich recognizes this Love as keeping so lowly a thing as a hazel-nut on her palm from falling to nothingness out of its littleness. Having lost this recognition of the self-evident, having lost a sense of ontological commonality in being shared by creatures created, we find ourselves "lost in the cosmos," the cosmos itself increasingly reduced to an uncaused mechanism as the only "rational" account of the unaccountable.

St. Augustine and especially St. Thomas, in their rational pursuits of the intuitively known, would advise us that ontological certainty may be recovered through a reflective pause out of our blind pursuit of progress toward illusions of absolute intellectual freedom of the self. Otherwise, the self becomes disfranchised from its own nature as the inevitable end. That is the end Edgar Allan Poe speaks, of whereby the self can conclude itself only "a dream within a dream." That is the panic conclusion to Cartesian Idealism when forced to its logical extremity. The Saints to the contrary assert that a recovery lies in accepting our actual experiences of discretely existing things, here and now, as the beginning point (as it is for Aquinas). Encounter through the senses of actually existing things, collectively designated in rational attempts at understanding as the orders of nature: that is the genuine, but slow, progress of *homo viator* toward the "self" recovered to its ordinating nature. For through that acceptance of the self-evident, the "self" may recognize itself *communally* grounded in being. It is this responsibility which requires our stewardship, of each according to his gifts. It is a responsibility with a spiritual depth seldom touched by our popular concerns for "ecology," by alarms over "global warming," and so on. Those concerns may consequently prove baffled by whatever resolve at last, because so dependent upon a limited version of the person's survival as materialistic integer in a global machine, the "Cosmos." Many of our greatest poets since Dante and Chaucer have recognized this necessity of recovery to their witness. Many more since then have, with some agitation of spirit, borne witness to our gradual loss of ontological certainty. Even so, by that very agitation of spirit reflected in their signs there abides at least a negative signal of that positive ground, uncertain though their signs may be. The desire for that ground (St. Thomas might say) cannot be out of nothingness formulated in a pursuit of power through that dark refusal, *non serviam.* Satan, in our myths concerning his reality, reacts negatively against the antecedent positive, but in doing so he bears witness to that Absolute Positivist by his continuous *non serviam.* Once the brightest of the angels, fallen through his willful sign (*non serviam*), Satan continues nevertheless the consummate philosopher, theologian, poet. He is so by his created nature, though a fallen one.

That is a shocking recognition for poet, theologian, philosopher to make. And especially perhaps for the poet, who may remember Dante's old treatment of Satan at the pit of Hell, devouring the prideful. Dante makes him imagistically repulsive by sensual detail in which the metaphorical implication may be obscured. It is true that this revolting figure in action is committed to "self" cannibalism, and is properly attempted in imagistic detail as Pride ravishing the prideful. Were Dante theologian more than poet, he might have appended arguments about Satan as the consummate "intellect," his perfect knowing because created perfect intellect his eternal dolor. Satan in this perspective is his own Hell because he knows, consummately though not comprehensively (given his limits as *created* the brightest angel), the Perfect Good. A human intellect, weakened by the dry-rot of sentimentality, might even be tempted to a pity for him, that being an aberration not unrecorded in the annals of the Church Militant. Indeed, there is something of this torture experienced by O'Connor's Haze Motes in his concluding agony. He has been a Countryboy Nietzsche, who attempted to deny God's very existence by acts of blasphemy as his self-creating principle, coming to confess at last himself as "unclean."

Our believing poets engage variously, each according to his specific gifts as maker, the Tupperware party into which he finds himself *thrown* (to appropriate a Heideggerian gesture). He finds himself where a celebration is in progress, hosted by Modernist gnostic intellectuals, and is reluctant to leave, since he feels called to bear a different celebratory witness. That very sense of responsibility, if not carefully approached, may even put at risk his gifts as poet. For what he feels required to reject is the plasticizing of being itself. The Modernist hosts to the contrary urge process as if it alone might procure a safety to the self against its sense of its own impermanence, a plastic lamination of the self as it were. By such witness in such circumstances, the poet may come to value the more the initiating and sustaining actions of his own intuitive intellect nevertheless. He may do so in responding to the actualities of things, among them even the spectacle of our Tupperware party as a sign of the possible and increasingly probable end of an intentional self-destruction in pursuit of absolute freedom. For though this Tupperware party is metaphorical, it speaks a reality – that of idol worship, however softened by arguments for "consumerism" as an ideal in the rejection of the deepest truths about the nature of the self. Our poets respond to these actualities by their immediacy to us, dramatizing the *possible* and *probable* waywardness of selves given to a defiance of the truth of things, attempting to make palpable a negative as it were – a waywardness – through attention to "objective correlatives" reflecting *here* and *now* in its increasingly wild disorder. For certainly, becoming lost in the cosmos is our most common experience in the moment, though not universal. It is not only a possible, but a probable circumstance to *homo viator* as a new millennium opens.

It is in response to the intuitively known, then, that our poet (in St. Thomas's words) becomes committed to reason in making, though it is not always easy for that poet in his desire to witness against false celebration to remember his primary responsibility as that to his gift of making. That responsibility requires his unwavering attention to the good of the thing he makes, in the light of the truth seen, and not to a rectifying of Modernist aberrations, his being lost in the cosmos. We have been concerned so far to discover in Walker Percy as poet a gradual unfolding of this recognition, he counterpointing and complementing his attempt by reference to Flannery O'Connor as one who seems to have been born already largely possessed of this understanding of the poet's responsibility, though she credits it to a reading of Thomas's *Summa.* It is an understanding that seems resonant in her signs, though some critics of her work do not respond to those vibrations.

Now both Percy and O'Connor share in this recognition, then, the one more gradually coming to it, or so a burden of our argument. Especially they share a recognition of the importance of reason to the deployment of the intuitively known, though it is Percy who comes to this recognition out of his initially formative address to the cosmos from the scientist's perspective. What he moves toward, we are suggesting, is an acceptance of a mystically perceived complement to his scientifically rational beginnings. In the evolving of his understanding, he will come to declare that the circumstances to man's having become lost in the cosmos is man's having lost ontological orientation. What we are emphasizing about Percy's concern, of course, is that we have lost metaphysical vision as properly related to our rational deportment as finite intellectual soul incarnate – to our deportment as *homo viator.* That is a considerable development of understanding, pursued by reason in the poet's making. Given Percy's initial beginnings as skeptical Stoic turning to a science of signs in his quest for rescue, a transformation of thought toward mystical understanding in Flannery O'Connor proves a congenial counterpoint to him. For this reason, we might in our concern for the relevance of poetry to mystical vision revert once more to that openly mystical poet, their contemporary, who pursues myth with a fierce rational intensity. We might, that is, once more summon J. R. R. Tolkien to our concern for an ontological certainty in the poet, a certainty more fundamental than being a mere *feeling* as a counter to *thought* in a dissociated reduction such as that argued by logical Positivism through "scientific" reductions of signs to instrumentalities over being itself. In dire straits, threatened by this version of Cape Horn conjured by Modernist ideology, we need all the help available.

Tolkien labors as both poet and explicator of poetry to recover metaphysical vision against the Puritan inclination which evolves into Positivism. It is in this attempt that he distinguishes between art's "Secondary" use of myth to approach a visionary truth which is at once analogous to yet dependent upon the "Primary" myth we discover through creation itself. That primary truth we absorb intellectually from existential reality. It is truth attributed through creation's witness to intellect of that Primary Artist, God. This is not a recognition unique to Tolkien, of course. It is a recognition to be also acquired by our relation to the cosmos. St. Augustine dramatizes the recovery as out of his own reflective memory, his witness left us in his *Confessions.* At a point of his conversion out of Manichaeanism, he turns to the cosmos, asking "the earth, . . . the heavens, the sun, the moon, the stars" whether they are his origin – as they seem so certainly at last a food to the hunger of homelessness to his consciousness, wandering the cosmos. Then he turns to things immediate, things that "stand around the doors of [his] flesh," insistently demanding that they speak to intellect in witness of reality. But the signs they "speak" do not yet satisfy. Things in particularities assure him. "We are not the God whom you seek," they tell him, but then they cry out with "a mighty voice, 'He made us!'" Thus "the whole fabric of the world" bears that insistent witness: "I am not he, but he has made me!"

That is the decisive point of turning for St. Augustine as *homo viator* in the narrative he leaves of his recovery as intellectual soul incarnate. It is also the progress which Walker Percy is to discover himself to have begun to make by his labor of signs called *The Moviegoer.* Later, that novel behind him, he realizes that it is St. Augustine who proves a more fundamental father supporting his quest than Jean-Paul Sartre, though he had at the time of his making supposed his labor most deeply indebted to Sartre. What is revealed through this mystery of encounter, for both St. Augustine and for Percy dramatically caught in signs, we are explicating as the reality of connaturality, the principle which Aquinas engages philosophically. In the light of that principle, *homo viator* may better understand himself as, by his given nature, a maker. For that is a peculiar gift most immediate to him in relation to the signs he uses in making. What may properly orient his reason in the making – whether of a novel or poem or even of systems, whatever the species of *made order* – is the recognition of a proportionate brotherhood in being by virtue of a common dependence in being. That is the necessary limit if any thing is to exist at all.

It is by that shared dependence that each discrete thing *is,* though it is as well uniquely *this* thing. That is to say, by Creative Action of Love, each thing is the thing it is within the connaturality of being. That is the truth Gilson makes insistently, in his *Spirit of Thomism,* in saying that "if we want to philosophize" the problem of *being* is "really *the* problem of problems." We approach that problem, Thomas has argued, most immediately through the experiences of our senses, through experiencing those "things that stand around the doors of my flesh," in Augustine's words. Augustine adds that things thus serve "through ministry of the outer man" toward the "inner man," the inner and outer thus reconciled toward a perfection of a simple unity as a person, as intellectual soul incarnate. We begin, as Thomas would have it, within a reality: within our connaturality as created beings among disparate beings, within a shared existence as initially sensually experienced. Thus begins that enlarging of our awareness as sojourners of the cosmos.

What we come to know and then to understand (if but partially, because of our finitude) is that existing things are created and sustained by a Creating Love. The challenge to philosophy which must follow from that revelation to intellect is to come to an understanding of things as proportionate in their being within complex reality, requiring us through reason to distinguish things held inclusively by Love in a connaturality of being. Things differ in proportionality as specific things though sharing in connaturality. For stones and stars, hazel-nuts and persons participate in being, but disproportionately. Thus the importance at last of our recovery of an ontological point of departure to intellectual journeying in being. It is a point not to be established precipitately by reason, though reason must aid understanding in its alliance with intuitive knowing. The point of intuitive encounter, a revelation through intellect's openness to being, we may observe in the small child who is held in wonder by a kitten. The child's is an act of consent to an existing thing through love. It is also an action imitative of the action of that Causing Act, Love. In this beginning lies the possible recovery of an ordinate piety toward creation, out of which hazel-nuts yield food, as trees yield board feet with which to build through a responsible stewardship. It is, in sum, a sacramental deportment to creation which is required of our gifts, through our makings and our signs of making. A deference to things themselves as good.

It is this juncture of experience understood by reason moved beyond mere analytical knowing to which Tolkien points. Thus he emphasizes the necessity of distinguishing creation itself as Primary, art as Secondary. The whole of creation, recognized through particularities of discrete things as experienced, feeds the artist in his making of things at a Secondary level, a making of paintings or poems, gardens or houses. That is the point Flannery O'Connor makes when she says that "The longer you look at one object, the more of the world you see in it; and it's well to remember that the serious fiction writer always writes about the whole world, no matter how limited his particular scene." This is also the argument, both implicit and general, in Tolkien's address to myth, in his fiction and in letters and essays. He makes his argument in a concentrated way in his essay "On Fairy-Stories," so that by that argument Tolkien proves a helpful counterpoint in our concerns for Percy's address to the making of fictions, as it is confirmation of O'Connor's Thomistic commitment. Tolkien, by his insistence on truth as borne by what we often call dismissively fairy-tales, proves (*tests*) the same truth which Percy pursues in his more naturalistic diagnostic tales, fictions he playfully enlarges out of his scientific origins in becoming a diagnostic maker of fictional tales.

By this juxtaposition of unlike artists (Tolkien and Percy) as fundamentally like in their pursuit of the truth of things, we may better understand our own disquiet, verging on fear with the accelerating technology of the Machine, insofar as the agents of that acceleration would command us to submit to the magic of their signs used alchemically against being. For they are often persuasive in their evangelical enthusiasms, sometimes verging on totalitarian insistence upon technology as ultimate salvation. That evangelical enthusiasm, born of Positivistic certainties, is the spirit abroad at the moment, especially evident in the promises of the latest genetic engineering of being. Tolkien would observe this scientific enthusiasm with disquiet as parallel, and so a kindred, violation of the reality of our human nature. It has been born in part out of the theistic Puritan's suspicions of myth, his suspicions having been subsequently adapted to pragmatic Positivism. That is the prophetic suspicion of Hawthorne, who sees his recent fathers as foreshadowing the emerging scientific Puritans such as his Aylmer of "The Birthmark," who in his devotions to "scientific studies" values those studies over his love of his new bride Georgiana. Aylmer is so possessed of a degree of "faith in man's ultimate control over Nature" that he is led to kill Georgiana in attempting to remove the one mark of imperfection in her nature, her birthmark.

What we might ourselves discover of Hawthorne is that he *tends* to be intuitively a Thomist, for he recognizes our loss of metaphysical vision, our loss of the ontological ground necessary to our journeying the cosmos. If we should wonder why Flannery O'Connor finds Hawthorne her ally, then, it is not because she sees him as a consummate maker of "tales." It is rather (as she says) because Hawthorne in writing what he called "romances" was "attempting . . . to keep for fiction some of its freedom from social determinisms, and to steer it in the direction of poetry." He was, that is, attempting to be a prophetic poet, recalling us to known but forgotten truths about human nature. In respect to her own craft, it is evident that she learned much more about the science of making from Henry James and James Joyce than from Hawthorne. But it is Hawthorne as poet in whom she finds something of that "natural Catholic" which makes him akin to her Old Tarwater, whom she values as prophet.

Hawthorne, though lacking the metaphysical sophistication of a Tolkien, anticipates him, though dependent as maker upon the allegorical. Tolkien eschews the allegorical as rationally distorting the complex mystery spoken through myth. One nevertheless finds likeness between Tolkien and Hawthorne in Tolkien's defense of myth against the magic of the machine as evolved by science. For instance, in "The Maypole of Merrymount," and "Young Goodman Brown," as in "The Birthmark" and "Rappaccini's Daughter," there are themes parallel to Tolkien's concerns. In Hawthorne, one finds the religious Puritan on the one hand and the religious scientist on the other. Each is committed to a manipulation of reality through sign gnostically employed. It is also a concern dramatized in *The Scarlet Letter*. The concern common in these works is a concern for the authority of rescue through sign (*vide* the title of the novel) from the mystery of evil in creation. Is science the answer, executed through an imposed control of nature by the agency of abstract sign? Is Puritan theology bearer of the answer, rejecting nature for a Manichaean dream of transcendence – through the agency of sign?

Hawthorne sees these seemingly antithetic solutions to the problem of evil (for the Puritan) or the problem of environmental comfort for the secular gnostic. Reflection suggests them proximate in their misunderstandings of creation itself. And if Hawthorne's Puritan fathers would be more radical in their rejection of art, for they hold art to be the Devil's mode of seduction, he sees as well that emerging secular gnostic as a version of the same rejection of creation though differently clothed by signs. This new "Puritan" is already moving toward dominance. And he tends to be more condescending to art than tolerant of it. Poems and novels, for instance, may be suited to ladies in their gardens no doubt, but hardly plausible as capable of a rescue where theology and science seem to be failing in that rescue.

In his "The Custom House: Introductory Sketch," Hawthorne provides a preface to *The Scarlet Letter.* He has just lost his political appointment at Salem as custom's agent the year before, finishing his novel in the interval. While holding that political sinecure, he had had occasion to think about and observe the coincident merging of the old Puritan and a scientifically and politically progressive spirit. (The novel is finished in February of 1850, a decade before that wrenching war called "civil.") The common aspect of these only seemingly divergent perspectives upon nature he could recognize as reflecting another emerging civil war over the definition of *evil,* over the nature of *sin.* If he could have but been aware of the increasingly secularized perspective upon economic matters as addressed by the Federal tax concerns that involved him at the customs house, he was nevertheless already prepared to recognize correspondences between a burgeoning secularism and a decaying old Puritanism. He had already had occasion to see this intellectual process underway in Concord, in that close neighbor Ralph Waldo Emerson. For Emerson contributes largely as an influence upon those specializations of the self that will become the academician's ideal as justification of the self quite different from that old Puritan principle which at least held that man is created in God's image. That is a doctrine not yet abandoned despite the Puritan aberrations of that old dogma by Manichaean separations of grace and nature. No wonder that when Charles M. Eliot becomes President of Harvard in the late 1860s he turns to Emerson as a model for the new intellectual to be produced by academic process. For that new president sets out to establish an intellectual process at Harvard, toward establishing ultimately what he called and defined as "The Religion of the Future," to be established through specializations of intellect. It is this process which will lead to the constrictions of intellect whereby the Machine becomes the god over man in Tolkien's argument.

In his "Custom House" introduction to *The Scarlet Letter,* then, Hawthorne imagines those "stern and blackbrowed Puritans," his recent fathers. He hears them still speaking, long after their day, and about him specifically: "A writer of storybooks! What kind of a business in life – what mode of glorifying God, or being serviceable to mankind in his day and generation – may that be? Why, the degenerate fellow might as well have been a fiddler!" That bandying about between Hawthorne and his "great-grandsires" is made "across the gulf of time." We suggest that Walker Percy will have heard a similar version but from a different quarter. He will have read it in gestures from fellow scientists, especially as he risks crossing from one of C. P. Snow's "two cultures" to the other, from science to art. If his peer should be a psychologist of the behaviorist school, interested in data relevant to the biochemical certainties hinted at in signs, that behaviorist might plunder a Hawthorne or a Melville – or a Percy – for relevant data, as O'Connor's Rayber plunders the Tarwaters. But in doing so he would not speak of the *soul* or of *God*, at least not as if thereby to give the concepts credence, as if we were naming realities. Much safer, then, for the physician novelist if he cultivate indirection by signs' trickery, practice a deliberate deception in the mode of a psychological diagnostician of looniness. That mode might even give the behaviorist pause at last, especially should he be unaccustomed to irony. He might, that is, be given an uneasy feeling that something is going on in Percy's signs beyond scientific diagnosis, beyond the powers of mere logic to rationalize by formulaic signs the actual nature of looniness. He might as reader of Percy, indeed, begin to find himself in a position analogous to Tate's speaker at the cemetery gate, in "Ode to the Confederate Dead," having experienced more than reason, constricted to an absolute through logic, can accommodate.

Looking into Percy as diagnostic-novelist, then, might give one a sense of looking into a kaleidoscope rather than into a telescope upon the cosmos from the position of the lost self, in our instance the "behaviorist," or into a microscope focused upon intercells of a particular self as biochemical machine. Even so, and discomfortingly so, he might nevertheless discover a constancy of dark elements yet unanalyzed and so unnamed by science underlying the shifting patterns of light which yield diverse "colors" of the self. If we find ourselves in this uneasy state of mind, we may attempt at best a formal (as opposed to an academically *specialized*) attempt to understand his attraction to us in his role as diagnostic-novelist, a deportment amenable to his calling as artist at this juncture of history with the self, but hardly a deportment comprehended by science. When we encounter that dark element of thought in Percy which underlies his imaginative projections of the self, disguising somewhat a dark thought through satiric playfulness, we may discover as well something akin to the darkness which Melville finds in Hawthorne perhaps. The formal designation of that shadow which is always steadily present to anyone lost in the cosmos, one of the polar attractions in Percy's thought: *death*. Not death as a violence external intruding upon the self in spectacle, as in the general destruction which so horrifies Melville in his war poems, but a violence blossoming darkly from within: a shadow foreshadowing the possible actual event Percy toys with, the threat of oblivion countered by suicide. In posing this as an always underlying theme in Percy's thought, and one which carries a personal resonance to us, we need not – and perhaps best not – explore it as an effect on his thought out of the specific history of suicide in his family, though we are aware of that "history." We might rather take it that the tension between *life* and *death* which he engages within his *present* moment is in response to the always *present* mystery of reality itself to any discrete person. For the question in this perspective becomes whether the self is victim of an illusion of life, even as that self poses those disparate poles of death and life in suspending action itself. (That is an underlying theme in Eliot's portrait of the intellectual, Prufrock.) It is less a Percy family history that attends such moments than the actual present moment to this person named Walker in his tensional balance *here* and *now*. The threat of the abyss, this is to say, is the nadir from which here and now one may move at last beyond spiritual arrest as an "ex-suicide."

What seems necessary to this self, Walker Percy, waking to his own condition of having become lost in that large and ambiguous machine, the Cosmos, burdened by a consciousness which is itself so ambiguous as to defy naming? The necessity, he concludes, is to descend deeper into the self out of that suspension, in a journey imaginatively made, though colored by art's underhandedness with the perspective of the scientist. It is, we need reminding, the same necessity St. Augustine experiences, though undertaken by Augustine from his perspective as devout Manichaean. Thus that multitude of possible *modes* of the self in Percy's mischievous address to a serious personal concern for "transcendence" becomes the unifying theme of his *Lost in the Cosmos*. This, he declares, with mischief prepense, is his gift to us of *the* "Last Self-Help Book." Ostensibly, the address of the title is to a reader, but beneath the playfulness at work – such is our repeated point – we come to suspect that the most central reader of all these signs is Percy himself. He provides a resting point, occurring in the middle of his way in this 1983 book, aware no doubt that it appears almost midway the body of his work. As he himself has reached a midway in his actual journey. Almost at the middle of the book itself, we come upon that "intermezzo of some forty pages" whose concern is semiotics, a parenthesis as it were which he encourages us to skip.

We have come to this mid-point of *Lost in the Cosmos,* having been delighted by our guide's playful and often imaginatively fantastic projections of possible "selves," encouraged to measure our own self against each. For along that way, we are instructed authoritatively to judge these hypothetical selves in relation to our own sense of being an actual "self" lost in the cosmos. A cleverly dramatic preparation for Percy's central and at least quasi-philosophical concern put as scientific speculation about signs. He encourages us to skip – his "intermezzo." Consider the last two "selves" just before this semiotic intermission. The last one is that of "The Impoverished Self," a rather anticlimactic prelude to the purported "aside" of forty pages. It is a sort of calming of disturbed waters, after which our guide will address the mystery of sign, but put that address in relation to the dilemma of a polar suspension of consciousness – the "self." The dramatic strategy is to suspend us between questions of life and death. And that is the darker aspect of the self presented in the penultimate drama, "The Depressed Self," a portrait which now requires our attention.

Concerning this "Depressed Self," we are given circumstantial difficulties that oppress it, dragging it toward darkness. In the light of circumstantial evidence, we are to consider "*Whether the Self is Depressed because there is Something Wrong with it or whether Depression is a Normal Response to a Deranged World.*" Italicized in accord with the consistent format of the presentation of "selves," there is as well a playful capitalization. The ordinary syntax, the ordinary flow of signs toward meaning, appears counterpointed by signs elevated: Self, Depressed, Something Wrong, Normal Response, Deranged World. These are signs worn smooth by careless discourse, carrying themselves as a flow of clichés. The subtitle is followed by a very flat statement bearing a shocking report, as if casually made: "The suicide rate among persons under twenty-five has risen dramatically in the last twenty years." See the official statistics, if in doubt of the pervasiveness of depression. For scientific data is undeniable. Then in juxtaposition, in a sentence placed as a separate paragraph: "A recent survey disclosed that the symptom of depression outnumbered all other medical symptoms put together." So the accumulation of "facts" reveals depression as overwhelming many selves to the point of suicide.

The rhetorical stage thus set, in repetition of the manner of presentation already established, two "Questions" are put to the reader, resting on the irony that our civilization as "the rightful legatee of the greatest of fortunes, the cultural heritage of the entire Western World, its art, science, technology, literature, philosophy, religion," with the self by its depression a "second-class consumer of these wares," encouraged as consumer to devour its inheritance. If that depressed self pray succor of our *first-class* consumer, namely the expert theorist, the theorist may deign to rescue us as a self from the ashes of depression but is enabled only by a technology governed by psychology – drugs and therapy. There must be "an expert for everything that ails me, a doctor of my depression, a seer of my sadness."

What remedy for this self as a second-class consumer of its own inherited culture? No remedy which the novelist as diagnostician – as "art" theorist – will advance, though as diagnostician he seems able to describe our collapse as a self – describe our symptomatic state but confining his description to the symptoms of an unidentified disease, rather than engaging the disease itself as a spiritual one. Better a psychology supported by statistics than theology or philosophy to the rescue. In that light, we are given the rare hazard of a treatment, a resolving remedy. "The only cure for depression is suicide. This is not meant as a bad joke but as the serious proposal of suicide as a valid option." And so in the midst of our guide's playfully ironic detachment, darkness breaks in, though quickly followed by a return to playfulness. This "valid option": " . . . as Ivan said to God in *The Brothers Karamazov*: If you exist, I respectfully return my ticket." But having merely elected suicide, the self has not completed the ticket's return. He finds himself as a self rather like "a castaway on an island," who can't believe his "good fortune," provided only that he does not drink arsenic or pull the trigger. Thus he becomes an "ex-suicide." Our diagnostic-novelist, addressing us about the consequences of *seriously* considering suicide to cure the malady of our depression, suggests we will have "been freed by the serious entertainment of . . . hypothetical suicide," but seriously considered as active option. Only consider: "Are you not free for the first time in your life to consider the folly of man, the most absurd of all the species, and to contemplate the comic mystery of your own existence?" Which, then, given this comic mystery of the self, is the more absurd plan attracting the self: that predicament of manifest absurdity whereby one finds himself "lost in the Cosmos and no news not even from experts blathering news of how you got into such a fix or how to get out"? Or that other "even more preposterous eventuality that news did come from the God of the Cosmos, who took pity on your ridiculous plight and entered space and time of your insignificant planet to tell you something," that good news whose sign is the Incarnation? The Pascalian wager, but a bet on the nature of reality made valid only when one has seriously approached that "valid option" of actual suicide. *Playing* with theory through statistical evidence as toy (here, a fifty-fifty option, a one out of two) is insufficient to the nagging necessity of resolution. One must come, with Ivan Karamazov, seriously to the brink of self-obliteration, risking that collapse which Dostoevsky dramatizes as Ivan's.

After such a darkly serious putting of the question, with the reader perhaps feeling almost bullied by his guide up to a precipice, Percy pulls him back playfully once more, though the dark shadow of oblivion as a fifty-fifty-possibility lingers, turning humor somewhat toward sardonic irony. We are offered two line-sketches, one of the "non-suicide," the other of the "ex-suicide," each "leaving the house for work, at eight o'clock on an ordinary morning." The non-suicide is swollen with depression, "sucking care with him from the past and being sucked toward care in the future." But the "ex-suicide" is comic in his deportment. He "opens his front door, sits down on the steps, and laughs. Since he has the option of being dead, he has nothing to lose by being alive. It is good to be alive. He goes to work because he doesn't have to," that other option of actual suicide still his. One cannot escape recognition that our "expert" on the self, while denying his expertise, has himself very likely been in this state, and perhaps is yet in it. If so, the words are a disguised witness to his own private experience, an acknowledgment of his position as an "ex-suicide" who has made Pascal's wager, at a last moment affirming that it is "good to be alive." Yet in making that wager he still holds close to his chest that hidden trump card which he might yet play, his "ticket" which he may yet return. The option of suicide remains for the ex-suicide, and it governs future moments in underlining that "It is good to be alive."

In that good moment of suspension, this present of our being drawn into the world by this comic self, one finds himself relieved from the spectacles of history, relieved of care for the past or for the future. It is a moment of suspense which bears dark analogy to Eliot's encounter of a "still-point" at the center of the Cosmos, a Point which paradoxically permeates the Cosmos with the "good news." Analogous, but differing in that it is tinged by a lingering darkness of a contingent surmise that in the next moment life may prove not good. Eliot emerges from such a moment of suspense between life and death with a faith in the Word as continuously at the center of the word, the Word in that desert which Percy calls the Cosmos. Percy, this is to say, keeps his options open at this midway of his journey. That is a mode of intellectual deportment of the "self" which will become less optional to him as he draws near the end of his journey. For we see a growing certainty of faith in life, including life everlasting, reflected in his late essays and in his *Thanatos Syndrome*. That last novel's title, indeed, suggests the novel an excursion into the mystery of the self as lost in the cosmos, seeking dependable signposts in a land permeated by the syndrome of death. But our guide, more or less hidden by his art, presents the seeking with a more cheerful prospect as an ex-suicide. One might thus not simply hold onto Ivan's return ticket as an accusation against the "non-suicide" as it were. In charity he may perhaps even toss it away as detritus of the self's history now past.

Here is the moment so effectively dramatized but unresolved in a scene we know: Will Barrett in *The Last Gentleman*, standing outside his old home in Mississippi darkness, remembering his father's suicide, but turning his eye to the hitching post at hand, which is vaguely present in the darkening evening. For Will is yet a long way from that simple deportment of Percy's Tom More at the end of *Thanatos Syndrome.* The gesture (and there are others) which we chose to signify that deportment is Tom's sailing paper airplanes into his yard, waiting the last courier but with a content of spirit. That earlier touching of the immediate outer world through the senses mediates Will's eye and hand to the tree next to the dark iron. And though Will cannot, we through the image of the closing bark of that tree upon the hitching post may, "feel" an enwrapping of the hitching post, that manmade imposition on nature – an enwrapping by some presence greater than pied spectacles of nature itself, let alone of a presumptuous ordering of nature as if eternal monument. Percy remarks the moment as one of a pending vision to his "last" gentleman lost in the cosmos, Will Barrett. Will does not experience in himself that opening, the novel's resolution coming to rest in the pathos of Will as a lost self.

There is some rescue of Will in *The Second Coming,* for Percy recognizes the possible in that moment. He does not force the recognition upon his signs in the novel's scene, knowing that a transgression of the good of the thing he is making. There is in the scene something very like what is expressed by Gerard Manley Hopkins directly, reflecting Hopkins's experience of a "pied beauty" in all "dappled" things. Percy as poet must engage that beauty as it is revealed to him to be "the comic mystery" within his own existence of himself as person. Man is "the most absurd of all the species," and he does not presume to exempt himself. Hence Percy makes his witness as artist in response to "the folly of man." And so Will's suspense through his eye, holding the bark of the tree, is short of a resolving epiphany, a revelation. Hopkins's vision releases Hopkins from that pathos of the self which otherwise threatens to leave any poet in depression. There are his close-ups in signs as witness: "rose moles all in stipple upon trout that swim." A shock of recognition for Hopkins of that presence of the Word as Creator, present in such small ordinary things, so that his gifts as an "Imagist" poet are more resonant to us. A poignant recognition of the moment is in Percy as well, who, not fully rescued by awe nor yet fully beyond being an ex-suicide perhaps, "sits down . . . and laughs," knowing it "good to be alive." It is a laughter qualifying joy in response to the contingent challenge to make a new song as poet. That is, his laughter carries still a touch of uncertainty, almost to the end. If it were not so, then he might well turn from his *Thanatos Syndrome* to engage philosophically the conundrum of semiotics, as he wrote Jan Gretlund he intended doing. But he might then do so sans uncertainty. That might prove fit occupation as he himself waits the courier. That might be a deportment akin to, if more sophisticated than, playing with paper airplanes. It might be a last toying with this world's straw, as St. Thomas might put it, waiting a summons.

IX

If we are right about a nagging uncertainty in Percy's thought about his "self" in the world, prompting that self to impose *a world* upon the *cosmos*, we suggest we might take his strategy of indirection to be in part a shielding of himself against the contingent cosmos. The comic dimension of his art then serves something like the turtle's shell, armor against uncertain contingencies. That is why we are not surprised by his finding Herman Melville so companionable. Melville, too, moves through the cosmos protected by a world he makes, though for any artist it is that cosmos out of which he must make his world. Propelled by uncertainty, fearful of the rocks of the world upon which he may wreck himself: that is the aspect of Melville's deportment to the cosmos which W. H. Auden memorializes in the poem we cited earlier to which Robert Penn Warren and R. W. B. Lewis call our attention. In a footnote comment, they observe that Melville "sees" only through disaster. But the gamble is that, by running aground on the "rock of Eden" (Auden's phrase), man may perhaps gain a true paradise, at that risk of destruction of the self. That is a pursuit almost to the point of suicide. Auden's words on this theme, projecting Melville's deportment:

> Goodness existed: that was the new knowledge
> His terror had to blow itself quite out
> To let him see it; but it was the gale had blown him
> Past the Cape Horn of sensible success
> Which cries: "This rock is Eden. Shipwreck here."

We return here to Melville, the Melville to whom Percy is drawn by mutual uncertainties that make action – especially heroic action – ambiguous, and darkly exciting. For Melville, that uncertainty is not simply the nature of our human engagement of the world, an inadequacy of will submitting to its own evil inclination. For evil is rather an active presence in both nature and in man, a presence hardly deniable. There is "something like Original Sin" permeating creation itself we heard him say. That he suspects evil incipient in nature as well as in man is a Manichaean conclusion which he declares no "thinking mind" capable of denying. High and noble causes advocated by man prove always ambiguous. That dilemma centers dramatically in Melville's unfolding of Captain Ahab in contention with the spirit of the cosmos, with Leviathan. Almost at once in actual history, after this imaginative engagement of the dilemma in *Moby Dick* and on a panoramic scale as large as that of the rolling ocean, Melville's whole nation becomes torn apart between a high and noble cause proclaimed for Union and a dissent from it, embroiling brother against brother, father against son, in deadly destructions.

In that widening storm, Melville writes the poems he publishes at war's end as *Battle Pieces*, in 1866. But in those poems, high and noble causes are echoed ironically against the realities of the general slaughter. Though he might wish to do so, and makes some pretense of doing so in words that are then ironically undercut, Melville cannot advance the high cause of the Union as bearing an heroically epic energy to the poet's vatic intentions. The poems are occasional, not epic, though bearing a certain thematic unity out of his dark misgivings about the war. Wherever he looks in those years between 1860 to 1866, he finds the destroyed residue of once lively persons, named and unnamed, scattered across a shattered landscape. The darkness at the heart of existence gnaws relentlessly, through what may appear to vain youth grand spectacles put on heroic display in the war reports. Those official reports Melville follows all the way to Appomattox, but as well he presses on to a darkness surfacing most disturbingly beyond that surrender of the Confederacy. There is an ominous Congress gathered under that new "Iron Dome" of the White House. Under that dome lies "Power unannointed," even as he had observed it at the outset in 1860. It is a power bent upon a "Dominion (unsought by the free)."

The iron dome of his opening poem receives thematic variations, in symbolic uses of the new instruments of a technology serving war – canon and rifle, and especially the ironclad replacing his billowed sail ships. The "Iron Dome,/ Stronger for stress and strain," may will "Fling her huge shadow athwart the main," but thereby "the Founder's dream shall flee." How indeed is he to be an American writer while also a Calvinistic Yankee, to turn upside down Percy's question puts to himself, "How to Be an American Novelist in Spite of Being Southern and Catholic"? How indeed be such a writer encouraging hope if one is Calvinist and Northerner? A question to be asked, despite uncertainty about the role of the novelist as seer to a disoriented people. But the question will settle at a more personal level for Percy, the level of his private concern for the uses of his peculiar gifts as maker, whenever he must recognize the maker himself as a made thing – a created intellectual soul incarnate. That is the unavoidable reality he must hold as "Catholic."

The question requires rephrasing for Percy, in his response to that upside-down conclusion which Melville tends toward in resolving his own uncertainties about evil and its origins. Melville as a "thinking mind" discovers signs to be helpless in dealing with the problem of evil, as he might well have concluded from the public's reception of his work just before the American Civil War. Given the fate of *Moby-Dick* (1851), Melville writes a last lament for his scribbling inadequacy, his "Bartleby the Scrivener" (1853), though of course much later he does return to fiction. But then on the eve of the wrenching war, almost as an act of revenge against both signs and the pretenders to sign as if truly signifying, he writes his *Confidence Man*. It is his own version of the elusive self lost in the cosmos, the cosmos reduced to the ill-fated riverboat with ironic name, the *Fidele*. These words are a farewell to fiction, and he withdraws from his own diagnostic undertakings such as that in *Moby-Dick*. "Ah, Bartleby! Ah, humanity!" The last words of his sad elegy made just before the more mischievous (and in its technique very "Modern") farewell to fiction, *The Confidence Man*. Thirty years later, he returns with *Billy Budd*, about which Percy talks in counterpoint to Dostoevsky. In that brief essay on Melville, Percy declares *Moby-Dick* a great work because it does "no straining for a symbol of truth," while to the contrary "*The Confidence Man* is so boring." But here that lover of James Joyce as craftsman, Percy, seems not to observe Melville in this "boring" work as close in technique to Joyce and, in a degree, to Percy himself. It is following this quoted remark that Percy abruptly defends himself as novelist, as himself a confidence man in his use of signs. He is given to playfulness, trickery, malice, underhandedness, naughtiness, and is especially concerned with "hoodwinking the reader."

It is a question to be asked, of course, whether the maker of novels if too much concerned with audience becomes either ally with or antagonist to his audience, thus tempted away from the most central of his obligations: his responsibility to the good of the thing made. For by that dislocation, by a concern for hoodwinking the reader, he may distort that responsibility as maker. (Some objections to Joyce's *Finnigan's Wake* take this tack, reading that work as if it were primarily an affront to audience.) How does the novelist, under the necessities of his art, as a maker, accommodate to his primary responsibility for the thing he makes? If he is a Catholic Christian, rather than a Calvinistic Manichee, there is a further burden, the responsibility of a Christian humility, especially as he must distinguish himself as maker from "Creator." It requires as well an *ordinate* "Yes" to creation itself, preventing such an absolute "No" as Will Barrett's father pronounced with his shotgun blast, a haunting signpost throbbing in Will's memory. One *makes,* in fulfillment of and in recognition of the limits of the gifts peculiar to himself as maker. He attempts to do so through a charity uncontaminated by inclinations to judgments of the contingent world, a responsibility of the maker which St. Thomas articulates. The virtue of art, he argues (*Summa,* I-II, Q 57, Art. 4) lies in "right reason of things to be made," so that the artist's primary responsibility must be to the good of the thing he makes. Thus "the good of things made by art is not the good of man's appetite, but the good of those things themselves; wherefore art does not presuppose rectitude of the appetite" as its final end, rectitude of either the artist himself nor of the community receiving his made thing. For that first error involves the poet's attention as primarily to himself, the second a traducement of art to some species of tract. Through a charity toward things, when the maker is uncontaminated by inclinations to judge things as if thereby to dispose of them, or to compose or reorder them in themselves – that is the proper deportment of the artist in his making according to the possible or probable. But not with an intent through his art to determine – to cause – the potential to actuality in persons. That, at last, is also an intent conspicuous in some scientists, whereby they incline to be artists transforming being into an imagined world. It is an intent made into a formal obligation to the artist, we remember, by political power where it forces the artist's service to political or religious ends. We need only recall the role of the artist in service to the U.S.S.R. under Lenin and Stalin to the point witnessed to us by Solzhenitsyn. The state would enforce an obligation that the poet become subservient rhetor to a quasi-religious cause in the interest of the state's gnostic power over being. But it is as well the subversion of any ideology commanding art, even in the best of temporal "causes." Thus the poet's responsibility, through a perfection of the thing he makes, bears only a secondary role of the *vatic,* if considered in St. Thomas's perspective. But insofar as art is dependent responsibly to the truth of things, that art will necessarily bear a vatic effect, in that it recalls us to known but forgotten things.

Under his recognition of this limit to art, then, Percy attempts a balanced intellectual deportment in a trying time, inclined to take refuge as maker in what might be called a "Title IX" of human rights under the rubric of Original Sin in its orthodox, not its Manichaean, sense. All have sinned and fallen short of the mark. Hence, a *care* for the spiritual rights of all manner of mankind – from racist redneck to silly sentimental liberal – must not put him off his primary responsibility as artist. Reformation of such creatures is not the primary end of art, he knows, though as a secondary effect that becomes a possibility through a right will of the person responding to the well-made thing. Rilke celebrates such a response, a possible effect of encounter with that made thing, the "Archaic Torso of Apollo," dedicated to the God of Art. In that famous sonnet, Rilke attempts to respond to the *instress* of the made thing, which (having been made) exists as a thing. He would make a suitable *inscape* in a Hopkins-like sacramental celebration of that thing by open response to it. That thing is the bust only, the head and limbs lost in the sands of time. And yet that torso "glows like a candelabrum," with a light that breaks out from all the torn edges where once the head rested and limbs extended. "Here is no place that does not see you," the work's essential unity still radiating, so that in response "You must change your life."

How sharp a difference we recognize if we juxtapose to Rilke's sonnet that even more famous one by Percy Bysshe Shelley on the self-adulation of Ramses II, Shelley's "Ozymandias." Shelley's account of two "vast and trunkless legs of stone," of a "shattered visage," and the general "decay of a colossal wreck" in the midst of desert sands speaks the human inclination to self-love (though Shelley would not call it *sin*). Through spectacles turned toward human self-glorification by power in autonomous intellect. But Shelley does not celebrate art in his sonnet as does Rilke but man's inclination to set aside, to abandon, what he calls in another poem "Intellectual Beauty" as that Beauty may be paid tribute to through art, not himself recognizing an affinity of himself as poet to that ancient Egyptian monarch. For both are oriented to the cosmos in a pursuit of power, the one political power in nature the other the poem's power in establishing the poet's autonomous "self." Hence Shelley's famous remark that the poet is the unrecognized *legislator* of mankind, a remark which at once romanticizes the poet's alienation but pronounces his power nevertheless.

And so a sharp contrast of poets, Rilke and Shelley. Rilke, by such witness of words to abiding beauty, responds to that beauty as immanent toward a perfection, even in that wasted torso of Apollo from an anonymous artist who lived perhaps halfway back in time from us to Ramses. In that recognition of distinction, one may the better appreciate why Percy's early mentor, Gabriel Marcel, praises Rilke at length in *Homo Viator,* under the title "Rilke: A Witness to the Spiritual," even as one finds in Rilke's poetry itself a labor with signs while Rilke recognizes (as he says) that "Words still melt into something beyond their embrace." In that recognition is signified his own surrender through love to things both created and those made by love. One may discover in him also an anticipation of our loss of that response, a response which is Tolkien's concern to recover. For "machines" erode our capacity to love. Machines are the "Source of our weakness now, and in vengeful rage ruining our heritage." So Marcel has it.

For Rilke, as Marcel says, this means the loss of a "reverential love of the created," a loss of what Percy will call "the holiness of the ordinary." In his two essays exploring this reverential love in Rilke, Marcel concludes (his essays coincide with the end of World War II) that our triumphant world has instead chosen to doom our souls "to aridity in the most miserable desert of self-adulation." The "mechanical world," he adds, thus becomes also "the world of pure consciousness, that which burns without giving any light and gives light without any warmth." And then Marcel juxtaposes community divided, in terms that well might prompt Percy to juxtapose the consumer and the theorist, or St. Augustine the "Hearer" and the "Elect" of the Manichaean provenance. Both are eluded by false transcendence. "Thus," Marcel continues, "we see a gulf widening between the masses who are literally *denatured* by a more and more inhuman way of life, and a small company of super-naturalised elect whose life's foundations are more and more fragile and unsteady and who for this reason are in danger of falling a prey in the end to the most fatal mental disorders, and the worst inner collapse." These we shall meet, encircling a native corn dance in the desert near Los Alamos in *Lost in the Cosmos.*

And so if the poet, Percy, engaging his own making in the guise of a pathologist of the self, eschews the role of being also apothecary as artist – demurring from providing an elixir – his reader from the Left or the Right might exhibit restive irritation with his refusal. Art is not, as art, salvific, a replacement of grace, Percy would respond, if forced to respond. That same irritation was exhibited in questions put to Flannery O'Connor as well. What was she trying to "prove" by her stories? Her rather caustic response, suggesting that such questions were simplistic and her questioner perhaps too far gone for rescue: no one ever *proves* anything with a story. Even so, if one as poet presents himself as diagnostician, though it may save him from some questions by his rational incisiveness with signs used as ironic scalpel, that may seem a process which runs parallel to the Modernist reductions of art as salvific, with an intention to save a culture or the state. Percy, of course, sees the human condition much as does Marcel at this confusing juncture of history – with a clear eye. It is ripe with symptomatic evidences of dementia, threatening to unleash Marcel's "fatal mental disorders" and "inner collapse." Everywhere are those spectacles of "looniness." Why will he not then *prescribe,* that being an action proper to the analytical physician?

A part of our irritation (which is a sign of dis-ease) is that we recognize in Percy such a clear diagnostic eye. It is a perception revealed to us through his signs, which in their unfolding begin as well to reveal his own growing delight in existence itself. How good life is! So good, that we may experience through his signs a deportment which is somewhat that of a child, as sophisticated as his presence to us through those signs clearly is. A precocious child? Or perhaps more aptly, it is the deportment of the adolescent, in that he takes delight in horseplay as it were, a delight in being given to playfulness, tricks, malice, underhandedness, naughtiness – epithets Percy embraces as his own by virtue of his being a diagnostic novelist.

A part of our irritation may lie in the appearance to us that our maker-player Percy seems himself exempted from our own disquiet by his innocent openness, as if he were somehow pointing to us as an Emperor "self" naked in the cosmos. Insofar as such pointing prove prophetic of a reality we have ignored, it might suggest that we suppose ourselves clad in self-protecting clothing, in some "role," as Adam and Eve were clothed in fig-leaves after their sinning. Hence that discomfort if we solemnly address those questions posed directly to us in *Lost in the Cosmos,* or undertake those "Thought Experiments" set for us as selves. Strip away the "role" as camouflage, and one has left only that invisible self which allows no naming. That is the dark secret of the Modernist self, a secret protected by all sorts of stances, roles, pretensions to some "being" by the willful authority of our autonomy. Hence, where autonomy lacks sufficient authority, it can only be comic to the child-adolescent. Percy, then, is playful satirist. But in his satiric observations he does not exempt himself as perhaps also being on occasion at least an empty self. It is as if he recognizes the tendency toward emptiness as a tendency in fallen man. And a part of the "role" making is resisting acknowledgment of that tendency. For him, in *part* as reminder to his "self" is his adopting the role of the "physician as novelist." He is a self which recognizes as well that, through grace supplied to his ordinate deportment toward existence, he may as a self become substantiated, fulfilling the discrete gifts to him, Walker, as journeyman.

That is a grace experienced as a continuing, a sustaining, act of love to man, despite man's temptations to emptiness. How great to be alive, his ex-suicide says. The emptiness, then, is at last only an illusional "effect" of our skeptical rejection of being, especially a rejection of our *own* being in that slow suicide called self-love. That is a species of suicide not directly and seriously engaged by most of us, which is why the shock effected by the poet's direct address to actual suicide proves unsettling to the addict of Marcel's "self-adulation," a gradual addiction to nothingness. Thus when we almost empty our self, we do not achieve a self almost emptied (by willful intentionality) though we may dream we have accomplished the illusion of the self transubstantiated. By a will independent of grace – *non serviam,* its emblem – we may believe through pridefulness that accomplishment, only to discover that a presumed "transcendence" by will when some mischievous poet points to the nakedness of "roles" assumed substantiation of our "self." Percy will come up to this point again and again, but hesitate to make it, taking refuge from resolution by hinting at remedy. "But that is another story." He also seems sometimes to shy away from the mystery of grace, that incarnate word our age stores in moth balls in the attic of memory. But he does ponder with a sardonic irony grace's effect upon his own personal history. In respect to grace, it "leaves one unclear about who does the choosing," a remark almost suggesting that he continues to hold Ivan's return ticket to the Agent of Grace, a possible final rejection.

Among the difficulties Percy seems to create for himself as novelist, while longing for the transparency he sees in a writer like Flannery O'Connor or G. M. Hopkins, is his undertaking the mystery of *being* as if perhaps limited to the necessities of science. Specifically, he seems to attempt solution to that mystery by a science of signs. The Thomist would no doubt concede, even insist upon, the importance of such a science, but with qualifications. For there is a science in the root sense of the term regarding art: reason in making. Reason here is more inclusive, more fundamental to the given nature of intellect than science comes to mean (at least popularly) since the Enlightenment.

Thus reason must engage more than may be comprehended by all of our scientific accomplishments in riddling reality, evidenced by biochemistry or biology, or by the uncertainties sometimes built upon these hard sciences by the soft sciences of psychiatry or psychology which assume a power of mediating hard scientific "knowing" in relation to the social and natural context. There underlies these attempts, to be made *ordinately* welcomed as those attempts must be made in our concern for the mystery of sign, that reasoned recognition out of experience which is spoken to by the poet, a knowing deeper than finite knowings. Rilke speaks witness to this recognition about the sign's limit when he says, "Words still melt into something beyond their embrace."

The difficulty in Percy's pursuit of the science of signs, then, lies in his seeming to be, in his own reasoning, attracted to that prospect not only by Charles Peirce and his triadic epistemology but moved as well by the mystical science of Teilhard de Chardin, whose argument in defense of evolution posits a "leap in being" out of a Darwinian evolutionary theory. That Teilhardian leap in being is into a self-consciousness, which argument intersects (in Percy's thought, one suspects) Peirce's version of a similar leap out of a sudden discovery of sign as consequent to the simply organic-dyadic man. For he seems suddenly by this theory to become a human-triadic creature through the agency of sign. It is a leap, a Maritain or Gilson would argue (judging from their reactions to Teilhard), which implies a transformation of man's *essential* nature at some point in his evolutionary history. That concern Gilson engages in correspondence with his friend Fr. Henri de Lubac, who is more kindly inclined to Teilhard than Gilson can be. There is for Gilson "the problem of materialism" in Teilhard de Chardin, leading him to wonder "if he isn't an advocate of a kind of materialism, as Auguste Comte understood the word, that consists in explaining what is above by what is below," that is to say by what is evolved (letter to de Lubac, April 7, 1967). If so, then the transcendent appears dependent upon the immanent, rather than the other way round. Put bluntly, God must then depend upon the cosmos. Indeed, that is the direction already taken in speculative philosophy by Henri Bergson, whose *Creative Evolution* (1911) at first appeared a rescue from mechanistic determinism through that "*élan vital,*" through creative evolution. A vital spark fuels the material cosmos. But that proves a problematic vision of the cosmos, though based in the latest science. (It is an obverse of Melville's suspicion of an *evil* spark permeating creation in its essential nature.) It is problematic because it consents, or seems to consent to the seemingly stricter but limited Positivistic readings of deterministic materialism, whose supporting myth has been Darwinian evolution. At the end of his life, Bergson concedes this point in declaring that "The universe . . . is a machine for the making of God" (*Morality and Religion*).

By Bergsonian speculations into the heart of a materialistic cosmos, the immanent becomes endowed theoretically by a spirit. But it is a spirit quite different from that sustaining Presence which Christian orthodoxy calls the Lord and Giver of Life. We nevertheless remember that Bergson's intellectual venture nevertheless proved at once stimulating to the thought of some poets and philosophers, those sensing an increasing entrapment of intellect itself through the rigors of logical Positivism, those Puritan materiallogians denying all spirit. Maritain responded briefly to Bergson, hope sparked in him, as among the poets so did Ezra Pound and Robert Frost to name familiars. So, too, Eric Voegelin. It was an understandable effect, since Bergsonian arguments were at least making a crack in the concrete walls (poured around creation by unrelenting logic) of the doctrine of materialistic determinism that had come to so encase not simply creation but the intentional intellect itself. That Positivistic materiallogian doctrine pretends to have lifted the heavy weight on intellect, thus freed absolutely to a transcendent freedom of the material cosmos, when instead it was collapsing upon itself by its angelism. Through Bergson the question of the "spirit" (however variously interpreted) at least reentered speculative thought – both aesthetic and scientific thought.

But just what is one to name that recovering spirit, however it might recognize itself as desiring recovery by experiences of the immanent world? That remained problematic. Once mentioned as a common experience, this recovery of "spirit" immanent seemed increasingly an undeniable aspect of intellect's response to the material world. Certainly the poet became bolder, though he might insist that the vital spark should be associated only with his own imaginative actions. That was the point of departure we remark for Ezra Pound and Robert Frost, as it was to become the central theme of poetry itself for Wallace Stevens. Eliot made a pilgrimage to Paris shortly before World War I to hear Bergson, only to conclude that Bergson as prophet provided no substantial food to his own spiritual hungers. It was on that visit that he discovers the work of Dostoevsky. What, then, is the name best suited to a community of consent, whereby we may mutually recognize a term in reference to our common experience of things? "Élan vital"? Perhaps. But there were questions about Bergson's argument unsettling to both Eliot as poet and to Jacques Maritain as philosopher. By the time Maritain comes to write his memoir, *The Peasant of the Garonne,* he will have long since rejected Bergson, evidenced in that memoir by his scathing dismissal of another of Bergson's early disciples, Teilhard de Chardin. For by then for Maritain (as for that other Thomist, Gilson) the nature of the act of naming attaches to the metaphysics of being, but not to *being* as the prime causal source of this reductionist view of being itself, whereby it is mired in the limits of the materialistic.

Neither can Percy subscribe to that limitation fully. But, though much encouraged toward Gilson's or Maritain's perspective upon the cosmos by his own reading of St. Thomas's *Summa Theologica,* Percy's own approach to the science of intellectual naming proves more Modernistic than Thomistic. It is a somewhat staining effect upon his intellectual approach to the mystery of signs, we are suggesting, out of his anticipation that science, not philosophy or theology, may be best suited to solve that mystery. A severely logical science (semiotics) may at last account for the sign in its mediation of intellect and the perceived thing in a common consent. Thus he introduces difficulties in supposing such a science of signs sufficient to the mystery of our experiences of things. Gilson to the contrary will insist as philosopher that semiotics as a science is at last insufficient to that mystery whereby intellect possesses truth in consequence of encounter of things. That is the concern he addresses in his *Linguistics and Philosophy,* arguing that linguistics as a science crosses a line and becomes a pseudo-philosophy. We might put Gilson's Thomistic position in opposition to this pseudo-philosophy in summary of a possible solution: naming *follows* a sacramental experience of the created particularities of a discrete thing from among those things which Percy subsumes in his term "Cosmos." Percy, too, would recover this sacramental relation of the self to the thing at last, but he believes the recovery possible through a science of sign in his early concerns. And in that attempt, he requires as theoretically necessary a coincidence of selves to each other, accomplished through sign. By that coincidence occurs an effect, a leap in the being of the discrete self. He is concerned for a recovery of community, an admirable concern. But his argument does not at last speak directly to the reality of a community of the discrete consciousness as it experiences a thing, in relation to the sign as mediation of that community first of all to the experiencing "self." Thus he sees a dependence of one self upon another self *in sign* itself, an action committed to intellectually *in media res*. To the contrary we suggest that a community already exists between consciousness and thing in relation to *being* within the experiencing moment. That is the reality of experience, certified only subsequently by sign – sign in this sense being any historical witness to the reality of a *communion* with the thing. There has been a precedent communion by a *person,* according to his created nature as intellectual soul incarnate, with a *thing* – a communion effected initially by the person's openness of love to that thing.

It is this entwining of Modernist dislocations of the self, though with vague Thomistic echoes, that encouraged Percy nevertheless to his initial Pascalian gamble, for which much thanks. But we must consider the inherent problem with his argument as argument, a concern quite other than any question of Percy's own actual rescue as person through what he will ascribe later to grace. Our concern is that a confused thought on this mystery may itself prove an obstacle to grace for some soul who is not given the bravery of risk such as his, the willingness of such risk as he attributes to Melville. There is then an inherent endangerment of the "self" in the argument out of Peirce, reflected in the language Percy uses, as when – in a very serious moment – he argues a distinction between a *world* imposed by sign and the separate *cosmos*. For he is insistent that a "world is imposed upon the Cosmos" by the sign. This is the point of danger, not only to Percy's argument in the moment of these words, but in each moment to each person in whatever his circumstances as *homo viator* if he presumes himself arbiter of order by sign's authority. It is a moment of an "in-between" at which the person is suspended between a movement of the self in retrogression toward the Old Adam or a movement toward rescue by the New Adam. The dilemma is the temptation to a "self" to assert autonomy by naming or of a "self" surrendered *through* a consenting name in an openness to grace – that "other story" Percy knows to be so foreign to Modernist thought that he is hesitant to name it publicly.

On the one hand a "closure"' which has an illusional effect of "transcendence," but which is as closure dependent upon the assumption of intellectual angelism energized by intentional will. On the other an "openness" which may at first appear to be a submergence of the self in existential reality (such is the deceptiveness of the self through pride) – that movement of intellect which may be falsely seen as an obliteration of the self as opposed to the counter aggressive angelistic transcendence. (For it may be especially so seen by submission to Positivistic dogma.) It is the moment of the will's suspension, then, between a self-love imposing a barrier to any other (cp. Prufrock) and an ordinate self-love which is a self-forgetfulness through the action of charity – through love. Put in relation to that tension in Percy himself between his Southern Stoicism and Catholic openness to being, it is a suspension between the Stoic's self-love supposed sufficient to keep a distance from the "cosmos" by imposing a "world" of signs (out of an assumed "role") and that Christian self-love which is a surrender to the Cause of the cosmos, made *through* the cosmos in recognition of the connaturality of this opening "self" to the immediate things toward which it opens in moments of charity. That, from the Thomistic perspective, is movement toward the truly transcendent. What is effected by an openness of love, a consent to existential reality, is a modification of the "world" man would otherwise impose by his attempt at a pseudo-transcendence. If we express the distinction by reference to poets, the French Symbolist makes his signs a mirror reflecting the self in this art version of pseudo-transcendence, in contrast to Dante's sense of sign. For Dante, that journey called the *Divine Comedy* unfolds his gradual discovery of sign as opening upon the transcendent through a translucence gained as governed by the poet's love, the transformation of his "seeing" under the inclusive auspices of Divine Love. An imposed world (such as the French Symbolist would command) becomes an obstacle to a truly transcendent end, becomes an obstacle to grace Thomas would say. It becomes a stumbling stone to rescue, however well polished as reflecting the self. That is the paradoxical Christian mystery uniting two admonitions: (1) we must love our neighbor (2) but as we love ourselves – remembering that love requires a loss to the self of its presumed autonomy. He who would save his life must lose it in this manner of spiritual action. It is a manner of action one might describe as possible only out of a proper humility. Humility, in this respect, is the initiating ground of charity – of active love. So that we might put it that *charity* (love) is the active deportment of *humility* toward that which is not the self, an act removing obstacles to a grace thereby substantiating the self toward its perfection. Thus a communion, transforming the self within the connaturality of *person* to *thing,* occurs in a proportionate mutuality of *beings created.*

It becomes then a danger to the self lost in the cosmos if it erect a barrier called the world (*Welt*) against the threatening mystery of the Cosmos (*Umwelt*). The Cosmos as a mystery seems to threaten any revelation of the self to the self, or to imply that in such revelation the self discovers only its emptiness – consciousness thus but a dream within a dream. In that concern, Percy may prove more generous in his response to Nietzsche or Heidegger or Jean-Paul Sartre than it may be safe to practice intellectually save through a charity held with a knowledge of those thinkers' inadequacies as pilgrim intellects to be in any wise emulated. It becomes, if this be true, a concern of importance to our reflections on that section of *Lost in the Cosmos*, Percy's "Semiotic Primer of the Self," in which he underhandedly says that the "intermezzo [is] easily skipped," his strategy in underlining its importance. To Percy, these are the most important pages of the work, as we have heard him declare on a later occasion. If so, they require our closer concern, especially in relation to any foreboding about the intellectual consequences of opposing *Welt* and *Umwelt*, the self's world and that Cosmos which the self would in some wise "transcend" by its own actions, too often tempted to eschew any aid save that supplied by its act of imposing a "world."

Percy begins his "intermezzo" with an "Emphasis" upon a "Short History of the Cosmos," echoing the concurrently emerging "Chaos Theory" in physics, turning that theory to serve the interaction between entities in a linear emergence of cause-effect out of the chaos of the "self." In respect to this perspective upon entities in collision, "When I take a single step, I affect the rotation of the earth." How is one to "stand" against this entrapment by the Cosmos, this sense of being "thrown" as Heidegger might put it? That becomes the problem for an "I." And the answer lies in signs as instruments to a transcendence of the linear as a constricting movement upon the self trapped in what (in a Teilhardean sense, perhaps) is the Cosmos as reduced to the horizontal dimension of the energy of physical action (as opposed to Teilhard's "vertical energy"). How gain the desired vertical inclination, how gain a "transcendence" of the self? The answer for Percy is as "sign-user."

"For the sign-user, a world is imposed upon the Cosmos – to which he responds like any other organism." Here is the crux of difficulty for the Thomist, and a point of danger to intellect from that perspective. For in this apparent event, the sign-user cannot respond to the Cosmos "like any other organism," his intellectual nature disallowing that. To respond *like* any other creature (other than another intellectual soul incarnate) is to begin a falling away from what has already occurred: a visionary moment to intellect. Note Helen Keller and her reaction to actual water in relation to the sign given, a witness Percy summons. She has arrived in a "world" now to be lost only through a willfulness intending *either* a *power over* all other organisms *or* a will to a *submergence into* that "cosmos" in a rejection of the vision by attempting to become thereby "like" all others. Willfully assuming a transcendence by the power commanded through this vision (which is for Thomas rather a gift of grace) becomes the Modernist's orthodoxy. On the other hand, a willful submergence must end in despair if pursued to its end, in contrast to that alternate pseudo-transcendence which cultivates the presumption of intellectual autonomy in a heresy of angelism. For by that presumption of autonomy, knowledge is intended to a use in an exercise of power, enthroning intellect beyond its finitude as knower: it attempts to usurp Godhead by its act of angelism. In the end, it too becomes subject to despair, the danger Eliot has dramatized as inevitable in his "Gerontion."

Percy's address to man as sign-maker does not address man as *partaking* in creation through his openness to the "other," to that *not-the-self*, in an action according to his already *given* nature. Rather, what seems to be required in Percy's view is a *taking* by the action of sign-making, a naming action characteristic of intellect in a mode which we usually ascribe as the calling of the analytical scientist. And so a difference can be seen here between the Thomistic address and Percy's address out of Saussure concerning the relation of the *sign* to the *thing* signed and to the *signer*. From this perspective both signifier and signified "are interpenetrated and the former transformed," says Percy. If by *signifier* we mean the *sign-maker,* the statement suggests that maker reconstituted. If by *signified* we mean the *thing* named by sign, the implication is that by nominalist action the thing is changed – a "world" imposed upon it. The difficulty to this approach to sign is engaged specifically in relation to Saussure by Gilson in *Linguistics and Philosophy,* as we anticipated earlier. From Gilson's perspective, sign-making is an effect of an action of openness to the Cosmos. Properly engaged by the Thomist, it is a *sacramental* gesture toward the "other," memorialized as it were by the sign. Thus sign becomes the locus (independent of time and place) in which occurs a *communion* of sign-maker and thing which allows a subsequent presence of intellects in communion. That is a circumstance to sign allowing a communion of the living and the dead, popularly "signed" as *tradition.* As sign-maker, as rational orderer of his own experiences, man assumes his office as steward of being, a sacramental relation to the particular other.

Percy (as indicated in his long note in *Lost in the Cosmos*) would escape from the Modernist prison of solipsism conjured by willful Nominalism by stressing "the social origins of language." But even so, "zoo-semiotics," however fine a distinction we may make in arguing this approach to sign as dyadic rather than triadic, is itself in a degree a social language, at least insofar as *social* as a sign is overwhelmed, made opaque, by the immanent cosmos reduced from transcendent cause. For the Thomist, man by his created nature differs *essentially* in his nature, so that only by denial of that nature does he effect his solipsistic illusion. His *intuitive* (not *instinctive*) sense of community rests in his unique gift as created intellectual soul incarnate and as such a creature participates in the transcendent as well as the immanent by that property to intellect called natural law. Percy will declare as his own conviction that "you have to point to an apple and name it for me before I know there is such a thing" existing "outside ourselves." But what is more arresting than this elementary level of "communication" through pointing and naming is the mystery of our recognition of a common experience, as discrete persons, of the thing itself, Percy's apple. Neither *I* nor *you "have* to point" in order that *you* or *I* know such a thing to exist outside our "world." (And, indeed, one may wonder whether Eve did not simply *hand* Adam that old apple.) Certainly not from a Thomistic position may one conclude the apple, nor a knowledge of it, dependent upon sign. In the simple act of knowing, we are suggesting, the person already participates in the transcendent because created in the image of God.

From this position one might argue that the action of intellect through event – through encounter of discrete things – effects a truth of the thing *in* the responding intellect. That is, the intellect comes to know a truth of the thing through the correspondence between thing and intellect as an actual event under the "connaturalizing" agency of being, within that ground of connaturality which we call *being.* That is the ontological nature of the person's experience of encounter with a discrete thing, becoming collective experience of that intellect suitable to contemplative memory inasmuch as the person is journeyman, is *homo viator.* We speak here of the complex of encounter, in which complex is effected a communal relation of intellect and thing. It is a context to action which we subsequently term *event.* Given contemplative memory, we recognize a *co-responding* between mutual but not always proportionate agents to such encounter, a respondency partaking of *community* at an elemental level. It is that *active reception* of the thing experienced which bonds person and thing though they are essentially discrete. They are bonded by truth through their connaturality. That is the promised recovery of community promised by Christ in the Comforter, the "Spirit of truth." By that active reception, the person may open toward a larger community, discovering thereby the in-membering of discrete persons in community as that term is generally used.

We bracket here a movement of the specific intellect toward that larger community, that larger community itself a way station toward reconciliation of the journeyman person as *member* in the *body* which St. Paul speaks of. For St. Paul and St. Augustine and St. Thomas, that is a body of discrete parts (members) discovered members one of another in a proportionality governed by its Head, Christ. Concerning this elementary encounter by intellect of the discrete thing, we find Gerard Manley Hopkins speaking of it as a visionary moment, in which he communes with roses in stipple on trout, or fire-coal falls of turned sod: such are lowly instances of encounter. That is the poet's way. The philosopher's is argued by Thomas in declaring that our first movement toward God is through our senses, as we begin to experience discretely existing things proximate to that "outer man," the body, and so stirring our properties as an incarnate nature into a pilgrimage. Hopkins would witness this close encounter of things in the signs of poetry, concerning which as poet he speaks of his attempt to capture the *instress* of the thing encountered in a visionary manner through a corresponding *inscape* of signs. That is the responsibility of art to use reason in making. But we observe that, from the Thomistic perspective, the reality of a correspondence of truth to essence is not effected by sign itself at the primary level of our knowing, by that event we call post facto a discrete experience of a thing. Rather, intellect finds itself already possessed of a *truth* corresponding to an *essence,* from which devolves a concern for memorial sign. Such a possession, we must be reminded, is not a comprehensive, inclusive possession of the thing in itself. In Thomas's argument, comprehension is reserved to omniscient God.

Thus in the action of thought toward sign-making, intellect discovers that it already knows things by their truth, held experientially out of the essence of things, but not comprehensive of essence. And that includes as already possessed some stock of signs, along with the discrete "communal" experiences of such things as apples. Indeed, the infant is born already possessed of many signs. It may be for instance already attuned to the voice not only of its mother but of its father through experiences held in common with them. In his book *The Secret Life of the Unborn Child,* Thomas Verny, M.D., brings research evidence to bear. Thus "The newborn [proves] able to pick out his father's voice in a room even in the first hour or two of life," evidenced by his stopping crying on hearing that voice – if the father has "talked to his child in utero using short soothing words."

And one may even measure the child's reaction in utero to music, measurably soothed by Vivaldi or Mozart, though "Brahms and Beethoven, and all forms of rock . . . drove most fetuses to distraction," as experimentally recorded. In addition, there has been clinical evidence suggesting that in utero the fetus distinguishes among signs in such a way as to witness recognition of signs, though its "vocabulary" is small, perhaps some ten actual signs.

Responses to experiences perhaps merely physiological? But then, how explain a fetus's severe agitation when its mother only *thinks* that she *might* smoke another cigarette? This is to suggest that already while yet in the womb there is communal *knowing* which is precedent to signs, deeper than any signification of name. We might be reminded of a happier event, the effect of St. Mary's sharing her condition with Elizabeth when the future John the Baptist not yet born leaps for joy in Elizabeth's womb. We must underline, however, that such *knowing,* even for that future John Baptist, does not mean *comprehension* lest seers or prophets be worshipped. We rather speak to a condition of the intellectual soul incarnate according to its given nature, where in a fulfillment of that nature through proper action it perfects a sacramental openness to things: a proportionate accord between the intellect's created and providential nature and the discrete things which it progressively certifies by love as actual, through a natural law independent of any letter of law. We must underline this distinction as crucial: in a sense strictly governed by the reality of our nature, any *thing* is subject to *comprehension* only by that Sustaining Love whereby it exists. That distinction nevertheless does not obviate truth as known by intellect though in a limited manner, despite the created finitude as agent. Out of that knowing, according to our given nature, we respond, or may respond, in a sacramental openness that is progressively enlarging our person on the journey of the cosmos.

And so, Dame Julian of Norwich requires no pointing by some other person to the hazel-nut on her open palm nor is she required to point it out to some other person for a memorial naming to certify the event in actual signs, though she witnesses her vision in signs to us. Hers is a vision independent of any other person, and out of that experience rises her wonder that such a small thing should not collapse to nothingness for its very littleness, a meditative accommodation of her "self" to the visionary experience. She moves from intuitive awe in knowing, to a wonder requiring rational meditative reflection. That is a progress toward her witness of reality *through* signs, but not dependent upon those signs as external, as *in* the possession of some other sign-maker. She brings back news of the hazel-nut as evidence of a vision of the interpenetrating love which at once sustains both signifier and signified in a communion vested in *being*. What is already spoken, before any sign exists, is the commonness of all as *created* and *sustained* creatures through Creating Love. That is the witness borne by St. Augustine in recording "words" spoken to him by all those discrete "things" that he experiences as standing about the doors of his senses. They are "words" which he commands of them though those things by their very existence are already begging entry in support of his *knowing* more deeply significant (though yet unworded) than any reductionist response of the senses affords. And those "doors" of the "outer man" to the inner man are opened by more than a merely sensual opening to the sensed thing. For St. Augustine and St. Thomas, for Dame Julian of Norwich, this aspect of encounter of a thing is to know at last, and understand (though not comprehend), a continuous action of the Lord and Giver of Life, a Presence in and to things. That is to know an abiding Presence which is both more fundamental to and so comprehensive of the cosmos than a theory of the *élan vital* affords.

And so, from a Thomistic position there appears a possible danger hidden in Percy's confident phrase pronouncing the self as the agent enabled by signs to effect "a world *imposed*." For this is a language residually infected by a Nominalistic "reading" of an event, an encounter by intellect of a thing of the Cosmos. It is a self-conscious (and so self-withdrawing) recognition of that self's disposition as a consciousness to impose a "world" on the thing. But it is not an encounter of a "world" with the "Cosmos." It is rather an encounter of a discretely existing – an "ordinary" – thing. As an experience of communion, through which speaks the continuous Act of Love, such event stirs a desire to witness as an action of intellect, a movement of making. Thus it is here that Thomism diverges radically from Percy's Saussure and from Peirce and their implied dependence on Darwin. Thomas argues in the *Summa,* I-II, q 91, a2, as follows, concerning man's given nature: "Among all others, the rational creature is subject to divine providence in the most excellent way, insofar as it partakes of a share of providence, being provident both for itself and for others. This participation of the eternal law in the rational creature is called natural law." It is a participation *in* the creature antecedent to the rational letter of that law externalized by an intellectual making. Long before Aquinas, St. Augustine had discovered this communal sharing through his ordinate participation in created creatureliness, his sharing in being out of his created nature. That is, he recovers his ontological ground in being. That is a discovery adumbrated in the *Confessions* in relation to the mystery of memory itself – that place which is no *place* in intellect which is susceptible to limited rationalization, even by biochemical science in whose limited province Saussure's semiotics becomes entrapped at last.

Thomas takes a position out of his faith in Revelation, to which he brings the support of his considerable rational gifts. For that reason, we must see Thomas first of all as a mystic, though he is seldom so considered. How surprising it may be to us to discover that Thomas argues that reason is an "imperfect" form of the intuitive – that the necessity for thinking is a burden because of the imperfection in us of our intuitive intellect. Percy finds himself in a "world" of persons for whom that faith has been excluded in the interest of a progressive imposition of "meaning" through signs *upon* the Cosmos, a *world* as a "role" forced upon creation. That imposition has led to the illusion of an evolution of intellectual autonomy as if it were the primary cause of the self. That principle by the end of the 20th century has rather been established as the orthodox law to the required separation of our imposed world in distinction from the Cosmos, an action of indirection by intellect whereby it separates grace from nature. A consent to world imposed becomes primary, to resist which imposition raises totalitarian anathema. But that is an illusion reflecting on gnostic intent, in recording "stages" of human history, a point addressed by Voegelin in his *Science, Politics and Gnosticism.* Though Percy sees the destructive consequences of this evolved staging as dogma of a Modernist orthodoxy, its destructive horrors everywhere about us, Percy seems not to recognize as buried in the theory he himself propounds as descriptive of actual reality the hidden agenda of an intent to power, to be wielded by intellect when it imposes its *world* upon the *cosmos*.

There is in his argument, then, an ambivalence in which his signs at once accept a Darwinian perspective and continue baffled by its inadequacy to account for Darwin. Percy's early distinction between *science* and *scientism* does not engage the possibility that science as he approves it may already incline to impose error (when not governed by metaphysics) through mistaken presumptions about the complexity of creation. The quest for certainty, insofar as we discover ourselves lost in the cosmos, tempts us to an imposition of a world as if intellect's primary authority through reason were thus credentialed. Percy is nevertheless uneasy about this difficulty, returning again and again to it, often from a somewhat amused and detached perspective as a satirist of the conditions of man in the world as a "looney" presence devoted to the magic of technology. He is more interested in man's "looney" dimension, then, than in man's diabolical inclinations through power to force a "world" upon the "cosmos," a *Welt* upon that *Unwelt.* Hence his distinction between himself and Flannery O'Connor on this point.

Percy is, of course, acutely concerned that we, no less than he, are betimes "lost" in the cosmos, but he is particularly concerned as pilgrim with his own restlessness one suspects, allowing our listening to him along his way. It is in this respect that he observes Modern man to have substituted the virtue of Power for the virtue of Love, in a confusion none of us quite escapes. By that presumption of freedom as absolute to the self, certified through the imposition of signs (the inheritance to Modernist man out of Nominalism), intellect first presumes, then assumes. Then it may deport itself almost "unconsciously" as autonomous. So pervasive that climate of thought that we all breathe it, whatever the degree of allergic reaction we experience. Thus Modernist man becomes confused in his gift for the making of signs, increasingly reduced to the magically instrumental: blueprints to machines, means to the maintaining of that heresy of angelism. Thus his suspension above the Cosmos by means of an imposed "world," denying the givenness of the Cosmos – save as an "it" to be transformed by power through will. And so emerges *system* as a grace serving *angelism*.

This, then, is the Modernist presumption which Eric Voegelin names *gnosticism.* He defines its intent to be the self-empowerment of intellect by gnosis, in order to transform being itself to the will's desire. What is required to that intent is a reduction of being by system, accomplishing thereby a reduction of being, disallowing along the way any questions that might invalidate his system. Thus the imposed *Welt* supercedes the *Unwelt.* For of necessity "system" is the only "form of reasoning" to be allowed (Voegelin's words). Voegelin poses this distinction succinctly (in *Science, Politics & Politics*): "Philosophy springs from the love of being; it is man's loving endeavor to perceive the order of being and attune himself to it. Gnosis desires dominion over being; in order to seize control of being the gnostic constructs his system. The building of systems is a gnostic form of reasoning, not a philosophical one." We should add here that some Thomists, disregarding Thomas himself, might themselves on occasion be guilty of an attempt to impose Thomism as a system, that inclination in some of his disciples leading to a disaffection with Thomism as esoteric, when it is rather reason's exploration of common sense response to existential reality, certifying by reason the intuitively – mystically – known. Against this possibility of a "gnostic" Thomism, Thomas himself forewarns us. "The purpose of the study of philosophy [to which we should add science and art at least] is not to learn what others have thought, but to learn how the truth of things stands." Both philosophy and poetry serve prophetically this principle of our limited being, recalling us to known but forgotten things, as science also serves by its restricted concern for the particularities in things leading to recognition of the orders of nature.

Percy, given his intellectual circumstances and his discomfort with them, is making his way out of the closed Modernist "world," but from an initial position as scientist we have suggested. That is indeed one of the virtues of his witness to us, a rarity among first-rate poets. We must be cautious nevertheless in reading some of his signposts along the way. Hence we are specifically cautious of his suggestion that man as sign-user effectively *imposes* a world upon the Cosmos. We might recall Adam as sign-user to our cautionary concern. Adam names the creatures of the Cosmos, *Genesis* says. The poet in us may imagine Adam's growing enthusiasm as analogous to the account Percy recalls of Helen Keller in her discovering signs, her naming "water." God approves Adam's naming, not because the names are "right" (though they are) but because Adam's deportment to the Cosmos is right. Adam responds; he does not impose. But he *will* come to a point of imposing, in response to that proffered apple.

A poet might well be tempted, then, to the conundrum of signs and to his own temptation to naming in order to recall known but forgotten things. And so here, concerning Peirce, Percy, and the *triadic* in relation to the *dyadic*, with Percy's playfulness a version of old Adam at his naming game, an event occurring even *before* Eve is created, according to *Genesis*. An old poem as commentary, as old at least as Occam though not so old as Adam's imaginative action, yet *almost* that old:

Would You Like to Try for Infinite Years

When Adam was a little boy, his God came walking in the afternoon
    and He said, "Adam, Adam. You're old enough to name some."

And Adam said, "Yes, Lord."

And God called up an elephant. It walked around them, stopped and turned.

And God said "What does that look like to you?"

And Adam "Well . . . "

"Look at it closely, Adam. Take your time."

"It's not a whale?" said Adam.

"It's not a whale. We'll get to whales directly," God said. "Look at its tail and ears. Look at its lithe proboscis. Now what does this old pachyderm remind you of?"

"Rhinoceros?" ventured Adam.

"You're getting warm," said God. "What did the Greeks call ivory?"

And all creation watched boy Adam anxiously to see how he would do.

"An Elephant!" cried Adam as it ran off into Eden.

"Good. That's very good," said God, amid applauding centuries.

So all afternoon with God's good coaxing Adam named, till finally, proficient, when a rabbit came, "A Rabbit!" Adam shouted.

"That's getting pretty good," praised God.

And after animals came birds till Adam named the owl in darkness and God said "That's all today. We'll do the fish tomorrow, and you'll find them twice as hard. You'd better get a good night's rest."

"Yes, Lord."

"And Adam . . . "

"Yes, my good Lord."

"We're running out of things to do. Next category after fishes will be trees. Then I must entertain you somehow else."

"No hurry, Lord."

X

Always for us: the difficulty of naming with a prudential justice to the thing named, in our present concern Percy's *Lost in the Cosmos* in its differentiation. Midway this fascinating work, one might be tempted to see it as an autobiographical novel perhaps. But then with wider reflection, we might rather call it an intellectual autobiography, one disguised by the underhandedness of art. *If* this latter naming, we might suggest it a work bearing some analogy to St. Augustine's *Confessions*. Both come at the end of a span of history in which civilization seems threatened by a total collapse, though in this respect we might rather see St. Augustine's *City of God* as the more telling parallel witness. In *The City of God*, St. Augustine, in a deliberate address to the general spiritual collapse all about him, sees the threat as interior, though the symptoms are spectacular in the external invasions by barbarians from the North. The hidden danger lies within Rome itself, in what St. Augustine perceives as a resurgence of an old Roman paganism intent upon overthrowing Christianity.

In this respect, then, Percy's last novel *The Thanatos Syndrome* might prove analogous to *The City of God,* if we allow such comparisons, acknowledging the differences between them in respect to their literary genre. *Lost in the Cosmos,* of course, engages an emergent "New Age" paganism, which Percy addresses often in essays and fiction and interviews. The putative mode in his last self-help book is to dramatize the self in representative specimens declared lost in the frictional disintegration of intellect and spirit. What may interest us, by the time we are halfway through the work, is a growing suspicion that a very central concern is with a hidden self whom we may think of as Walker Percy. Indeed, that is why our first suggestion of appropriate analogy to *The Confessions.*

There proves a difference, however, beyond the first and most obvious one that in the *Confessions* we hear the saint, in the other a novelist wary of the epithet of sage. Thus we borrow a distinction from Heinrich A. Rommen's *Natural Law: A Study in Legal and Social History and Philosophy.* We might adapt his discussion of the relation of the Stoic to the Christian and suggest our difference between the Christian saint bearing witness and the Stoic sage-as-scientist very much desiring the certainty of the saint. Or more aptly for our present speculative concern: we might say that in Walker Percy we have both the Christian and the Stoic as *two* "selves" trying to become one. This speculative hazard gives us a transition whereby we may explore tensional circumstances to that discrete self,

Walker Percy, who is first and last (but usually very privately) concerned with his own journeying. By this hazard, we set aside any judgmental dimensions to our concern, certainly. But by this speculative view, we may come to see Percy as poet in a role as an Everyman witness to our own difficulties in reaching certainties about our "self." Nevertheless, he denies to us in his analysis of our Modernist circumstances in *Lost in the Cosmos* the certainty we desire. The self in tension is, he suggests, unnamable – though attempts to name it yield tensional symptomatic evidences that we actually do exist as a "self."

The certainty St. Augustine holds, after his conversion, is that he has till then been a most sinful child of God, crafty in his intellectual speculations to such a degree that he weeps contrition throughout his *Confessions.* What he knows with most certainty is that he is an intellectual soul incarnate, through the sustaining grace of God's love for him as this specific person. It does not follow from such certainty that he believes as well that he fulfills the responsibilities called forth by that belief, except insofar as God's grace enables him to those responsibilities as a person. Walker Percy is initially steadied by a Stoicism, largely learned from his Uncle Will and then strengthened through his conversion. But all along his way he finds himself held in suspense, and with a degree of suspension discomforting to him. How well he knows that anxiety we hear even from St. Paul, which St. Augustine also expresses: "I believe. Help thou my unbelief." There is a difference, however, in that St. Augustine engages that threat of suspension directly, while Percy engages it by indirection: as a novelist, not as philosopher or theologian.

Of course we engage this distinction, if it be such, with our own risk of prudential error. We do so by considering the witness of signs which each leaves to us for our own engagement of the desert of this world. They leave us, in Percy's phrase, signposts in the desert. And if, considering Percy as poet rather than as philosopher or theologian, we dwell on the aesthetic dimension of his work, we might even argue collaterally that certainty such as St. Augustine's might well become the death of poetry – the death of imaginative explorations of the *possible* or *probable* insofar as the poet must engage these as pilgrim poet.

St. Augustine had to deal with the same, at least early on. That is, we remember that in fact he too was a poet, having written a poem winning a public competition. And as a teacher of literature, he also wrote a treatise on the nature of beauty. But with his conversion, though he does not at last reject his speculative concerns for literature, he values literature in an ordinate subordination to his deepest concern for his (and our) salvation as intellectual soul incarnate. Percy, however – early and late – continues with the conundrum of the sign, not only in its relevance to truth, but with its possible service to his explorations of the *possible* or *probable* dimensions of human nature. This is his concern in relation to the making of novels.

As for the sign's relation in a witness of beauty, the poet's abiding concern, St. Augustine already fears a danger, one rather generally neglected by most of our own recent poets. The perfection of art in and of itself, he knows, is insufficient to rescue any self lost in the cosmos. That is nevertheless a "Romantic" faith of poets for some two or three hundred years now. It is appealing in that it seems to promise rescue of the lost self by words artfully ordered. And we might notice, in reading the *Confessions,* that this temptation to believe the sign to be sufficient to such a rescue is the repeated theme in a rejection, for St. Augustine is anti-Romantic.

And so let us suggest speculatively – that is with prudential concern in relating Percy as pilgrim and to St. Augustine as pilgrim – that Percy very often reflects uncertainty about his own calling as poet, while St. Augustine, rather, reflects growing certitude about his own calling as a child of God, one whose most special calling is to a witness of that calling. In its exercise, however, St. Augustine yet reflects a discomfort over the necessity to bear a *literary* witness. Willy-nilly, in order to witness he must use signs, and use them persuasively, but toward an end beyond aesthetic effectiveness. He seems, in the *Confessions,* almost embarrassed by this "literary" necessity. And he is so because he remembers with deep contrition his own career as rhetor. The rhetor (especially as he remembers himself as such) seems rather by his professional strategy to be all those things Percy declares necessities to him as novelist – indirect, sly, tricky, underhanded. But above all the rhetor is intent on misleading his audience, at least in that earlier practice for which St. Augustine is so redundantly contrite.

Looking back on his teaching days, St. Augustine now sees himself back then as a remote and foolish figure, "falling about on slippery ground and in the midst of much smoke." It was a great relief when he could retire quietly from his "post as a salesman of words in the markets of rhetoric." From the beginning, his ambitions to an academic career as rhetor was to achieve a civil and social advantage such as was made possible in his day through liberal arts. Now he sees the liberal arts as possibly dangerous to the soul, though it was that very training, perhaps even a Sophist's practice of those arts, which had prepared him to escape from the Manichaean absurdities to which he devoted a decade of his life. As a "Hearer" to the Manichee "Elect," as member of a lower strata of that heretical movement, Augustine mistook the true nature of *form*. That heresy would impose its own form regardless of reality as a means justifying its own ends, anticipating thereby the later triumph in the West of Nominalism. Thus it held that there is substance evil and substance good, rather than that substance as created is necessarily good and evil a falling away from substantial goodness through willfulness, in which failure, the will is adamant to enslave its own intellect. Indeed, when Augustine comes to recognize the absurdity of the Manichaean aversion to Christianity, he recovers a measured respect for the classical literature he had so long taught, though now he approaches it with a caution not practical earlier. For in his professional days as rhetor of a Manichaean persuasion, he believed himself thereby justified in his distortion of the form of argument by his Manichaean intent. Later he can recognize that the liberal arts require a relation of intellect to reality which proves subversive of Manichaean rejections of the real, though those arts in themselves may also tempt a person to a worldliness, to which St. Augustine found himself most susceptible.

One of the sub-themes of Augustine's *Confessions* becomes his studied rescue of his "professional" training in liberal arts from Manichaean corruption of those arts on the one hand, but also a proportionate ordering of these arts to the glory of God on the other – lest worldliness overtake him. Thus, if one look closely at his literary and philosophical explications of *Genesis* in his *Confessions,* one finds him an ancient father of the Modern "New Criticism," but of that theistic faction within the New Criticism which includes T. S. Eliot, Allen Tate, and especially Cleanth Brooks. In retrospect, then, he sees himself to have been "Publicly . . . a teacher of the arts which they call liberal" to the affluent, the paying public, while "privately I professed a false religion – in the former role arrogant, in the latter superstitious, in everything vain." His first treatise following his conversion in 186 A.D. is *Contra Academicos,* exposing both of these – his public and private errors – which he had cleverly practiced in his own office as rhetor. The object now, in his self-examination, is to restore an ordinate service of intellect to God through intellect's arts recovered to a subordinate service to the God of all the arts of being, to the Creator as Supreme Artist. Thus the *grace* of art through which beauty is revealed is not in itself evil as the Manichaean religion required him to suspect, except if made the artist's own final end to the destruction of his soul.

The rhetor through vanity, this is to say, may see himself as the ultimate artist, the superior grace of his formal "post as a salesman of words" in the market stalls of the liberal arts proving his self-proclaimed virtues as intellect. The ancient Manichaean was suspicious of the liberal arts, and particularly of the *fine* arts and poetry. In this respect he proves precursor to the New England Puritan. Nathaniel Hawthorne feels the shadow of those recent of his fathers, as in his "Maypole of Merrymount." And both that ancient Manichaean and the more recent Puritan are a continuing presence, the suspicion of the liberal arts transferred to secular society in the interest of Pragmatism. From a Manichaean perspective, to take refuge in the pleasures of music or painting or poetry evidences a failure, an impurity as Manichaean. It is to fail from a pure intent to a rejection of the world as evil. If one is tempted by those arts, he thereby reveals himself as worldly – as given to a world which on principle must be declared evil. That is, there must be a *formal* disjunction from existential reality. Of course, there is that Sophist's strategy, perfectly legitimate as intellectual manipulation of form, whereby the world may be used against itself. That is a strategy which St. Augustine took great pride in when he was by worldly profession a rhetor. Even one's carnal appetite could be accommodated – for awhile – by the logistics of the rhetor as Sophist by turning the sensual world upon itself.

It is, of course, a species of heresy which will rise long after St. Augustine, intellectually justified by the Albigensians in their pursuit of scandalous worldliness. Later than the Albigensians, Hawthorne we have recalled is haunted by the presence of this inclination in his Puritan forebears, themselves influenced by St. Augustine though not having read him with a full consent to his insistence on the goodness of creation itself. The Puritans were especially suspicious of literature and of the "fine" arts as they might purport to be celebration of God's glory. But what a forceful rhetorical poetry one finds displayed in some of those Puritan sermons, practiced in a rhetoric to be envied by the "metaphysical" poet! Thus by poetry, poetry itself is condemned as it were. That is what Hawthorne hears echoing across the interval to his own day from his Puritan fathers. Hawthorne had as well been a fiddler as a writer of stories! St. Augustine to the contrary will locate evil, not in art but in the artist. Insofar as ordinate to existential reality in the making of a good – the work itself – art is itself good. And this is a theme St. Thomas will develop at considerable length after him.

Hawthorne has intimations of this truth about art, though he lacks the formal capacity of a rhetor sufficiently oriented to that truth to make the case. He might have found it made for him in St. Augustine or St. Thomas. That failing, he is left to struggle darkly for that truth in a world within which New England Puritanism is rapidly becoming transformed toward pragmatism, a pragmatism bearing a Puritan solemnity in its public rhetoric. That Pragmatism will come to serve Positivism. We might well ask whether we encounter Positivistic scientists who allow poetry any validity, save perhaps as "R and R" to intellect, a recreation not to be taken seriously. For the Positivist is not likely to escape a "puritan" depreciation of art. As mediator of Puritan to Positivist authority, recall Ralph Waldo Emerson, Hawthorne's near neighbor. Emerson is our first philosopher of the "self," extolling the self as capable of "transcendence" by its own will. Thus Emerson in his "American Scholar" is emphatic that "In self-trust, all the virtues are comprehended." And in "Self-Reliance": "Nothing is at last sacred but the integrity of our own mind." In Emerson one has, not a "Transcendentalist" as popularly supposed in mistaking that elevated Kantian term. Rather, he is advocate of heretical angelism as the means to self-rescue, the fundamental principle to Emerson's doctrine that intellect is autonomous.

That is, incidentally, why Emerson was recognized at once by the new president of Harvard University, Charles W. Eliot, as a suitable sage to his redeployment of the liberal arts to specialization – toward secular, pragmatic ends in his own intention to that "new" religion which he spells out in farewell to the Harvard theological students at the end of his tenure. His sermon is called "The Religion of the Future," which religion will be by his argument a bare, secular humanitarianism whose end is the reduction of the person to a worshipful service of the state. In that farewell, the retiring President remarks that "the religion of the future will not be based on authority, either spiritual or temporal." As for the catechumen of this new Modernist religion, he must remember that "the primary object will not be the personal welfare or safety of the individual in this world or the other . . . but . . . service to others, and . . . contributions to the common good." Above all, it must not be "propitiatory, sacrificial, or expiatory." Specialization in service to the state, at the expense of Renaissance Humanism – or so Irving Babbitt and George Santayana recognized in opposing President Eliot. Nor was the message lost on President Eliot's distant cousin, T. S. Eliot, a skeptic increasingly given to self-reliance and self-trust and increasingly suffering alienation. At that moment, the poet is struggling to finish his famously ironic poem about self-love, "The Love Song of J. Alfred Prufrock."

Now St. Augustine will declare that evil may be in the artist, but it does not follow that art is itself evil. Nor does the aesthetic dimension to art bring suspicion upon it. But then neither does the absence of that aesthetic grace in the art of the sign foretell the sign itself as evil. He declares (in his *Confessions*), "Ignorance of the liberal arts is compatible with holding authentic piety, but not if one is a Manichee." For "a statement is not true because it is enunciated in an unpolished idiom, nor false because the words are splendid." St. Augustine, we may discover, is revealing a progress in his own understanding of the grace allowed to sign when oriented to the truth of things. It is a quest which Percy's Binx of *The Moviegoer* may be said to begin as he stands on the library steps baffled by Modern Rhetors. In a quietly comic conclusion of that quest, at the end of *Thanatos Syndrome,* Dr. Tom More is making paper airplanes and sailing them into the world, in a Josef Pieper-like celebration – a "contemplation" of – the holiness possible in small things and actions.

Indeed, *The Thanatos Syndrome* proves very much Percy's own *Contra Academicos* in this respect, though *Lost in the Cosmos* serves as well. That this seems true appears to dawn gradually on Percy himself, who as he wrote *The Moviegoer* had supposed himself very much a part of a modern school of Existential philosophy (by his own account), which St. Augustine might well have suggested to us is only our version of the Manichaean philosophy with which he had struggled. Within that new version of a very old philosophy, Jean-Paul Sartre was being much honored as an "Elect" by academic "Hearers" at the time Percy undertakes that novel. In his "Physician as Novelist" (1989) Percy remembers writing his *Moviegoer,* an experience in which he "almost by accident . . . landed squarely in the oldest tradition of Western letters: the pilgrim's search outside himself, rather than the guru's search within. All this happened to the novelist [Percy is speaking of himself in a third-person detachment] and his characters without the slightest consciousness of a debt to St. Augustine or Dante." (Cartesian Idealism prepares the ground for pagan embraces of the guru in New Age versions of being *Lost in the Cosmos,* on which see Gilson's *Methodical Realism.*)

In his *Confessions,* St. Augustine along his narrative way must deploy signs in which he nevertheless recognizes a lingering infection, knowing as he does the manner of the academics of his day. This in contrast to Percy, who rather discovers a fortuitous inoculation of his own signs through Augustine and Dante. In his own intellectual deportment as a teacher of literature Augustine had allowed and even encouraged subversions of sign to Manichaean ends, a purging of which infection in himself is one of the principle attempts of his *Contra Academicos.* But literature proves superior to the empty uses of sign by Manichaeans. "How superior are the fables of the masters of literature and poets to these deceptive traps" of the Manichee's version of evolution, with their "Five Elements" posited as dwelling in caverns of *darkness, water, wind, fire* and *smoke,* each a specific cause of (respectively) *reptile, fish, birds, quadrupeds,* and *bipeds.* No wonder that he should, on coming to himself in the dark wood of Manichaean denials of the goodness of creation, see himself as biped "in the midst of much smoke," fallen on "slippery ground." But as inheritor of those old literary masters to the contrary, their "verses and poetry I can transform into real nourishment."

Even so, a masterful art in those old works, if unordered to the divine, may easily serve only to enslave the appetitive self to the world on the one hand, or arrest it in a "virtual reality" divorced from the real world on the other, as is the inclination of James Joyce's Stephen as young artist for instance. Thus the experience Augustine recalls as his own addiction proves analogous to Joyce's Stephen in his pursuit of art as transcendence. Incidentally, St. Augustine's passion was for the theater, in which regard one might also compare Binx Bolling's – and Percy's – fascination with movies. (How hauntingly Plato's allegory of the cave returns to us!)

By retrospection and through art (despite its danger), then, Augustine undertakes to dramatize with art's *transparency* (a theme important to Percy) his own pilgrimage as more than a species of literary indulgence in "virtual reality." It is agonizingly immediate as art in his recapturing of it, an agonizing immediacy which Dante will raise to a higher perfection as art in praise of creation and of the Creator God in his own recovery of an *ordinate* celebration of creation in that great poem *The Divine Comedy.* Dante's is an attempt through art which Percy will recognize himself as having hit upon as if by accident, though he adds "or was it accident?" implying it an intercession of grace to him in his blindness. Thus *The Moviegoer* proves a discovery to the writer himself, after his having written it, of his own experience on a pilgrimage in which he once was lost but now seems almost found. St. Augustine submits himself to a severe inquisition in his own self-interview, summoning his failures with contrition, but most of all with a conviction of the steady presence of God as a present judge of his signs, a judgment made here and now as he sets them down. Percy forces himself to such inquisition, by indirection usually, his "confession" a gradual, seemingly less self-judgmental one, than Augustine's.

The unfolding is in the fiction, but also in his other work. If Augustine leaves us his witness of a rescue through grace – as a literary maker he casts the work as an address, not to us, but to God – he seldom acknowledges any other possible audience to his self-interview than the Living God. That theme of regret for his early "literary" concerns – as first those of a socially ambitious rhetor and then as a rhetor devoted to Manichaean ends – he underlines with his regret, again and again in a literary mode which reveals to us St. Augustine's continuing literary influence upon us, though seldom acknowledged by us as Percy does. That last Stoic born of Puritan fathers, Henry Adams, however, is very explicit in acknowledging his own memoir, *The Education of Henry Adams* as modeled on the *Confessions,* though he distances himself by his mode of third person narrative, as does Percy in recollection of his accidentally hitting upon "the oldest tradition in Western letters." His narrative of a pilgrim's pursuit of rescue beyond the inadequate self in *The Moviegoer* is conspicuous, once it is seen in the light of "St. Augustine and Dante." Adams is quite explicit in letting us know that it is St. Augustine's *Confessions* that he has in mind, a work shadowing the *Education* as the *Odyssey* shadows Joyce's *Ulysses.* The fundamental unlikeness between the two works lies not in one's being first person, the other third person narrative however. The unlikeness is that between a Christian openness in the one, heavy with contrition, and a testimony of self-justification in the other by a last Puritan Stoic, in a work heavy with pathos.

Of course if our concern is for a literary aesthetics proper to the science of making, a concern with how to be an American writer, though also both a Southerner and a Christian, we might well argue that the saint's certainty may prove the death of poetry to such a writer. We find evidence to that point in our critical responses to great works of art. The dramatist, Aristotle suggests, must deal with the *possible* or *probable* in relation to human nature and actions, and so he must value uncertainty, ambiguity. While that may well prove an advantage to art, even a necessity to art, it is not necessarily an advantage to the artist as *person* in actual pilgrimage. For as person we most likely discover that we are fundamentally moved by a desire for a certainty beyond art's ambiguities, an inclination disorienting to us as artist perhaps. Thus a problem possible to the devoted Christian if he would be novelist – even a buried danger. Through art he may be drawn into risk, endangering any comfort he might otherwise hold in being either a Southerner or a Christian. It is the risk of exile, which our "Romantic" inclination has celebrated in the artist as hero, whether he leave "home" or not. Thus art's risk requires a courage in the face of this danger to the person in his "role" as artist. That is the danger Herman Melville risks, gaining Percy's admiration. It is also the danger omnipresent to Dostoevsky, whom Percy associates by contrast with Melville in an essay.

We have thus prepared a suggestion: Walker Percy, in his case-history of the hypothetical "self" in his *Lost in the Cosmos,* as artist risks any certainty he may hold about his own "self." Therefore, with some of Percy's own playfulness borrowed to our present concern for the *possible* or *probable* to the novelist-maker, we may suppose that the Modernist malaise he engages as diagnostician-novelist has been and continues to be evidenced to him within himself, his attention to it exacerbating his awareness of it. But we may even suggest that he recognizes his own situation as analogous not only to that of Melville, but also to that Christ-haunted pilgrim poet, Dostoevsky, who fears the Ivan Karamazov within himself even as he woos the Alyosha in pursuit of a pilgrim victory. As malady bearing pilgrim, then, Percy ostensibly witnesses to us our own burden of that malaise, almost universal to us at this opening of our century. But still he knows it to be most acutely his own "personal" problem.

Now the drama underlying his engagement of the Modernist malaise in *Lost in the Cosmos* is one he undertakes midway through his journey of life as novelist, to echo Dante's famous lines. Appropriately, midway this work itself we come upon a section carefully prepared in what Percy calls an "intermezzo of some forty pages" concerning a "Semiotic Primer of the Self," a more personal testimony to his belief that he has discovered a *science* of sign through which the self may recover from randomness in the cosmos and perhaps make a way toward certainty at last, having come to itself in the dark semiotic wood. After that "Primer," there follows a sharp turning away from an increasing intrusion of seriousness upon his present venture in words, a playfulness bordering upon farce, as in the "13th" engagement of this illusive self: THE TRANSCENDING SELF, a section concerned with "*How the Self Characteristically Places itself vis-à-vis the World, particularly through modes of Transcendence and Immanence.*"

Given some of the terminology in this later section, we recall Percy's reading of that serious philosopher of the self, Eric Voegelin. (Their mutual friend Cleanth Brooks pointed out some time ago Percy's interest in Voegelin.) Terms like *transcendence vs. immanence,* of *gnosis* and *gnostic* as we encounter them in *Lost in the Cosmos* might well imply an indirect tribute to Voegelin. And Voegelin's own engagement of a theory of consciousness, his *Anamnesis,* was in translation from Gerhart Niemeyer four or five years before *Lost in the Cosmos.* Earlier there had been Voegelin's *Science, Politics & Gnosticism,* much talked of in intellectual circles, engaging as it does a closing of the self by gnostic denial of the transcendent through the intellectual exploitation of the immanent in post-Renaissance philosophy.

And so if St. Augustine is a companionable presence to Percy, though late in Percy's recognition of that presence, there is also this additional one. Percy was well aware of his fellow Louisianian Eric Voegelin, an exile settled for some time on his own pilgrimage from Germany at Louisiana State University, before going on to California and then completing his journey by a return to Germany. (That journey made symmetrical, he could at last settle quietly in California to wait the courier's last call.) Voegelin's was an exile from Europe, and we note that among his own immediate intellectual progenitors in Europe are several recent thinkers whom Percy had already discovered, among them Husserl, Heidegger, Bergson. But Percy sees himself as poet-analyst, as diagnostician depending upon analytical science as instrument to discovering the Modernist malaise. Voegelin is rather the philosopher, exploring the Western "self" in its wanderings in the desert, from ancient Egypt into our century. In their mutual concerns for the "self," for self-aware consciousness, they respond to Modernist dislocations. As novelist-physician, Percy is more deeply committed to philosophical questions than he at first supposes. That is, he addresses the Modernist dislocations of the self, not as philosopher but as a scientist committed to semiotics. Voegelin explores the philosophical tradition more directly, as a political and social philosopher recapitulating the Western intellectual journey from Egypt and its closed world, through an opening of that world by Revelation, down to the gradual reclosing of that world through a post-Renaissance thought in which that closing effects in the sign – the word – what Voegelin calls an "opaqueness." His explorations, then, provide a certain philosophical resonance for Percy to his own pursuit of the philosophical questions he raises out of that indirection of science serving art, centering for him upon the "scientific" nature of the sign. Our point here is to emphasize a considerable body of speculative work, most of it philosophical, which constitutes Percy's own intellectual awareness, a complex presence to his speculative thought, underlying his scientific concern for the sign. His "academic" familiarity is more extensive than his mischievous role as merely diagnostic novelist might suggest.

A central theme in *Lost in the Cosmos* becomes the self's defense against confusion through its assuming dramatic roles, a defense by assuming persona in response to the impinging Cosmos as desert. The material suited to these multiple disguises, if one is committed to St. Augustine's profession as "salesman of words," is the sign. Thus when Percy himself, in essays and interviews, talks about his own role as a maker of "agents" in his dramatizing a variety of assumed roles – a maker of fictional personae intextured by signs – he returns again and again to the untrustworthiness of the *novelist* – that very popular species of salesman of words. The novelist first and last is out to "hoodwink" his reader, he says, speaking of himself. No easy task for us, then, to make our own explorations beneath the defenses of artfully assumed roles, and especially difficult to us in that *tour de force, Lost in the Cosmos: The Last Self-help Book.* Perhaps there is some purchase for us in this undertaking if we hear Percy's indirection as he stands before us – before an actual audience of other persons as he delivers his signs. Thus by a sort of triangulation, given two of his talks made before quite diverse gatherings, we may the better be prepared to test our conclusion: namely, that *Lost in the Cosmos* on its surface intends to bring the reader to the test concerning his own assumed roles as a self, while at its deeper dimension it is a drama of Percy examining his "self" in its role as writer. He is putting himself to the test, exploring lingering effects of Modernist reductions through programmed denials of *homo viator* as the creature understood by Augustine and St. Thomas. Consider two of Percy's talks before live, or almost alive, audiences. In these at least he seems to encourage persons to life beyond Modernist reductions.

In the first, "How to Be an American Novelist in Spite of Being Southern and Catholic," he gives to a local, almost hometown gathering at Southwestern Louisiana University, an encouragement cast as if he himself is a local member of that community. That in 1984. A year later he speaks to a more formal literary conference at Cornell whose subject is Chekov as writer. He moves from a regional state school, among neighbors, to that Ivy League gathering of sophisticated literati. Or if we may put the distinction playfully, borrowing Allen Tate's terms: he moves from an audience which might be suspected of being largely local unsophisticated provincials. At least so considered by a foreign audience which itself may be suspected of being caught up in the currents of a worldwide intellectual provincialism. At least they might be so considered local by an audience caught up in the currents of intellectual provincialism worldwide. As Tate remarks, this "new provincialism" of the intelligentsia is "that state in which regional men lose their origins in the past and its continuity into the present, and begin every day as if there had been no yesterday." This provincialism is "limited in time but not in space." It is a denigration of intellect, for when this provincialist "extends his own immediate necessities into the world, and assumes that the present moment is unique, he becomes the provincial man." These words from Tate's "New Provincialism," at the end of World War II.

To the Louisiana audience – addressed as regionalists, not provincials and sounding a Voegelinian theme – Percy remarks impediments to the literary assets of any Christian novelist, Catholic or Protestant. That writer's problem has to do "with the devaluation of the Christian vocabulary and the media inflation of its contents. The old words, God, grace, sin, redemption, which used to signify within a viable semiotic system now tend to be either exhausted, worn slick as poker chips and signifying as little, or else are heard as the most random noise of radio and TV preachers. The very word 'Christian' is not good news to most readers." Thus the writer-believer, whether Catholic or Protestant, "feels like Lancelot in search of the Holy Grail who finds himself at the end of his quest at a Tupperware party." Such then is the uncertainty of Christian signs available to the believing Southern writer at the moment, one who sees his South now become the "Sunbelt South increasingly informed by a flatulent Christendom and Yankee money-grubbing. . . ." The old signs, as Voegelin says, are now "opaque."

The occasions of the two talks differ, so that the matter at hand in his Cornell talk (Chekov) is more restricting to his appearance before that "Yankee" audience. However, one cannot fail to sense a different level of comfort with that audience nearer home at Southwestern Louisiana. To his "Yankee" audience he begins, not with questions of a relation of signs to Christian belief, but with a "scientific" theme. For "if I believe anything, it is that the primary business of literature and art is cognitive, a kind of finding out and knowing and telling, both in good times and in bad. . . . The pleasures of literature, the emotional gratification of reader and writer, follow upon and are secondary to the knowing." As for Christendom, it would hardly do to charge its erosion to Yankee money-grubbing before that audience, nor to that down-home flatulence inflating Southern locals, preposterously on display through TV evangelicals – those whom his Louisiana audience would at once recognize from their own experiences of such "preachers" as Percy variously satirizes in essays along the way and in his interviews. (Does New York have such radio evangelists? The answer is *Yes*.) Nevertheless, Christendom, he says to his Ivy League audience, has rather begun "to crumble, perhaps most noticeably under the onslaught of a Christian Søren Kierkegaard, in the last century." And so the Christian notion of man as wayfarer in search of his salvation no longer informs Western culture. In its place, what most of us now seem to be seeking are such familiar goals as "maturity, creativity, autonomy, rewarding interpersonal relations, and so forth." The ubiquitous suburban housewife, in this explanation of the decline of Christianity, has replaced the evangelical, at least at the national level, corresponding as a figure in Percy's rhetorical strategy to his Northern audience to the Yankee money-grubber in the Sunbelt South. Not that such caricatures aren't to be found in Dallas or Atlanta.

One might here reflect how differently a Flannery O'Connor would put a similar point, a point not far removed from Percy's, whether she makes it before a Louisiana or an Ivy League audience. For the Christian writer, she insists, "moral judgment will be implicit" in his vision, so that when we are invited "to represent the country according to survey, what we are asked to do is "to separate mystery from manners and judgment from vision," thereby to "establish the relative as absolute." Thus by contemporary dictates, conscience itself must be made to conform to statistical survey in order to make our isolation a bit more palatable in accepting whatever candidate or service or product offered ("The Fiction Writer & His Country"). Those who believe that art understood as proceeding "from a healthy, and not from a diseased, faculty of the mind will take what [the artist] shows them as a revelation, not of what ought to be but of what we are at a given time and under given circumstances; that is, as a limited revelation but revelation nevertheless." And since the moral dimension is necessarily implicit to such revelation, art serves a prophetic office, but by an indirection differing from Percy's sense of indirection, insofar as it recalls us to known but forgotten things about human nature itself at the spiritual, not the psychological, level. Thus, Flannery O'Connor's position is uncompromising in her manner to any audience.

Percy's words to his Cornell audience are similar we said, though put more cautiously. Art's primary business is "cognitive," being "a celebration of the way things are when they are right, and a diagnostic enterprise when they are wrong." Meanwhile, speaking for that diagnostic dimension of art, Percy does so with a sense that he is an outsider to both Yankeedom and to the South, "having been born and raised in Birmingham, Alabama, in a new house on a new golf course," as he observes on another occasion. As for himself as diagnostician, and from a point outside that diseased creature the Modern self: "The real pathology is not so much a moral decline, which is a symptom, not a primary phenomenon, but rather an ontological impoverishment; that is, a severe limitation or crippling of the very life of twentieth-century man." Thus man is left with the limited reality of "sex, violence, and death." Art becomes, then, an "instrument" for pathological exploration for Percy. Thus the "contemporary novelist . . . must be an epistemologist of sorts," exploring "Homo Sapiens *alienateus*."

We know what Flannery O'Connor's response would be to any "writer" who might seem to excuse all human weakness because human weakness is "human."

(See her "The Grotesque in Southern Fiction.") As for the suburban working housewife seeking consolation through a vague togetherness, she speaks of one of them who wrote her from California, complaining that "when the tired reader comes home at night, he wishes to read something that will lift up his heart," as some story of hers had failed to do. Her response: "I think that if her heart had been in the right place, it would have been lifted up." One such complaining reader wouldn't be so bad, she continues, but if "you multiply her two hundred and fifty thousand times . . . what you get is a book club." Or, she might now say, by two million to five million, what we get is the talk-show audience of afternoon television. O'Connor's words are from an address to a gathering in Macon, Georgia, but her deportment remains much the same when she is at the University of Scranton or at colleges in New York state, or writing for that liberal literary editor of the *Saturday Review of Literature*, Granville Hicks.

She gives no quarter, and indeed on occasion must have struck her audience as unmannerly, as Percy does not. She herself remarks that bad manners are better than no manners at all. (The lack of manners she tends to suggest is endemic to most audiences, but especially to Yankee ones.) As for heart and head set in radical tension by the spectacle of her fiction (as in her use of the "grotesque"), that is out of her charity of "bad manners," since for the hard of hearing she must shout (she says) and for the almost blind she must draw large and startling pictures. It is not that she lacks concern for epistemological questions related to ontological ones that occupy Percy, her steady attention to Thomas Aquinas evidence to that concern. It is rather that she is less willing than Percy sometimes is to flatter intellectual pretensions to those concerns. She is likely to declare nonsense to be nonsense more directly to her audience than will that Southern gentleman Walker Percy.

Reading them, then, we discover that they share a common vision, though witnessed in diverse manner, sharing a common acceptance of our given nature as *intellectual soul incarnate* – the sum of our givenness. They share as well a recognition of the severity of our dislocation at this juncture of history, our contention with givenness in consequence of will's insistent autonomy over the mystery of our *given* nature. It is a disjunction whose spectacle is that of enthusiastic delight in being lost in the cosmos, though haunted still by a desire to be found by – we know not what agent we hope for. Increasingly uncertain of our own capacity to "find ourselves," we enter a new millennium with false hope raised by millennial speculations, especially a hope vested in science and science's consequent technologies as devoted to the imputed sovereignties of the self. These two to the contrary, Percy and O'Connor, as prophetic poets recall us to hope through intellectual and spiritual mentors now largely discarded, especially to St. Augustine and St. Thomas. Each poet according to the manner suited to his peculiar gifts as poet.

XI

In reflecting on the rhetorical stance Percy chooses to address his Cornell audience or his Southwest Louisiana audience as differing from what we might expect of Flannery O'Connor, we nevertheless discover his arguments bearing a common recognition of the malady of spirit in the current state of Christendom. He is quite aware that the South is still haunted by Christ, aware as well that it is not Christ-centered. In demurring to her on this point as authority, he knows as does she that in this haunted country the con-agent flourishes, feeding upon the residue of the Southerner's concern as Christ-haunted soul and so vulnerable to a flatulence through a trickery of signs, insofar as he allows desire to become disoriented. In this regard, O'Connor's Bible salesman in "Good Country People" and Mister Shiftlet in "The Life You Save May Be Your Own" prove rivals as conmen to that invading Yankee moneygrubber who is a concern to Percy. The one as scalawag the other as carpetbagger depend upon rubrics rhetorically sold to rubes. St. Augustine would recognize them as akin in tactics to his own spiritual subversions as rhetor in those days when he was a "salesman of words in the markets of rhetoric," though they are hardly so learned as was he. Thus the South is to be made a province suited to a "Sunbelt Economy" by appropriation of the good to appetitive limits as if ultimate on the one hand, or to a charity perverted from its Christian purities, though conjured out of residual inclinations to love, on the other. Nor are the two mutually exclusive. Everywhere good country people find themselves victimized by scalawag or carpetbagger, though in the dramatic issue (at least in O'Connor's reading of the conflict) such conmen are already sufficiently prepared against by those "good country people" themselves, who are wily and adept in manipulations of the ambiguously "good."

Perhaps a conman strategy against such con-artists may prove effective defense, then? As artist, Percy rather insists upon such a strategy for himself as novelist, declaring himself as artist given to "playfulness . . . tricks . . . malice . . . naughtiness," in order to accomplish a "hoodwinking" of the reader. But he is openly so in an engagement of the Modernist malaise struck in North and South. By that gambit perhaps he may lure the reader toward self-recognition. In the interest of drama, perhaps his native – or almost native – place provides sufficient milieux, since it has to some extent escaped an absolute pervasiveness by that malaise. If we put it as O'Connor does, many Southerners still recognize the truly grotesque, in no small consequence of their being "Christ-haunted." And so good may yet be at least ambiguously good still within that locale, suited to Percy's game as diagnostic novelist. In respect to this advantage to him as novelist, he found reassurance in the correspondence between his own experiences of the South and Flannery O'Connor's, both of them attuned to a lingering in the South of old visions. One should notice here, in respect to Percy's or O'Connor's recognition of the South as a viable place to their prophetic concerns (remembering as well that the prophet's responsibility is to recall us to known but forgotten things), that they welcome the Southern cultural matrix for reasons more fundamental than, say, Tom Wolfe's choice of Atlanta and South Georgia in which to explore his Stoic theme of *Man in Full.*

One might even argue, sustaining the proposition by analysis of Wolfe's recently popular novel (1998), that when his editor persuaded Wolfe to shift his setting from New York to Atlanta for the novel, this was a collusion of scalawag and carpetbagger from one perspective. The congame played with setting seems intended to disguise what are at last pseudo-Stoical ambiences, lulling critical addresses to that novel. (Such has been the effect of that novel that it has encouraged pockets of Stoic revivalism.) Put another way, with Percy in mind, if one would seriously engage the theme suggested by Wolfe's title, the nature of *man in full,* he might better turn to Will Barrett of *The Last Gentleman* and *The Second Coming* as more persuasive than Wolfe's Charlie Croker, whom we first see "astride his Tennessee walking horse." In such a critical reflection and aware of historical, philosophical, theological complications embedded in the materials but used by Wolfe through selective excisions of a convenient matter to represent the "Southern culture" (in the manner Donald Davidson charges to Cash in *The Mind of the South*), the critic well remembers the Fugitive-Agrarian response to the Western infection of intellect as threatening both mind and spirit. That is the malaise imported and imposed by deracinated intellectuals. Eliot, in response to the Fugitive-Agrarian concerns as we have noted was fearful that they might in opposition defend only *tradition,* only the "Southern Culture" as unexamined in the light of *orthodoxy.* (Perhaps Eliot did not respond to the implications of Stark Young's argument in *I'll Take My Stand,* in which Young insists that "we are concerned first with a quality itself, not as our own [as Southerners] but as found anywhere; and that we defend certain qualities not because they belong to the South, but because the South belongs to them.") To defend a culture as history, Eliot had learned at some expense to his own spirit, is inadequate – is doomed. He had failed to effectively riddle the malaise by a skepticism served by an intensely rationalistic intellect.

Reaching such an impasse and reflecting as critic upon the uses of cultural symptomatics as they may serve art, the poet (Eliot had become convinced) must at least consider whether spiritual concerns attach to reality, some immanent perceived through symptoms but speaking toward the transcendent end of the person. (Hence a sudden popularity to poets of Bergson's *Creative Evolution.*) If in that reflection he turns literary critic with philosophical concerns, as does Eliot, he may reach some understanding of the inadequacy of symptoms taken alone, of spectacle as the limit of art to a world limited to the immanent. So Percy does also as he comes to concentrate upon the symptoms surfacing in Southern culture in the 20th century, those symptoms Percy speaks of as man's "looniness." There had been, by the time Percy must engage such concerns as relevant to his prospects as novelist, a considerable literature already addressing the concern, not only that from the Fugitive-Agrarians and Eliot and Gabriel Marcel on the one hand, but as Percy had discovered from Kierkegaard and Camus and Sartre on the other. Julian Green records in his diary Camus's encounter by an "ex-revolutionary" who says to Camus, "Monsieur Camus, I tell you very humbly that you are not [in a state of grace]." After a few minutes Camus responds, "I am your Augustine, before his conversion, I am struggling with the problem of evil and can't get to the end of it." He is struggling with those questions which brought Dostoevsky's Ivan Karamazov to the brink of madness, a struggle which Percy will declare necessary so that one may emerge an "ex-suicide."

Closer home there had been the essays of Richard Weaver out of his concern with the complexity of the South since Appomattox (now collected recently as Weaver's *Southern Essays*). And these had been written as preludes and postludes to Weaver's wider and deeper concern in *Ideas Have Consequences* published at the end of World War II – a small work stirring the intellectual community. In a conjunction with Marcel's *Homo Viator: Introduction to a Metaphysics of Hope,* and de Jouvenel's *On Power: The Natural History of Its Growth,* and of that small signal book by C. S. Lewis, *The Abolition of Man,* the poet-novelist might well be stirred beyond the established limits of art as a service to social and political concerns, a dislocation of his responsibility accomplished in both the East and the West. These works and many more become a new intellectual context to our discovering the poet's forced pandering to the modern malaise through his appropriations of cultural surfaces to ideological ends, from the Leftist literature of the 1930s (in both Russia and America), down to the Rightist literature in its new Libertarian mode, perhaps represented by such a recent novel as Tom Wolfe's *A Man in Full,* to be read (we suggested) in contrast to Percy's quest for truth immanent in symptoms in his *The Last Gentleman.*

By such reflections upon the intellectual climate as it evolves to Percy from the 1930s to the 1950s, we may appreciate his strategy of deliberate indirection. We recognize as well that he is finding himself as an intellectual among a curious lot of "traditionalists," some of whom are very open in their concern for the spiritual starvation of community, an aspect of the intellectual malaise controlled largely by an intellectual elite. And for many of these somewhat strange "Southerners" there appears as well an aspect of the heroic in their assuming the spiritual burden of intellectual lost causes. For knowing their limited prospects in their opposition to Modernism, they nevertheless attempt to recover the viable out of lost causes to a present witness, without becoming sentimentalists through temptations to nostalgia. In such circumstances to Percy, then, one may better understand his uneasiness when some early critics associate his concerns with those of the Fugitive-Agrarians. He is already fearful of "traditionalism" as shallow – as indeed it tends to be at the symptomatic level, the level dear to media attentions. So much for those writers of an imputed political "Right." But there is already as well an ancient tradition of the political "Left," reaching back to Occam as Richard Weaver argues.

It is easy enough, without careful reflection, to overlook, for instance, the rather defiant statement of intention of those young Fugitive poets, who in the initial issue of *The Fugitive* declared that "THE FUGITIVE flees from nothing faster than from the high-caste Brahmins of the Old South," the influence of which upon Southern literature has been that the literature "like any other stream whose source is stopped up" becomes stagnant. And again, the reflective critic might explicate that initial pronouncement as thematically central to Allen Tate's novel *The Fathers* and to Faulkner's *Absalom, Absalom!,* works appropriating even those stagnant cultural waters in a pursuit of the sources of stagnation. He might emphasize a contrast of the notoriety of *Gone with the Wind* in relation to these works, in tandem to an exploration of Percy's different uses of the symptomatic in *The Last Gentleman* as counter to Wolfe's uses in *A Man in Full.* Indeed such a critic might order his concern by a critical metaphor, the dangers of the carpetbagger and scalawag in contrast to Percy's or Melville's sense of the artist as conman.

Nevertheless, Percy does not abandon the seemingly ambiguous currency of signs though they be worn down by easy exchanges in confidence games played at the expense of spirit. By such uses occurs a devaluation of terms like *sin* and *grace* and the like, terms engineered as malleable by psychological theory in order to restamp the faces of such coins, reissuing them as poker chips in the appetitive game, with face values like Percy's satiric listing of some of them: *personal growth, emotional maturity, consciousness-raising, creativity, rewarding interpersonal relations.* Those are the goals prescribed, bought with such new coinage processed to stifle and conceal the immanence resonant in our experience of things. Our present experiences are residually echoed in those terms stored in the attic and labeled as the flotsam and jetsam of history. Not yet thrown out of the progressive ark of progress but soon. Thus signs are reduced Nominalistically. By calling that alchemy in question as but smoke and mirrors distorting the surface of the real, Percy might gain some eventual purchase in the reader's intellect, a stirring of a doubt about magical Modernism. Somewhere along the uncertain way, then, the diagnostic novelist might even help recover immanent truth to the Cause of truth, a Cause both immanent in being and transcendent of it. Meanwhile, he knows that "The very word 'Christian' is not good news to most readers." Thus he might well set aside those old actual terms which have suffered an inflation and collapse by autonomous intent to those diverse species of angelistic transcendences. He must get at such realities by an indirection. To puncture inflated signs (the *self* principle among them as a substitute for *soul*) reveals an emptiness filled by that willful self, if filled at all. That has been the strategy to appropriate a distortion, declaring the sign's sheer dependency on intellectual intentionality as the ultimate authority of truth. What if, with the authority of psychology as limited to creation's evolutionary immanence, the poet might push that dependence toward its collapse against the walls of mystery itself? To do so might require an acknowledgment by Modernist intellect of the transcendent, requiring a new accounting of psychological truths as themselves limited by a spiritual reality of man himself as intellectual soul incarnate. It is with such sly trickery, then, serving the intent to hoodwink us as Modernist readers, that Percy teases us toward recognition of our profound responsibility as *homo viator*. But that would prove a responsibility inadequately engaged if allowed to remain a concern only at the level of "social adjustment."

His strategy as "diagnostician" of the Modernist malaise, then, becomes that of the con-artist, conning us Modernists (if he can) into some recovery of known but forgotten ends proper to man as intellectual soul incarnate. His address to the problematics of art, as art may touch the truths of our spiritual nature, differs from that of Flannery O'Connor, though they share in a concern for man's ultimate end to his journeying of creation. That end, potential to our nature, unavoidably impinges upon art since the action of making is not *ex nihilo* but dependent upon givens. Both as Christian artists would dramatize the possible and probable spectacles as born of that given human nature itself. Both recognize as well that their instruments to that engagement (signs) have been severely decayed. There remains yet a difference. Percy's friendly delight lies in what he characterizes as that "looniness" consequent upon man's fallen nature, become now exacerbated by language in its rapid collapse. Flannery O'Connor's delight appears rather in her strategy as artist to a climactic arrest of her protagonist as conman, revealing the inadequacy of his easy confidence in his own signs in that his use of them proves sacrilegious, non-sacramental. The signs turn back upon him with ruthless effect. Consider Haze Motes's sign *clean* as thematically pervasive of *Wise Blood,* in relation to his denial of the existence of *sin* by a denial of the actuality of sin. He walks up and down in a desert territory where signs proclaim a locale of denizens who (many of them) suppose themselves clean – good country people – but cleansed of that historically resonant sign *sin*. They are clean because innocent of their own fallen nature, by their estimate, appropriating an uncleanliness as if cleanliness as Haze must finally concede. By the very intention to a seeming good, they present themselves as if but local yokels to any conman's estimate, but they become rather easy prey only when they are oblivious of self-deception about man's given nature as fallen. Because they in fact are acutely aware of fallenness, at least in others, they themselves prove counter-conmen, a lesson Haze learns at painful cost.

O'Connor's climactic moment in a story very often involves for her as artist an ironic recovery in her art of the Joycean "epiphany" to its orthodox signification, Joyce's use having become a sophisticated technique popular to our criticism as mere technique, a play of irony in signs suited to witty and clever exercises in explication (for the critic) and to the teaching of "creative art" at the time O'Connor writes. (Yes, she will say, there is a kind of "creative" writing that can be taught: it is the kind you must then teach people not to read.) What she recognizes is that the Joycean epiphany, especially as revealed in his *Dubliners*, borders fictionally upon sentimentality, being heavily dependent upon irony for a rescue from that sentimentality. For Joyce, the climactic moment, the moment of epiphany to his protagonist, is the disillusionment of a naive or worldly but unsophisticated protagonist, who through circumstance is forced into the "reality" of the sordid world in a psychological reversal. It is a world to which the mystery of good and evil seems hardly relevant. Joyce's "Romantic" hero thus is shattered in some degree only in his psychological deportment to a world that is suddenly revealed to him as other than he had supposed or wished it to be. But epiphany to a Joycean agent remains at most a psychological threshold to any spiritual concern. Thus it is a moment in that fiction yielding, not tragedy, but pathos. One might even (after long meditation upon Joyce's fiction) be tempted to conclude it restricted in its parameters to man as if man were perpetual adolescent. Especially Joyce's young protagonists prove at a far remove from O'Connor's adolescents, who know more thoroughly than their older antagonists the possible and probable perversity in man himself.

O'Connor's adolescents, let us say, are not yet so far removed from reality that they fail to recognize conmen when encountered (shades of the 1960s?). That, for instance is the occasion of a confrontation of Mr. Shiftlet in the denouement of "The Life You Save May Be Your Own." Mr. Shiftlet, having conned Mrs. Crater out of her automobile and escaped her idiot daughter, his "legal" wife, as well, nevertheless feels "more depressed than ever," and so he picks up a boy hitchhiking, a runaway obviously. Shiftlet, feeling oppressed, opens up a cheerful lie: "Son . . . I got the best old mother in the world so I reckon you only got the second best." To the response of the boy's dark silent suspicion, he enlarges. "It's nothing so sweet . . . as a boy's mother," his own being "a angel of Gawd." The response from the boy is "You go to the devil! . . . My old woman is a flea bag and yours is a stinking pole cat!" – shouted as he leaps from the moving rattletrap. Mr. Shiftlet, stunned, speeds up. Though he cannot deal with it at the moment, he has at least an intimation of having experienced a formidable rebuke, an epiphany more fundamental, that is, than merely psychological. He accelerates toward Mobile, carrying his depression with him unrelieved, evidence of the spiritual vacuum he has not yet named.

And so O'Connor, in her adaptation of the epiphany to her own ends, dramatizes an effect in her protagonist (one thinks especially of the extended treatment of Young Francis Marion Tarwater in this respect) who is as protagonist hardly innocent or naive in respect to the outer world's threatening perversity, though having yet to discover that perversity in himself. Indeed, her protagonist makes his defense – self-esteem, in an evaluation of himself as a "self" enabled to a transcendence through clever deceptions, conquering the impinging world by a deliberate separation from that world's threatening presence. He dreams the strategy made effective through his virtues as con-artist, enabled he supposes to out-con his antagonist of the moment. In varying degrees of self-violence in her protagonist, then, her epiphany to a protagnoist shatters his pretense to self-salvation, sometimes leaving such an agent devastated, as is Mr. Shiftlet or Asbury or Hulga in their stories. But they are sometimes set upon a road to spiritual recovery as is Young Tarwater in *The Violent Bear It Away* and Haze Motes in his final admission of uncleanliness. There is an encounter with an intended victim, supposed less clever than the protagonist as judged by surface signs. But usually it is this intended victim of an intended exploitation who proves more con-artist than the would-be predatory journeyman himself. How very old evil proves to be to her arrested protagonist.

One of her most effective presentations of this tensional action leads to an "epiphany" in that contest alluded to between the Bible salesman and that intellectually adolescent Hulga of "Good Country People." Hulga takes him as one of those pious country folk, much like her mother. Hulga has already provided herself with a defense against these silly country creatures by her conversion to Existentialism, having pursued this new "religion" in a rigorous academic training. She occupies a world to which she is superior by virtue of that trained intellect. And so, encountering the "good" Bible salesman, she intends to play a destructive game upon him. She does not notice that he is walking to and fro in the land, selling Bibles to good country people in something like a parody of the old Adversary in the Book of Job. She will seduce him she thinks, thus showing him he isn't "good" for all his pretended deportment as good. That game will serve as well a spiteful revenge against her mother, a revenge possible to her because she herself is intellectually committed to nothingness. How shocking, then, to discover at the moment of her intended triumph in the barn loft the contents of the Bible salesman's fake Bible: a whiskey flask, a deck of cards, and a box of condoms. And how humiliating then to have him take her false leg as another trophy, to add to the glass eye from an earlier seduction. But above all, how devastating to be left simmering in the acid of his final words to her: "You ain't so smart. I been believing in nothing ever since I was born!"

Through her fiction, O'Connor allows us to see the fundamental ground of human nature itself: all have sinned, all have fallen short of the mark, and so all have become dependent upon the grace of Love's Sacrifice. Miss O'Connor shouts to an "American" audience which no longer recognizes the grotesqueness of its denial of sin, and she does so through the common shibboleths of sentimental tenderness toward "mankind," whose shocking spectacle becomes at its most grotesque the gas chamber at Auschwitz. Nor was she unaware of how convenient to sinful man his failure to recognize his situation. Hence her shouting through the megaphone of grotesquery. Her "American" – her Modernist – audience resists this recognition, especially relieved to respond to her with enthusiasm if they are allowed the illusion that she intends a social satire depicting the provincial South, rather than delivering a devastating revelation of that larger intellectual provincialism so crucial to the sophisticated intellectual in his pseudo-"transcendence." Ah, those loony Southerners – how well she pictures them in her fiction. They must be the object of her wry humor, since she renders so acutely their comical voices!

Such then is the strategy of Flannery O'Connor as diagnostician of the perennial malady of the soul, a strategy I have pursued more thoroughly in *Why Flannery O'Connor Stayed Home* and *Why Poe Drank Liquor*, but more especially in *Why Hawthorne Was Melancholy*. O'Connor finds in Hawthorne a concern to keep alive man's relation to creation through "Romances," in which he would reveal the futility of that Puritan address to *homo viator,* through which man must be denatured as it were so that the soul may be exalted by severe denigration of the body. To see what she is talking about, one need only look closely at Hawthorne's uses of Eliot's "objective correlatives" in that story already introduced, his "The Maypole of Merry Mount." When Governor Endicott (that actually historical Puritan whose ideological spiritualism Hawthorne appropriates to his "Tale") interrupts the woodland wedding festival, he can see only a violent paganism underway at the expense of soul. He comes clad in armor. Indeed, this man seems "wrought of iron," an iron somehow "gifted with life and thought." The gaiety of Comus and his creatures, celebrating the woodland marriage, is chilled. Their images flit as reflected in Endicott's polished armor. In many of his tales, then, Hawthorne attempts emblems that are at once imagistic and symbolic. There is that scar on beauty in "The Birthmark," we noticed. And there is the scarlet "A" which Hester must wear, matched by that secret emblem on her lover's breast that is a torment to him such as is the barbwire Haze wraps around his chest. The new scientist and Puritan divine are troubled on either hand by their gnostic reduction of man from the old recognition that as intellectual soul incarnate man is radically fallen from grace. Theirs is an address to man as *homo viator* but from a perspective awry from the vision St. Augustine and St. Thomas witness in their theology and philosophy.

Hawthorne already senses what will become of this distortion as it becomes transformed into a popular doctrine: the abuses of nature and human nature through pragmatism, which as a persuasive doctrine becomes helpmeet to Positivistic autonomy. Or so we argue. It is with the consequent effects of this transmogrification of the spiritual to secular limit that O'Connor and Percy must deal – the one as prophetic poet, the other as diagnostic physician. And so they share in a vision of the progressive deracination of intellect, accomplished through careless or intentional dislocations engineered through signs, until the Modernist mind becomes lost in the cosmos. Percy finds himself required to examine all along his way the nature of his own personal difficulty as an "American" novelist, to a degree not affecting O'Connor. He recognizes a seemingly personal handicap in being both Southern and Catholic, a burden hardly pronounced in Flannery O'Connor's concerns. The difficulty is of such a complexity to Percy, or so he takes it to be, that an initial engagement of the loony spectacle of *homo viator* in the Modernist context seems the necessary gambit as artist, requiring his being the diagnostic pathologist of cultural symptoms.

In the course of his development of his peculiar gift as novelist, his strategy of indirection, he might well fear himself threatened by his own arrest in the hidden depths of loony mankind. Such a writer may discover along his way, after many arrests but always unwilling to surrender either his ambiguous "Southernness" or the ascent to the Pascalian gamble that draws him into Catholicism, that he is (at the end of his journey) even closer as *homo viator* to O'Connor's understanding than he at first supposed. She seems to have been born believing Something, rather than as the Bible salesman as con-artist, believing Nothing. She resists from the beginning the act whereby intellect abstracts form from created things to the convenience of making an abstract "world" in which consciousness may be safely detached into the "self," a world of art "created" through a disembodiment of the givenness of the cosmos. In sum, a "Supreme Fiction." That is the artist's version of what his scientist kinsman would manipulate, actual persons and things reduced by a form extracted, adjusted, and then reimposed upon givenness through ignoring the *possible* or *probable* as it resonates out of the *given*. Such a gnostic Modernist would become as *homo viator* the god of his own closed world. He, too, is moved by faith. But his faith rests in the authority of autonomous, willed action, that being his only apparent rescue.

Though granting O'Connor's assertion that "The modern world is a territory largely occupied by the devil," Percy is interested not in "the malevolence of man – so what else is new? – but in his looniness." This difference between them we might explore by juxtaposing *Love in the Ruins* and *Thanatos Syndrome* to O'Connor's two novels. But in doing so we will discover an issue of interest beyond looniness for Percy, despite such an occasional lapse (as he concedes) into the self-indulgence like that of his "Marx-brothers moviescript" aimed at "certain semioticists, primatologists, and post-structuralist critics" in *Thanatos Syndrome.* If indeed Flannery O'Connor sets out in her calling as prophetic poet as one already largely escaped from the entrapping suffocation of Modernist ideology, Percy comes to discover his calling as poet by struggling with that very entrapment, emerging by his labor from those oppressive ideological swamps – from the Modernist version of Dante's "dark wood" to be more clearly seen from his gained perspective. This is not to say, of course, that somewhere along her own way Flannery O'Connor did not dawn to herself as lost in such a world. We are not attempting to establish any actual moment for either poet like that of Saul of Tarsus on the road to Damascus, though we cannot escape a recognition that in both these Southerners there is an attempt to dramatize just such moments in their fictional agents – an epiphany more resonant than psychological recognition of a circumstantial arrest to the agent's "self" in its social context. We need only look more closely at Haze Motes peering down at the museum mummy, or at Binx's encounter of a stranger with an ash-cross on his forehead outside the church (Binx on his way to that version of Plato's Cave, the neighborhood moviehouse). Binx's moment measures a movement from the library steps, where he is agreeing with antithetic cultural-political doctrines encountered in the library's journals. His, too, has been a progress *toward* a resonant epiphany, one that Eliot would recognize as involving an encounter of the Word in the word at last.

Our concern is not, therefore, with biographically personal experiences of O'Connor or Percy, such spectacle as has made the fortunes of *People Magazine.* It is rather to remark that, in dealing with the signposts each poet has left us in our common desert, each erects those signposts in differing circumstances to his own journeying and out of differing gifts as poets. This is to speak of the *personal*, the discrete *personhood* of each as created. Out of such unique particularities – inherent accidents of an essential nature as *this* person – they engage our common responsibility to make. Reading their made signs accurately, then, we may acknowledge such difference as somewhat affecting their signs. That leads us to speculate that the one deploys signs as one already escaped entrapment (O'Connor), while the other engages signs in the process of escaping from an entrapment of the self as an intellectual soul incarnate (Percy). Percy discovers himself called by his nature to the offices of the poet by engaging the mystery of sign. It is a difference through which we may gain some purchase of understanding of both as seen by analogy of their kinship. And along our own reflective way in these pages, we have recalled and shall recall analogous kinship to other poets.

Eliot, for instance, in his *Collected Poems,* reveals a closer correspondence to Percy by his actions of art than to Dante (or to O'Connor), though Dante almost from his setting out is for Eliot his Virgil to Dante's journeying as *homo viator.* On the other hand, Dante as *person* becomes an imagined agent to Dante's own mythical journey, a fictional agent in the *Divine Comedy.* As agent in that fiction, he unfolds a journey somewhat awkwardly paralleled by Eliot and Percy. The maker of that poem, Dante the actual person, is projected as a fictional agent who has been rescued as a self. As person in the office of poet, he is now obligated, as a present actual poet, to witness the imagined journey – the *possible* journey – in a confessional reminiscence. His recapitulation of that journey is his made poem, an incarnation of signs by Dante as an actual person. Eliot (and Percy), to the contrary, work out their possible rescue as proceeding concomitantly with their making of signs along their actual way. Both, at their end and in their final "poems," arrive at the place from which they had set out as actual persons. And as persons (poets) they recognize, *see*, that point of departure with an understanding for the first time – Eliot in his *Little Gidding,* Percy in *Thanatos Syndrome.* It is the relation of the personal to the unfolding of their art in both Eliot and Percy that differs from the unfolding for Dante and O'Connor in their work. Eliot articulates this point at the close of his last important poem, *Little Gidding.* The end of all our exploring has been in order that we might arrive "where we started," at which point we "know the place for the first time."

If such a speculative suggestion – that the inescapable *personal* is intrinsic to the poet's work – is tenable, we might well anticipate some recognition by the poet of his having arrived at his point of departure, but only at his end as poet. As we have already suggested, Percy reaches that point in his *Thanatos Syndrome,* in which a dramatic ambiance suggests the affinity Percy feels to his Tom More. He had anticipated as much at the outset, when he writes Caroline Gordon that, if her husband Allen Tate intends "forming a St. Thomas More Society I want in" (April 4, 1952). But at his setting-out as poet, Percy first assumes then sets aside a direct engagement of evil as of no immediate or primary concern. The potential malevolence, endemic to human nature as fallen, is not central to his address as it is to Flannery O'Connor's. What else is new? he will ask. He does not deny evil as a reality. His interest is rather in the symptomatics of evil, as if by that attention he might lessen somewhat the agony of spirit that threatens us in our "modern malaise."

By that address he makes comic man's ridiculous pretensions to self-sufficiency. Though acknowledging evil by indirection, he is sympathetic to man's symptomatic consequences. Perhaps thereby he makes more tolerable our sojourning of what O'Connor insists is territory in which the Adversary has established a subtle sovereign, maintaining power over the world through that trickery whereby intellect is persuaded that the Devil does not even exist. That has also been Ivan Karamazov's denial, though one hardly calls *The Brothers Karamazov* a comic novel. How arresting, to both O'Connor and Percy, must be that scene in which Ivan attempts to persuade Alyosha of an actual encounter with the Devil, followed by Ivan's physical, intellectual, and spiritual collapse. It is a scene far other than Percy's "Marx-brothers moviescript" aimed at semioticists and others of a similar persuasion, the zoo scene in *Thanatos Syndrome.* More closely allied to Dostoevsky's manner, O'Connor gives us the scene in *Wise Blood* in which Haze comes to a self-recognition, leaning over the museum display case at the center of Taulkingham's zoo. She provides a comic dimension to the scene, but the dramatic effect proves Haze closer to Ivan in his spiritual collapse than to the hilarious spectacle of Percy's zoo scene of doctors regressed to primates. Percy wittily presents Darwinian evolution forced into a reverse through machinations of science, in contrast to Haze's recognition that he is not "clean" as he has so insistently pronounced as an "innerleckchul" up to that point. His epiphany begins when he sees the mummified "A-rab" through his own reflection in the glass case, with a consequent violent resistance to an acknowledgment of his fallen state.

From the beginning, then, O'Connor feels more confident of Hawthorne and Dostoevsky as prophetic witnesses of a malign world, become malign because allowed by man to be governed by Satan. It is a world evolved by the individual will in a retrogression from that Epiphany of all epiphanies, the coming into the world of God in Jesus. The pursuit has been of an absolute freedom, requiring rejection of all givenness. For her, the primary sin at issue is called Pride, widely manifest in her view by the Western intelligentsia. That bumblingly malevolent conman Onnie Jay Holy (Hoover Shoates) leaves his dialectical argument with Haze Motes unresolved with a bitter observation: "That's the trouble with you innerleckchuls. . . . you don't never have nothing to show for what you're saying." O'Connor would not gainsay him. But how fascinatingly complex that saying! To arrive at that unsayable nothingness, human nature must be declared the sum of blind evolution's thrust upward, through biochemical but accidental existences. In making that theory acceptable, as if it were comprehensive of human nature, we are required to undergo an intellectual purging whereby intellect sloughs off any residual waste still clinging in it from old visions of itself. Otherwise it cannot levitate by its purified angelism.

That is a purification made systematic under the auspices of Pride as converted into a governing virtue. Be your self, an ambiguous charge which Socrates spends his life riddling, becomes "You can be whatever you want to be" in its diabolical reformulation. And so at our own moment, in the current stage of transcendent angelism of intellect on the threshold of a new millennium, how welcomed the magic of the gene has become, refuting all our Onnie Jay Holys. Everywhere, things are transformed, justified by what the genetic innerlectual says. Behold reconstituted soybeans! And genetically altered corn to be fed to cloned cattle and sheep and monkeys! And so, perhaps inevitably, we shall produce on order not only a girl or a boy baby, but one destined to rival Einstein or Beethoven. Or so the false freedom of intentionality seems to suggest.

A liberated intellectual might (though perhaps reluctantly) grant there to *have* been – in history past – a certain advantage to the ancient makeshift readings of human nature as sinful. Historically (he might say) that illusional concept served toward ordering social machinery, that primitive ordering accomplished under the universally enchanting rubric of the "common good." This old reading of the "common good" depended upon a *metaphysics* revealing *good* and *evil,* under that other false rubric of *sin* as if a reality descending in man as *fallen* from *grace*: quaint terms. But that historical misreading was but an *accidental* use of Nominalistic power, innocent of the unreality of *sin.* Such old awkward service nevertheless allowed time to evolve the authority of autonomous intellect over social and biological beings. Now is the time when genetic science must replace all that old awkward labor of intellect. Genetic science itself may therefore replace and slowly eradicate the residual false concept of Sin as explaining the inadequacy of what was once called *being.* Put more decisively, genetic science obviates grace.

That (Miss O'Connor might suggest wryly) is the illusion required if system is to be sustained in gnostic impositions of a "world" upon the cosmos. From her perspective, that becomes the last defense against an intuited suspicion that the cosmos is created, a suspicion inevitable to the truly philosophical mind. For that reason, philosophy born of awe in the presence of being, becomes a mode of intellectual address (through wonder) to the self-evident cosmos. And it is a haunting possibility revived in intellect again and again. From the Modernist perspective therefore philosophy must be forced to a subservience of systematic science. If an Eric Voegelin sees philosophy as springing from "the love of being," that is not sufficient. For what is this "love" but a sum of biochemical energy seeking an object to dominate? Hegel or Hobbes were prophetic on the point. Gnosis in its Modernist aspect must desire "dominion over being," must require the building of systems. But, as Voegelin adds to his phrase, to maintain system requires a universal prohibition of questions put to system or to any intellect originating a particular system. It must be a law stringently enforced (one adds), more stringently than that against alcohol in the XVIII Amendment to the Constitution. By the severity of this new prohibition, system becomes ascendant over philosophy, replacing metaphysics as authoritative governor of intellectual action. Unlike our Modernist circumstances, Voegelin observes, it never occurred "to the Greek to prohibit analytical inquiry as such," ours being "a phenomenon unknown to antiquity that permeates our modern societies so completely that its ubiquity scarcely leaves us any room to see it at all: the prohibition of the examination of gnostic premises," that prohibition elevated as a "part of dogma," and always in the name of the common good.

The consequences to our world has become random civil wars, ideologically motivated. But even so, these struggles are not over whether system is the ideal – system abstracted from the cosmos by logical Positivism. Rather, the question is over *which* system is to dominate. And the resolution of embattled ideologies depends upon power in the moment. That is why Stalin's sardonic response to Papal opposition makes suitable epigraph for the spectrum of these wars: "How many divisions has the Pope?" By the ascendancy of *system* as a mutually honored universal principle, though among contentious gnostic intellects, there rises the dominance of particular totalitarians according to the relativity of power to each. We are used to genocide and ethnic cleansing from Stalin to Balkan tyrants yet with us. What we have not yet recognized is the pervasive destruction of intellect sanctioned by the dogma of declaring the person sovereign within the cosmos. In the past decade, for instance, this has led to the shocking destruction of the academy under the impetus of the "politically correct" as codicil to system, a dogma established thereby which is aimed directly at any philosophical questioning of system.

Not that such totalitarianism is as yet conspicuous through spectacles such as have been frequent in the history of actual wars in the century just past. But one need only look closely at the fate of some academics who resist this sophistry as practiced increasingly by the academy for the convenience of diverse ideological causes. That such academic heroes still survive needs only a survey of issues of *Academic Questions,* the quarterly published by The National Association of Scholars in defense of the academy to verify. (An instance to the point: not long ago some of the radical faculty at Duke University, in secure tenured positions, attempted to have banned from that institution a chapter of this National

Association of Scholars which a few brave scholars were attempting to form.) Nor that some freedom of questioning is not allowed, within parameters. The parameters nevertheless rather strictly require that such questioning deal with the *further* perfection of system, not with possible problems in the foundation of system itself as if our ultimate salvation. This limited freedom, indeed, is encouraged as the means to an evolution of system to a transcendent perfection as instrument overpowering being itself. Restricted philosophy is useful to system, as restricted poetry proved useful to Lenin and Stalin. It is only by submission to the system as beyond questioning, however, that the philosopher may gain admittance to the Courts of Autonomous Intellect.

There is an Armageddon at hand to Modernist man at millennium's close. He faces his own abolition, self-induced. It seems a general movement toward the last act of rejection possible, save one – Ivan's (and Percy's) serious contemplation as a person of returning his "ticket" to creation. But in that event general or particular, the only God available to accept that returned ticket is the God called Nothingness. As Percy would have it in respect to Armageddon at the personal limit, the serious contemplation of that precipitous action becomes for the discrete (the specific) Modernist intellect a possible rescue, his becoming not an actual but an "ex-suicide" through his recognition that his old gnostic "truth" about the self is but illusion. At morning that ex-suicide "opens his front door, sits down on the steps, and laughs," knowing his option: if he does not laugh he can always commit suicide. In that knowledge, he "has nothing to lose by being alive." And so he discovers that it "is good to be alive," a consent to his own *being* that refutes flirtations with nothingness. He may even go to work happily, "because he doesn't have to," that return ticket safely hidden in his billfold, no doubt along with credit cards. Such is the point for Percy, in relation to which we the better understand that for him life is made tolerable, whereupon he practices signs as a diagnostic novelist of that more general flow of his fellows toward Armageddon. He makes the Pascalian gamble, but holds on to that ticket. It is here that we may once more make a contrast to Flannery O'Connor, the better to understand Percy's pleasure in life, a life embraced with gusto, as if thereby he is better enabled to observe the looniness of *homo viator* without temptations to despair.

To remind ourselves of this contrast between these two Southern Catholics, we advert once more to that difference Percy makes quite explicit between himself and O'Connor. It is the passage in his *Paris Review* interview (1987), already introduced: "I am perfectly willing," he says, "to believe Flannery O'Connor when she said, and she wasn't kidding [as we might take Percy to be kidding had he made such a remark, leaving his reader uncertain of the position taken], that the modern world is a territory largely occupied by the devil. No one doubts the malevolence abroad in the world. But the world is also deranged. What interests me as novelist is not the malevolence of man – so what else is new? – but his looniness. The looniness, that is to say, of the 'normal' denizen of the Western world who, I think it fair to say, doesn't know who he is, what he believes, or what he is doing. This unprecedented state of affairs is, I suggest, the domain of the 'diagnostic' novelist."

There is in this argument, one is tempted to say, a naiveté about the relation of the derangement of such a "normal denizen," the everyday American we might say, as it occasions his condition of being lost. For, from the Church's position that disorientation is inevitable consequence effected by malevolent will. That no one doubts the malevolence abroad in the world misses the point from this perspective, as Percy himself on other occasions (especially in his last essays) is quite aware. It is, indeed, the confusion within the popular spirit, the "everyone" as aware that something has gone awry, that Percy himself attends through his fiction. The drama in his agents depends upon a spectrum (by degree) of restlessness, a diverse awareness that ours is an age increasingly lost in the cosmos. That is why Percy will say that, having abandoned Christian belief, our concerns are with "maturity, creativity, autonomy, rewarding interpersonal relations." Such the cliché terms yet popular, not yet removed to the attic of terms outworn, though well on the way.

Those terms speak symptomatically for Percy as pathologist of the Modernist malaise, leading him by satiric playfulness to address the malady at the level of our age's psychological disorientation within the grounds of being. To address it directly as evidencing spiritual deracination might risk (or so he seems to conclude) his alienating most of us from his witness. To address spiritual malady by satiric indirection allows us as reader, for the moment at least, to think the person pilloried must be someone quite other than ourselves. Indeed, that is the address which he supercedes by playfulness in *Lost in the Cosmos,* putting his reader on the spot again and again by requiring a direct address to a systematic exploration of the reader's own "self," turning the Modernist confidence in system back upon itself.

Since system depends upon signs made acceptable to a degree sufficient to concentrate force toward ends, even ideological ends, it is the nature of sign itself which requires Percy's consideration. Our recent history is so strewn with effective manipulations of signs to ideological ends as to call attention to the problematic nature of sign. One need hardly rehearse the growing recognitions of language's decay in our time, alarms sounded as variously as by Orwell and C. S. Lewis and Richard Weaver. What may be overlooked in this concern for the symptomatic evidences is that the roots of this disorder lie in human nature itself, principally in pride. Given pathological evidence of the disorder, established on slides suited to the microscope of analytical logic, we might discover those slides evidencing excisions from history, so that history itself may become suspect, rather than man's fallen nature as manifested historically in his pursuit of power over being.

There is, then, an attention to that "parenthesis" that interested David Jones in his poem addressing the Battle of the Somme and his participation in it. Jones discovers subsequently that he has entered a larger parenthesis of history, the Modernist world as measured from the Renaissance calendar down to World War I. He will in his reflections, however, conclude that the truly significant parenthesis in history was an intercessory rescue, largely ignored or by now unrecognized. The historical signs of that enclosing of history by that parenthesis are largely buried in desert sands or – as Percy suggests – stored in the attic. That is the parenthesis between the Incarnation and the Ascension, a closure at a point in history subsuming history as it were, an event which proves a mystery enclosing all time and place by Love. The Modernist wanderer enters, experiencing at first perhaps a wrenching of his own signs as they fail to correspond to the truth of things. And so a poet such as Eliot discovers that "objective correlatives" already touch a reality into which words so often dissolve as inadequate to that reality. In the penultimate section of his "Ash-Wednesday," that is for him the new experience he undertakes to touch with signs.

That section of his poem is atumble with signs, in which there is hardly a reassuring music accompanying them. For some critics of the poem, here is a failure of poetry. It might rather be seen as reflecting dramatically a nadir to intellect, out of which issues the resolution of the final section of the poem. It is, we might say, Eliot's attempt to capture in signs an experience out of which he himself has escaped as an "ex-suicide." A few lines, in which there is an awkwardness of internal rhyme, as opposed to our usual sense of orderly prosody using rhyme, a sense of metrics and prosody as under the poet's strict control. That order may prove inadequate to an immediacy of actual experience, so that the disorder Eliot attempts rather speaks a possibility of order not yet secured. In this respect, he attempts a spiritual realism.

> Where shall the word be found, where will the word
> Resound? Not here, there is not enough silence
> Not on the sea or on the islands, not
> On the mainland, in the desert or the rain land,
> For those who walk in darkness. . . .

The lines go on in similar manner, echoing as it were an inception of spiritual despair such as we might remember Keats to have experienced in far more orderly lines. In his "Ode to a Nightingale" Keats attempts to force fancy's signs, declaring that "Haply the Queen Moon is on her throne clustered round by all her starry fays." But then the falling away from false language, back into "embalmed darkness" such as threatens the voice.

In Eliot's poem, though in a mode quite "modern," Eliot catches a moment not unlike that Keats experiences. In such a juxtaposition of "Romantics" (Eliot and Keats) we counter Keats's concluding stanzas of his Ode to the final section of Eliot's "Ash-Wednesday" and discover that Eliot rises, not falls into his sole self. There is an almost palpable presence in the signs rising above entrapment. We note as well that the voice is not a mask as in "Prufrock," but an active witness of the poet. In rising beyond an entrapment by despair as a "sole self," he does so through signs recovered as *proportionate* to the actualities of an existence which has become almost lost in the cosmos. His witness is to a labor toward purifying the dialect of the tribe, enacting a possible rescue in the hope of maintaining in the "tribe" a sense of community as persons. Such a labor as poet may require the seemingly awkward attempt of his Section V of "Ash-Wednesday," the penultimate section of that poem, concerned with the "lost . . . spent . . . unspoken, unheard . . . word," leaving "the unspoken word" destitute since separated from "the Word unheard." An awkward, stumbling deployment of words as poetry. We might discover it a revisiting of the experience of being lost, echoing a common experience, in our words that have become separated from that Word which already was "in the beginning." As such, this is a preparation, out of the experiences of lostness, for the prayer that concludes the poem: " . . . let my cry come unto Thee," unto the Word as a mystery attending even our weak words though we be separated from that Word. In this respect, that next-last section of Eliot's poem of penance, "Ash-Wednesday," is a dramatic *tour de force,* imitating our sense of confusion when we are lost in the desert, our experience of being lost as a person in what we declare an accidental cosmos. And as such, Eliot's poem proves also akin by analogy to Percy's extended *tour de force,* his *Lost in the Cosmos,* especially bearing a parallel in its next last section to that penultimate section of Percy's work to which we have paid special attention, that section engaging the possibility of rescue in the desert but as an "ex-suicide."

What we may remind ourselves of at this moment, lest we too become easy victim to the cunning of history's deceptions, is that it was ever thus, since Adam. And the cause of our disaffection with givenness, leading us lost in the desert, is our own distortion of or ameliorating of signs. That loss disjoins sign itself from the ontological ground we call being. To see this self-destruction through perverted sign, we recall an argument from Josef Pieper, that steady Thomist who views Western history with an inclusiveness reminiscent of the largeness of the view we value in Eric Voegelin. A decade before Percy's *Lost in the Cosmos,* Pieper addresses our concerns in an essay translated as "Abuse of Language, Abuse of Power." His concern is at once to alert us to a common dire predicament as selves lost in the cosmos and to reveal by his own diagnosis of our lostness the causes occasioning it. Pieper reveals this malady as both an ancient and an abiding circumstance to any self. Pieper does not, save by implication, go all the way back to Adam. Nor does he introduce out of that Parenthetic moment in history of the Incarnation-Ascension the witness of St. Peter (in his Second Epistle). St. Peter warns against those who "with feigned words make merchandise of you." Instead, he is concerned for the mystery of sign and the abuse of sign through magic. He turns to that steady philosophical presence Plato, exploring Plato's "lifelong battle with the sophists."

Pieper insists that word and language form the medium that sustains our existence in common as persons, sustains "the human spirit as such." Both word and language, he knows, are always under perverse attack by those intent upon power over being. Remember Gorgias, the sophist as early Nihilist, whom Socrates contends with. It is he who asserts that "nothing is," – that is (in Pieper's words), "there is no such thing as *being*." It is Gorgias who argues therefore, concerning signs, that by our use of signs we intend only pure form, form emptied of substantive implications, an argument subtly revived in Nominalism as an instrument against being. That is, Gorgias contends for a "pure aesthetics" of sign. But as Socrates is aware, it is not aesthetics that is at issue, as if Gorgias would be a poet superior to our own Mallarmé. There is rather a hidden agenda, an intentionality to power through signs by means of their dislocation from reality. Again, as Pieper puts it, the "word is perverted and debased to become a catalyst, a drug, as it were, and is as such administered [as an] *instrument of power. . . .*" Socrates, in his amused recognition of this strategy of the Sophist, responds to Gorgias's argument toward power: "You are truly experts in this; you must have a deep understanding of human nature; you know exactly which spot to hit." Gorgias thinks he knows that spot in Socrates, who himself wonders whether his own calling has been that of poet rather than philosopher. To play the "aesthetic" card against Socrates is his sophistical (his sophist's) gambit against the almost caustic humor in Socrates' opposition.

And so Pieper, in his essay on the abuse of language in order to make it the means to power, pronounces ours an age of sophistry, in which by a deliberate "degeneration of language" language itself is turned "into an instrument of rape," an instrument serving a variety of totalitarian intents to power. For "on the one side a pseudoauthority, not legitimized by any form of superiority," would establish itself over, "on the other [side,] a state of mental bondage." That is the sophist's adaptation of dialects to the end of dominance over person. In his conclusion, Pieper turns to our current academy as the last hope of recovery from our self-enslavement executed through language, though he is not very hopeful of our prospects. He makes a passionate defense of the "Academic" against the sophists' version of the academy, an argument "antisophistic." Pieper's anticipation of endangerment to the academy by sophistry become the dominant intellectual principle has unfolded to us, self-evident in the years since his essay.

Such is the academy as Walker Percy and Flannery O'Connor are making in their fictions. Those academies bent toward sophistry as if the only truth at first fascinated them. Both writers already recognized, as does Pieper and as had Eliot and Lewis and Weaver, that the academy is endangered. They could but deport themselves warily when "on campus." (Flannery O'Connor on one occasion I witnessed, having given a reading of "A Good Man Is Hard to Find," excused herself from the festivities that were to follow, saying she had to get back home to Andalusia, her farm near Milledgeville, to "feed the chickens.") Percy uses a somewhat different approach, not much given to actual peacocks and chickens as a rescue. One might, even at such festivities "on campus" in which he participated, come to suspect that he was more like Dante doing research in dark regions, sojourning intellectual Tupperware parties, perhaps making notes toward *Lost in the Cosmos.* His very public and playful assertion of his wily position as novelist serves his necessities as poet – he not apt to excuse himself to go feed alligators in his Louisiana swamp. By such deprecation of his intentions in his fiction one need not take him too seriously, if instead one suppose his fiction largely an entertainment of the intellectually sophisticated.

Such indirection itself: that he may well have discovered in that early mentor of his, Kierkegaard. Josef Pieper in his essay on our abuse of language, seeing our age as perhaps more pervasively sophistic than Plato's, reminds us of Kierkegaard's awareness of sophistry in its Modernist revisions. In Kierkegaard's late *On the Approach Employed in My Literary Activity,* Pieper reminds us that the outlander Dane pronounces as necessary to his addressing his reader that he must "Cajole them into the truth!" The argument runs on, in Pieper's summary: "First, . . . you have to tell them something nice, aesthetic, to capture people's attention – launch the boat as it were. Then, when it is floating along, let it run aground: namely, on the rock of truth. Better hurry, though, to get away from there immediately; they will try to kill you." W. H. Auden, that sometime disciple of Kierkegaard, perhaps recognized a similar inclination in Melville, whom he declares to have heard the gale of the world that blows him "Past the Cape Horn of sensible success" and raises a siren song in doing so: "This rock is Eden, Shipwreck here." Too direct? Better to skirt that rock by posting signs of indirection, running aground on a more comfortable beach, cajoling those in sophistic bondage so that they might risk the truth of things. Most centrally for Percy's indirection, that truth is of the self as a thing created, an intellectual soul incarnate.

XII

From a direct engagement of the Modernist malaise from the Christian perspective such as Percy professes, one must conclude it an effect of spiritual deracination out of a turning of the self to itself in order to command creation to the sole or at least primary benefit of that self in its appetitive nature. That is the sophist's mode of indirection, diverse in manifestations within the social body. Nor is it unlikely that such a sophist, though lost from the Christian's perspective, may glory in his very lostness. That is an aspect bordering on frenzy in that totalitarian who is successful in his accumulation of power, from the Roman emperors to Stalin and Hitler. But we find it as well in lesser orders of tyrants within the social body down to very remote manifestations – even to be discovered in the "rural" South, as Flannery O'Connor's fiction suggests. Whatever our place or station, we may become lost in the cosmos as a consequence of participating in evil at the expense of the spiritual good. How, then, may one persuasively argue that by a neglect of the spiritual good, the good of both intellect and even of that incarnate dimension to the discrete existence of the self – the body – is sacrificed? To engage that truth about our given nature directly would most likely only raise alarm, as it did for St. Augustine who early on was able to pray for rescue, but "not yet." It would confuse the lost person and no doubt cause automatic antipathy to suggest that it is out of self-love that has led us to become a lost and wandering self, usually encouraged by a chorus exhorting us to "feel good" about our self. Such old truths about man's potential to evil: the primary victim always is the "self" as lured into becoming a citizen in territory declared sovereign to the Antichrist. After all, those old truths seem always to lie blurred in a dusty residue in the attic of intellect. Or so it appears to Percy as diagnostic novelist. There is that other concern, proper from a Thomistic perspective upon art as well: namely, that the artist is responsible to the good of the thing he makes, which sets aside the poet's tractarian intentionality even as he recognizes a propensity to self-destruction, a danger in devotion to the good of the thing he makes. Art, St. Thomas insists, is not concerned with the rescue of any audience from its appetitive dislocations. But, then, that tractarian temptation is not the emphasis here at immediate issue. Rather, our concern is for the manner in which the poet may and must adapt current realities to art in his devotion to the good of the thing he would make without compromising his primary responsibility to that good.

Percy's address to the problem of evil, then, in respect to his adoption of indirection as his mode as artist, is quite other than that of Flannery O'Connor. He is therefore "perfectly willing to believe" our world very largely ruled by that Ancient of Darkness who is resolute in his opposition to the Ancient of Light. O'Connor, however, concentrates rather more intensely not upon the "self" as a popular concept in her concern for our dislocation. Instead her emphasis is upon the "world" of the specific consciousness as the most local arena in which the struggle for sovereignty between Light and Darkness occurs. That is the suspension of soul which feeds her drama. For her that small world is endangered by terrors more decisive than either psychological disorders (to be adjusted by the latest science) or by the more spectacular evidences of terror in larger spectacles of war – the destruction of Kulacks or (currently) ethnic cleansing in Rwanda or Kosovo or Chechnya. Or in the armed conflict between random gangs in our own inner cities. Like Dante, she orders her selected matter to a making out of the circumstantial reality which she observes manifest locally. But she orders it in relation to a principle which art cannot set aside. At issue, in respect to her dramatic art, is the intellectual soul incarnate within its locally enveloping circumstance as this person who exists here and now. That imagined agent represents a recognizable possible or probable of human actions. Both the actual person, and so the fictional agent derived from that reality, are at risk in consequence of human nature as fallen. Such is the reality governing her vision in her making. It will lead her on occasion to speak of this reality to our personhood as it is independent of her own calling as artist. That is, she will speak of actual terrors to the actual person as a consequence of his having divorced sentiment from the "source of tenderness," whereby sentiment is reduced to sentimentality and leads to "forced-labor camps" and "the fumes of the gas chamber." It is that recognition of a close relation of evil to looniness which engages Percy more intensely at last. He comes to an O'Connor-like emphasis upon the *person* as beleaguered by evil in his agents of his *Thanatos Syndrome.* Fr. Smith gives an impassioned sermon on the point, echoing O'Connor almost verbatim.

What Flannery O'Connor knows is that pity is not love, that pity is amenable to a detachment of the pitying self from the object of his pity. Thus one might even be tempted, we said, to pity Satan, the ultimate scientist, theologian, philosopher, poet who is self-doomed by his cry *non serviam.* What a relief, then, to such a creature to practice love by donations to the Community Chest or to Doctors without Borders in withdrawing from the painful and continuing terrors revealed just at hand in social and political destructions. And it seems even some relief to have the local enlarged as worldwide, given in vivid technology on the evening news. Flannery O'Connor proves much closer to Dante as poet, dramatizing the risk to the intellectual soul incarnate as *this* created creature *here* and *now.* She does so through such agents as Haze Motes or her young Tarwater. What she knows (perhaps out of Dante, whom she knew through his *Divine Comedy*) is that Aristotle's concern for "catharsis" in tragedy, an *exorcising* of "pity and terror" in intellect, requires our moving beyond pity and terror into that country of high comedy, the country into which young Tarwater is about to enter at novel's end and whose border Haze has reached at the conclusion of *Wise Blood*. That is a reality necessary to recognize for her, governing her making by an over-arching visionary ambiance as a reality to the things she makes.

Thus O'Connor would reject that range of diagnosticians of the deracinated soul who operate from the perspective of the Modernist, as if that were ultimate authority on the reality of the "self," though they may provide grist to the mill of her making as does Rayber in her second novel. These would give malevolence a more comfortable name. Not evil, but "maladjustment" out of genetic or environmental misfortunes, rather than out of that possible will to evil whose rubric is *non serviam*. Flannery O'Connor's response, then, might well be that Percy somewhat misses the point of her own insisting upon the reality of evil as actual and to be confronted. Not merely confronted, she adds, in the passage from which Percy quotes her on the devil and his territory. She insists on the devil "as a real spirit who must be made to name himself, and not simply to name himself as vague evil [as for instance some species of "maladjustment" attributable to nature or society], but to name himself with his specific personality for every occasion." Dostoevsky would applaud, having dramatized this necessity in Ivan Karamazov's encounter of that bourgeois devil who effects Ivan's collapse. For Ivan's most destructive encounter with the Prince of Darkness is made, not in that celebrated figure of his imagined Grand Inquisitor, whom he projects in a Romantic poem. That has been a strategy allowing Ivan an indulgence in pity out of his intellectual sentimentality. It is rather that ordinary devil who leads Ivan to a self-conviction, to an admission that he is after all but a "Romantic."

It is in her "Memoir of Mary Ann," engaging the evil of cancer wasting the small child Mary Ann, that O'Connor remarks this intellectual sentimentality as leading at last to the gas chambers, as we have recalled. Since her observation, we see it leading increasingly to formal endorsement of abortion and euthanasia, the new symptom of the Spectre of Death giving our age a name more ominous than if we call it the "Age of the Theorist-Consumer." Percy becomes more and more agitated by that Spectre, which has become an idol fascinating naïve humanity. He does so to the point that he writes a letter to the editor (January 22, 1988) of the *New York Times,* never published, though he asks after it in a follow-up letter. Earlier, in a milder letter, he had insisted that "religion, philosophy, and private opinion have nothing to do with the issue," as if by man's marshalling of signs in controlling the letter of the law, death as a convenience to the living might be justified. This one was published, in June of 1981. In the letter which the *Times* refused publication in 1988, he reminded us of "the most influential book published in German in the first quarter of the century . . . *The Justification of the Destruction of Life Devoid of Value*." Its authors were "the distinguished jurist Karl Binding and the prominent psychiatrist Alfred Hoche." Though Hitler may not have known that book, it reflects the preparation of a consent to the horrors Hitler will presently unleash. Theirs is the answer posed by enlightened intellectuals as the "solution" to Ivan Karamazov's dilemma. O'Connor says, "Ivan Karamazov cannot believe [in God], as long as one child is in torment." His has now become a "popular pity" in which "we mark our gain in sensibility and our loss of vision." And that loss is what Dostoevsky addresses in juxtaposing Alyosha Karamazov to Ivan, culminating in the conclusion of that great novel in the scene in which Alyosha speaks for Love as mediating our inevitable sufferings as the circumstance to our journeying. And Alyosha, we recall, speaks to children mourning their small fallen companion, children who cheer Alyosha with shouts of "Hurray for Karamazov" in recognizing the truth in Alyosha's witness.

How appropriate, from this perspective upon suffering, upon evil eroding good in us to the point of our indulging pity as if self-exculpation, that Dostoevsky and O'Connor prove companionable. Both see Baudelaire's truth about the Prince of Darkness. In one of his several "Prefaces" to *Flowers of Evil*, Baudelaire remarks that the Devil's most subtle strategy in the Modern world has been his having convinced us that he does not exist at all. By that blindness we resort to "nature" as the only agent, a blind agent, of evil. As for Ivan Karamazov, his encounter with this subtle presence in the world leaves him devastated. Not the Grand Inquisitor of his Romantic projection as poet, we said, but a minor, unspectacular little bourgeois devil, a very Russian devil, to which we might compare C. S. Lewis's devil as an apprentice, probationary servant of Satan, in *Screwtape Letters.* If Ivan falls into a madness, or a seeming madness, wracking mind and body, making him the pathetic ward of his brother Alyosha, both Dostoevsky and O'Connor see this as the terror which lies not in Ivan's psychological disorder, a mere symptom, but in consequences of his dark spiritual encounter of an Evil which Ivan himself has conjured through his Modernist mode as intellect, his presumption being that he has *logically* purified Romanticism. What he discovers in his collapse is that he has only succeeded in focusing, by a diminution of his self, the conjured evil of self-love as disguised pity, through a sentimentality dogmatically derived from Positivism.

Here then let us explore Dostoevsky's Ivan Karamazov in his encounter of the devil after his self-excitement of that intellectually Promethean exercise in "creating" his Grand Inquisitor. The details of that encounter, we observe, foreshadow the "Southern" concerns of both Percy and especially Flannery O'Connor as they become concerned with the "modern malaise." The "objective correlatives" Dostoevsky chooses to make concrete Ivan's encounter are most ordinary. Ivan's paltry Baudelarian devil, as contrasted to the Grand Inquisitor, gives him "the appearance of decency on rather slender means." He declares himself but a "sponger" in society. How apt, in relation to the Thomistic point that evil depends upon the good, sponges upon the good for its very existence as it were, evil being defined as an absence of good.

As a devil, that presence to Ivan declares himself "very sensitive and artistically susceptible," though much committed to "common sense." Even so, he feels a responsibility as prophet and so gives Ivan's philosophy an articulation through which Ivan only gradually comes to recognize those signs as reflecting his own mind. And then a shocking prophecy: "Man will be exalted with the spirit of the divine, titanic pride, and the man-god will appear," a prophecy in two parts of an apocalyptic Second Coming, but as so divided not necessarily the Nietzschean prophecy of the Superman. (We remember that Nietzsche was much taken by Dostoevsky's *Crime and Punishment.*) In the moment of a seeming triumph of the Antichrist, Christ's return would follow in Dostoevsky's reckoning. How comfortable to Ivan's fiction, his setting his version of the Second Coming in the past, at the late Middle Ages-Renaissance turning of the world into Modernism. Instead, in his own present moment, there is in prospect an apocalypse imminent, as indeed it proves for Ivan in his descent into madness. Ivan's fury smolders toward an eruption as he begins to recognize those echoes of his own arguments, redounding upon him with ironic implications from this commonsensical devil.

In this respect there are notable parallels between Ivan's confrontation with his devil and Haze Motes's confrontation of Onnie Jay Holy (Hoover Shoates) in Flannery O'Connor's *Wise Blood.* That rather pedestrian redneck con-man is a comic echo of the same confrontation, the comic dimension obscuring for some readers the high seriousness of the encounter. Onnie Jay Holy, after all, is only bent upon conning the nondescript, unimportant denizens of Taulkningham (née Atlanta), doing so with Haze's own words in advancing the cause of a new system of belief, soliciting paid membership in the Church of Christ without Christ. If Haze Motes proves a self-made country boy Nietzsche, unlettered in those Western intellectual patrons of that position, the same is not true of Ivan. He is highly educated, a sophisticated interlectual who cons himself. His ideas, defiant of his own created givenness, have been supplied by formidable Western minds, from Voltaire and Descartes to Diderot and Rousseau, to Hegel and Marx and Comte. How shocking to Ivan, then, when his conjured devil proves more subtle than Haze's "devil," Hoover Shoates. But as always, the devil knows the principle of proportionality – proportionate unto the person is the devil therefore.

Both Haze and Ivan reach a point of collapse, consequent to their disparate gifts of intellectual conjuring, an epiphany at a spiritual nadir. Ivan's collapse bears more complex intellectual origins in Western science and philosophy as known to him than does Haze's, of course, though at risk for each in common is his own soul. With Ivan, the final fillip is Alyosha bearing news of their bastard brother Smerdyakov, who has turned in his ticket – has killed himself. Given that news, Ivan sees himself as an intellectual Frankenstein who has created this pseudo-intellectual monster Smerdyakov out of his own intentionality, in an opposition to brother Alyosha's God. By Ivan's doing so, Smerdyakov has served him as an instrument, a machine-like creature adjusted to diabolical ends. Smerdyakov has been the instrument of the murder of Old Karamazov (who as *man* is reduced to the bestial in Ivan's judgment). Ivan's conscience burns. The event is actual, not speculative theory about the relation of God to his creation. Playing God, even in a role disguised as a Renaissance Grand Inquisitor, proves quite other than Ivan has bargained for because complicated by the mystery of evil in Smerdyakov and the entanglement out of Byronic romanticism of Brother Dmitri in a public trial. It is a trial replete with persons assuming "roles" in defense of theoretical positions on the question of justice.

Ivan in his dark epiphany, contrary to his deportment earlier, begins to insist that the devil he has just engaged (one evidence, his wrecked apartment) was a real presence. That is his last self-defense before his collapse into Alyosha's care. His concluding recognition: "And *he* – is me, Alyosha, me myself. All that's low, all that's mean and contemptible in me. Yes, I'm a 'romantic,' he noticed it . . . though it's a slander." That is the recognition which Haze comes to at last, in a sequence leading from encounter with Hoover Shoates, to the Arab mummy stolen by Enoch as a present to Haze. The mummy corresponds to all the particulars Haze preaches about the nature of man. Haze in his collapse, self-blinded and with barbwire wrapped about him, holds on to the one truth irrefutable: "I am not clean."

Another of Flannery O'Connor's versions of such an epiphany is that moment of violence on a back-country Georgia road when the Misfit shoots the grandmother for what he takes to be her ultimate betrayal, her attempt to absolve him of evil by a confessional gesture of love – as social institutions and their agents have been unable to do by theories of social adjustment. The moment of violent recognition to the Misfit is of the reality of his own fallenness, susceptible of rescue only through love, a certification of which possibility is made by the old woman with devastating effect on her. He, too, has submitted to evil, under the considerable pressures of his being Christ-haunted. When the old woman makes her final gesture, it is one of genuine love toward him, as if the first gesture of love she has herself been able to make, judging from her family deportment in the story. (Is she by this action, in her short happy moment, a martyr?) The Misfit leaps back, shooting her and declaring that she would have been a good woman if there had been somebody around to shoot her every day of her life. Our poet Flannery O'Connor with great care gives us a final image of the dead grandmother: she "half sat and half lay in a puddle of blood with her legs crossed under her like a child's and her face smiling up at the cloudless sky."

Again, as Percy observes, Miss O'Connor isn't kidding here, knowing (as she says in the same passage which Percy uses) how helpful to her own making of fictions the devil proves. He "accomplishes a good deal of the groundwork that seems to be necessary before grace is effective," she says. That is, before an effective removal of obstacles to the mystery of grace, there is often necessary a dark night of the soul. Percy speaks of it as that ordeal whereby one becomes an "ex-suicide." O'Connor knows that necessity as witnessed by St. John of the Cross, whose *Dark Night of the Soul* precedes that rescue of an *Ascent of Mount Carmel*, as in turn it has been preceded by St. John's exploration of the "Dark Night of the Senses." An epiphany in her story proves quite other than the psychological unfolding of a protagonist to a point of his uncomfortable recognition of his "self" such as Joyce employs in the epiphany used as but a fictional technique borrowed from a limited psychological reality. Joyce's is a fiction reserved to the level of man's mere looniness. In this difference lies the confidence with which O'Connor says of her Misfit – again in the passage Percy cites – that she would not "equate the Misfit with the devil," preferring to think that "the old lady's gesture, like the mustard-seed, will grow to be a great crow-filled tree in the Misfit's heart, and will be enough of a pain to him there to turn him into the prophet he was meant to become. But that is another story" – that story she writes called *The Violent Bear It Away*. For her there is a mystery attendant upon the violent act, the Misfit by his violence – in spite of it – in some degree is exorcised of evil potentially. For even the Misfit, she suggests, may escape full submission to the Governor of Evil. Given Miss O'Connor's witty mischief, one might even suppose a spiritual analogy made seriously comic: the Misfit in relation to the grandmother in the story's dénouement might be likened to Saul of Tarsus at the martyrdom of St. Stephen. The Misfit is without a shirt (we notice almost in passing that fact of attire), the escapees having buried their prison garb. The grandmother suggests that maybe an extra shirt is in Bailey's suitcase. "I'll look and see terrectly," he says. (*Acts* 7 records that at Stephen's stoning "the witnesses laid down their clothing at a young man's feet, whose name was Saul.")

O'Connor's Misfit reminds us by his actions that a good man is always hard to find. He seems very much in quest of such a man, though that quest is through bloody actions. He wishes he had been at the Crucifixion and thus known that Good Man Christ up close. We, unlike the Misfit, may continue amused by looniness, though becoming uncomfortable if it become too grotesque as it seems to do in the story. And so, perhaps, we are relieved by the Misfit's judgment of the old woman he has just killed. We are content to enjoy the comic aspect of looniness in relation to our supposed distance from it. For O'Connor, however, that is in itself an evidence of that dangerous looniness through which we become lost in the cosmos. Responding to such comfort in us, she becomes very caustic, even unmannerly as when at one level of her concern she observes the degree of removal of "New York critics" from the realities of human nature upon which her fiction depends. She remarks that "no matter how favorable all the critics of New York City may be, they are an unreliable lot." In contrast, the Southerner has an advantage, if he is alert, in that he is still attuned to "the general conception of man" in his theological dimension, according to his created human nature. That is an aspect evident to her even in her Misfit. Not the "looney," but the "freak" – the grotesque character – is of fictional interest to her, since "the freak can be sensed as a figure for our essential displacement," attaining a depth in the literature addressing the "freak." Provided, of course, that one can recognize the freak, as the unreliable critics in New York City seem unable to do. In her "The Grotesque in Southern Fiction," she remarks that "the freak can be sensed as a figure for our essential displacement," and that as such a figure "he attains some depth in literature." But alas, the "reader of today looks for the motion [of the redemptive act]" but that reader's "sense of evil is diluted or lacking altogether," so that "he wants either his senses tormented or his spirits raised. He wants to be transported, instantly, either to a mock damnation or a mock innocence."

By her strategy, then, the grotesque figure is such because, haunted spiritually, his disfigurement is a prophetic reminder of displacement from spiritual orientation. And she reminds us in this regard of the nature of the prophet as revealed in the Old Testament: he recalls us to known but forgotten things. In this respect Haze Motes in *Wise Blood* is such a prophet, with the added dimension in his actions that the recalling is most immediately to himself lost in spiritual blindness, making his self-blinding at the novel's end a fictional resolution speaking something more than does the self-blinding of Oedipus in Sophocles' play to which O'Connor's denouement of *Wise Blood* is often compared. Haze declares himself "unclean," we said, which is not the same as being unknowing. What he now knows about cleanliness has brought him to an understanding. Sin is the issue, pridefulness, and not that more secular arrogance of Oedipus, which incidentally troubles Sophocles as insufficient so that he attempts to make Oedipus prophetic in some dimension as human person, beyond mere psychological or even philosophical and certainly beyond a merely political recognition of his flawed character. It is as if something more profound than any historical resolution must be summoned to an account of an Oedipus. Sophocles pursues this mystery in that ambiguous play *Oedipus at Colonus,* with its Old Testament ascension of Oedipus. It is as if the poet Sophocles longs for some Revelation to solve the baffling circumstances of Greek philosophy, as Plato will struggle to summon revelation through those philosophical dramas centering in Socrates as protagonist in his dialogues.

O'Connor's grotesque figures differ from Percy's loony figures in respect to her intense concern for the soul in those agents in their contention with evil. They are haunted by an intuitive hunger for the good. And so there is a dimension to her violence more directly dependent upon a spiritual evil struck into the soul than with the symptomatic looniness. Her thematic concern, this is to say, is in recognition of the reality of Original Sin. As for that violence, her confused prophets as protagonists commit bloody acts against their enclosing worlds, acts recognized at the popular level as very bloody indeed. They seem to act violently in a rejection of that entrapping secular world, though not understanding that threat as the cause in their shedding of the blood. To miss this aspect of the dramatic action which is implied in her agents is to mistake the violence as evidence only of social maladjustment. For her, their reaction is at least in part a resistance to an accord with that agency governing the "territory" they journey, the sovereign of that "country" being the ancient Adversary. That is a world intellectually reduced from the spiritual dimension of reality which she holds more largely by vision. By her vision she holds created things divine by virtue of Love's creation. (I have explored this point in relation to O'Connor in my *Why Flannery O'Connor Stayed Home*, especially in such chapters as "The Separation of Grace from Nature" and "Getting to Know Haze Motes: Nietzsche as a Country Boy.") This spiritual dimension to reality, if denied or ignored, leaves *homo viator* convinced that the devil does not even exist, as Baudelaire suggests to be our naïve conclusion. The naiveté of such citizens of the cosmos in their actual social presence occasions O'Connor's acerbic reflections from time to time. What is irritating to her is that violence, as she deploys violent actions to evidence the spiritually grotesque in her characters as they resist encounter with Revelation, is most usually engaged by the Modernist mind (among whom, those New York critics are prominent) at the level of mere social aberration.

Human nature is taken in that reductionist view as limited to the biochemical level of man. But if so taken one may conclude "ontologically" only that man is an accident of an accidental cosmos. In a presumption of pride out of this conclusion which might make Oedipus or Socrates blanch, the Modernist in his counter action sees the solution to random violence as requiring "adjustments" of the psychological machine, man, as if thereby he may be tuned as an instrument serving whatever system is supposed desirable by that gnostic authority. Such authority (as Voegelin reminds us) usually blindly presumes that his own system is transcendent (in Percy's sense) of man as machine. Thus order must be imposed by angelistic intellect, an imagined world externally pressed upon the chaotic cosmos thus writ small by gnostic intentionality. The person as a small world is to be forced as a new "individual" into an accord with the new divinity, *System*. Such is the dream of an ultimate act, engineered by a process whereby form is divorced from substance and a substitute substance conjured out of nothingness, in order to *in-form* a willed system. Thus the *individual* becomes a new world, by adjustment of the given which as dogma is denied as given. He is thereby to be accommodated in a constellation of like worlds into a decreed social order. Eliot, having at first responded wistfully to this aspect of Modernist system, speaks a sardonic conclusion in his early "Preludes" in a poignant figure: those little "worlds revolve like ancient women/ Gathering fuel in vacant lots." How sad a displacement of the old Greek chorus which the tragedian uses to counterpoint his failed hero, an Agamemnon or Oedipus, thus keeping open the mystery of existence.

From O'Connor's and from Percy's perspective, the gnostic strategy to social order (which we know in a spectrum of versions of "Great Societies" from Stalin and Hitler to Lyndon Johnson's version of it) is dominant in this latest of the last days. Percy, with a rich mischief as diagnostician, has at that strategy, especially in *Love in the Ruins*. For the reality is that *system*, however justified by science, must fail at last to recover a significant community since it ignores the spiritual center necessary to the soul's order. To that spiritual creature as person, the social and political ebb and flow of community are taken as peripheral, as vestigial to evolution, though they are in reality made viable only by reference to that common center. The true center, then, must be the specific person as intellectual soul incarnate, a reality now deliberately set aside by denying man's actual nature. (Hence Percy's observation to his Louisiana audience that such a term as *soul* has been retired to the attic of our language.) These "Catholic" writers (Percy and O'Connor) both hold to the contrary of the Modernist position, to the necessity to see the person as *homo viator*. For then, the person journeys the reality of a created world toward a recovery from being a fallen person lost in the cosmos. He is a pilgrim seeking a lost country in which his givenness is fulfilled. The metaphysical depths to this ancient metaphor turn upon the reality that *homo viator* is lost in that he cannot "see" that the longed-for country is always at hand, declared to be present to him by those ordinary things as experienced by St. Augustine in his recovered experience of created things.

It is with a marvelous economy as artist that O'Connor brings this journey into a spiritual focus, with a subtle "naturalistic" context which makes the lost country immediate to a waking pilgrim reader through epiphany is a waking protagonist. It is a rendering which is often upsetting to a reader. Young Tarwater, almost despite himself, has returned to the geographical place from which he set out, that Georgia country place where he had lived with Old Tarwater. He returns to the grave of that old prophet, O'Connor's "natural Catholic." And as he approaches the grave of that dead patriarch, with reluctant steps, we are told that now "he saw the clear grey spaces of that country where he had vowed never to set foot." But this is no longer simply a present geographical place, though in the moment initiating his epiphany it seems thus limited to the waking boy. Presently we shall see, in the final words of this drama about *homo viator*, young Tarwater plowing ahead into the "jagged shadow" of himself as cast by a fitful and actual moonlight. He is once more on his way to that city to which he had first fled as if it were a refuge, a sanctuary suited to his absolute freedom, only to have found it otherwise. Now he returns in order to bear the message heard moments ago as he lay on Old Tarwater's grave: "GO WARN THE CHILDREN OF GOD OF THE TERRIBLE SPEED OF MERCY." The last words of all in the novel: Tarwater moves, "his face set toward the dark city, where the children of God lay sleeping." In the "naturalistic" context, it is night, with moonlight casting a fitful shadow of himself ahead of him. But the "dark city" will continue dark, held by an "embalmed" spiritual darkness under the rising sun, if it continues to reject Tarwater's message brought out of the burning grave of old Tarwater. It is a message brought out of a seeming darkness from the perspective of that disaffected world, but young Tarwater no longer sees from the brink of that abyss of nothingness. That "nothingness" has been hollowed out in the cosmos by the fallen soul in its pursuit of evil. But even by that retreat from light, Light proves always present on the instant through grace, as Old Tarwater insists, with the terrible speed of mercy.

And so in O'Connor's fiction we find a celebration of a mystery in the spectacles of violence, speaking a tensional spiritual circumstance which lies within the person as he struggles toward a love beyond his own willfulness. That is the central conflict, an aspect of her fiction which (if but rarely) has raised an orthodox eyebrow over whether Jansenism is afoot. And it may be that in response to suspicion which is reflected in her note on reissuing *Wise Blood* in 1962. She remarks that from the Modernist perspective "Haze Motes integrity lies in his trying with such vigor to get rid of the ragged figure [Christ] who moves from tree to tree in the back of his mind." For the author, however, it lies quite elsewhere, in his not being able to do so. But that does not mean Haze is not free, since "free will does not mean one will, but many wills conflicting in one person." Freedom cannot be conceived simply, she says. "It is a mystery . . . which a novel, even a comic novel, can only be asked to deepen." It is within this complex of conflicted wills, within her protagonist, that violent action breeds – in the *person* caught up in his own civil war. It leads her for that second novel to the Gospel of Matthew for her title: "From the days of John the Baptist until now, the kingdom of heaven suffereth violence, and the violent bear it away."

Like many of her predecessor poets, we conclude, her center of concern is with that "little world" as Shakespeare or Donne or Eliot speak of it, the discrete specific soul, whose revolving as lost in the cosmos sparks spectacles of violence in creation. It is those sparks on the surface of the social and natural cosmos, appearing as spectacle, which govern the choice of suitable "objective correlatives" (Eliot's term) to the drama of that deeper violence contingent in the soul itself, that willful self-undoing toward chaos in that entity which Percy talks about as the "self," since "soul" is a term now long since stored in the attic. A remnant, even in the current academy, will take this point about the self as a "little world," remembering perhaps the incredulous student who, when given Dante's belief about the effect upon the soul of willful evil, finds Dante absurd. It seems to make no "sense" to insist that for Dante the most terrible consequence of the act of murder is the destruction to the murderer's own soul, of which the death of the hapless victim is a circumstantial effect in the light of eternity. One might as well attempt to persuade that student that Percy, in his ever-so-playful *Lost in the Cosmos*, is indeed serious in his argument that suicide is an option to be contemplated as a possible solution to the sense of alienation. In a sense, of course, that final act might resolve questions by issuing consciousness into oblivion. The shock of that gamble gave old Socrates pause long ago – long before that famous "to be or not to be" soliloquy of Hamlet. But the issue, the centering concern, is for a recovery beyond such dark questions, a recovery to a Light stronger than Tarwater's fitful moonlight as he struggles toward that sleeping Southern city.

That Light transforms the specific person, not creation in itself, since creation is already transformed, constituted by the "holiness of the ordinary." That is why what seems a desert proves an imperfect garden to opening eyes, those eyes enabled by grace to behold creation in a visionary encounter, in a still point of the turning world. This is the distinction which John Keats could not make, standing in his actual darkness under trees with flittering moonlight breaking through as the actual breeze moves the leaves above his head. He descends into despair within an "embalmed darkness." But when our seeing is itself transformed (through grace), when the pilgrim comes to know his present place for a first time, even in darkness he discovers an incommensurate Love lying actively and sustainingly in the very depths of the rubble-strewn world as littered by man. And so, though given such destruction, he may know (with Gerard Manley Hopkins) that "There lives the dearest freshness deep down things," the grandeur of God's Love sustaining things however much trodden down or "seared with trade, smeared with toil." What is opened, in seeing this place at this moment for the first time, is a spectrum of Divine things existing through Love. We recall to such possible vision always, as St. Thomas reminds us, that such grace cannot be commanded. Rather, by an openness to creation we remove obstacles to that grace. This failure of distinction, surely, is the most considerable distortion emerging out of the Reformation, in a pursuit of the individual conscience as supreme earthly arbiter of truth. That becomes a Puritan excess out of which occurs inevitably a Manichaean separation of grace and nature.

It is in relation to this unwavering perspective that Flannery O'Connor engages her version of Love in the ruins, her comedy coming to rest in the self-violence of her protagonists, making hers not only a fiction with comic overtones along the way but a fiction much closer to that sense of a "Divine" comedy pursued by Dante in his great poem. We may see a difference then between her fiction and Percy's, a difference which on occasion he sees and speaks of in relation to her gift of "transparency" as artist. She is not committed to satire, as Percy tends to be in much of his work. One sees this point by summoning his reflections about his own *Love in the Ruins*, made to a press conference arranged by the National Book Award committee in 1971. He tries in that novel, he says, to provide by means of satire "a little something . . . to offend everybody: liberal, conservative; white, black; hawk, dove; Catholic, Protestant, Jew, heathen; the English, the Irish, Swedes, Ohioans, to mention only a few." He intends thereby to "call a bluff," as an "American" novelist. In such a work as *Love in the Ruins* he can enjoy the mischief of satire portioned out broadly. For he is by then convinced "that for the first time in a hundred and fifty years the South is off the hook and once again free to help save the Union." Not that the South has rid itself "of its ancient stigma [slavery]," but that "the rest of the country is now also stigmatized and is in even deeper trouble."

One might wish to dwell in explication on such a passage, knowing that Percy stands here in the mode of analytical novelist and so must be taken as perhaps wily in his argument. But at the surface at least, in admitting the South's "ancient stigma" as now pervasive of the Union, he does not appear to make that stigma specifically grounded in the Fall of man except by implication. O'Connor would more likely do so directly. Percy would undoubtedly grant that ground if pressed on the point. But he is rather concerned, as he says in reflecting on his novel, "not with the takeover of a society by tyrants or computers or whatever [as George Orwell or Aldous Huxley may be said to be concerned], but rather with the increasing malaise and finally the falling apart of a society which remains, on the surface at least, democratic and pluralistic." Through that encroaching malaise upon the intellect, signs themselves are but the more revealed as in a rapid decay, so that the "ruins" of the moment of the novel reflect thematically the dislocation of meaning in such a term as *love,* underscored imagistically by the *rubble,* the *ruins*.

Such a reflection requires our remembering, of course, that the protagonist of this novel is Dr. Tom More, and from our perspective of hindsight on Percy's remarks we may also remember that this is the same Tom More who will at last be central to Percy's final engagement of the theme of Love in opposition to Death, *The Thanatos Syndrome*. Nevertheless, in juxtaposing Percy's and O'Connor's concerns, in such terms as Percy's *stigma* and his declaration that now "the rest of the country" is similarly *stigmatized* and in even deeper trouble than the South, there is a limiting of the arena to the political and social spectacle that fuels the devastating satire which he intends in order that he may "offend everybody." From O'Connor's perspective, one might engage this concept of *stigma* quite differently, as we have seen in considering her concern for *epiphany* in her fiction. One remembers the formal theological sense of *stigmata*, the mystery whereby human persons receive the violent wounds of Christ. The "stigmata" of interest to O'Connor, we suggest, is not in actual bodily wounds but in that spiritual wound in *homo viator* as a singular fallen person, leaving him "Christ-haunted" in both intellect and soul. From her perspective indeed it is a stigma bleeding into and out of sinful denial, affecting not simply the Southerner or the "rest of the country" but each discretely existing intellectual soul incarnate, insofar as any person in any place stands in resistance to Love.

In each of the two public talks that we singled out from Percy earlier, he addresses his audience as one convinced that life is wonderful, since he is an "ex-suicide." He engages each audience through signs rich with his diagnostic indirection. In doing so, he maintains a manner of mannerliness, very much aware of distinctions between the gatherings he addresses in those public "talks," though no less acutely aware that such audiences (wherever encountered) must be in varying degree already engulfed by and infected by the Modernist malaise. The one however – his Louisiana audience – he believes (or at least hopes) still has a residual sense of place such as he recognizes possessed by that other "Southern" writer, Eudora Welty, whom he defers to as early as 1969 as a significant witness toward our recovery. In "Eudora Welty in Jackson" he anticipates a time coming "when the American novelist will tire of his angelism" and will find his way "back into a body, live in a place, at a street address." Become, this is to say, a quiet participant in the cosmos, abiding the necessary journeying of it, as Eudora Welty does at home on Pinehurst in Jackson, Mississippi.

With that concern in mind, we have been preparing, enlarging, our own observations about Percy as seeking just such a comfort in such a place. It is a quest for a moment of life's goodness despite his stalking that goodness through the strategy of the novelist as con-artist, the rhetorical stance revealed in his work. His craftiness in this pursuit is evident in his craft-managed distancing from audience. We see this strategy engagingly effective in *Lost in the Cosmos*, making this work not an "essay" but a dramatic work, so deployed as to make it sufficiently "underhanded" that it may put the putative reader on his guard if he is alert. By his rhetorical stance, Percy can as writer *enjoy* his deportment as "diagnostician," that epithet he ascribes to himself repeatedly in essays and interviews. It is also especially present in that other *tour de force*, his "Questions They Never Asked Me, So He Asked Them Himself." Percy, in explication of a portrait of himself hanging on his wall, identifies "the subject of the portrait" (himself) with his character Lancelot in his novel of that title, but he enlarges by adding that the portrait is "a composite of the protagonists of my novels." That protagonist is anything but "attractive" as person and is indeed "something of a nut besides." Indeed *Lancelot* is by a person as novelist whom he might with some justice describe as being as "mean as a yard dog," a characteristic Percy openly embraces as another self-epithet.

We may properly note, then, that in the self-interview, because interviewing his "self" which he poses to us as it stands in the role of writer, Percy can be more brutally direct than his good manners would otherwise allow, were there an actual second person as interviewer. He can be quite rude to himself as it were, though the cunning strategy underway involves a rudeness which is made even more underhanded in that it is aimed, not at Percy himself as interviewer, but beyond himself – to readers, especially ex-interviewers no doubt. The "literary" mode here we have already introduced – that of St. Augustine's *Confessions*. But the audience before whom St. Augustine appears in his self-inquisition is God, though he shares his confessional audience with us as well. With Percy, the immediate audience (the readers of *Esquire*) are better described as academic, or pseudo-academic – an audience believing itself both seriously and deeply concerned with the mystery of "creativity" but which as a collective of "selves" has lost the orienting importance of terms like *Creator* and *creation*. For we are aware that *Esquire* at the time is given to "serious" fiction and social issues from a sophisticated perspective. It is an audience which nevertheless, Percy would say, has lost ontological concerns proper even to art, let alone to science or sociology. One might suggest Percy's position in his self-interview to be that of the Stoic as mean yard dog, gaining a rhetorical purchase thereby which allows his castigation of at least that part of his audience he must endure – the silly, stupid, repetitious intruders with their endless questions born of their own unrecognized condition of being lost in the cosmos. Not knowing themselves lost, they are remiss, reluctant to put heart where it ought to be, in a significant conjunction with head, as Flannery O'Connor would say directly to them. In the self-interview, then, Percy reveals a brute honesty, possible only in that moment through a rhetorical strategy whereby he is both interviewer and interviewee. If he is rude and unmannerly, he seems to be so to himself, though that is but a strategy of sly indirection.

In this respect, we may see a kinder deportment in that very late essay addressing the endless and therefore betimes tiresome question from the baffled secularist perspective, "Why Are You a Catholic?" (1990). But in contrast to both these essays, we may observe Percy's use of his mannerliness to pursue a subtle indirection in his deportment as a guide in *Lost in the Cosmos*. That mannerliness in his self-help book proves an artfully deceptive presentation of his own "self" as guide to his reader. In this work his stance is somewhere in between that mannerly deportment assumed on stage before an actual audience (Southern or Yankee) or the more gentle one in "Why Are You a Catholic?" and that fierce stance as a mean "yard dog" in his self-interview. In *Lost in the Cosmos* the reader (hearer) is anonymous, until we recognize it to be ourself as his reader – put on the spot as self. On stage, Percy must look into the anonymous faces before him, but there are present also his host or hostess or the inviting committee just behind him on stage. In "person," then, he feels obligated to a mannerliness which must acknowledges the presence of actual persons, as his printed signs need not. For he is a Southern gentleman. In a "literary" withdrawal from audience such as his self-interview, or in a role as a stranger among strangers in *Lost in the Cosmos* – that is another matter. Freed in his deployment of signs, in a safety of his privacy on the edge of a Louisiana swamp, he may enjoy teasing the (to him) anonymous audience.

And so in the address of advice of this last self-help book (which despite his relative freedom does not free him at last of the pursuing *paparazzi*, the interviewers), his words are to an anonymous self, the reader, who is projected as if but the hypothetical reader. In reality of course no actual reader is so simply hypothetical. Of that reader, Percy supposes him (among other characteristics) to have been affected by watching as much silly television comedies, of having seen as many bad movies and listened to as many silly commentators on the tube or radio, of having read as many advice columns to the lonely, as Percy himself so clearly has. The reader as hypothetical, then, becomes along the way a partial projection of a character closely akin to the speaking voice of these signs of this self-help book. Such a projection draws both reader and his guide (Percy) into speculative explorations of the modern "self," exploring in it the symptoms of an epidemic called the "Modern Malaise." The speaker-reader, this is to say, is citizen of a culture-worshipful age – this age of the "Theorist-Consumer."

And so this rhetorical gambit would entrap the actual reader holding the book, especially in the deepest pit at that section midway *Lost in the Cosmos*. We come upon Percy's diagnosis of a general deracination shared by us as Modernists who have lost ontological certainty. It is a section which functions dramatically in the structure of the book as if he were using a fictional technique borrowed from Henry James, who in his late aesthetics argued for the "climax" of a novel as properly placed at the center, as a fulcrum to the rising and falling action thus balanced equally on either side. And so it is here at this middle of a way through this work that Percy gives us his scenario of "selves" in a local setting – at a Corn Dance staged by Taos Indians for diverse tourists in the vicinity of Los Alamos. A witty presentation of characters, as if notes made in anticipation of a novel yet to be written. As such, it carries the elements of a novel to be dramatized by the reader himself, through which imaginative action (prompted by the questions posed) that reader may find himself drawn into the drama as himself a "self" – become a character witnessing the dance: become a protagonist lost in the Cosmos.

This strategy proves complex in its implications. Percy, we have seen repeatedly along his way of words about words, warns us to beware of his guile as guide. As guide he is always untrustworthy because he is given on principle to the deviousness of indirection. That warning is given once more, here in this now jointly autobiographical "novel" called *Lost in the Cosmos* (the reader become an author to his own self). It is a work the reader must help *inform,* as we are repeatedly encouraged to notice ("check one" or "Thought Experiment" or "Question"). And so it is the reader who is required to complete the "self's" action, by which action that reader is put in a self-judgmental position, exposing himself – often an uncomfortable exposure if he submit seriously to it, as when he is encouraged to consider his own prospect as an actual suicide. The artful mischief afoot is Percy's treatment of the reader as a live psychological specimen, teased into submitting to his own (and to Percy's) analysis through the exercise of a Keatsian "negative capability," as if by that entrapment he might emerge with some of the relief of an "ex-suicide."

It is at this deeper level of exposure in the work that we might come upon an interesting speculation. For in this scenario of a gathering of a variety of characters into a circle about a Corn Dance, we begin to suspect that this "last self-help" book has as its hidden impetus Percy's own self-analysis which we are tricked into sharing as our own by his novelistic indirection. It is a diagnosis of the malaise with which he has contended personally all along his way and which infests his own consciousness intolerably, even as he sees it infecting Western civilization to its roots. It is this common dilemma thus discovered which affords a community between our guide and our own "self." By degree, we all find ourselves isolated as selves, he concludes, in that we are denizens of the cosmos at the lag-end of a nameless age. We stir fitfully before the threat of a "new age" yet to be named by retrospection. For even as the self cannot name itself, neither can this age of isolated selves declare its significant banner. Such is the mystery of human experience in relation to human signs used to name a common experience. We begin to emerge from an intimate personal experience of this unnamed age into a country we cannot name. Meanwhile we are delayed, fumbling intellectually for a significant naming of the country we are just leaving. Nearly all of our signposts erected in that century named the 20th after the Birth of Christ seem to lead us now stumbling in a circle – a contracting circle of history – unless we choose to sit withdrawn indifferently on the side – outside – that circle, one of the modes of almost surrendering our ticket to the Cosmos.

Is the novelist, aware of this stumbling dance, responsible to establish as scientifically as art allows our problematic circumstances as a warning? And if so, to what authority may he appeal as prophet? Science? But science reveals itself increasingly refined to an abstract sophistication, a safe angelism exhibited by novelists intent upon becoming "American" novelists. A byproduct of that refinement, turned in upon itself, is that "scientific" technology overwhelming us, consuming us even as we consume. And so we have as common, it appears, only a sense of isolation, an arrest which as Modernists we may hope may be one between two ages of history. One dying, the other unnamed and struggling to possess the Cosmos, struggling to be born as history *now*. In this arrest, we recall William Butler Yeats as prophet at the old century's delayed turning, but a prophet able only to pose such a question as we have done. In the chaotic aftermath of World War I, Yeats speaks what he "'knows," reaching as his conclusion only a question. He ends his "Second Coming" with allusion to that ancient event which Eliot will engage soon after Yeats's poem in a reflection of his own personal journey as Magi to Bethlehem in his "Ash-Wednesday." As for Yeats, now he can only know, he says, "That twenty centuries of stony sleep/ Were vexed to nightmare by a rocking cradle" in that old day – at that point in Western history from which we number our years as Western Civilization. That was a bad dream if not a nightmare for Yeats, who cannot believe the Incarnation actual, cannot believe that God become man. (*Pace,* O'Connor's Misfit.) Disturbing – even nightmarish – even to Eliot's Magus on his journey, who cannot resolve the complex signs he encountered on his desert passage as imagined for us by Eliot. That Magus cannot yet engage the mystery he has actually witnessed a mediation by the event of the Incarnation. What can he make of the signs *life, death*. And what of this 20th century, given that ancient point as our measure out of history, the point now two thousand years ago? As Yeats puts the question, "what rough beast, its hour come round at last" in our turning world, with its revolving souls lost in the cosmos. But Yeats has a vision of that beast nevertheless as it "Slouches towards Bethlehem to be born?" Yeats, concerned with the "growing murderousness of the world," anticipates a radical antipathy to Christianity in this new, unnamed age about to be, an apocalyptic anticipation akin to what Percy sees settled upon us more certainly at century's end. Percy with ironic humor presents his version of it: that ancient Corn Dance, with a residue of selves out of the interval since the Incarnation, settled into their private selves on the periphery of a dance which is or seems to them to be at most but a cultural artifact. One to be encouraged and supported, no doubt, by grants from the National Humanities Foundation – public and private grants for recovering Corn Dances or writing the great American Novel.

XIII

Percy finds himself somewhat in Eliot's position as reflected in *The Waste Land*. Also somewhat like that of the English-Welsh poet David Jones, who in his poem *In Parenthesis* points to World War I as the deepest collapse of Western history. It is a poem, Jones says, "which has to do with some things I saw, felt, and was part of . . . from December 1915 and [ending] early in July 1916," an understatement of his participation in the brutal Battle of the Somme. (Eliot as editor at Faber & Faber publishes *In Parenthesis*, with his own introduction to it as "a work of genius.") Or we might find Percy in his reading of the closing of our age as somewhat near that of the Christian historian Paul Johnson, who sees our century at an *In-Between*, to borrow a famous term from Eric Voegelin. In his *Modern Times: The World from the Twenties to the Eighties*, Johnson explores our century in its unfolding since World War I, first gathering a context to that war from social, philosophical, literary and other cultural evidences to which that War is such an arresting spectacle.

Thus there are kindred intellectuals – philosophers, poets, artists, theologians, scientists – mutually aware that our civilization drifts lost in the cosmos in this past century. In Percy's own day Alexander Solzhenitsyn came West, we have recalled, bearing that message, shocking Western Modernist intellectuals content with the drifting. Percy, then, is in a company of prophets in writing his last self-help book, those prophets who see our last century as an anomaly in respect to its In-Betweeness. He will say in his "Diagnosing the Modern Malaise": "If one had to set a date of the beginning of the end of the modern world, 1914 would be as good as any, because it was then that Western man, the beneficiary of precisely this scientific revolution and Christian ethic, began with great skill and energy to destroy himself."

But we might also note that in these words Percy's address differs from these other prophets we have cited. He seems to suggest, and there is other evidence scattered in interviews and essays and in this essay in particular, that the scientific revolution beginning with Bacon and Christian ethics as devolved from the Church Fathers were at first more comfortably compatible than some of his allies do. That is a position which Eric Voegelin would not grant, then, on the evidence of his *From Enlightenment to Revolution* and his *Science, Politics & Gnosticism.* Nor would that deeply Thomistic poet David Jones, who nevertheless agrees with Percy on the significance of World War I as marking an inescapable spiritual nadir. There is also Jones' richer, compact (and still too much neglected) poem, *Anathemata,* in which his concern is to lift up the sacred things so widely reduced by post-Baconian philosophy and science. As a soldier in France in World War I, he had found himself in the waste land disaster of Western civilization. There, he happened upon a ruined chapel and experienced an epiphany dramatized as his rescue in his *In Parenthesis*. But it is the *Anathemata* which proclaims hope, proclaims with Eliot and Julian of Norwich that all manner of thing shall be well.

Given this complex of confusions to the modern self robbed of hope, its confusions in attempting to reconcile science and religion, we might call our past century one "in parenthesis" as considered within the larger flow of Western history. We may argue that, at least metaphorically, we experience as a civilization a closure, a separation from the past, finding ourselves increasingly alienated from both history and nature – from the complex whole of the cosmos – leaving us uncertain of and fearful of whatever future age may lie on history's horizon. The "self" suffers spiritual and intellectual dislocation, as witnessed in great profusion in our century's art. Percy makes the point again and again, but it becomes the intense subject of this late essay (1989), "The Fateful Rift: The San Andreas Fault in the Modern Mind." And there, so radical the change about us as he sees it, Percy remarks ours an age still lacking a name.

Percy, given this chaos of the self in the world, feels keenly his responsibility to diagnose our mental malaise in his own "personal" interest, the circumstance to the self of its being trapped in a parenthesis of history, with nature become an outer world seen as an ambiguous cosmos. The dire circumstance to the self is that it finds itself teetering over its own internal abyss as a consciousness. He has experienced acutely his own isolation which, with a considerable will against despair, he has overcome, aided in that long struggle (he declares) by Kierkegaard and Thomas Aquinas and Gabriel Marcel. But he nevertheless still finds himself "in parenthesis," insofar as he must establish a starting point from which to set out to escape that closure. It is initially a position as scientist, as physician. But then he discovers himself better engaged in diagnosis of the malaise through the instruments of art. Thus he also finds himself ambiguously discomforted in his attempt to reconcile science and art, lest the two prove the closing ends of a parenthesis upon the self at either side.

And so in this new and strange world, as the old frontier humorist of Southern literature put it a century before World War I, it "pays to be shifty" in such a new country of the self. Nevertheless the self, assuming such a deliberate shiftiness, is likely to discover itself exposed as but using shifty disguise for self-protection. *Lost in the Cosmos* cannot fully hide Percy from our suspicion that in some degree he is engaged in his own self-analysis beneath that clever strategy of artful rhetoric. We are often reminded by him, as we hear him as guide, that the relation of *science* to the psychologist-psychiatrist in the *art* of the novelist is uncertain, though he is careful to be apologetic in assuming his diagnostic role as that of perhaps a pseudo-psychologist. We might put it that the ontological ground limiting the psychological symptomatics isn't yet comfortably accommodated. We observe this as a thematic concern in many essays. The novelist's responsibility, he holds, is to diagnose the malaise commonly shared by selves in this century, though he is shy about prescribing remedy. Science and not philosophy or theology are preferred as appropriate initial mode to the novelist as pathologist. But from a Christian perspective, the acceptable remedy lies in theology, involving a defense of a creed outworn, so far as the contemporary intellectual community will allow.

In neither art nor science may the conman as maker dissociate himself from the thing he makes through a fiction of role playing. The scientist especially (and sometimes the artist) may falsely suppose himself capable of accomplishing such a dissociation from responsibility to his actions, though he call that dissociation "scientific" (or, if a poet, "aesthetic") objectivity. Eliot had thought such self-protection possible through skeptical philosophy, only to discover that truth proves contrary to intentional willfulness of any resolute skeptic, whether he go dressed in robes of philosopher or poet. Recognizing the impossibility of an *impersonal* art (for which the early Eliot argues), Percy unlike Eliot acknowledges that limit at once. But he takes refuge nevertheless in a shifty indirection through wit satirically deployed – in his non-fiction as well as in his fiction. *Lost in the Cosmos* thereby partakes of fiction in disguise, through the fancy of an indirection hiding its serious dimension, since our guide through assuming a "role." That is why we are alerted to it as something of an intellectual autobiography. If he were more innocent as artist in this parenthetic century of our history, he might be more openly philosophical or theological, perhaps even more "serious" rather than playful in his address to our moral responsibility to the signs we use. Or if he were more certain in his own judgment as a transient in this parenthetic century, as *homo viator*, he might even succumb to the dangers of allegory or parable, though thereby putting the more at risk the virtue of his made thing. Thus Faulkner failed in his attempt in this direction, in which his setting is World War I as the turning point of his *A Fable.* It is an undertaking as if Faulkner were Dante. That flawed work would be sufficient warning to Percy against such a gambit as artist. And so the satiric, mellowed by a humorous acceptance of human folly, proves more comfortable to Percy. That approach to signs, artfully deployed by "indirection," involves the playfulness of a nonjudgmental irony. And yet again and again, as is evident in *Lost in the Cosmos*, judgment proves an obligation difficult to set aside by ironic detachment.

The point we are attempting here is a delicate one, delicate in more than one sense, including especially the danger of presumptuousness. But we attempt it in tribute to Percy. We are not so much concerned with an aesthetic question – whether through some "distancing" from the making (as we have called it) through role-playing, the made thing is put at risk by the making. That is a legitimate question, one which is a most personal one to the artist as person. That is, the person as poet, fearful of the "personal" as endangering his made thing, puts himself at considerable risk. That is why we turn once more to Eliot in making this point, since he is thematically (in his art) and personally (in his pursuit of transcendent rescue) dealing always with the terrors of the spiritual dimension to making which for him proved inescapable at last.

It was this engagement of the relation of the "personal" to art, spoken to in his early criticism with a presumptuous arrogance (as it subsequently appeared to Eliot himself), which brought him to that spiritual collapse occurring at the time *The Waste Land* is at last brought to its public form. That spectacle of his collapse as person, as if but personal circumstances to Eliot himself, his close associates took to be a "breakdown," as if his psychological machinery were the only problem. Eliot knew it a spiritual dilemma, having come to recognize himself as intellectual soul incarnate. The spectacle of his breakdown lacked that degree of the spectacular which Dostoevsky gives it in his portrait of Ivan Karamazov. But in recovering from it, Eliot would certainly have recognized correspondences of his "personal" experience to Ivan's, as Percy recognizes something of his own intellectual and spiritual dilemma caught in Dostoevsky's fiction. What we are about, then, is the engagement Walker Percy makes with the terror possible to the poet on his own spiritual journeying as made through his calling as maker. We might thereby better value his witness to us as an "ex-suicide." And in making such an attempt, we may see Percy a Modernist Everyman in recovery, his role a witness of the possibility to us of emerging from the swamps of Modernist despond. It is in that interest that a close comparative reading of Eliot's *Cocktail Party* alongside *The Thanatos Syndrome* reveals a kinship of Percy to Eliot, both initially caught in the historical circumstances of Modernism but discovering a rescue, not in or by art but through art into that country ruled by Love. Recall his subtitle to "Physician as Novelist," "Why the Best Training for a Novelist in These Last Years of the Twentieth Century Is an Internship at Bellevue or Cook County Hospital, and How This Training Best Prepares Him for Diagnosing T. S. Eliot's *The Waste Land*."

Self-judgment always becomes an especially complex presence to the writer himself, and not simply at the level of craftsmanship: his concern (as he must continuously remind himself) must be for whether the thing he makes is good or not in itself. With such thoughts in mind we might return to the scenario involving the Corn Dance and discover underlying the manner of Percy's address an increasingly *sardonic* humor. Now the nature of sardonic irony is that it turns back upon the ironist. Put another way, sardonic irony is that flavor of words suggestive of self-satire, most effective in art when the self-satire is most artfully hidden. Sardonic irony colors much of our century's literature. Percy would notice it as particularly evident in James Joyce's work. It intrudes in Eliot's work, up through *The Waste Land* (hence Eliot's later characterization of his poem as "a personal grouse"). And in our turn, we may notice it emerging here in *Lost in the Cosmos*, in which our guide within this great wilderness of the cosmos is present to us, self-amused and yet somewhat uncomfortable in his assumed role as our guide. There is, we might put it, a sense of his personal presence in his signs, though that "person" is not always comfortable in being a presence.

In consequence of this very personal awareness of his presence as guide, we respond to the climate immanent in the words, the sardonic irony. It hovers in his posing of characters who are almost caricature, made such through satiric art's removal of *character* (the realities of personhood), which deportment as rhetor leaves the agent he is making somewhat incarnate in the words thereby somewhat more a caricature than character. A verisimilitude of characters to persons to the contrary (through a maker's openness of consent to them) seems of a quite different order of making. That is the more persuasive effect Percy achieves in *Thanatos Syndrome*, to such a considerable degree that even Percy's "self indulgence" in his "Marx-Brothers moviescript" (as he admits) proves somewhat intrusive. By that slap-stick treatment, his scientist is made to revert to primate and loses that "sense of everybody as human beings," as Jan Gretlund objects in his letter to Percy.

Percy must, as any writer must, address the inadequacy of signs to the complexity of persons, and that obligation is increasingly in his awareness in his later essays, especially evident in "Why Are You a Catholic?" and in "The Holiness of the Ordinary." The difficulty might well make even more appealing to the writer, as he finds himself under that pressure of responsibility, that he take recourse through signs in caricature, effective and even persuasive in pillorying looniness by exaggerating the symptoms of human failure. But to do so may lose thereby something of that "sense" of characters as dependent upon "human beings" in their actualities. We might take this inclination to caricature as more conspicuous in Percy's early work, somewhat endangering *Love in the Ruins* for instance and coming to a focus in *Lost in the Cosmos.* In part one suspects this response in making to be from the growing pressure upon Percy out of his growing popularity. He is badgered to submit through his words to the role of public guide. Having once submitted to making this thing of words, but protected by a playful mask, his pathological fascination with the Modernist malaise as infecting the "self" nevertheless draws him into contemporary circumstances to the self in its actualities the more deeply.

Percy finds himself drawn into a current "culture" in decay, and thence drawn further into its historically derived inception out of late Medieval philosophy and Renaissance science. Through that drawing, his attempted detachment through rhetorical mask (the poet's version of "scientific" objectivity), leaks somewhat into the thing he makes, evidencing his personal presence. We might put it that his is a circumstance, as maker of signs, analogous to Eliot's in his early poetry. Eliot will discover by his attempted detachment from his poem – a withdrawal into the impersonal through the device of the mask, a positing of speaking personae – that he cannot escape "personally" thereby. Intending to sterilize the personal as it were, he but exacerbates his own actual struggling as the person he is in the act of making. This is to suggest that Eliot, in his attempt to submit to the responsibility of the poet to employ "reason in making" (as St. Thomas remarks that responsibility) is yet deeply committed to a rational skepticism well into the separate poems drawn together as *The Waste Land* (with the perceptive aid of Ezra Pound). By that rational skepticism, he is constrained as person from an intuitive openness, especially suspicious of Romanticism's "feeling" as damaging to the English poet in the 19th century. In this respect he continues as a rationalistic philosopher as much as poet, with a decidedly 18th-century rationalistic suspicion of "Romanticism," shared with his companion in the war against Romanticism, Ezra Pound.

Not a scientific rationalism, except insofar as Eliot has been drawn to the science of mind that has been opened out of William James's speculative writings. Eliot will write of Hawthorne at this time, for instance, as our first "psychological" novelist, avoiding as did James the question of "sin." Put in another aspect, Eliot is himself given to a dissociation of sensibilities at the level of epistemology, catering to the *ratio* in fear of the *intellectus* – to reason in fear of his intuition. It will come as a surprise to his contemporaries, then, that after "Ash-Wednesday" he praises the English Romantics, declaring Wordsworth a "seer" and "prophet," praising him as a great "philosophical" poet. And he will be drawn very close to Keats, recognizing affinities between the young Keats and the young Eliot. What Eliot discovers is that the device of the mask does not prevent a leakage of the personal into the projected voice. To take a distinction here, a close reading of "The Love Song of J. Alfred Prufrock" in relation to "The Journey of the Magi" or "Ash-Wednesday," in respect to the poet's proximity to his personae of his poem, reveals a difference in the poet's relation to his mask early and late. He is more comfortable with the "voice" of his poem in those later poems.

The device of the mask may prove particularly faulty, then, if employed in the primary interest of the poet's escape from the personal entangled in his making. That is a concern quite other than Keats's concern for "negative capability" as person. In Keats's own attempt, what is sought is a comfortable submergence of his own personal presence into a thing, a conjoining in a consent to its actuality. That is why it is important to remember that, when Keats talks about his concept of negative capability in a letter, he is not talking about a concept in relation to his making a poem. His concern is to come to an accord with existence other than his own "self." Not that he doesn't recognize a relation of this attempt to the art of making. Indeed, it is a gift he sees Shakespeare possessed of superlatively, moving Keats to admiration and some envy, since he dreams of becoming playwright himself. What Keats understands is that negative capability is a gift to the poet as *person,* a gift which may serve in relating his personal presence to the thing he makes. It serves the dramatic voice, for instance (again, Shakespeare notable in this regard), in projecting and so making more persuasively incarnate a simulacrum of person. Insofar as by this surrender of himself to a dramatic making, the voice he projects as maker makes an incarnate presence in signs. The poet participates in his character as "possible" or "probable" in relation to the potentialities of person, dependent upon that actual nature in his commitment to a making. He may be thereby endangered, we suggested, as Dostoevsky is endangered in projecting a Raskolnikov or an Ivan Karamazov, insofar as there is a sympathetic attraction to his made agent. There is required of the poet, then, a courage hardly recognized, though Walker Percy recognizes it in Melville and praises Melville for this very risk he takes.

If the poet intends a craftiness of indirection, then, his signs may well prove more crafty than his intentional control of them. That has been, we remarked, an abiding problem to the poet especially since Henry James. For since the appearance of Jamesian "Realism," the intellectual, social, spiritual circumstances of the poet himself threatens to shadow the thing he makes with autobiographical material, the "craft" of making becoming something obsessive as a self-protection. This is especially so if the autobiographical seems a rich plunder at the moment, as psychological science evolves into psychiatric science (with Freud), it may present a most unwelcomed challenge to the poet. In his concern for the good of the thing he makes, his poem, he may risk words by an indirection, lest his "psychiatric self" as a matter to his making dominate at the expense of the possible or probable in complex human nature. The struggle may only exacerbate his personal sense of alienation. That, let us suggest, is the "psychological" matrix to the poet's "autobiographical" making, out of which evolves sophisticated techniques – some of them critically celebrated in Conrad and James and Joyce. In turning from philosophy to poetry, Eliot learns much from all three of these predecessors, his essays and allusions in his poetry revealing an awareness of his having done so. But even so gifted a poet as Eliot, profiting from the techniques of a "new" literature, cannot establish an effective barrier between himself as person and his role as poet inclined to an imaginative voice of an imagined persona.

His skeptical irony dissolves gradually, becoming evident in those *Poems, 1920*. Of these poems most of them ("Gerontion" aside) depend on the old folk ballad for structure, both in metrics, verse line and stanza. Not that there isn't a sophisticated adaptation of old measures, but in comparison to that arresting first volume, *Prufrock and Other Observations,* whose title suggests a cool detachment, the difference gives pause. Though a few are in French, and there continues throughout a kinship in the ironic as a counter to sentimental inclinations that one might trace back to Baudelaire, there is emerging another quality. The irony is turning sardonic, a prelude we may speculate in retrospect, hinting certain intellectual agonies in Eliot himself more conspicuous in *The Waste Land.*

One detects beneath the ironic detachment of the poet in his "role" as singer an ironic deportment to current miseries encountered at an intellectual dead end. An adaptation of the role of "folk" singer from popular ballads dominates with cultural "tales" in Eliot's second volume. It is a perspective in the volume's notable poems speaking a dead end, which proves personal, Eliot beginning to come to himself out of ironic skepticism, though but gradually. For a comparable Eliotic "folk ballad," see the "Two Corbies" as a response to that sentimental version of the same story, "The Three Ravens." The anonymous singer of the "Two Corbies" intends to shock his present audience with a cynical version of the possible or probable. Eliot's irony turns sardonic, then, a point made by that poem with the confessional title, "Mr. Eliot's Sunday Morning Service." It might well be, given that title, a signal somewhat discomforting to his close ally Pound, who will presently participate in bringing *The Waste Land* to issue, in a neighborly service to "Parson Eliot" in his crisis. Pound was long practiced as diagnostic doctor of signs in relation to intellectual circumstances. His career had been as such a practitioner, dissecting culture as it were in relation to its signs, in an internship well-preparing him for (in Percy's phrase) "Diagnosing T. S. Eliot's *The Waste Land.*"

In another place, I have suggested that Ezra Pound uses the mask, more boldly and audaciously, almost as if in a defiant reaction to what he considers a cowardice in some of his contemporaries who use the mask as self-protection. Pound will have done so in part perhaps with one eye on his ally Eliot, whom he begins to refer to after *The Waste Land* as "Parson Eliot." He is rhetorically ruthless as well in directly ridiculing those using the mask as an excuse for sentimental blather, as in that perversion of Imagism which he calls "Amygism" in order to pillory Amy Lowell. His collected shorter poems, *Personae,* is rich with the audacity of his masks. It is this tendency to a consumption of the simulacrum as it were, Pound insistently a presence at the heart and mind of his projected personae, that signals his inevitable alienation from his close friend Eliot once Eliot becomes Christian. The breach will become conspicuous after *The Waste Land.* Meanwhile, Pound praises that second of Eliot's collections, its English version *Ara Vos Prec* ("Now I Pray You") its title from one of Pound's good poets, Arnout Daniel, though the words are put in Daniel's mouth by Dante on *Purgatory.* But what is especially pleasing to Pound about the volume is Eliot's recovering prosody from the abuses of "free verse" as practiced by lesser poets than he and Eliot.

We might look at Eliot's second volume ourselves, then, suggesting it to be concerned with the personal as controlled by the poet's role-playing, a theme Percy speaks of as learned by him from Jean-Paul Sartre. It comes at the end of that disillusioning World War I. In the context of Eliot's *Collected Poems* we might call it comparatively Eliot's version of *Lost in the Cosmos.* To do so recalls Percy's remarking the "Physician as Novelist," his own "Internship" at New York's Bellevue or Cook County Hospital as if that had prepared him to read *The Waste Land* with understanding for the first time. Percy recognizes a "personal" affinity to Eliot through that famous or notorious poem. Percy very seldom, however, mentions Ezra Pound, to whom Eliot dedicated the poem, Pound already notorious as our post World War II villain. But in the years preceding World War I Pound himself is in an active pursuit of a science of the sign, to be commanded by reason, leading Pound to the Chinese ideogram as the way "back to the thing itself." Confucius becomes his St. Paul.

There is underway, at the time of that parenthesis of World War I, a widening fault in the intellectual community in regard to sign, Pound's participation in that civil war among poets over the nature of sign is worth our remembering since it bears consequences to us. Pound is resolute in advocating the poet as arbiter of order through signs, established by the poet's intentionality as a discrete intellect. Thus the poet is to be recognized as arbiter of order, both social and political. That is the address Pound makes, resting his authority in Confucius (see Pound's Canto XIII). What we might remark, however, is that Pound is acting in a resistance to Positivistic reduction of man toward machine through science, though often Positivistic himself in his resistance. We remark him here, then, as an initiating influence in the civil war between art and science, Pound's influence less and less acknowledged or even recognized in that role. His position early and late rests nevertheless in autonomous intellect's presumption of transcendence, and that becomes the point of contention between him and Eliot. Incidentally, he does so initially directly out of Bergson's *Creative Intuition.*

Percy, in his "self-interview" for *Esquire* (1977) makes a rare mention of Pound, very interestingly in a context discussing the relative "hospitality" of the South in contrast to the isolated community, an allusion to that New York enclave of intellectuals removed from "community" into a self-contained group, a gathering almost as famous in our literary history as that gathering of writers called the Fugitives at Nashville. "There is a good deal of talk about community," Percy says, "and the lack of it, but one of the nice things about living an obscure life [as a writer] in the South is that people don't come up to you, press your hand and give you soulful looks." That is, one doesn't have to endure the pity one may encounter in Northern condescension to the "South." Percy's next sentence: "I would have hated to belong to the Algonquin round table, where people made witty remarks and discussed Ezra Pound." The writer in the South has an advantage in his "obscure life," since "Most of the men in the South don't read and the women who do usually prefer Taylor Caldwell and Phyllis Whitney to Faulkner and O'Connor."

We remember this self-interview, its questions put to this Southern writer in his "obscure life" among Southerners by himself. What he calls attention to as a "Southern" virtue is a cultural bonding which is not dependent upon sophisticated "roundtables" where intellectuals gather at a safe remove from the Bellevue or Cook County Hospital, in the Algonquin Hotel, into a sort of "King Arthur's Court" of knights serving literature by wit, ideas isolating them from community. If they conducted themselves as Percy playfully suggests, if indeed a popular entertainment at that court Ezra Pound is laid upon the table, the witness of his words to such a court that failed to recognize Pound as *homo viator,* as Modernist, might well suggest the roundtable itself in advanced decay. It had seemed possibly other to Pound in those days from the time of King Edward up to that somber November of 1918, with the dark clouds already gathering toward 1940. He had looked to New York (rejecting Washington, D.C.) as culture's capital. Pound thought that by sign strictly ordered we might recover the social body, whereupon he went to war to establish a *pax Romana* through sign, becoming disillusioned in doing so with New York as a possible Ecbatan, a possible shining city, as he was to do in London and then in Paris.

Pound, just as he is becoming aware of that strange Puritan refugee T. S. Eliot in London, has become the principal father of Imagism, a new mode of poetry derived directly from Bergson's theories of the *élan vital.* As poet, through his authoritative action in a control of signs, there could be engineered intellectually a direct recovery of things in themselves, ordered by art and thereby effecting as a deterministic inevitability a social order. This in contrast to Eliot's philosophical, speculative address to that continental movement Phenomenology. By that authority of the *élan vital,* centering in the intellectual poet, there was to be drawn all the past into the vortex of intellect, to be issued "imagistically" in effecting an order irresistible to social and political minions. Political and social order would follow, giving rise to a City on the Hill analogous to Ecbatan in contrast to that City on a Hill preached by our Puritan fathers. New York will be followed for Pound by London, then Paris, then Rome, in his progress of disillusion – leaving him at Rapallo at the close of World War II charged with treason. Not the Heavenly City sought by St. Augustine, nor a city Eliot becomes accommodated to, London despite its decay, that "Unreal City" lamented in *The Waste Land.*

What had not been calculated because beyond calculated measure was the possible, even probable, uses of Pound's theory of order (given human nature itself). Thus Imagism, initially exciting (see the early numbers of that famous periodical *Poetry*), became hostage to pseudo-Imagists. There began, after that first assault (Pound's recollection of his and Eliot's contribution), the overthrow of the iambic pentameter line in its 19th-century dullness. But that led to an abandonment of prosody through sentimental self-indulgence of the poet, leading Pound to abandon his movement, his departing anathema declaring it *Amygism,* Amy Lowell having succeeded him to high office in that movement by popular consent of her peers. Vorticism failing Pound's larger intentionality to rescue Western Civilization, he goes at last to Rome, romanticizing Mussolini as poet-emperor. This, at about the time Walker Percy is visiting Germany and observing youthful arrogance rising to political power, recalling that on one occasion he was somewhat intimidated into giving the Nazi salute himself.

To dissociate himself from irresponsible "Imagists" then, Pound summons a new term, *Vorticism,* as World War I is getting underway. Vorticism is a name which catches somewhat a Bergsonian ambiance of the *élan vital,* with the poet (in Pound's version) the specific locus of an immanent force. Eliot to the contrary will be increasingly drawn toward a surrender to things rather than a command of things as ordered by the sign, though that is a gradual change – celebrated at last in "Ash-Wednesday." That will become his habit of being which will earn him the epithet from Pound, "Parson." By a more ancient allusion than Bergson in our seeing Ezra Pound, we might call Pound Promethean. In his poetry, especially his

Personae but in the succeeding *Cantos* as well, we see him at an exercise as poet, summoning consciousnesses (often historical personages) to his service, his rescue of tradition involving his "making it new" as poet.

The poet's strategy of adapting a mask against the intrusive world, a means of self protection, usually allows an irony threatening to become sardonic and thus rupturing that mask. That is an intention unacceptable to a Pound. Pound intends to risk himself, to the considerable irritation of his contemporaries very often. He is particularly irritating in his disdain for that tendency of a growing intellectual deracination, given rather to the bravado of *becoming* his mask in a very personal way. As for Walker Percy, he shares with Dostoevsky in his intent rather than with Pound, perhaps having encountered Kierkegaard's remarks in *Works of Love* (1847): "The actor's art is one of deceiving; the art of deception. . . . It is the pinnacle of art when the actor becomes one with what he represents, because it is the pinnacle of deception." Perhaps Percy was encouraged to this strategy as deceiver (through adapted role) not by Kierkegaard or by Sartre entirely. He tends to associate that strategy with these "Existentialists." But his more companionable ally Dostoevsky deploys the mask as means to deception in his *Writer's Diary* in sacrifice as surrogate. That is, he intends to lead the "Russian soul" out of the bewilderment and disorientation which he sees occasioned by the Russian intelligentsia's having embraced Western ideologies, theirs a citified manifestation which he could not escape in Moscow or Petersburg.

I say "citified," since that intelligentsia assumes a condescending deportment toward the Russian "peasant" who is embarrassing to its own version of Russianness. It is a peasantry migrating to those cultural centers and forced to live in degradation unsettling to their idealistic projections of social Edens out of Rousseau. In such imagined Edens savages might be transubstantiated by idea into noble integers, unlike those we encounter in *Crime and Punishment* or *The Brothers Karamazov.* Such the dreams lovingly dwelt upon in Moscow and Petersburg saloons, within which Dostoevsky could only be a strange presence. (And Walker Percy, a *Southerner*? A Roman *Catholic*? Such condescension becoming a sentimentality assumes (in Dostoevsky's observations of it) of an embarrassment to the Russianness reformed by the intelligentsia. It would reject an unlettered savagery of nature, an unsophisticated beastliness, which Dostoevsky sees as rather a spiritual disorientation caused by pretenses to sophistication in adopting Western philosophy and literature as models for a Russian rescue. As for a sophistication in the use of the mask by the poet, Dostoevsky is more subtle than Sartre. In his analysis of Dostoevsky's "role-playing" in *A Writer's Diary,* Professor Gary Saul Morson provides an "Introductory Study" of the *Diary* for the 1994 publication of Kenneth Lantz's translation of the *Diary.* The *Diary's* diversity of genre ranges from fiction, to pseudo-fiction, from speculative adaptations of current history to the ambiguities of art, to direct commentary on current events, to ambiguously autobiographical accounts of the writer himself, then widely popular in Russia – the author of *Notes from Underground,*

The Idiot, Crime and Punishment, A Raw Youth. How is it held together as *a* work of art, as Dostoevsky rather certainly thinks it to be, though a monthly publication, a journal published by Dostoevsky who is its single contributor, editor, publisher?

It is held together, it gains a certain unity, by a singularity of an intense intentionality in Dostoevsky himself, though in his deportment in words his is often an ambiguous presence as actual person. Among his observations: "I keep thinking that we have begun the epoch of universal 'dissociation.'" His dissociation we find relevant at once to that action of arrest in Eliot's Prufrock mask, as a means of Prufrock's withdrawal from the impinging world. It is a key term as well in that famous critical phrase we have concerned ourselves with, the "dissociation of sensibilities," the separation of "thought and feeling," which phrase Eliot laments having burdened graduate students with in their defenses against academic committees as it were. (Again, one might here remember the first "graduate student" of the Modern academy to run afoul of such committees: Kierkegaard, in defending his huge dissertation *The Concept of Irony.*)

And so, Professor Morson wonders: "Could the unifying theme" of the *Writer's Diary* "be 'dissociation' itself?" If so, then how, as a work of art, could the *Diary* "achieve any wholeness on the basis of utter fragmentation?" Having remembered Eliot's fragmentary "Prufrock" or his fragmentary *Waste Land,* our own answer to the question Professor Morson poses and explores is that the unity must lie in a projected consciousness posed through that mask, a world projected in a "fictional" response to being lost in a chaotic cosmos. Thus a drama of dissociation, a portrait of consciousness lost. In respect to Dostoevsky, there is a concern for a dramatic unity through the mask, always identified by the "editor" Dostoevsky with the actual person Dostoevsky – despite ironic manipulations of that mask which leave us often uncertain of how to take "Dostoevsky's" testimony. There is a deep and unifying intentionality nevertheless, whose analogy one might find in the *Divine Comedy.* For as *homo viator* himself, Dostoevsky as person undertakes a surrogate journey as Russian soul, projecting himself in the role of exemplum to a recovery of the latent, the incipient virtues in the Russian soul. He sees those virtues, in a reaction against the Westernizing decay of that Russian soul by a Russian intelligentsia turned sycophant to Western modes of our being lost in the cosmos. It is in this aspect of *A Writer's Diary* that it becomes, from Dostoevsky's point of view, a last self-help book to the Russian soul, lest that soul become irretrievably lost in the cosmos. As a hidden thematic unifying concern, there is a Kierkegaardian "Either/Or" running through it: either Western dissociation or Eastern recovery of unity as community through Orthodoxy.

Interestingly enough, there is in the *Diary's* "Dream of a Ridiculous Man" an other-worldly visit by the protagonist, into a prelapsarian community, in consequence of which this space traveler (through his dream) becomes as man already fallen he becomes the contaminant of the innocent community. One remembers Percy's concluding scenarios to an Either/Or in his *Lost in the Cosmos:* a space journey, or a retreat to a common fallen ground in backward Tennessee. What Dostoevsky is intent upon, in his "experimental" work – though he takes it but a development out of already-existing Russian literature – is a transformation dramatized in himself as surrogate Russian person faced with contingent options to his becoming. He assumes a role of representative figure of the Russian soul on its possible journey, buffeted on every hand by Western perversions of soul.

In Professor Morson's words, Dostoevsky's intent is "to transform his real [his *personal* experiences as *homo viator*] into a collective myth of the Russian people as he is simultaneously transforming journalism into art." Transforming, we add, even the making process of art as itself a part of that myth. But here *myth* carries for Dostoevsky – as it does for Tolkien – a sense of a prophetic and visionary relation to transcendent realities, the "author" mediating that vision toward a possible awakening of that Russian soul which might even be recognized by the intelligentsia as desirable. For, after all, Dostoevsky's considerable audience for his *Diary* is a middle audience, one between the vast peasantry intuitively joined to realities of places through spiritual hunger and that smaller contingent of Russians so confidently defensive of their intellectual dissociation from that visionary reality. We have had, and will have, much to say about Walker Percy's concern to perfect a role as poet which he describes as that of diagnostician, and so we here remark that Dostoevsky is a very constant presence to him in his pursuit of that role in part through a shared concern for the writer's "role." For this reason, we may the better understand his own *Lost in the Cosmos* as a version of his own *Writer's Diary.*

Dostoevsky might well have recognized this exercise of signs as involving a deception putting the writer himself at risk, despite his own intent to underline the dangers of *possession* in its theological sense in relation to evil. For by intent, one hazards, Ezra Pound would occupy his own inkpot, dislocating even the devil. One sees this in his "Ballad of the Goodly Fere," a "Scotch" ballad (by its diction) sung of Christ's Crucifixion by one of the "brawny men" who are his followers. It is the same assumption of personae at work in a more celebrated of the early poems, Pound's "Sestina: Altaforte." An anecdote reports Pound shouting this poem from a table top in a London pub. Given Pound's penchant for outlandish garb to shock people, particularly the British, he might thus have shocked further by impersonating vigorously, through the "effete" form of the Sestina, a presence of Bertrans de Born, declaring (in his epigraph) to have dug that old warrior up from Dante's having buried him in hell because "a stirrer up of strife."

That is the possessive appropriation through mask which becomes the technique of the *Cantos,* then, in what one might (to Pound's horror) call a Miltonic masque of control to an epic intent. That is, Pound would dictate the limit of sign by an autonomous dictation. In respect to this manner, we may juxtapose David Jones in his version of an epic attempt, his *Anathemata,* the "voice" of that complex poem Eliotic in respect to the poet's devotion to a recovery of things in themselves. His deportment is a sacramental response to things, since Jones is concerned with a proper stewardship as poet both to and through signs. It is in this respect a poem attempting to "purify the dialect of the tribe" in a deference to the holiness of both ordinary and extraordinary multiplicity of the creation he inherits as an intellectual soul incarnate.

Pound might well be dismissive of Jones – as he tends sometimes to be of Dante – seeing Jones as but another instance of the Poet as Parson. One might suspect that inclination in Pound to lead to the poignancy of fragments of the *Cantos* late in his making. In one he laments that "I am not a demigod,/ I cannot make it cohere," though he will insist that though "I cannot make it flow through," the late voice is still that of the poet as medium of the vortex, the agent of order. For "it coheres all right/ even if my notes do not cohere." Thus the painful consequences, in this late confessional mode, of "Many errors,/ a little rightness,/ to excuse [Dante's] hell/ and my paradiso." Almost a transcendence, though not that understood by Dante or Eliot. Rather "a nice quiet paradise/ over the shambles" of this century's world, "some climbing/ before the take-off" in his own version of transcendence. A little later, a fragmentary lament: "That I lost my center/ fighting the world . . . that I tried to make a paradiso/ terrestre." A last lament for his Modernist response to givenness.

XIV

A pursuit toward caricature as the ironist's species of allegory is a temptation, one might suggest, as opposed to the more demanding responsibility to the reality of agents as persons to be celebrated in art in their possible or probable manifestations. Each of the writers, of course, will differ as to whether he himself is "Romantic" or "Realistic," categories adapted to academic cataloguing of our literature of the past two centuries. (Eliot will counterpose Romanticism to Classicism at first, but argue subsequently that such division is rather facile.) Flannery O'Connor, in her devotion to Hawthorne would hold him more realistic than Henry James, given that James shies away from the realities of man's sinfulness. Nor would she consent to Eliot's early characterizing of Hawthorne as primarily a "psychological" writer. One might differentiate one art from another in this distinction, making the one less resonant of human realities through a tendency to caricature (including even that very serious species, the caricature of person called allegory, differing thereby from formal satire such as Swift's in contrast to Bunyan's *Pilgrim's Progress*).

Perhaps Percy himself recognizes this dilemma, measuring himself as artist against others he admires in relation to his own novels. For an interest in loonies is a temptation to caricature. He sometimes seems to feel that Flannery O'Connor speaks through a more resonant art than his in her attempt at an "incarnational" effect difficult to achieve by any poet. The term *incarnational* he uses in specific reference to her, and in praise of her achieving this quality in her prose to a considerable degree, speaking as well of her "transparency" as maker. In such "transparency" is evidenced, we would suggest, the poet's escape from a discomfort about his presumption in making, which presumption leads to a confusion between "making" and "creating." He may, alas, as maker be tempted to become "guide," abandoning in some degree his responsibility to concentrate on the good of the thing made in a response to the truth of things existentially real, signified in this relationship by the *possible* or *probable*. That is a weakness in Hawthorne, as O'Connor was well aware – his temptation to allegory. And we recall as well the lingering discomfort in Dostoevsky from his intuition that art in its concern for the possible or probable *depends* in a most fundamental way *from* his own person as maker. We might discover also that this relation of the poet to his made thing becomes a terror to Tolstoy, in reaction to which he declares himself sinful if he writes a story. Not surprising, then, that Percy, praising Flannery O'Connor's "transparency," will turn increasingly to a consummate artist who seems to achieve a perfection of balance between himself as person and things, through an art partaking of that "negative capability" which Keats so much desired but which seemed always to Keats only to leave him isolated in his "sole self," revealing art's inadequacy as salvific to the person.

That is, Percy turns to Gerard Manley Hopkins, an early interest of Percy's. Hopkins appears to be of increasing importance to him as he wrestles with the difficulty to the artist in his dependence *from* the reality of his own person through signs in his making. In Hopkins there is a "transparency" achieved through the poet's openness, his signs made the more adequate through an open love of actual things. What stirs Hopkins's love is the "inscape" of a discretely existing thing seen ordinately, as it may be related by sign to that thing's "instress," to use Hopkin's terms once more. Sign as a gesture of love out of an openness to the holiness of things, the "holiness of the ordinary" which Percy praises in his late tribute: that is the deportment of the person as poet whereby self-love is rescued toward a "transcendence" quite other than the false transcendence represented by angelism, whether an angelism in poet or scientist or philosopher. But a high desire for self-forgetfulness to the artist – the maker of a thing ordinately celebratory of the "instress" of the holy things constituting the cosmos – is perhaps not to the fore in *Lost in the Cosmos.* In this work the concern is for "characteristic" characters as "selves," loony denizens of the Modernist world such as those posed in the scenario of the Corn Dance. We are reminded of this difference by the tone of Percy's own presence in this text. (We might also be reminded of another rather close analogy, the presence of Tom Wolfe in his *Bonfire of the Vanities*.)

But here, having reminded ourselves of a steady presence of Hopkins to Percy, we turn to a less comforting presence, a writer already introduced passim, a writer who seems almost to haunt Percy on his way, engaging his interest more deeply than can Tom Wolfe's satiric "reporter" fiction, more deeply even than can a Chekhov as diagnostician of the Modernist malaise. Again and again, it is Dostoevsky whom Percy summons to points he makes about the novelist and his discomfort in the Modernist world. Dostoevsky is, from the time of his *Notes from Underground* (1864), a dedicated adversary of the new Western science and philosophy. Those enemies of the "Russian soul," certified by the Enlightenment to the popular spirit which is thus set on its way to Percy's consumerist age, have replaced poet and priest, making the more difficult Dostoevsky's role as prophetic, rather than diagnostic, novelist. If a Diderot or, subsequently, a Nietzsche commands deference to his theories that man is autonomous intellect, Dostoevsky is already attuned to such dangers to the Russian soul of that presumption, anticipating the alienation accompanying intellectual arrogance. It is he who explicitly announces the circumstances to *homo viator* as "antihero," though himself heroic in his attempted confrontations of Modernism and his attempt to recall us to known but forgotten truth about our nature. What troubles him especially is the inclination of autonomous intellects to dictate the actions proper to man, with a certainty denied the prophetic novelist. That is as well a comfort Percy finds increasingly suspect. He is drawn to Dostoevsky, sometimes uncomfortably so, discovering that they share common spiritual and intellectual difficulties and anticipations. Percy will become increasingly acerbic toward those scientists, though not with science itself as a suitable intellectual discipline. The scientists seem increasingly false to their calling precisely in that they assume a comfortable office as sage to society. They tend to that certainty which makes the pejorative *scientism* the more apt description of their ideological practice, as if they were philosophers. Looking about the cosmos as affected by scientific impositions upon it, Percy finds himself the more inclined to what he might describe as the "looniness" of a Dostoevsky.

If sometimes perhaps reluctant to do so, Percy recognizes this affinity to Dostoevsky, as in that essay on Melville. There, though Melville is the protagonist of his reflection, it is with Dostoevsky that Percy sides at last, though not associating himself so openly with Dostoevsky as Flannery O'Connor embraces Hawthorne. She celebrates Hawthorne's concern for keeping "romances" as a defense against "social determinisms and to steer [fiction] in the direction of poetry," as she says. In that tribute to Melville, we recall, Percy juxtaposes Dostoevsky, as if to elevate Melville. He declares himself impressed by the bravery of Melville's attempt in such a work as that late *Billy Budd,* which bears a "flawed originality." It does so since Melville endows his hero with an unacceptable "innocence." It is not an innocence "from human nature" but from "outer space," as if Billy Budd were "man before the Fall…dragged in from some loony planet invented by Melville and Rousseau." What results is "a readable science fiction."

As for any relation of Melville's fantasy version of the good man, Dostoevsky would make something quite other of Billy Budd, says Percy. Billy Budd would turn out to be "a child molester." The interesting undercurrent in this praise, ostensibly of Melville, follows in a subordinate aside. Billy Budd would be, in Dostoevsky's version, "therefore a good deal more believable." Differing though they do in vision, both Melville and Dostoevsky (Percy argues) impress "Southern writers for the same reason. . . . Neither was afraid to deal with ultimate questions" in relation to that spiritual disquiet which gains the Southerner the epithet of "Christ-haunted." We notice nevertheless that Percy invokes the name of Dostoevsky very regularly in interviews and essays, Melville seldom.

After the publication of his *Moviegoer,* interviewers begin to swarm. For *Library Journal* (February 1, 1961) he acknowledges its antecedent in "Dostoevsky, Rilke, and especially Albert Camus." In a more extended acknowledgment of antecedents a year later: "in this order, Dostoevski, Kierkegaard, St. Augustine, Lawrence, Joyce, Gerard Hopkins, Marcel" as those who have been most important to him in his apprenticeship. More interestingly, in his association of Dostoevsky with his concerns as pathologist of the spirit and a decade after *The*

Moviegoer (in 1973), he says that the last few pages of that novel "were meant as a conscious salute to Dostoevski." But then with the erosive effects of interview questions after receiving the National Book Award for the novel, he begins to grow tired of such fruitless attempts at requiring his "naming" influences to be listed, that professional parlor game of the academic mind in the years contemporary to Percy's early labors. To an interviewer for *Esquire* (1977) at the outset he says, "Please don't ask me about Dostoevski and Kierkegaard." It is from these two "influences" as affording interviewers easy questions that he begins to shy, as he does increasingly shy from questions put him about the "South" and himself as "Southerner." That brings us to the caustic rejection of such questions about the South in his "Self-Interview" for *Esquire* (December 1977), his "Questions They Never Asked Me, So He Asked Them Himself." But it is he who introduces the theme. In this attempt he is in charge of the questions no less than of the answers. What one observes is that much of this lengthy self-examination, if not most of it, dwells on the "South" and "Southernness."

What we are suggesting is that, similarly, Percy's fascination with Dostoevsky at the outset continues with him, less noticeable to us perhaps insofar as his witty indirection obscures the intensity of his own pursuit of "ultimate questions" that almost becomes an obsession with that great Russian. As a person, responded to from our distance geographically and through the curtains of a separating language, Dostoevsky proves nevertheless a presence to many "Southern" writers. It is somewhat as if he were a Hazel Motes, rather than a Tom More. And that he continues a presence to Percy to the end one might discover in that fictional presence in *Thanatos Syndrome,* Fr. Smith. Father Smith is a spirit, as it were, who encompasses by his history as an imagined person much of the disparate intensities of Dostoevsky's Karamazov Brothers, coming to his climactic position in that fire tower with the convictions of Alyosha, the passion of Dmitri, and something of the intellectual incisiveness of Ivan, having confronted and even somewhat escaped by his remove an encounter with evil at its darkest. He bears witness to us of that continuing presence of evil nevertheless, present even in the green swamps of Louisiana. He is, this is to suggest, an accusatory presence – a prophet – whose diverse experiences of having walked to and fro in the world from Germany to Louisiana swamps, increasingly both reflecting and reflecting upon in his works the recent history of our failures, brings him to charge mankind at this juncture of history as responsible for having become lost in the cosmos. Man has become so through intentional flirtations with the dark beauty of the Abyss. Fr. Smith's recognitions parallel Dostoevsky's as revealed in that Russian's fictions and notebooks from those *Notes from Underground* to *The Brothers Karamazov.*

If Percy is not more conspicuous than Dostoevsky in agonizing over his circumstances as both poet and person, he nevertheless shares with that dark Russian a recognition that the *person,* by his given nature and "after the Fall," risks his soul through willfulness. And since Percy is – as is Dostoevsky – a person, he must be also at risk despite or because of the roles he assumes. In this recognition lies a common belief that the person fallen puts not only himself but community at risk by willfulness. In our Modernist circumstances, community's intellectual guardians – poets, philosophers, scientists – present clear and present danger to community, insofar as they advocate the willful denial of our endangerment in the interest of whatever ideological theory they would advance in order to effect whatever earthly Eden they propose by theory. Especially the scientists, ascendant as venerated sages to the popular spirit, seem less and less aware of the endangerment to community through their theories that are to be executed by sophisticated technology to our pragmatic conveniences. They seem given to a resolute faith in method, out of which they devise clever systems, extrapolated as ideals to the proper order of society: specifications decreed by autonomous intellect, produced by machines to please man as himself a machine. And they do so, as Dostoevsky recognizes, out of Enlightenment philosophy.

Concerning this tendency to a blind faith in theory, Percy will speak (in his "Diagnosing the Modern Malaise") of a "misapprehension of the scientific method, its elevation to an all-encompassing world view." He will say in that essay "the scientist, in practicing the scientific method, cannot utter a single word about an individual thing or creature insofar as it is an individual but only insofar as it resembles other individuals . . . whether the individual is a molecule of NaCl or an amoebae or a human being." And he adds a complicating mystery: "the catch is that each of us is, always and inescapably an individual." It is the intrusion upon our recognition of this inescapable *limit* to human knowing out of our limited human being, indeed, which must underline the necessity to us as knowers that we find a solution to our Modernist "ontological impoverishment," to which impoverishment science itself seems to have so largely contributed. (We have attempted in supporting Percy's position here expressed, to use *person* consistently, where in this passage he uses *individual,* we reserving *individual* to signify *person* as gnostically reduced from the reality of personhood.)

We discover like discomfort in Dostoevsky. He is troubled to discover in himself an affinity to Ivan Karamazov, desiring to be instead an Alyosha Karamazov. But if Dostoevsky is so troubled about his own inclinations, he is quick to locate the source of the infection of his beloved "Russian soul" put at intellectual risk in Western philosophy and science (as indeed Tolstoy shares with him a similar conclusion about the origin of the "modern malaise"). Thus, if Percy's essays, and specifically his self-help book, may be considered speculative reflections on his own difficulties, we may fruitfully recall Dostoevsky's own speculative notes in comparison. In his notebooks, this is to say, we find a version of Dostoevsky's own attempts at riddling his calling as novelist, for instance those notes made in preparation to write such a work as his *The Idiot*. His notebooks by their manner suggest a parallel to Percy's *Lost in the Cosmos*, being analytical of characters as measured against the note-taker himself, though as a self-help book they are notes private to himself. We have already hinted at a significant difference, as Percy would have noticed – perhaps even with some envy of that dedicated, committed, and tortured soul, Dostoevsky. In those notes toward dramatizing Prince Myshkin, for instance, Dostoevsky reflects a hope struggling to escape despair. Dostoevsky is himself in exile from his beloved Russia as he brings that work itself to completion and publication. His struggle is spiritual, not intellectual, and his concern is deeper than with the aesthetic possibilities of his anticipated work, as well as it is also beyond that mounting burden of literal poverty burdening him in exile. He is living hand-to-mouth, with his wife expecting a child. (They are forced to pawn clothing off their backs for food to survive.)

For his novel, Dostoevsky wants above all a protagonist persuasive to us as one of God's fools, to be dramatized as constant in his Godly foolishness, though increasingly pressed in upon by a collapsing world. Rather specifically, in respect to Dostoevsky's uses of "objective correlatives," the milieu is to be that of St. Petersburg. Now that milieu, personally dear to him, he sees as affording tensional relations of persons. He does not concentrate on the actual history and geography of Petersburg, though he nevertheless pays these a sufficiently careful attention. In this concern for *place,* then, there are interesting correspondences to Percy's concern for his world, the South. St. Petersburg at mid-19th century, at the heart of Russia, is counterpointed in its Modernism somewhat by Moscow, which Petersburg society is all too eager to emulate. (In Percy's "South," Atlanta has this reputation in relation to New York City.) It is an environment well known to Dostoevsky, within which he may posit agents caught up in political and social and religious contentions similar to those encountered by Percy in New Orleans at mid-20th century. As Dostoevsky was drawn to Petersburg, New Orleans and Louisiana are becoming for Percy similarly a comfortable place within which to contend with man's looniness, after his Alabama youth and his young manhood in Germany; an academy in North Carolina and New York City in self-exile from the South. Those absences, in retrospect, prove Percy's version of exile from his Southern origins, parallel in spiritual connotations to Dostoevsky's exile to Europe to escape imprisonment for debt.

In Russia as in America, granting the century interval (the 1860s in Russia, the 1960s in America), youth finds itself in revolt against corrupt fathers, though the youth are fundamentally corrupted by their own revolt as Dostoevsky sees it. For the Russian novelist, there is a species of intellectual war underway, which he anticipates as more destructive of Russia than Napoleon's invasion had been. Dostoevsky speaks of it as a war between the fathers as "Liberals" (his designation of his own generation) and their sons who have been deeply infected by Western radical philosophy through their fathers. They have subsequently become Nihilists, their faith resting only in science and so their actions a studied destruction of tradition and especially of that Orthodox religion to which Dostoevsky is devoted. The youthful Nihilists had as "Liberal" fathers many who paid a mannerly deference short of believing to Orthodoxy, a sign of hypocrisy setting their sons' teeth on edge. But they are even more radically destructive of a recent tradition, that Liberalism of their fathers. Against those "Liberals," Dostoevsky's own generation, the Nihilist sons, are in an increasingly violent revolt with terrorist acts. And Dostoevsky is in sympathy with their revulsion, those destructive actions understandable to him. The young are in revolt against what in our 1960s would have been dubbed the "Liberal Establishment," though often pronounced "conservative" by our own youths in opposition. (Lyndon Johnson, the advocate of a "Great Society," is hurt personally by that charge.)

It is in writing his *Idiot* (1869) that Dostoevsky would attempt (as he says) "to portray the positively good man," speaking to the necessity of a rescue of the "Russian soul" from both the Liberal fathers and their Nihilist sons. "There is nothing more difficult to do," given that there is "only one positively good man in the world – Christ." Dostoevsky finds that, in Western literature, the closest attempt and nearest success in rendering the good man is in that satiric novel by Cervantes, himself something of a conman as novelist. *Don Quixote* is beyond merely a gentle and farcical satire, a persuasive image of a good man. A part of the irony in that great mock epic is Quixote's foolish failure to accomplish good on the scale he envisages, though he stirs a certain goodness in others by their response to his very failure. (One is tempted to suggest in Percy's manner that had Quixote been a novelist at a later date, he might have written his own *Billy Budd.*) Cervantes, then, does not by his art deny the good, treating it as a gentle foible in his hero. Dostoevsky on the other hand is given to scathing rebuke of human folly, which complicates his own attempt to render fallen man in quest of the good, possibly rescued by grace, by dramatizing a good man as protagonist in his Count Myshkin. Indeed, he is much given to dramatic representations of evil destructions, painful to experience in his narratives even in *The Idiot*. In this respect Dostoevsky differs from Cervantes in both gift and given nature. Cervantes by his detachment does not at last threaten to sever himself from a sympathy with humanity, despite humanity's looniness, as Dostoevsky is so threatened, making him temperamentally the more akin to Percy one hazards. There is a considerable tenderness in Cervantes' treatment of his failed knight and a degree of suspension of judgment, even of those taking advantage of the knight's naïveté. Consequently, the irony is relieved by sympathetic humor, in which respect no doubt Dostoevsky discovers hints of a Christ-like presence in that foolish knight – one of God's fools, though a bumbling one. We might detect echoes of this same deportment by Percy to his characters, such as in his treatment of Tom More in *The Thanatos Syndrome*. (That is a deportment largely absent from *Lost in the Cosmos,* our present concern.)

Dostoevsky's difficulty is that he cannot, as does Cervantes' in his good humored response to human nature, present a character sympathetically endearing without coming dangerously close to sentimentality by that sympathy. Thus in his presentation of Dmitri Karamazov in *The Brothers Karamazov* as a Byronic Romantic, victim of Western philosophy's dislocations of heroic intentions to honorable actions, he borders upon an excess of sentiment. Dostoevsky cannot always maintain detachment sufficient to his task, so that he will be more persuasive in his incarnation of an Ivan than of a Dmitri. He is somewhat rescued from sentimentality in that great novel by Alyosha, in part because of a careful ambiguity attaching to Alyosha's uncertain future. Thus Alyosha seems a portrait of the staretz as a young man, one might put it, remembering that it is Alyosha whom Dostoevsky would have as protagonist in the novel he intends just before his death. It may be said as well that Alyosha is clear-sighted, seeing the circumstances of the Karamazov clan prudentially, and with an endurance through a love which is substantive in his presence, not a passive futility.

In the event, in the execution of *The Idiot* as the first of his most celebrated novels, Dostoevsky discovers that the complexity of spiritual reality as besieged by the Modernist world does not allow him to be tempted into allegory or parable. The actual present world – social and spiritual – restricts his fancy and as well restricts his sympathy for foolish man. If he were writing a satire in an *ad hoc* response to the moral chaos abroad in Petersburg, he would be less restricted. We may see this well enough if we contrast *Notes from Underground* to his more ambitious attempt, *The Idiot.* He is at once fascinated by and fearful of the current social and spiritual realities of his beloved but decaying Russia, circumstances the effect of which is to inflame his prophetic concerns. That sense in him as poet is of a responsibility to community, a sense which exacerbates his role as novelist. For he would make *real* to his reader the alarming reality of the pending community collapse of the local world he inhabits as person. It is as if his *idea* of a positively good man, to be set in the midst of that reality, must yield at last to realities, reflecting the dark struggle of the Russian spirit toward the good at that particular moment of history, agonizingly centering in Dostoevsky himself. Dostoevsky, then, shares with Flannery O'Connor in uses of the grotesque, knowing as does she that for the hard of hearing his art must shout. But he seems less able than she to maintain the spiritual serenity necessary to a "transparency." Hence, following his attempt to embody the idea of an ideal good man in *The Idiot,* he recognizes that he has not realized his *idea* in *art*. He turns immediately to a concern for what he calls in his notes and in letters "The Life of a Great Sinner." And this turning leads to that novel sometimes called *The Possessed* (1871), more accurately called *Demons* as it is titled in some translations.

Dostoevsky, in those notes and diaries and in his letters, reveals himself intense with desire beyond any possible refuge through a detached irony, or any escape into art itself as a substitute for his Orthodoxy, especially in those last years from his *Idiot* up to his death. He is not drawn, after his *Notes from Underground,* to the erosive skepticism of the cruel protagonist pilloried in that work, nor by a skepticism tempting him to substitute "art" for "religion," the refuge so often attempted by Western Romantics from Keats to Joyce and Yeats and Eliot (up to his *Waste Land*), encouraged in the Western poet by Descartes and Kant. We might put it that he is evangelical as artist, though seldom succumbing to tract (as does his rival Tolstoy) and often given to a severe irony of judgment on human folly, concerning which folly he is seldom ambiguous. This is to say that Dostoevsky submerges and risks himself beyond cautionary self-interest. He is *prophet* rather than *diagnostician*, in that old sense of *prophet* meaning one who would recall us to the once known but now forgotten vision of man as a spiritual creature. But in similar circumstances of the decay of community, it is with the term *diagnostician* that Percy is most comfortable, especially when he is trapped into talking about his own work or his intentions in it. His has nevertheless a sense of being drawn as prophet despite himself, aggravated by interviewers. He resists most carefully, lest as novelist he risk that looniness we hear attributed to Dostoevsky as person. That, after all, is what he senses in the perennial question: Why are you a Catholic?

Speculative comparison, this between Percy and Dostoevsky, though encouraged by Percy's own comments on that Russian as an antecedent father to the 20th century's "Southern" writers from Faulkner to Flannery O'Connor. The role of prophet is hardly a promising one to Percy in the post-World War II American South or North, so that he might well choose a protective cover as "diagnostician." But even by that choice he cannot avoid the intensity of a growing interest in him occasioned by the initially arresting if puzzling nature of his work. There is that further complication, from his point of view: in the interval of the century between Dostoevsky and himself there had continued an erosion of any primary concern for the *work* itself and a shifting of attention to and adulation of the writer of current reputation. Such a writer inspires, if not a cult, then at least a fan club. Flannery O'Connor, we saw, observes this caustically in reference to the Book of the Month Club.

The explosion of the media in the interval since Dostoevsky is toward making the writer himself an instant popular presence, with the emergence of the "interview" at first in quarterlies, then in Sunday supplements, and at last in that mode of virtual reality through the television camera. It is a tendency which has proved gradually a disservice to the made thing, *this* work by *this* person. A hundred years and more ago, one might have a thoughtful version of this tendency in such a work as Coleridge's *Biographia Literaria,* a work unhampered (metaphorically speaking) by the necessity of commercial breaks. Earlier there had been Boswell's testimony of Samuel Johnson as a formidable presence, a work perhaps more popular at mid-20th century than at the time of its publication, given the "discovery" of Boswell's own "notebooks." By the 1960s, with the poet a welcomed presence on the academic scene, the interest concentrates upon his personality, the more celebrated if his life has been scandalously spectacular. It tempts the poet to an adaptation of a public "role" exciting to students and faculty and so desirable to administrators in evidence of their public service as it were, justifying public largesse to poets like Dylan Thomas, more famous for boozing and womanizing than for his poetry one suspects.

Those young Fugitives at Vanderbilt, laboring to teach undergraduates the Western canon, were hardly welcomed presences as poets on that campus, though since their day considerable government and Foundation funds have been poured into many academies in an attempt to capture local and current images of those randomly gathered poets who found themselves by accident almost at Vanderbilt just after World War I. We need only remember how a Dylan Thomas might have fared in those old days, not only at Vanderbilt but at any "respectable" academic institution, as compared to the excitement of his erratic presence on campus after World War II. Walker Percy (as was Flannery O'Connor) was aware of that concentrated attention to the poet, his poetry often but an excuse for an attention to him as celebrity. What has now superseded the poet (or novelist) as phenomenon, "visiting" writer, is almost any visiting celebrity, provided he or she has become sufficiently notorious. From Hollywood as commencement speaker or a politician bearing scandal or rumor of scandal, preferably already having as credentials some prison time behind him as fillip. The world, it is the old world yet.

In that shifting climate, Percy could only have recognized that, despite the labors of the "New Criticism" in the late 1920s and 1930s (Pound and Eliot salient in that movement), such attempt had failed to return intellectual attention to the poem and away from the poet. This despite the phenomenal influence in the academy of such a work as Cleanth Brooks's and Robert Penn Warren's *Understanding Poetry* on the teaching of "English" in the post-World War II academy. Nor could Percy have failed to observe a burden upon the sign itself inherited out of that attempt, a "spin-off" of one aspect of the New Critic's concern for the text. And so not an interest in the possible diamond but rather a fascination for the diamond merchant prevailed. Thus Percy pays caustic words to "Deconstruction" as an academic concern, centering in the Deconstructionist as a rebel against reality. He remarks this late academic fact in that note to his "Semiotic Primer of the Self," in *Lost in the Cosmos.* Having set aside "French structuralism" as "the self-proclaimed foe . . . of the very concept of the human subject" which is proper to semiotic concerns, he adds, "I do not feel obliged to speak of the deconstructionists." That dismissal, avoiding even a collective honorific capital D, comes at a point in the ideological history of the American academy (the early 1980s) when Deconstruction has already invaded the provincial academy as the new critical rage, the latest importation from the continent. Concentrated in its purported interest in the sign, Deconstruction (Percy saw) was the most self-centered address possible to the mystery of the sign, though all through the academy the Deconstructionist as Intellectual Dandy rose as academic personality, to be celebrated for outrageous pronouncements about the sign. That fad is now faded and outworn since Percy's dismissal, exhausted by the initial enthusiasm for spectacle as the principle "product" of the academy, a "theory" for a moment marketable.

Such looniness of intellect, academically revered, Percy views with an ironic distancing from it, though aware of it as part of the local atmosphere whenever he is "entertained" on any campus. In such an intellectual climate, then, how may he avoid being merely a presence on campus as a celebrated loony, being both "Southern" and "Catholic," especially if he aggressively assumes responsibility as prophet as his much admired Dostoevsky had done? To so address himself to the academic Babylon might be to reduce to spectacle any depths in his own prophetic vision. The residual deference to analytic deportment in the academy, somewhat surviving the dislocations of the academy, might at least allow by indirection some movement of mind toward the truth of things intellectual and spiritual, a counter to the overwhelming malaise of mind becoming more and more concentrated in the academy. If he assume the role of diagnostician of the Modernist malaise, perhaps. . . . Dostoevsky in his address would appear a decidedly wild presence in the 1960s, and so much celebrated as a sensational as to exacerbate his risks as person. (Remember Solzhenitsyn at Harvard in 1978.) For were Dostoevsky a presence on our present campus he would be instantly a wild darling of intellect as an intellectual celebrity, as Dylan Thomas had been. Most likely he would have self-destructed in the circumstances to choruses of sentimental lament. By indirection, then, though remembering always the courage of Dostoevsky in his engagement of the ambiguous manifestations of our given human nature.

If Dostoevsky is concerned with a protagonist presented as God's fool in *The Idiot,* or with a protagonist as the greatest sinner imaginable in his *Demons*, not so Percy. He demurs from such temptation by making a distinction between himself as novelist and Flannery O'Connor. We have heard him already and, with Dostoevsky in mind, recall his words once more from his *Paris Review* interview (1987): "I am perfectly willing to believe Flannery O'Connor when she said, and she wasn't kidding, that the modern world is a territory largely occupied by the devil. No one doubts the malevolence abroad in the world. But the world is also deranged. What interests me as novelist is not the malevolence of man – so what else is new? – but his looniness." Percy's *matter* as novelist then, as we have also heard him say, is this "looniness . . . of the 'normal' denizen of the Western world who . . . doesn't know who he is, what he believes, or what he is doing." For this "unprecedented state of affairs is . . . the domain of the 'diagnostic' novelist," the role in which Percy finds himself most comfortable. His is a perspective quite other than Dostoevsky's upon Prince Myshkin who is shown struggling in pursuit of goodness as God's fool, only to find himself responded to as a loony by other characters. Given his spiritual concerns, he appears "deranged." The surrounding agents of that fiction are nevertheless revealed as drawn to this strange presence beyond reason's protection, attracted by his looniness as Percy might put it. It is of this spiritual abnormality that Flannery O'Connor speaks, declaring her commitment as fiction writer to the grotesque. But as she says in "The Grotesque in Southern Fiction," "I have found that anything that comes out of the South is going to be called grotesque by the Northern reader, unless it is grotesque, in which case it is going to be called realistic." Here, in her defense and against a misreading of this caustic response to her work as if she were provincial in her concern, let us note carefully her "Northern reader." Her term is less a geographic designation than it is her version of Tate's term to designate the intellectual *provincial,* such a person as that Tate on another occasion than his essay "The New Provincialism" speaks of as "possessed" through fallen nature in a way Dostoevsky might recognize. For such provincials are "born Yankees of the race of men" under "the modern power." They are "Damned souls, running the way of sand/ Into the destination of the wind!"

Well enough, then, if we grant our harvest of looniness to be unprecedented as Percy implies it to be in countering a concern for "malevolence." But one might also ask what is new about looniness, save perhaps the "scientific" language evolved as descriptive of it, lest its roots in malevolence intrude upon the concern and stir those attic-stored terms like *sin*. One might, with Modernist indirection, declare it more often than not "normative" rather than "grotesque," given its pervasiveness. Another question to put: Are God's fools loony? And if not (as Percy must agree that ultimately they are not in the light of eternity, to which light he subscribes) what then of this current anomaly of "'normal' denizens"? Put more searchingly, is this "normality" intimately related to malevolence as Flannery O'Connor would insist, whether turned destructively upon the "self" or upon others? We notice that in his conclusion to the *Paris Review* interview, answering the question his interviewer urges him to pose to himself on that occasion, he asks himself "What is the main target of your anger in *The Thanatos Syndrome*?" In his surprisingly angry answer to this actual interviewer, he begins with a description of "a certain mindset in the biological and social sciences" as having corrupted "educated folk" with "a quasi-religious orthodoxy." It is a mindset one might name (he suggests) as the "Holy Office of the Secular Inquisition." (An echo, here, of Eric Voegelin.) Expressed in anger, his title is an epithet very much adapted as a chilling indictment of a very similar mindset which Dostoevsky reveals through Ivan Karamazov's poem, his "Grand Inquisitor."

Dostoevsky, as we discover by reading his letters and notebooks, seems personally acquainted with the likes of an Ivan or Raskolnikov. It is as if in his reflections about the characters he would incorporate in his fictions in various guises (dare we say it), he practices a personal therapy. This seems evident through his notes especially. John Keats might recognize the address, as dark as it is, as partaking of a "negative capability" in response to malevolence. To put the point another way, Dostoevsky is given a gift which Flannery O'Connor speaks of as the writer's "incarnational" gift. But it is a gift less free of risk to him than to her in requiring of the novelist, in his actions of making a fiction, a self-endangerment in making a character palpable through sign. The possible or probable reality of malevolence itself may be stirred in the person of the poet. The mystery of this gift, the source of such an *informed* art – the *carnate* dimension of it – lies most immediately in the potentiality of the poet himself as person. He enters into diverse characters, so to speak, in order to *incorporate* the possible or probable dimensions of human nature itself, but the ultimate authority to the possible or probable lies within his own discrete nature. This is a necessity to the poet which

Goethe will also find required to the "good" of the thing made, and his *Faust* is his great accomplishment by his own submission. The gift to the poet as maker – as novelist – requires this openness to potentialities in human nature ranging from the saintly to the demonic, then. And it is both a terrifying and endangering gift to discover such potentialities in oneself. To "make" through this necessary openness therefore endangers, in that what the maker discovers through his actions is his own deepest possibilities as person, including even the possibility of demonic inclination. The protection for the poet undertaking the risk, for a Flannery O'Connor, lies in an unshakable vision of the good, a relation of nature and grace beyond the finite power of the person to dissolve absolutely. Thus she sees her misfit as possible to a rescue as the prophet he "was meant to be."

It is this risk which I suggest Dostoevsky was uncomfortably attuned to through his making of fiction and which Percy recognizes in him. He is shaken from certainty beyond risk by obsession, not only for the good but exhibited in his own obsessive failure. A fictional exorcism of that danger he attempts in his *Gambler*. As a person, a presence, in Petersburg and elsewhere, he is seen as disturbing to those he encounters – to Tolstoy or especially to Turgenev, both of whom incline to believe Dostoevsky mad. But it is the risk he takes, which makes him such an arresting presence to us as person no less than poet. There is, in relation to our argument here, an interesting analogy to draw between two poets, Dostoevsky and Kierkegaard – worth our attention because of Percy's early and enthusiastic discovery of Kierkegaard, and his lifelong fascination with Dostoevsky. The Dane is painfully and angrily aware of his local reception as a "loony." One might see in him as well an intellectual assault upon the citadel of the growingly effective Modernist spirit. At the extremities of Modernism, he might even be supposed a cause of Modernist excesses. That is a theme one might explore in following his influence upon French intellectuals leading at last to Jean-Paul Sartre.

After his early reading of Kierkegaard, Percy refers to him often, but cautiously. It is almost as if Percy gradually begins to wonder whether his initial fascination with Kierkegaard was not a delight in the audacity of Kierkegaard's confrontational energy. For Kierkegaard, ideas were worth whatever ridicule that Dane suffered from a stagnant intellectual community, and for this courage Percy admires him. We notice that Percy later, after a history of fielding questions about Kierkegaard's influence on him, makes a challenging statement recognizing a danger in the Dane. In his "Diagnosing the Modern Malaise" (1985), Percy remarks that "Christianity began to crumble [after World War I], perhaps most noticeably under the onslaught of a Christian, Søren Kierkegaard, in the last century." The consequence of this general crumbling, he adds, is that "the Christian notion of man as wayfarer in search of his salvation no longer informs Western culture," having been replaced by "such familiar goals as maturity, creativity, autonomy, rewarding interpersonal relations, and so forth." That is a consequence of philosophy's turning to the self as the ultimate concern, to which turning Kierkegaard contributes.

If Dostoevsky as "loony" cares less than does Kierkegaard for local ostracism, he is no less painfully angry at the rejection of the "Russian soul" by those who should be defending it. He would do so by enacting possibilities of rescue as it were, "becoming" his endangered protagonists, but with a fearful sense of risk as opposed to the arrogant possessiveness of Ezra Pound as poet. We might say that Dostoevsky does not so much *transcend* as a self through his making (to use Percy's term for the will's act of angelism, to which the poet is always susceptible). He seems rather to inhabit his characters through the virtues of – and so endangerment of – a self-forgetfulness (again, contrast Pound), in a devotion to making the character immediate to us and therefore persuasively real as a warning against or parable about Modernist triumphs, probable threats to us as persons. As poet, then, he is himself one of God's fools, his ancient predecessors found in the Old Testament from Jeremiah to Malachi, prophets whose poetry about imminent destruction is persuasively realistic, made so through rhetorically violent imagery – through objective correlatives drawn from the violence of local cultural and religious clashes in the desert. In the recent history of literature, this aspect of the "science" necessary to art's making reveals an irony whenever the poet does not recognize his personal endangerment in his devotion to making. It is almost a cliché that the "Romantic" poet (especially if we summon him out of his 200-year development into our century as the "alienated" person) becomes lost in the cosmos by his very intensity as poet. Nor can we but recognize in such poets (Shelley or Pound for instance) a self-celebration of their alienation. It is as well a cliché that in attempting recovery from intellectual deracination, such a poet may but the more concentrate upon his art as the ultimate salvific instrument. By an intensified attention to art's perfections, he comes to suppose that his rescue is possible, though the attempt seems only the more to isolate him from those others "lost in the cosmos" – those fellow wayfarers moving in circles for whom Percy writes in his self-help book. (This tendency of the Romantic poet I have engaged at length in *Romantic Confusions of the Good: Beauty as Truth, Truth Beauty*.)

Concerning this intention to art's perfections by the Romantic poet, which Dostoevsky laments at times as isolating him in an attic out of the social world: it is a critical commonplace that as maker Dostoevsky is not so "polished" a "Romantic" artisan of signs as is his contemporary, Tolstoy. But the pressures he feels as novelist, which might be taken as primary cause of Dostoevsky's unpolished art, proves too handy an explanation. Especially so when we are tempted to summon those personal difficulties associated with his family travail as explanation. Of course he was in constant debt, partly through his addiction to gambling. He *was* often ill, not dying old and full of years as does Tolstoy. He took on family responsibilities to an extended family, including that irascible family left to his care (or so he believed) by his dead brother – with little thanks for his services from those unhappy survivors. It is out of these circumstances to him, as he reflects on his distraction from worldly responsibilities to his gifts as poet, that near the end of his life he made extensive notes for a novel about a "poet" who is prevented his blossoming because he is married and has complex family distractions – hardly a work intending a portrait of the artist such as Joyce will write. For Joyce's "poet" concludes that his responsibility as poet requires in the beginning his resolute rejection of family, country, and especially the Church.

But there is perhaps a better perspective to take on Dostoevsky's circumstantial difficulties that prevented his being so polished a novelist as Tolstoy – or more especially so polished in his work as is his own elected antagonist Turgenev. What Dostoevsky himself concludes is that accidents of circumstance interfere with the spiritual depth of his concerns, to which those actual "worldly" realities speak only symptomatically, insofar as his art is concerned. For he endures an increasing spiritual agony within himself, a sense of failure as a created intellectual soul whose troubles are exacerbated by that additional limit upon his given nature, his being called to be a poet. He is incarnate as spiritual intellect, through which givenness there opens the prospect to his art of an "incarnational" imagery of personhood. And through this very personal circumstance is reflected his own agony as poet. If by that agony, reflected in his work, we discover an opening of the spiritual way, that seems to offer the poet himself scant comfort. Nevertheless he has as a sacrificial concern as poet the ominous circumstances to those Russian souls he believes exceptional through their very "Russianness," though they are progressively eroded by the Modern world. They are God's entrapped agents, who by their spiritual recovery might rescue the world. That is the Quixote in him. Not that he will declare art itself salvational. Yet art might serve (or so he must believe) to remove obstacles to the rescuing actions of grace to such persons. Even to himself perhaps. That prophetic hope will lead him to declare the failure of the early Church, then the failure of Rome, leaving as humanity's last hope of rescue the possible triumphant survival of the "Russian soul" through the Orthodox Church.

He speaks constantly of that "Russian soul." It is threatened because it has become most dangerously entrapped by Western intellectual influences through the intellectual treachery of the Russian intelligentsia. Not the least by that Western importation from that Roman Church to which Percy and O'Connor are devoted. Indeed for Dostoevsky, the whole complex of the post-Renaissance West becomes his "Yankee" enemy, intensifying his uneasy commitment to a Slavic "Southernness." In this almost mystical address to his gift as poet, Dostoevsky understands his labor to be always a celebration of his Creator, a Creator abandoned not only by the secularized Western intelligentsia (poets, scientists, philosophers), but particularly betrayed by the Western Church. A recovery of the celebration requires his own descent into the darkness of his endangered soul. One is tempted therefore to suggest by descriptive epithet that Dostoevsky is the poet as prophetic staretz, putting himself at risk *in* the world rather than withdrawing from it as a monastic writer. Father Zossima lectures Alyosha against such withdrawal, requiring of him as demanding Alyosha's spiritual advisor that he participate in the world, even to the extent of getting married and having children. To the contrary, a withdrawal was to be Stephen Dedalus's gambit, but as a secular monk devoted to the self as God, as he proposes for himself in *The Portrait of the Artist as a Young Man.* We find him still unable to do so in *Ulysses,* immersed in Dublin still. And that final monument to Joyce's intellect, his *Finnegans Wake,* seems an attempt by Joyce to exorcise once and for all the Ireland always actual and pressing upon him. He carries Ireland within him, so rich a presence that it is palpable to him in his Paris exile. That last work as exorcism in one of its aspects is made as an act of magic to arrest a fictional world out of that actual world. Joyce leaves Ireland for Paris, in a self-exile reminiscent of Dostoevsky's circumstances on fleeing imprisonment for debt in Russia, and he experiences similar experiences of personal poverty. (Pound on one occasion we are told carried a "care package" to Joyce, including shoes and clothing and the like, arousing Joyce's indignation.) As prophetic staretz, Dostoevsky endures the agony of that celebrated Western victim of Yankeedom, Ivan Karamazov, with resonances of our sense of being lost in the cosmos which Joyce or Eliot or O'Connor or Percy can but recognize. And as poet he treats the pathos of such a soul entrapped. But Tate's "Yankees of the race of men" he also sympathetically explores in its Byronic mode, whose imaged personae is Dmitri. Yet always he is most drawn to Alyosha, leaving us fascinated but disappointed not to have seen the novel he promised us in which Alyosha was to have been his principal protagonist.

XV

Such a poet as Dostoevsky struggles, through an openness of himself as poet to creation, to make his imitation "incarnational" out of the possible or probable depths of human nature. And insofar as he accomplishes a persuasive fictional incarnation of characters through "objective correlatives" artfully deployed, he gains a measure of the truth of things human and thereby proves himself prophetic poet. For certainly he recalls us to known but forgotten or ignored truths about human nature. Thus his art serves, in a service secondary to art, to call us from our age's exacerbation of spirit, our spiritual deracination as persons. Spiritual deracination is everywhere evident to Dostoevsky in his country, in the mid-19th-century Russia, as it is to Percy in mid-20th-century America. If politician, philosopher, scientist fail us, such an address by art might prove a gift recovering us to reality, even through its dark tribute to the complexity of our spiritual circumstances. For to engage spirit as actually endangered by natural and historical circumstances recognizes that the truth of things as affected by history is awash both in and over our given nature as intellectual soul incarnate in this place at this time. Such are the circumstances to our reality, inescapable to our concern if we are to gain an ordinate address to the possible or probable of our "self" in its actualities. Nor need such an attempt, when made in signs, become necessarily a tract rather than art. The dangerous temptation to any visionary poet is to reduce art to polemic. Art uncovers the reality of our potential, our contingent actuality as persons, but it does not *as* art bear a responsibility for our salvation. The possible or probable, made prophetically palpable to intellect as a reality of *homo viator*, is a worthy risk, a sacrifice through which the artist may even prove martyr, as Dostoevsky seems sometimes to have felt himself to have become when he considered the critical derision aimed at him (by his version of "New York critics"), or his practical difficulties of surviving and supporting dependents.

In our century, Yeats will argue poetry sufficient to a rescue of the "self," but Yeats has been insufficiently lessoned not only by such sufferings of spirit as Dostoevsky knows, but by the example of his predecessor Keats, whose similar attempt leaves Keats forlorn, isolated to his "sole self." Yeats seems disinclined to engage the impinging and disturbing history of the moment to the poet despite his nationalistic devotions. In this respect, the early Yeats in particular is Byronic. And he will at last turn from responsibilities in the local moment of clan or family to a dream of art's rescue of the forlorn self as his primary desire, poetry becoming for him a mystical theology of the self, celebrated by him in his *Vision*. The poem itself becomes an analogue for him to that golden bird set upon art's evergold bough to sing to emperor and lords and ladies of what is past or passing or to come. Thus art allows a transcendence of the ravagements of time, at least for a moment. Joyce is better lessoned than Yeats on the point, perhaps owing some debt to his Jesuitical training (which would horrify Dostoevsky, who believed Atheism in the West a deliberate strategy of the Jesuits, executed with Rome's blessing, for reasons the Grand Inquisitor justifies to Christ in Ivan's imagined Second Coming).

Perhaps Joyce is nevertheless hopeful that for a moment art is a vehicle amenable to an angelism powered by the imagination, at least making a tolerable moment. It might, through "objective correlatives" commandeered from ambiguous nature (including human nature), thus allow consciousness to rise in an independence beyond what the naive or the simple call "reality," that concept in the popular mind known as the "real world." If that strategy succeed, then there might even follow a jettisoning of the launching engines, freeing the artist to a gnostic angelism. But then the final necessity: a rejection of the thing made – the art object, the poem or fiction – in maintaining a severe skepticism. That is youth's dream as artist, at least as argued by Joyce's Stephen Dedalus. Joyce plays out that dream of youth in a "naturalistic-realistic" art which affects subsequent artists by its technical virtuosity. Thus neither Percy nor even Flannery O'Connor escape Joyce's influence upon the "science" of their art, widely explored in our criticism because so heavily influential on fiction for nearly a hundred years now. Nor should fictioneers not be influenced. For "visionary" distortions of reality by art's pseudo metaphysics as advocated by Stephen Dedalus and enacted as art by Joyce do not abrogate technical perfections discovered in the attempt, any more than the presumptuous anticipations of genetic scientists abrogate the genetic truths they uncover. As with the science of genetics, in which what becomes known as the truth of genes must not to be rejected because the discoverer himself distorts that truth by pseudo-metaphysical pretensions (as when Dawkins declares man, both mind and body, but the gene's robot); so too with the skills of art, the sciences of making, are not to be rejected because of the willfulness of the artist in choosing to reject truth itself as independent of his intentional "creating."

James Joyce plays out in his later work the inclinations of the artist as a young man intent on an absolute freedom, a freedom declared self-created by his young Stephen in *A Portrait of the Artist as a Young Man*. But what we observe as an aesthetic concern is that "metaphysical" questions raised in the early novel are not resolved. Young Stephen is left dangling, suspended among a fragmented dialogue with himself in his diary. His dream as poet has been to become the one god of an aesthetic world, which by his will as its "creator" he will then reject by an indifference to his own made thing. But first is that necessity of self-exile from Country, Church, and family for Stephen, *homo viator* whose banner is *non serviam*. Having escaped this "real" world, he may make an unreal world. And then the crowning action: a rejection of his own made world by an indifference which certifies his own omnipotence. Thus to achieve an absolute angelism by absolute skepticism. Or so he dreams possible, and Nietzsche would be proud of him! Such is the drama Joyce gives us in a portrait of his version of the Romantic poet, a very Keatsian Stephen Dedalus, but one who through a refined cleverness would manipulate the sensual world, procuring thereby a sufficiency of "objective correlatives" in his plundering and thereby thwart even that deceiving elf "fancy" which Keats laments as his betrayer. For it is "fancy" that leaves Keats trapped in his soul-self as his only interlocutor, his "self" buried in his private signs. (Again, compare young Stephen, talking to himself in his fragmentary journal.)

As Joyce makes his *Portrait*, he is himself already an aging artist, for whom such an arrogantly Promethean attempt as Stephen's seems only to threaten an arrest of Joyce as "juvenile" one might fear, his difficulty paralleled by his American counterpart, Hemingway. The *Portrait* is prelude to *Ulysses*, then, in which Stephen attempts, though at last he fails, a recovery to the substantial world of persons and place in Dublin. The arresting art of Joyce's attempt is unable to obscure the dominance of pathos in his work in general, against which his irony must struggle to prevent that work from collapsing into sentimentality. That is Joyce's own personal terror as poet. And from *Ulysses*, on to *Finnegans Wake*, we suggested, an arrested monument to an aging intellect – a monument upon which Joyce reflects at the end of his life in wondering whether he, Joyce, is not as poet a victim of *fancy* rather than a creative lord through the *imagination* – his terms alluding to Coleridge's famous distinction.

For Coleridge, the fancy distorts images – the "objective correlatives" in poetry – disjoining them from their proper anchor in the real world, a disjunction which imagination to the contrary maintains in Coleridge's view. Thus Coleridge makes that once famous distinction, in which the dangers of fancy are emphasized: "Fancy . . . has no other counters to play with, but fixities and definitives. The fancy is indeed no other than a mode of memory emancipated from the order of time and space." But in that anchor of the imagination in the realities of time and space, upon which are dependent "fixities and definites," the bond of intellect to thing is governed by responsibility to an ordinate consent to the limits of reality. Through that consensual bonding, the imagination operates. As Coleridge would have it, the imagination "dissolves, diffuses, dissipates, in order to recreate." It is a distinction which we may well riddle toward an understanding out of St. Augustine's *Confessions,* in which Augustine comes almost to similar understanding in escaping a false rhetoric serving a self-love threatening to doom him to spiritual alienation. A difference from Coleridge lies in that St. Augustine would deny that imagination "recreates."

If in Coleridge's distinction between the imagination and fancy he credits imagination with the struggle to idealize in response to "all objects" which "*as* objects" are "essentially fixed and dead," we may demur from his definition of *object* (since he would have it *fixed* and *dead*) but see nevertheless an attempt to articulate an epistemology suited to the reality of our experiences of the world. Similarly, St. Augustine dramatizes a recovering through his memory to the present reality of the "order of time and space." In this respect, when Coleridge declares the imagination "essentially *vital*" in its response to the realities of time and space within which those objects are encountered, he is speaking toward a necessity of an openness of intellect to "objects." This is the intellectual action which the Thomist would prefer to call the act of love reciprocated imaginatively toward the Cause of created things, Coleridge's "objects." It is love supported by encounter of divine things. From a Thomistic perspective, through this action the discovery becomes that objects are not "essentially fixed and dead" but sustained *essentially* (*actively in being*) by an action of Love, giving the *thing* what Hopkins calls its "instress." The action of intellectual "fancy" only *seems* to sterilize a thing of life, as Coleridge comes close to recognizing – though in reality it is intellect's choice to use its plundered truths of things in a sterile action that effects the illusion that the thing is *fixed,* is *arrested* into *object.* In a response to that active recovery, the "secondary imagination" which Coleridge defines as "co-existing with the conscious will," proves vital precisely through a communion, imaginatively witnessed as an ordinate coincidence of the *inscape* of signs in correspondence proportionate to the *instress* of objects and held by intellect (Thomas says) as truth. Wordsworth talks of this same effect when he speaks of vital moments to consciousness as those moments in which we "see into the life of things."

This inclination to openness, or to adapt Coleridge's terms, this inclination to imaginative action, is crucially "co-existing with the conscious will." But the conscious will is capable of perverse distortions through dissolving, diffusing, dissipating, in order as Coleridge says "to recreate" according to its fancy. How easily then may will seduce its own imaginative action (to continue with Coleridge's terms) through that agency of the fancy, willfully ignoring Coleridge's warning that the "Fancy must receive all its materials ready made from the law of association," from the storehouse of memory – that repository of truth out of the experiential reality of consciousness. Thus Fancy itself may become "blended with, and modified by the empirical phenomenon of the will, which we express by the word Choice." How apt a diagnosis of the fanciful actions of Joyce's young poet Stephen which he would endow as imaginative not fanciful, whereby the anchor of his intellectual action in existential reality is severed by his intentional will in the interest of an absolute freedom as poet. Hence his prospect of a "world," the poem which Stephen would thus "create" by the agency of fancy – by willful whim: that is, by "memory emancipated from the order of time and space." What will would thus free itself of if the primacy of truth over intellectual action, in order that it may assume itself creator – assume itself the agent of truth, presuming its own "self" by implication to be antecedent to the existential reality upon which it is dependent but which dependence it would deny. What it creates, it concludes, is truth. It is in this distortion by intent that Joyce's Stephen cries out his battle cry against God: *non serviam*. And Stephen's "creator," Joyce, is deeply attuned to the nature of Stephen's revolt, a revolt summoned out of his own deepest nature to his art's ends. And perhaps he succumbs to that summoning himself. At least this seems so as reflected in the pathos of Joyce's late question, put to himself as poet near his end: was he a poet of the imagination? Or only a poet of the fancy?

In this brief excursion into the Romantic poet as supplied a metaphysics by Coleridge, we may seem to have gone far afield, unless we remember just how pervasive these concerns which Coleridge engages have been to the artist since the rising dominance of rationalism as absolute authority, established through empirical science this past two hundred years. Through that dominance, the poet has felt himself exiled, replaced as it were by the scientist, whose tendency has often been to reject art, or tolerate it skeptically as a mere entertainment by fancy. Coleridge describes the poet in his "ideal perfection" as attempting to bring "the whole soul of man into activity, with the subordination of its faculties to each other according to their relative worth and dignity," presumably including the faculties of the imagination and fancy. Even so, that playfulness with "fixities and definitives" which is possible through the fancy may itself allow surprising enlargements of self-discovery, enriching the *imagination* itself. That is a relation (between fancy and imagination) over which so much ink has been spilt this century in pursuit of the "subconscious." Coleridge it appears then would neither deny fancy nor reject it out of hand. It requires rather a subordination as faculty to the wholeness of the soul. Indeed, the poet's inclination to this fanciful indirection toward reality itself, as opposed to the scientist's empirical and resolute assertion of a directness, may profit in an emancipation of memory, especially at points when memory itself seems closed upon itself and capable only of its own fanciful fears about that San Andreas fault within its Cartesian closure. In the ordinate wholeness of the soul pursued through ordinate faculties, Coleridge would suggest, there is made possible the soul's recovery from and acceptance of its own limits in responding to the mystery of the cosmos. One might even, with some of O'Connor's caustic irony or Percy's playful skepticism, argue a decided role for both fancy and imagination in the "rational" actions of the scientist himself. How interesting, then, this concern of Coleridge over the distortions of reality as experienced through fancy. His argument bears a parallel to a corresponding distortion Percy calls attention to in "Diagnosing the Modern Malaise," a distortion occasioned by the scientist's version of fancy, namely objectivity. For when the scientist would maintain objectivity as an absolute to intellectual action, justifying his speculative authority, he may well be said to name actualities fancifully. Percy's observation is that "the scientist, in practicing the scientific method, cannot utter a single word about an individual thing or creature insofar as it is an individual but only insofar as it resembles other individuals." Likeness in distinct things, a species of metaphor sterilized by abstractionism. By abstraction from the thing the scientist thus derives a "fixity" a "definitive" (to adapt Coleridge's terms), tending to be oblivious in doing so of the self-evident truth about it: it is a thing in itself, and is not by the operations of abstract fancy "emancipated from the order of time and space."

In this respect, then, Coleridge speaks of the deportment of the "whole soul" to the cosmos as the poet's responsibility through his deployment of the imagination (through signs) in response to the cosmos. By extension, we have argued also this to be the proper deportment of the scientist no less than of the poet. The imagination is "put in action by the will and understanding, and retained under their irremisive . . . control." Thereby there may be imaginatively recovered to consciousness

> . . . the balance or reconcilement of opposite or discordant qualities: of sameness, with difference; of the general with the concrete; the idea with the image; the individual with the representative; the sense of novelty and freshness with old and familiar objects; a more than usual state of emotion with more than usual order; judgment ever awake and steady self-possession with enthusiasm and feeling profound or vehement; and while it blends and harmonizes the natural and the artificial, still subordinates art to nature; the manner to the matter; and our admiration of the poet to our sympathy with the poetry.

One cannot but recognize in Coleridge's explication of the powers of the imaginative intellect his concern that the poet recover ground lost by both the philosopher and the theologian before those accelerating triumphs of Enlightenment science. But in our emphasis, we suggest the loss first of all that by the scientist. No wonder that he cites immediately to his support the poet Sir John Davies, that now somewhat obscure metaphysical poet who was to prove of interest to T. S. Eliot. (I have explored this point at length in "Around the Prickly Pear: Eliot on Coleridge on Sir John Davies," in my *The Reflective Journey toward Order.*)

And so our concern has been to suggest, though too briefly pursued here, the intellectual circumstances to any serious poet or scientist, circumstances which Percy, abandoning his medical calling to pursue art, was pressed to engage intellectually – in the interest of reason to be engaged in his making as a poet. They are circumstances not only on occasion affecting a bitter humor such as that in Melville's *Confidence Man* but a more general uncertainty to the poet as to his relation to existential reality, an uncertainty increasingly haunting the poet for two hundred years, including our Walker Percy. Such a poet may seem arrested by intellectual dislocation, or so it may seem to him in his confused circumstances when science begins to supersede art. At the close of last century, William James becomes more celebrated among the intellectuals than his brother Henry, the novelist, and that intellectual deference will increase as the "science" of psychology begins to replace Christian metaphysics as an underlying myth suited to imaginative literature. That was a recognition early to T. S. Eliot, for instance, he then a young intellectual dandy, an American Stephen Dedalus at Harvard where William James was in an ascendancy. It will lead Eliot to those essays on Hawthorne as our first "psychological" poet. At the same time Joyce, with a cleverness that would have frustrated Dostoevsky no doubt (given Dostoevsky's dogmatic commitment to Orthodoxy) is appropriating to fiction Aristotle and Aquinas as logisticians of his fictional deployments of the science of psychology, using both in the making of and choosing matter for his fictions. And so accomplished a strategy by his art that Joyce more than Henry James becomes the direct influence on subsequent poets, especially in that device of a reduction of "epiphany" to fictional technique on the authority of psychology. (Caroline Gordon, much devoted to James, on an occasion urged Flannery O'Connor to read him with care – which she already had done. The advice is given with a severe schoolmarm insistence, the which makes it difficult for O'Connor to respond openly.)

If Percy and O'Connor are inescapably "influenced" by Joyce, we note a difference at once in their response to that influence. Joyce appropriates the Christian mystic's visionary moment, that moment of an "epiphany," and makes it a dramatic principle as a secular psychological moment ordering a story aesthetically. It is a device deferential to psychological science, in respect to the recognition of limited social situations. This literary principle Joyce demonstrates to us "scientifically" as it were in the celebrated stories of his *Dubliners*. He does so, let us quickly acknowledge, through an enviable mastery of "objective correlatives." Though recognizing a cogency desirable to the *craft* of the maker in this adaptation of "science" to "art," however, we have seen that Flannery O'Connor would use the Joycean technique to recover a mystical dimension to "epiphany," as actual to persons beyond the limits of mere psychology. Hers is a reordering of art's authority as subservient to the truth of things, which she buttresses in her own thinking through Aquinas's arguments about the "science" of art. The realities of creation as creation must be the ground of art, but most centrally the *given* nature of *person*. In respect to this orientation of art, the poet must discover himself maker and not creator.

Joyce's young Stephen dreams himself creator, his own will a sufficient power as the god of art. Percy, appreciative of Joyce's accomplishment as craftsman no less than O'Connor, also sees an inadequacy in respect to Joyce's implied reductions of the nature of man through a haughty agnosticism that is deferential to science. But he also turns toward the sciences of psychology in relation to sign, more directly than to the philosophy of St. Thomas to recover art to reality. He does so in an attempt to recover more persuasively to the intellect the lost ontological ground to the sign itself. Not through a metaphysical vision, then, but through science. Our suggestion is that his recognition of this lost ontological ground grows in him along his way. It becomes the lost country, he will conclude, in whose intellectual absence to us we find ourselves almost hopelessly lost in the cosmos. His becomes a strategy adapting the perspective of science to his concern as poet, and in this sense he is allied to Joyce and James and to the early Eliot – Eliot as poet up to his own dead end in *The Waste Land*. It is a difference Percy recognizes initially between himself and Flannery O'Connor, this inclination as maker to justify sign by science rather than metaphysics. She, with a stubborn insistence, cuts to the heart of the anomalous "self" as addressed by Percy with her deliberately chosen orthodox instruments. For her the crucial signs (sin, grace, incarnation and the like) are already adequately anchored in the ontology and epistemology of the *Summa Theologica,* not in the speculative psychology of William James as rationalized by Charles Peirce.

Perhaps, then, Percy finds some relief in concentrating upon the instrument of signs to riddle reality, encouraged by Peirce, lest fancy deceive through an initial fascination with Dostoevsky or even O'Connor. Neither Dostoevsky nor O'Connor, of course, is ignorant of his and her own instruments as bearing a certain scientific validity to empirical necessities of craftsmanship. Signs deployed even in fiction do not escape laws of logic and depend necessarily upon rhetoric exercised through grammar inherent to the dialect of a given tribe. But they concentrate upon the spiritual dimension of reality as primary in the burden of fiction as that dimension may be made resonant with the aid of logic and rhetoric. O'Connor is concerned with the world as territory largely occupied by the Adversary to the Good, that preeminent logician and rhetorician, not to say poet and philosopher and theologian as well. Percy chooses to be concerned with the comic presence of man as "looney" in a world more engaging of his imaginative gifts in relation to Modernist spectacle. If good and evil are at issue, he would approach that concern at least by a comic indirection which, if it does not set judgment aside, suspends it in the interest of an often hilarious looniness. Not a head-on confrontation of the sovereign of that Modernist world, the Devil, who seems a clear and present danger to Dostoevsky and O'Connor, an inescapable antagonist to *homo viator*. Percy is very careful in controlling judgments about "looneys," adapting a witty dissociation from man's presumptions which nevertheless spawn wild spectacles out of that looniness which Dostoevsky or O'Connor would locate in relation to the diabolical. Indeed, he is in some degree even drawn to an artistic looniness himself. For his is a *role* as novelist, a species of "transcendence" as he plays with it. His tends to be a dissociated masquerade as physician diagnostician. And well he might incline to that tack, remembering as he does that intense poet Dostoevsky, whose deportment seems at points to border on madness. For Dostoevsky becomes almost possessed by his own spiritual unrest, the threat of possession a real possibility to him which intensifies his concerns as novelist. The effect is that Dostoevsky is drawn deeply, personally, and very dangerously, into his making. He may well fear that by his making, he exposes himself radically to evil in his almost fanatic pursuit of the good. That is, he may appear in retrospective summary to have been seeking martyrdom as artist.

Turgenev, important to Henry James and his concern for fictional "realism" as we have remembered, is reprehensible to Dostoevsky precisely for his primary interest in the new realism at the expense of any concern for the "Russian soul." He is for Dostoevsky the poet as Judas. Turgenev's primary interest is for an aesthetic perfection, through which he is elevated above spiritual concerns. That certainly is Dostoevsky's reading of Turgenev. It is also a tendency in the poet emerging in Western literature, in part through James's advocacy of a fictional "realism" such as that he finds impressively practiced not only by Turgenev but by Flaubert. Flaubert's phrase *le mot juste* becomes the rallying shibboleth to that new realism in literature, though the idea itself is already abroad in the arguments of Poe. It affects Joyce, who out of James and Flaubert (among others) concentrates the more upon his own psychological "realism." Joyce himself, insofar as one might think of him as lost in the cosmos in consequence of the radical intellectual effects of Cartesian Idealism, accepts as necessary to his own recovery a deliberate dissociation from that cosmos through a strategy of art which Coleridge as critic might conclude a tendency to the primacy of fancy over the imagination, as we have argued.

In relation to Pound's version of Imagism as opening poetry out of the prosodic closures of the 19th century and recovering as well a vital spark within the mechanistic universe out of Bergson, we might see that movement as a "new realism" as well. But it is a realism establishing the poet as arbiter of "reality." Pound's co-founder of the movement, T. E. Hulme, argues emphatically for a primacy of *fancy* over the *imagination* as they launch their movement just before World War I. His is an argument intended to dissociate the poet's authority from the more orthodox – the more widely accepted – position of Coleridge, in whom the remnants of Christian metaphysics survive Coleridge's fascination with German Idealism, though somewhat shifted by Coleridge from its center. The Romantic inclination we speculate will be more comfortable with his own word as the Word in the poem, his own created Word in the desert, calling the lost wanderers to the oasis of autonomy. Not that palpable presence of Christ as God-man revealed in the mystery of the Incarnation as the Word within his word. Put in a slightly shifted perspective, in relation to Wordsworth as Romantic, the poet in his revolution from Enlightenment advocacy of rational autonomy as dominant, may only at the end discover himself lost because denying the thing itself as experienced. One might thereby see "into [a] life of things" on such a return, even though such a limited recovery as Bergson suggests by his theory of the *élan vital.* Hopkins to the contrary affirms a recognition of the abiding and sustaining Lord and Giver of Life, the continuous presence of the Holy Ghost as Comforter and Sustainer of being, than the vagueness of Wordsworth's "something" or Bergson's evolutionary agent, an *élan vital.*

That is a perspective which a Pound or a Hulme find discomforting at last, both of them anti-romantic, resting faith in a reason closer to their grandfathers (the 18th-century Enlightenment) than to their fathers (the 19th-century Romantics). But fancy elevated *over* the imagination? That is a strategy out of rationalism itself to be deployed in *Vorticism,* the programmatic poetry succeeding *Imagism* in Pound's revolt against the current poetry establishment as dominated (he fancies) by the likes of Amy Lowell. The declaration of *fancy* as superior to the *imaginative* uses of the word (Hopkins's Word set quite aside) will authorize the poet to autonomous power over sign, justifying his manipulation of perspective upon Coleridge's "object," which object for Coleridge is as yet independent of both fancy and imagination. There occurs a brief *Blast* (edited by Hulme and Pound) in revolt against the incipient traditional orthodoxy buried deep in Coleridge's argument, perhaps a reaction against Coleridge as much as against "Amygism." Eliot will exhume Coleridge somewhat in his lectures at Harvard, *The Uses of Poetry and the Uses of Criticism,* soon after Eliot's conversion to Christianity, which labor could appear to Pound (in Italy) counterproductive to autonomous power. Pound in various editions of his work will attempt to memorialize the brief moment when he and Hulme founded "Imagism" and then moved on to Vorticism, publishing *Blast* (in two issues) as World War I is underway. And soon after *The Waste Land* (1922) Pound yet once more gives us *The Complete Poetical Works of T. E. Hulme* as an appendix to his own collected shorter poems, *Personae.* (His first gathering of Hulme was in 1912.) The collection consists of five poems, the longest only nine lines. There is, for instance, "Above the Dock":

> Above the quiet dock in mid night
> Tangled in the tall mast's corded height,
> Hangs the moon. What seemed so far away
> Is but a child's balloon, forgotten after play.

By *fancy,* make the world as one might will it – which by the extension of the poet's authority over sign might well reach into the ordering of social and political affairs. That was the fancy in Pound that appealed to Fascist Italy in the 1930s.

Coleridge, in approaching a distinction of fancy from imagination, distinguishes the poet's temporal manifestation of intellectual action as that of the "secondary Imagination," not to be confused with the "primary Imagination" which is the "living power and prime agent of all human perception, and as a repetition in the finite mind of the eternal act of creation in the infinite I AM." That is too close to insisting that man is created in God's image to be comfortable to the Modernist inclination so widely abroad at the time of the Imagist Movement. Fancy, then, and not the imagination, must be emphasized as the primary intellectual faculty certifying the intellectual independence of the poet, a weapon against the rationalistic scientist. By fancy, intellect finds itself autonomous, as Coleridge's Imagination will not allow. The dialectical strategy of Pound and Hulme is against both 19th-century Romanticism and deterministic science, though on this point their implicit opposition to is to Coleridge, thus emphasizing the pervasive influence of Coleridge's argument upon the literary and critical imagination at the turn of our last century. We cannot overlook Bergson's contribution to this attempted rescue of autonomous intellect toward angelism, out of what had come to be feared and glorified as a mechanistic cosmos. Bergson's *élan vital,* in relation to Coleridge's insistence on the primary Imagination as bonding the secondary Imagination to "the eternal act of creation in the infinite I AM," inverts that dependence to an immanent *élan vital,* increasingly identified as resident in autonomous intellect. And it is out of this climate to intellect that Percy's patron Charles Peirce begins to pursue a science of sign as philosopher.

We remarked the importance to the poet in a Modernist strategy, to Pound or Hulme at century's turning, that *le mot juste* be a *willed* sign, therefore presuming to gain an authoritative purchase upon the mystical *élan vital* permeating the cosmos, made manifest in respect to power over being as exercised by the discrete intellect. That purchase will be the means to the poet's ordering of any spirit immanent in the cosmos. Thus intentional ends are justified, not philosophically nor even scientifically: they are poetically pronounced. Hence Pound would elevate the poet king over Plato's philosopher king. There develops in this intellectual milieu an inevitable war among the poets, between fathers and sons, between the Romantic fathers (Coleridge and Wordsworth in particular) and their liberated sons (in our instance, Pound and Hulme – and the early Eliot). But we may see this civil war among poets as already well advanced in the social and political confrontations between fathers and sons in Dostoevsky's Russia. Dostoevsky by the 1860s was acutely attuned to the Russian version of the same ideological war, seeing it as grievously wounding the Russian soul. This is the time when Flaubert writes Turgenev in high praise of Tolstoy's *War and Peace*. It is a "very powerful" novel, he says. But Flaubert laments that the final third "falls off terribly," descending from art because Tolstoy "philosophizes," particularly on the theme of history as fate. By his speculation Tolstoy distorts his great novel from its proper center in which the author's greatest gifts are revealed as those of "a painter . . . a psychologist!" Turgenev shares that message with Tolstoy, as also on a visit to Tolstoy he mimics Dostoevsky from a recent encounter in Europe of that hapless exile from Mother Russia. Tolstoy is delighted by the mimic show, as they both consider Dostoevsky more or less mad.

Dostoevsky himself, of course, rejects artistry such as Flaubert and Turgenev would reserve from its fundamental dependence upon the current matrix of human confusions, the consequence of our having become lost in the cosmos. At the same time he must himself use that matrix, and use it to aesthetic ends. At a fundamental level, he knows his obligation to the good of the thing he would make. But for Dostoevsky, such an approach to art as Turgenev's, concerned with aesthetics as ultimate to man, is a betrayal of both art and humanity. He will repeatedly charge Turgenev, then, with being a deliberate traitor to the "Russian soul." And yet it was Turgenev who in his most famous work, *Fathers and Sons*, appropriates the contemporary political-social conflict between Liberal fathers and Nihilistic sons to the aesthetic reservation of art, less concerned than Dostoevsky with cultural spectacle as revealing the fraying fabric of community. At least it comes to seem so to Dostoevsky. How comfortably Turgenev abandons

Russia for a Western adoration of him as novelist! That is Dostoevsky's charge. That most fundamental conflict in community is of primary concern to Turgenev as but providing an immediate (current) matter to be borrowed to aesthetic ends – to fill an aesthetic form, regardless of any implicit spiritual implications in those contemporary dislocations of fathers and sons. The Russian soul is becoming lost in the cosmos, Dostoevsky cries out, and Turgenev is content to profit from that destruction in the interest of his art. By ignoring the danger, Turgenev (for Dostoevsky) becomes a diabolical presence as artist.

Turgenev is a traitor, not only to his gifts as maker, but more damning he refuses his responsibilities as maker to value his own Russian roots, severing them by ingratiating concessions to Western philosophy and science. Were Dostoevsky one of those Vanderbilt Agrarians (with whom there are many affinities on this issue) he would castigate this as Turgenev's betrayal of his "Southern" roots. It is Turgenev's literary polish, much valued by Westerners such as Henry James, which is a symptom to Dostoevsky of Turgenev's selling out to the "Yankees," becoming subservient to corrupt Western secularities in catering to aesthetes. That judgment is confirmed for him when he and Anna, destitute pilgrims in exile, call on Turgenev in Baden-Baden, just after the two have encountered Holbein's dead Christ – a devastating experience which Dostoevsky will dramatize in Prince Myshkin's encounter of a reproduction of that painting in *The Idiot*. The encounter in Baden-Baden leads to Dostoevsky's "Ends and Beginnings," attacking Turgenev as a Russian liberal seduced by the West. At this point of Dostoevsky's pilgrimage, on his way back to his beloved Russia, we may see his sympathy for the "Slavophiles" as allying him in sentiment to the similar position of the Southern Agrarians, some of whom severely castigate their own fellow "Southern" artists for selling out to the "Yankees" in similar ways. Dostoevsky, largely alone, takes his stand in defense of the Russian soul as it must be nurtured by local Russian history, against fellow Russian "scalawags" like Turgenev. No wonder, then, that the sophisticated, liberated Turgenev can entertain Tolstoy by mimicking the impassioned accuser who confronted him in Baden-Baden in a threatening way.

At the same time, however, Dostoevsky is not oblivious to an inclination to provincialism in some of those Slavophiles he otherwise admires. For as *historical* Russians they tend to substitute history as cause over the spiritual implications to be rescued, those implications betrayed by the likes of Turgenev. (That after all had been a weakness Flaubert objects to in Tolstoy's early *War and Peace,* though his concern is quite other than Dostoevsky's.) Thus in resisting the progressivist political reformers in Russia, who are engaged in an increasingly violent betrayal of the Russian soul with a growing intensity in Moscow and Petersburg, some "Slavophiles" tend to substitute a nostalgia for the past and thus neglect spiritual concern. It is this tendency to provincialism which Eliot feared might distort the Agrarians' own position, should they rest their case merely on a tradition unrescued by orthodoxy.

In reaction to intellectual scalawags, whether Southern or Russian, the dangers of becoming a species of the provincial (usually termed *reactionary*) troubled Dostoevsky – as it also troubled the Agrarians. Our point is to remark a parallel in Percy as well, who had to deal with a similar intellectual betrayal by progressivist thought, while uncomfortable with the Agrarians as allies, lest the charge of nostalgic traditionalism lodged against them by the Modernist's progressivism prove all too true. As is Eliot, Percy is uneasy concerning the soundness of the Agrarian position, those Southerners so immediate to him. His close friendship with Caroline Gordon, Allen Tate, and Cleanth Brooks as Agrarians might have been more reassuring on the point than it seems to have been. But the intellectual betrayal of a genuine Southernness by a pervasive "American" provincialism begins to be inescapable as he observes the South becoming a province of consumer-theorist doctrine, increasingly pervasive of the Southern public mind and threatening to transform it into a shallow "American" mind. That would be but a substitution of an enlarged provincialism in the vague public mind bent on a "transcendence" of any region, any anchoring place to community. Percy, then, becomes more concerned with rescuing a valid center to "Southernness," an orthodoxy addressing the ambiguities of tradition in replacing a failed Stoicism. Still, he is given pause, suspended by his own uncertainty about his position as "Southerner." He remembers, and recalls more than once, having been born into a country club, golf course enclave in Birmingham, and so somewhat "placeless" as person. How difficult to be an "American" writer, if handicapped not only by being Catholic, but a *Southern* Catholic as well. For he fears himself a Southern Catholic of uncertain credentials of *place* to orient him in the cosmos. At last, how complex the temptations to become either carpetbagger, in order to succeed as an "American" novelist whose "matter" is the South of history; or a scalawag who might then appear as writer to his fellow Southerners as a version of Turgenev as seen by Dostoevsky. At least good Southern bourbon might prove of some rescue, if divorced from the "mint julep" clichés about the South.

XVI

It is understandable that Percy summons Dostoevsky often to his own concerns as a "Southern" writer, for in that Russian novelist there is a deportment making him very much a kinsman. Dostoevsky's besetting problem was how to be a Russian writer in spite of being Slavophil and Orthodox, and he attempted to do so before an increasingly Modernist audience. Percy recognizes affinity, even as he properly notes along his way that he differs from Dostoevsky. For Percy has not only a sense of himself as a Southerner but also an uncomfortable sense as well of being in some degree an outsider to the South, differing in this respect (as his observations on his fellow writers suggest) from Southerners like Faulkner, Eudora Welty, even from Flannery O'Connor. It makes him value, as a part of those Southern manners which are deferential to such sojourners, "living an obscure life in the South" as a writer, for Southerners "don't come up to you, press your hand, and give you soulful looks," as if sharing a sense of alienation with you, the "neglected" writer.

Not long after *The Moviegoer,* he writes a tribute to Eudora Welty in which he raises the question troubling him as a divided Southerner. "How can a writer live in a place without either succumbing to angelism and haunting it like a ghost or being 'on,' playing himself or somebody else and watching to see how it comes out?" He could well have had in mind "Count No-Count" Faulkner at Oxford, Mississippi. We yet remember a swaggering Faulkner, deporting himself as superior to the locals since he had gone to the city and seen the elephant, as it were. He is back home with false tales of having served in the Canadian Air Force in World War I. He had actually inhabited Bohemian New Orleans, getting to know the likes of Sherwood Anderson and publishing a now largely forgotten novel about that city life as an artist, *Mosquitoes*. Our memory has it that Sherwood Anderson agreed to recommend the novel to his publisher if he, Anderson, didn't have to read it. That anecdote makes interesting ironic counterpoint to Percy, who himself an established writer more generously rescues John Kennedy Toole's *A Confederacy of Dunces*, a novel out of that same New Orleans milieu but some fifty years later.

And so Percy at the time of *The Moviegoer*, among the many things on his mind, is wrestling with the question of his "Southern" roots. Those roots seem too shallow in the soil that feeds Eudora Welty, who lives just up the road in Jackson, Mississippi, though she, too, "historically" is a newcomer to the South. Binx

Bolling drifts "Feliciana Parish," a homeless native son. His proximate biographical origins are in his maker, Percy, who has himself only recently come home from the American East. Having come home, he seems to become the more aware of having been "born and raised in Birmingham, Alabama, in a new house on a new golf course." Then as he begins to publish, he finds himself increasingly accounted a second generation "Southern Renaissance" writer, that categorizing a source of some discomfort. Out of a confluence of such experiences, he becomes more acutely attuned to the current effects of an earlier gradual infection of himself by the "modern malaise." He becomes a more self-conscious intellectual through his exile and return, recognizing in his own discomfort the disorienting effects of Cartesian Idealism. That is an intellectual circumstance inherited, within his individual thought, which leaves consciousness in some panic as suspended over that abyss – if too much worried over.

He will also become increasingly aware of consequences of Cartesian Idealism upon the general community, both that of the "American" and the "Southern" versions of it, into which latter manifestation he is increasingly drawn as writer. This is a consequence, he recognizes, that is quite separate from whether the individuals so affected even know the name Descartes. Indeed, the spectacles of "looniness" he observes and reflects upon are occasioned in some degree by unself-conscious effects of Modernist ideas that run counter to community as a body, making a person somewhat alien whatever his proximate community. These effects upon the "Southern" community had been addressed by Percy's older friend Allen Tate in his essay " Our Cousin, Mr. Poe" (1949), the burden of which is that Poe anticipated the "modern malaise," his work therefore somewhat inoculating the Southern intellectual against his century's plague of Sartrean Existentialism. For Percy in the 1960s, a decade later than Tate's argument, the source of this malaise is to be traced back through French thought to Kierkegaard's diagnosis of a "sickness" in the modern mind. Percy at first himself will have engaged this debilitating intellectual malady at a level more personal than general, given his disquieting experience of being threatened by despair. Does this vaporous disease have origin in his own family context? Or perhaps it may prove more general, more widely disorienting of the larger "Southern" family than if limited to the fortunes of the Percy's. Richard Weaver, at about the time of Tate's essay on Poe, in his *Ideas Have Consequences,* had argued that the plague now grown random and general in the West, had sources earlier than Kierkegaard. One might nevertheless discover the symptomatic "looniness" so attractive to Percy as novelist to be in somewise associated with that Kierkegaardian "sickness," especially if we remember that Kierkegaard in his reaction himself pursues causes as ancient as Weaver's.

Percy's first novel carries buried autobiographical elements – the more easily buried in that they are spiritual and philosophical concerns which are not yet oriented to community by place (hence the surface analogies Percy makes of his concerns in relation to Sartre). The cultural milieu inhabited by Binx is rather disoriented from New Orleans, in a world whose inhabitants seem adrift in place. Percy sets as epigraph to his novel words from Kierkegaard's *Sickness Unto Death*: ". . . the specific character of despair is precisely this: it is unaware of being despair." We might adapt Kierkegaard's words by an extension: the specific character of deracination, in which lies incipiently the danger of despair, is the person's not recognizing himself adrift, though of necessity he is adrift at *this* moment and in *this* place. The persons encountered here and now are likely to appear but foreign presences, rather than the drifting self beholding them the foreigner. And so a comic dimension of this novel involves Binx's deracination in familiar but strange ground, baffling to Percy's engaging protagonist. The comic drama here is "made" by Percy at a point when Percy himself is similarly disoriented by the familiar, having come home willy-nilly and bearing the shocking effects of his actual physical sickness. We remember that Flannery O'Connor comes home also, bearing her inherited lupus, which will occasion a sentimentalizing of her misfortune by some of her friends, particularly "Northern" friends, whose "soulful looks" and words she rejects, sometimes rather crisply. She writes with her head, not with her feet, she will say to one of them.

Was Percy's contracting tuberculosis at Bellevue or Cook County Hospital an accidental catastrophe to him, or an act of grace? He will ponder that alternative of causes. Confidence in science might be called into question by physical trauma, his contracting tuberculosis, from which rebuff of his attempt to be medical scientist he recovers slowly while reading Kierkegaard – and Thomas Aquinas. He gives us Binx, a Huck Finn on the threshold of the New Age, aimless in the latest city of man, New Orleans. This New Huck is partially equipped for survival by his analytical fascinations making him comically akin to Tom Sawyer as well. That curiosity is fed indirectly by his maker Percy, as Twain feeds his Huck with a similar naive curiosity. Binx is semi-scientific, semi-Existentialist – but with an important gift of that naive curiosity about the truth of the things he encounters on his way. Especially there are those things so strangely encountered in what we might call a modern version of the Allegory of the Cave. That is, movie versions of *homo viator* reduced from a spiritual nature but with lingering hints of that nature echoed in shadowy actions translated by celluloid. It is this unsatisfying reductionism that is the thematic thread holding Binx fascinated.

It is one thing to be able to dramatize such a complexity through an intellectual analysis serving art. It may be quite another for the poet-maker to recognize himself in the protagonist he reveals within his texture of signs as ordered to dramatic ends. The poet-maker in such circumstances might at once, at a personal level, be both admiring of and jealous of a Eudora Welty, suspecting his own inclination to angelism as diagnostician. That is the temptation to a transcendence which would leave him haunting an actual place like a ghost rather than joined incarnationally as a member of a local body. In such recognition, he might well incline to embrace the indirection of playfulness as novelist, thus "being 'on'" in practicing that role through the underhandedness of the con-artist of signs.

Perhaps this role is the most likely prospect to happiness. But in more thoughtful moments such a con-artist must recognize that the "time is coming when the American novelist will tire of his angelism – of which obsessive genital sexuality is the most urgent symptom, the reaching out for the flesh which has been chucked." He will "wonder how to get back into a body, live in a place, at a street address." At which time such a writer as "Eudora Welty will be a valuable clue."

This is a point to which Percy returns fifteen years later than his Welty essay, in that talk before his Southwestern Louisiana audience, in which he argues, with an O'Connoresque fillip a prophecy of "a Southern Jewish voice" as writer, now much needed to "articulate the fact, increasingly evident, that the modern world is in the grip of demonic powers." It would be a voice which could not be his, he implies. We might be reminded of his having earlier set that difference between himself and Flannery O'Connor, on the question of the devil's occupying local territories through demonic power. She is concerned with our world as territory held largely by the devil, he had observed, while he prefers, or must be content in treating, man in his "loony" dimension. That Jewish voice Percy prophecies will perhaps be that of "a Jewish mother . . . a shrewd self-possessed woman with a sharp eye and a cunning retentive mind who sees the small follies and tragedies around her . . . rendering it, with an art all her own and yet not unrelated to Welty, O'Connor and Porter." If so, "Like Isaac Singer, she might speak of demons; unlike Singer, she might mean it." One might suggest, indeed, that Percy's prophecy is very nearly a description of Flannery O'Connor as Jewish mother to her "Southern" children. And so he feels, even to the end, somewhat hampered as a Southern Christian voice – perhaps hampered in part because he has been taken at large as an "American" novelist, not really a Southern one, and perhaps only superficially Catholic – given his affluent urban Alabama Sunbelt roots fed by country club origins. Such a judgment might, of course, be almost an affront justifying acerbic remarks about such "New York critics" as might make such a suggestion.

Or so Percy might feel, sensing that his growing popularity as an "American" novelist may be due in part to a provincial *American* spirit which delights in his playful drama depicting "loonies," the playfulness a warrant not to take him too seriously. That warrant had been exercised earlier, as Flannery O'Connor remarks of her own reception, precisely by those New York critics who were delighted by her fiction because they read it as merely a "naturalistic" rendering of the Southerner with some exaggeration for satiric intent by O'Connor, as if that were her own ironic distancing from her Southern loonies such as her Old Tarwater or Haze Motes. Thus she might be received at their cultural party, in whatever Algonquin Club still operative. Hence Percy, considering this "American" (i.e., the deracinated Modernist) as a provincial not given to regional sensibilities, is very hesitant to associate himself with "Southern" expatriates, those writers with origins similar to his own: such contemporaries as Carson McCullers or Truman Capote perhaps. On the other hand, why would he be at once drawn to but made more uncomfortable by Faulkner, who before Percy has had to do so wrestled with the enigma of the South in coming to terms with the Southernness affecting his Tolstoyian writing with its Dostoevskian depths? It had been with awe that Percy earlier spoke of Eudora Welty as comfortably at home in Jackson, Mississippi. But he seldom seems to feel so at home as she does, though very strongly held by his immediate local South, grafted increasingly into Covington, Louisiana. Within this sense of disquiet as a Southerner now back home, one who fears he may rather prove a detached intellectual practicing an angelism through his art, he might well be tempted to put on a role, a personae, as novelist. These tensional poles to his attempt to feel at home in Louisiana, put analogically, are those pulling Dostoevsky between Turgenev as self-centered exile, successful in the ways of the world as a celebrated European writer, and the Slavophil as nostalgic sentimentalist. Consequently there is present in Percy an uneasiness about the epithet "Southerner," more especially whenever that title is spoken in some relation to the Fugitive-Agrarians of *I'll Take My Stand*. And so at times he finds himself as native son in a strange and in many ways distant country, the "South."

Walker Percy as "Southern" writer is interestingly complex, then. He is a self-conscious writer to whose consciousness clings undeniable evidences of his Southernness, so that he seems almost a character suited to a fiction on this theme of the ambiguities implicit in this strange sign "Southern," even as he continues somewhat lost in the historical and geographical cosmos called the South, a region yet in exile from "America." What is Southernness? Perhaps because that question is difficult to resolve, it energizes his fictions, which by that energy suggests the self-analysis underway through art. Rather certainly it is so – as he acknowledges in reflecting on that portrait of himself on his wall in his self-interview. This painting of Walker Percy is, he says, a composite of his protagonists. In this respect, Binx of his *Moviegoer* may be seen in relation to Percy, as Stephen Dedalus is seen in relation to Joyce. The fiction implies in some degree a personal response to the enigma of New Orleans (the South) as compared to Joyce's response to Dublin. The thread of an analytical intent controls his analysis of himself through fiction, the ostensible subject of which is a pathological exploration of the Modernist self uncomfortably located in a very local South. That analytical analysis of the self, with some bearing upon the actual self of the novelist, runs through the fiction, carrying "indirectly" by art that fiction's secret agent: Percy, on his own serious and quietly personal pursuit of his own "self." Concerned with the thread spun of signs out of contingent and impinging intellectual experiences within the world's Modernist maze, Percy seeks authoritative guidance in answering the questions raised about the self and its journeying – about the self as *homo viator*.

But in pursuit of rationalizing that concern, we have been arguing, Percy at first seeks guidance primarily in the latest science, semiotics, as if through that science (if rigorously pursued) the self might recover the ontological ground lost to it. Yet by our argument we contend that he engages a mystery which that science alone is insufficient to fathom. To engage the mystery of witness through sign, out of a consent to creation as a Christian, requires more than a rationalistic scientific riddling. For the Christian, mystery is spoken to with an authority derived from Revelation. St. John's gospel begins, "In the beginning was the word and the Word was with God." That Word enters history at another mysterious conjunction: a cosmos-altering Parenthesis holding the cosmos beyond time or place. God became man, in Christ Jesus. John's is an assertion out of the immediacy of his own personal experience, we sometimes forget. Remembering it, we may share with O'Connor's Misfit a dejected envy. If only we had been there! St. John's signs in testimony are born through a continuing faith as a primary authority to semiotic "sign" for the Christian. John's is the actual experience O'Connor's Misfit longs for and which the Christian anticipates through hope of Beatitude. It is precisely this mystery of the Word within the word, the Word justifying sign itself, which so troubles *homo viator* on his erratic way, sometimes even reducing him to the violence of Flannery O'Connor's Misfit.

If Christ was who he said he was, says the Misfit, and if "He did what He said, then it's nothing for you to do but throw away everything and follow Him." But "if He didn't, there's nothing for you to do but enjoy the few minutes you got left the best way you can – by killing somebody or burning down his house or doing some other meanness to him." The Misfit's agony of regret, simple "intellect" that he is, is that he wasn't there, along with St. John. "I wisht I had of been there. . . . It ain't right I wasn't there because if I had of been there I would of known." The signs in which he longs to believe have no acceptable authority, and so seem inadequate to him in relation to his experiences. And this is a consequence to the Misfit of his having experienced a treachery through signs themselves, employed as they have been by those Modernists who "have the papers" on him – signs he knows inadequate to his uncertainties about the relation of evil to good. Indeed, the Misfit has certainly "been there," in the Modernist world, a world in which signs are perversely used. That "head-doctor at the penitentiary" said "I had done killed my daddy but I known that for a lie. My daddy died in nineteen ought nineteen of the epidemic flu." The Misfit is hardly capable of dealing with the "Oedipus Complex" in the mouths of head-doctors. "They had the papers on me," and those papers explain his evil deeds by deterministic arguments, thus excusing the evil. Denied the historical witness of the Incarnation, unable to recover its continuous immediacy as a reality through faith, he resorts to "meanness" in an acceleration of evil acts, as if thereby to certify his own existence beyond that abstract "self" dismissed by the papers they have on him. How dramatically ironic that the Misfit should cling to evil against Modernist doctrine as his only hope.

The Misfit is, in this respect, a figure of the extremity inevitable from Modernist reductionism of the person, of the intellectual soul incarnate. It is as if he witnesses by his violence the necessary existence of the good. That is the paradox which leads Flannery O'Connor to speak of him as a prophet gone astray, the "old lady's gesture" of love at the end perhaps planting a seed in his heart that may "turn him into the prophet he was meant to become." One notes in the unfolding action at story's end how rationally and calmly and reflectively the Misfit rejects the old lady's attempts to excuse his evil acts with her clichés out of Modernist dismissal of the concept of sin – a bad family, society unsupportive, and so on. Her final gesture of acceptance, a gesture of love, precipitates his shooting her. For in response to her words and gesture, her shocking action, the Misfit "sprang back as if a snake had bitten him" and shoots her three times. Then he returns to calm sad endurance. Still, that seed is planted, the faint recognition of which is his final conclusion: "She would have been a good woman . . . if it had been somebody there to shoot her every minute of her life."

If the Misfit is bound toward becoming prophet (compare young Tarwater in *The Violent Bear It Away*), he has yet to deal with those other "papers," those Testament signs reaching back to the Incarnation and with terms like *soul* and *sin* and *repentance* and the like now stored in the social attic. Those are the old signs Percy regrets as now rejected by intellect, signs that seem to him hardly viable to the fiction he would make – given his audience. He is reluctant to invoke them in summoning a presence of the Word to signs. The relation of the Word to the word, then, in respect to the science of semiotics, is a complication Percy hesitates to engage in his speculative concern for the nature of sign at a metaphysical level. For Eliot, the presence of "the Word within word" becomes increasingly central to the growing discomfort he feels as an ally of our emblematic "New York critics," who flourished in London as well. But once he has opened himself to that Word, he believes the Holy Spirit pervasive of creation and so relates intimately for him and to him as a presence in the very words of his mouth and the meditations of his heart. At that crucial turning in the final section of his *Waste Land,* the speaking voice, lost in desert sands on ocean edge, turns head to heart, toward a reunification of sensibilities quite other than the "dissociation" that had disturbed him in his critical speculations, the dissociation he detected in the Romantic poetry before him: the "dissociation of thought and feeling." This said, we may realize to what extent his *Four Quartets* becomes a dramatic recapitulation of his earlier poetry, a revisiting of the experiences now admitted as personal to the poet and occasioning those poems in which he had been so studied in avoiding the personal. What is recovered by memory from those experiences is a recognition of the Redeemer of time as always present, though not always recognized by the pilgrim Eliot along that early way.

This is not to deny that Percy has a rich gift in respect to the texture of his signs as he deploys them to establish a fictional setting imagistically persuasive. He possesses as well a delighting gift of ear for nuanced speech in his agents, though his characters are more culturally sophisticated agents than Flannery O'Connor's. Their speech carries a local history of speech in which are borne resonances beyond the local – a gift he shares with both O'Connor and Eliot. And for all three this gift is crucial to their "incarnational" fiction – whether as poet they summon a presence as if real in such an agent as the Misfit, or of a Magus imagined on his journey to Bethlehem or of a clever adolescent like Binx. Percy, this is to say, has that gift of "negative capability" in respect to those dramatically persuasive particularities which Eliot labels "objective correlatives," "a set of objects, a situation, a chain of events which shall be the formula of that particular emotion; such that when the external facts, which must terminate in sensory experience, are given, the emotion is immediately evoked." This is in Eliot's essay on *Hamlet,* in 1919. It is a passage proving embarrassing to him later, especially because it had been seized upon by academic critics and belabored, even in doctoral orals he remarks. But we suspect that it is not the necessity of finding some common ground between poet and spectator in order to be dramatically effective that is troubling to him. Rather, it is the detached logical distancing in himself, reflected with terms he could no longer subscribe to. To seek a *formula* speaks an intention to manipulate the spectator through signs, for instance. And, having read St. Thomas more intensely (as he does in the 1920s) Eliot could not have remained comfortable with declaring that "facts terminate in sensory experience," thus evoking emotion. The position in the argument is of the rationalist as skeptic. The implied intent to justify "objective correlatives" is to use them in an emotional manipulation through signs. Here there is no recognition of the possible relation of the Word to his word, nor of a sense of stewardship as poet in "purifying the dialect of the tribe." There is rather a stance as intellectual critic to intellectual critics. When Eliot in 1928 supplies a "Preface" to a reissue of his "Essays on Poetry & Criticism," *The Sacred Wood* (1920), he observes of that critic now a decade older, looking back at this famous early essays, "a stiffness and an assumption of pontifical solemnity" which he (and perhaps other readers) may find "tiresome."

It remains true nevertheless that an acceptably concrete setting and a persuasively *characteristic* speech in an agent allows a triangulation by art as it were, persuasive of the fictional agent's presence to us in an immediacy – as if we witness a moment in a character's "biography" and thereby respond to such a similitude of man as art as if actual, as if the agent were an incarnate presence. Still, Percy seems not to value or relish this gift he has as he might be justified in doing. To borrow Flannery O'Connor's observation about the naturalistic writer, that writer may "by his responsibility to the things he sees . . . transcend the limitations of his narrow vision." Percy through his own gifts, which are affected by his Christian inclinations, "transcends" often in her sense (not that of the Modernist presumption of absolute freedom). He does so through his signs despite the constricting influence of semiotic science to which he is speculatively susceptible. In his arguments in his own person, as opposed to his dramatic fiction, he appears on occasion not to recognize as inescapable some presence of the Word within even his own speculative word. He will remark Eliot's famous phrase about the "objective correlative," for instance, a phrase Eliot proposes (we note) before he himself has become attuned to the Word as both in the desert and in his own signs.

Percy declares that "objective correlatives" are "easily" come by. That seems to have been a discovery emphasized for him from his experiences of making artfully incarnate his version of Huck Finn – Binx, in *The Moviegoer*.

Percy's remark on objective correlatives is offhand, as if any user of signs may easily come by efficiently effective signs. Nor does he seem to have noticed, until much later as he reflects on his own first novel, that Binx is constricted more than the open hearted Huck in respect to existential entrapment in the cosmos. Neither has Binx in his travels any West to "light out" for, so that he ends up wandering the maze of New Orleans. He attempts on his wanderings to substitute a retreat into the current (1950s) version of "virtual reality," into the Modernist temple of the movie house – a retreat dramatically counterpointed with a resonance only dawning fully upon Percy later: Binx's moment at the steps of a cathedral which he passes on his way to engage celluloid shadows within the new temple. He encounters a stranger with an ash cross on his forehead. It is in retrospect that Percy becomes acutely aware of the Word implicit in his own words, his recognition that, unrecognized by him as he is making the novel, he echoes in his novel the journeys of St. Augustine and Dante. He does so, Flannery O'Connor might say, "by his responsibility to the things he sees."

And so we may observe that Percy's Bixby is acute in his recording of the sensual texture of his world, both in respect to persons and places, giving us through his own chosen signs (as the fiction's protagonist) a palpable sense of a culture in a place, though it may seem to Binx a culture cut off from the roots of culture. (Indeed, one of the mysteries of the sign is its effect through the palpable of stirring sensual memory in a present encounter through "objective correlatives." Thus "objective correlatives" do not simply "*terminate* in sensory experience.") Percy himself will admit, given his considerable readings of the poor fictions about which he often comments, that he has a gift as novelist in respect to the sign. Indeed it is a gift and not simply a skill to be easily learned as if it were an external purchase. But neither is it easily perfected as gift, requiring "reason in making" as Thomas says. Objective correlatives depend at last on a growing vision embracing human nature itself, engaged by reason in ordering experience, so that they are not "easily" come by, any more than the sign's dependence on vision yields easily to the science of semiotics. Nor for that matter is Percy's incisiveness as analyst of the active mind – his interest in the pathology of thought – easily acquired through the science of psychology as if it were but another learned scientific skill suited to a technology applied to some species by analytic thought. (That becomes the superficial address of Freudian psychology.) Certainly, as he will complain, we have been burdened overmuch by the "psychological" novel in our century, a species which rises to such a commanding critical attention in the academy at mid-century. In most such fictions, as in the critical analysis of them as well, the psychological theory becomes a scalpel to expose character, though it may often appear rather an instrument borrowed and used against character – borrowed usually from Freud but imbued somewhat with magic by Jung.

Subsequent behaviorists become (to Percy's irritation) merely biological determinists borrowing the Darwinian myth to justify "zoo-semiotics," at the expense of the true ground to fictional presence, the mystery of personhood.

As varied as Percy's novels are in respect to place, ranging from New Orleans to New York, with stops along the way in Alabama and Mississippi and North Carolina, or a brief wandering into the Southwestern desert (which Percy himself loved as a geography counter to Louisiana swamps), the dominant perspective on place is that of a Southerner as protagonist. There is in consequence the sameness of a hovering intellectual mindset, with some suggestion of repetition rather than of a progress beyond the parenthesis of each separate fiction. The same judgment might be made of Flannery O'Connor's fiction perhaps, though there is a difference to be made, in that hers is a more comfortable certainty of her own position as a Thomistic realist, as opposed to an activist existential wandering which seems to hold Percy, suggesting a mind as yet not settled in an accommodation to place. She is confident, early and late, of the "ontological" ground of being. It is her Thomistic perspective that underlies her comment that "The longer you look at one object, the more of the world you see in it; and it's well to remember that the serious fiction writer always writes about the whole world, no matter how limited his particular scene." That is a recognition mystically acquired by Dame Julian of Norwich as she looks at the hazel-nut on her palm. It is the recognition Eliot comes to, through his own long and often agonized spiritual journey in the "desert." It leads Eliot to conclude the body of his poetry by echoing Dame Julian. At the end of *Little Gidding*, he declares that the end of all his exploring has been to return to the place from which he set out, enabled now to "know the place for the first time." It is as well, in response to that seeing, that he can declare with Dame Julian that "all manner of thing shall be well."

That, we are suggesting, speaks also the journey and its conclusion to which we arrive with Percy at the end of *Thanatos Syndrome*. Percy comes, through this work, to a breaking out from the Modernist parenthesis against which he has so long struggled. He resists becoming isolated by history and nature within the moment as merely temporal or by that reductionist sense of place as if it were only geographical in its resonances through an accretion of history – of event – in geography. Such is that limit to a traditionalism unmodified by metaphysics. In that breaking out, the things now seen in that place are known as never before. Percy does not, in this regaining of spiritual freedom, proclaim freedom so insistently as does Eliot, at least not *directly* in his art. But neither does he, with spectacular alarms and sirens, announce his own escape through grace. Rather we recall once more that moment in the novel which on first encounter seems but comic, when Tom More sits sailing his paper airplanes, out into the yard. Tom More knows, without being able to say it quite, that all manner of thing shall be well. Percy, too, is now largely freed of mean yard dogs in his own person, freed even of diagnostic analysis of cultural phenomena as if he were preparing to become a novelist. Percy's Tom More is shown freed, as never before on his fictional journey, from that earlier wildness of *Love in the Ruins*.

It is in this perspective of our speculative interest in Percy as journeyman, his going in the guise of analytical novelist, that he appears closest to the Eliot of *Little Gidding*. And at their common point of arrival, both he and Eliot find themselves closer to O'Connor in a visionary understanding. The journey, this is to say, is not one confined to linear time or sequential history in its conclusion, which is why Eliot (and others) speak of a presence, of "the living and the dead" in a community, a continuing body. Flannery O'Connor stayed home as it were, in respect to her worldly history and her visionary journey, almost from her beginning. Her fellow poets Eliot and Percy return to that common "home." These parallel journeys by Eliot and Percy one may explore further, though we need not do so here, through explicative juxtapositions of *Thanatos Syndrome* and Eliot's play *The Cocktail Party.* Here we need only remark that Percy, like Eliot, comes to a deeper knowing of what at the end of his life Percy will speak of in a telling title as "The Holiness of the Ordinary" (1989).

That quiet accommodation to the holiness of the ordinary – the objective correlative to which visionary recognition we pose as Dr. More's sailing paper airplanes in an apparently frivolous diversion at the very end of *Thanatos Syndrome* – lies yet before Percy in his early role as Dr. Walker Percy, who is still a presence as our guide in *Lost in the Cosmos*. In this self-help book there is a self-exposure (required of the "professional" psychologist perhaps) though Percy himself is somewhat uncomfortable in his public presence to us. In the work, his is a challenge to art's deployment of sign out of his very self, when his native inclination is to privacy. Not that he does not take a certain delight in the playfulness whereby he makes his own position often ambiguous to us, his "public." In that essay-novel *Lost in the Cosmos* , then, he makes the most of artful indirection, giving us a species of fiction more famously associated with that new fictional journalism of Truman Capote and Tom Wolfe. And the game afoot is one which no doubt Jean-Paul Sartre would appreciate, as Percy appreciates the sense of the "game" he finds in Sartre both early and late. This appreciation is evident in his suggesting in the late *Paris Review* interview that the "spark" for his *Moviegoer* may well have been Sartre's Roquentin in *Nausea*, Roquentin being "a Southerner of a certain sort."And so in contrast to any refuge possible to his spiritual privacy as shielded by his protagonist Binx in *The Moviegoer,* Percy seems more vulnerable in *Lost in the Cosmos*. He stands closer to the work as Walker Percy. One might see his recognition of this difference by reference to the earlier *Message in the Bottle* (1975) in which he is even closer to us, even more seriously concerned with semiotics as a rescue to his own person. There he addresses the concern very formally, in a more "scholarly" manner. Perhaps at that time there was some comfort in knowing that he has a very limited audience. But his reputation with a much larger audience by the time of *Lost in the Cosmos* is a recognition to him even as he writes it. In his "intermezzo" to *Lost in the* Cosmos, his "Semiotic Primer of the Self," the indirection lies in its being not "technical but . . . theoretical," an interesting distinction in the light of his subsequent reservation about "theorists" serving "consumers" through technical systems. He encourages his reader to skip the whole section, since it will baffle the uninitiated and will "irritate many professional semioticists by not being technical enough." His true audience for his most serious concern is by that pretense small indeed, though he intends a wider net of signs. In *Message in the Bottle* (for which he had suggested as title *Contra Gentiles*), he is the more comfortable perhaps because he is more confident that he will suffer a more limited intrusiveness of audience upon his "scientifically" technical concerns. The technical aspect of the concern at that earlier point protects him from readers in great numbers. But the challenge to such a self-protection is much greater in his teasing "Self-Help" book, and he risks himself there with a courage he praises in Melville. He *pretends*, as a strategy, to a necessity of removing his reader from these more private and technical concerns, as if they could be of little interest or importance. But that is a rhetorical strategy: these pages are the very heart and soul of the work itself, he confides much later. The pretense of hiding it from us as of little interest to non-technical readers trades on our vulnerability to such underhandedness. He has warned us honestly, again and again, to be on our guard against such a "novelist," always a tricky fellow, devious in his art, a con-artist teasing and toying with us through the worn currency of our common signs.

This pilgrim of the cosmos presents himself, then, as analytic guide at our service, uncovering to us a certain waywardness in us as pilgrims. He does so on the authority of his own experience as sojourner, often rhetorically associating himself with us as a "we." Considering our guide's emphasis upon his own wiliness, we might well be cautious of consent to the tall tales he gives us about our own self, unfolded to us with an excess of humor and satiric exaggeration which might lead the literary scholar (concerned with influences) to suggest the mode descended from that old Southwest frontier humor, a recent literary tradition associated with Mark Twain. But we might seek influence in another quarter as well, thereby enlarging the range of the pilgrim as witness in the history of our signposts as we find them scattered in the desert. There is that early wily storyteller who interested James Joyce, the conman Odysseus as pilgrim, perhaps more "socially" amenable than Dante's Dante in the *Divine Comedy*.

Odysseus as a pilgrim of the cosmos – our first Huck Finn we might put it – is made an active witness to his own journey by Homer. As does Huck, he speaks firsthand of his experiences, ranging from the depths of Hades to that arrested Heaven of Calypso's island. A ranging pagan version of *homo viator,* then, who explores creation from those depths of an intellectual dead-end (Hades) up to the dreamed perfection with Calypso like that we now conjure as virtual reality: a perfection of our appetitive nature made possible by a divine Calypso. Odysseus in Hades encounters the sad, defeated shade of that ideal hero, Achilles, who might (in Homer's day perhaps) seem a New Age idol as hero. How arresting, then, Achilles' message brought by Odysseus to us: "I had rather live the slave of a landless man than be king of all the dead." In that other state of life, on the island with the goddess Calypso, Odysseus has the promise of life arrested at its full, as we are naively prone to dream an ultimate end: immortal as the April rose in a forever-April – with heavenly food, the love of a goddess, calm weathers at the sea merge in a rich environment unthreatened by either man or perverse nature itself. On the one hand, the "theorist" rebuffed. On the other the "consumer," to adapt Percy's terms, discovering a consumerism perfected. But neither proves sufficient to human nature. We see Odysseus, morosely staring out to sea, Paradise behind him, longing for Ithaca and Penelope and Telemachus – and no doubt as well for that faithful aging dog Argus. Homer, more wily than his Odysseus, would con us into Odysseus' rejection of "virtual reality" as made eternal by the magic of Calypso. He, too, longs for the pied beauty of uncertain existence.

Percy, though temperamentally akin to Odysseus, discovers signs left him by St. Augustine and Dante within his own signs out of his making of *The Moviegoer*, as he discovers as well other presences, a range of poets, encouraging him to rhetoric as a trickery toward good ends. Those earlier "literary" pilgrims were for him a chance discovery, often after the actions of his making with signs, yet bearing some presence as ancient pilgrims within those signs. He will hint that such "chance," as considered by the Modernist world to be mere accident, is in reality a hidden action of grace. In that first novel, he had "almost by accident – or was it accident? – landed squarely in the oldest tradition of Western letters," so that on "a single weekend in New Orleans" (shades of Joyce's *Ulysses*) his character Binx "creates within himself . . . a microcosm of the spiritual history of the West. . . ." But there is that added manner one doesn't find in the *Confessions* or in the *Divine Comedy*: the protagonist guide (whose mask is Binx) has attempted a witty distancing of himself from the journey as it were, a deportment one might well anticipate as reflected in that portrait of the con-artist as mean yard dog novelist, a wily Odysseus. Certainly Percy's is a deportment suited to that older and in some ways wiser con-artist, Odysseus, who is intent upon a survival as a self, though also fascinated to explore the variousness of challenges to his survival as a self in the randomness of the cosmos. Odysseus sails on, glad as one escaped, albeit he has lost his dear companions, until quite alone in the cosmos.

Odysseus at the court of the Phaecians holds the King's board fascinated with tales of that already fabulous hero, the ancient world's *homo viator*, Odysseus. What a shock of delight, perhaps as near to revelation as that ancient Homeric world might imagine – to hear this so recently naked and exhausted stranger, rescued from the salt sea, washed up alone and stripped of all cultural appendages on the Phaecian shore – declare at the King's board (after a long and boring preamble) that "I am Odysseus . . . who am in men's minds for all manner of wiles, and my fame reaches unto heaven." Whereupon he holds his now rapt audience with detailed personal accounts of his wanderings as hero, including even that descent into the underworld to hear the moans of the great Achilles. There is his prolonged account of his escape from there, back into a world in which he will now tell all, as perhaps a pagan version of the "ex-suicide." Not that pathetic toying with an endangerment of the self which Eliot's Prufrock mincingly engages, with Prufrock's speculative threat to return to the tea party and tell all. Nor Percy's Lancelot as sojourner, assuming some of the intellectual qualities of a mean yard-dog. Odysseus is rather Homer's Lazarus "come from the dead,/ Come back to tell you all." Odysseus is the hero as con-artist, then, who by the wiliness of indirection, in response to the randomness of his fated journey of the cosmos, survives as hero at the King's table among the Phaecians. His is an ancient anticipation, we might suppose, of the somewhat later repetition of the necessary journey in which Dante is hero. And both Odysseus and Dante are prelude to the Joycean ironic juxtaposition of Odysseus to his antihero Bloom in *Ulysses*. But what a delightful indirection by our Greek (or *almost* Greek) Homer. The poet is transmogrified into Odysseus. One wily act of Homer, and an evidence of a presence in that great poem of an actual discrete maker – as opposed to committee composition: the built-in praise of the poet and the explicit advocacy by the poet hero as properly seated, by protocol, beside the king, the wine bowl between them. No wonder that the first of Pound's *Cantos* assumes the voice of Odysseus.

And so it is in this much wider tradition that we may see Percy as wily novelist (partial to bourbon, not wine), the "psychologist-physician" as an Odysseus-Homer, maintaining a defense of the self by an artful "transcendence," sometimes suspiciously akin to angelism – at least it must seem given his own fear of self-endangerment by wiliness. Meanwhile, Percy's present reader is again and again put in a judgmental position, put on stage by his author guide. There are those lists of possibilities concerning the self, adventures of encounter of the Modern self with the realities of the Cosmos, concerning which as they are posited this "psychologist" of the self – Percy – quite carefully balances. Each a possible choice, some even probable – seldom revealing his own choice made necessary by his Christian position as person as distinct from his presence as Dantesean agent in the work. One might, indeed, have some difficulty, did we not know already that the maker of this handbook for lost selves is a Catholic, to decide that "fact" about our guide. For Percy is very cautious in presenting the "Christian" position in respect to any of the "selves" on those checklists the reader is challenged to complete. A strategy then, leading to a command: "Check one." And a further direction often: reflect on your choice as it may reveal something about *you* as a *self*. Especially "Chart your own semiotic profile." That as prelude to "your" becoming surrogate to the speculative novelist at a Corn Dance in the Western desert. A careful strategy of self-defense for the perpetrator of this self-examination, but one which may nevertheless draw the reader as surrogate closer to a humanity shared with such a clever fellow as our guide, if that reader but play the game.

If, as I have suggested, Percy as a "self" through his making of the *Thanatos Syndrome* may be discovered as having broken out of that endangering parenthesis holding him (as it also holds most of us in a Modernist isolation, as if isolation were "transcendence"), we might find our speculation on this point strengthened as we read a late and more direct essay published the year he died, "Why Are

You a Catholic?" In it, he begins with his old warning, and repeats it. Novelists, he reminds us, "are a devious lot to begin with," for "their stock-in-trade is indirection if not guile. . . ." The essay, however, proves more open, more direct, less ambiguous about his own understanding of himself as *homo viator*. He has moved beyond a more restricted concern as novelist, that concern for his own and for our being *homo sapiens alienatus* (his phrase), a malady which he has so cautiously engaged. The analytical term he uses here well suits the detachment of the physician as novelist whose attempt is to diagnose disparately alienated creatures in our century. But he is in this late essay less ambiguous about his own position, more direct. He addresses his own experience as *homo viator*, as a pilgrim toward eternity. We see this especially evident if we compare this last essay with that somewhat earlier "How to Be an American Novelist in Spite of Being Southern and Catholic" (1984), or especially that much-earlier self-interview of 1977, "Questions They Never Asked Me So He Asked Them Himself."

It is in this late essay ("Why Are You a Catholic?") that Percy witnesses to having come to terms with his "Southernness," to having moved on to discover himself more comfortable as a "convert to the Catholic Church." His reasons for that progress as *homo viator*, seen in retrospection, "can be described as Roman, Arthurian, Semitic, and semiotic." He pays tribute to these explicit signposts as orienting his journey, recognizing in them a relation of Richard I to Marcus Aurelius. Recognizing as well that by his responsive encounters he was enabled to move beyond "the beau ideal of the South," that Southern stoic knight R. E. Lee, without rejecting that noble antecedent guide. And so he is comfortable with his Southernness. He can now more wisely accept limits, having been moved through grace beyond certain of those limits. But he recognizes that by his progress he is not required to reject the heritage through which he has discovered himself as on the way to a proper end. That inheritance of the Roman, Arthurian, Semitic complex of signs left in the desert is not sufficient to his rescue to that proper end. Nevertheless, whatever the insufficiency, he is obligated to a proportionate reverence of them. And so he adds, "After all, the pagans converted by St. Paul did not cease to be what they were. One does not cease to be Roman, Arthurian, Alabamian." No longer is it necessary to him to join with that other Alabamian, the character in the Southwestern literature of the early 1800s who, coming among those strange frontier folk in Alabama, declares it always necessary to "be shifty in a new country." It can now be no temptation to this Alabamian Percy to take a journey into exile, toward a sad breakfast at Tiffany's, as his fellow Alabamian Truman Capote had done, thereby reduced to embracing spectacle as an end of the imagination's journey. For that is what we have in that signal work of the new journalism as art, Capote's *In Cold Blood*.

As novelist on his way, Percy leaves us works rich in their indirection and guileful in "coming at things and people from the side so to speak, especially the blind side, the better to get at them." But he must do so without destroying his own progress toward eternity. Art's indirection therefore may be more clearly seen as a necessity to the "science" of art. But art may not be relied upon for his safety in the strange world he sojourns, North or South. Neither art nor science can reveal the true path for *homo viator* with the authority of Revelation – without the intruding of grace. In recognition of this insistent Love which poet or scientist encounters, there may dawn as a light to the self the mystery of the presence of the Word within his sign. That, we have seen, was the revelation Eliot came to witness in *Burnt Norton*, declaring that in such a dawn the roses he encountered in a decaying manor's garden along his own journey had "the look of roses that are looked at." But not looked at simply by the poet as autonomous. There is a Presence to him, whatever the desert of the moment, if he but recognize it by an openness. Whether in a decaying garden or in a New York hospital or in a boat in the Louisiana swamp, with a sunfish flopping in the boat and by its reality as sunfish speaking Presence even in the swamp – a reality such as Hopkins had recognized in "rose-moles all in stipple upon trout that swim."

XVII

When Percy received the Ingersoll Award for his fiction in 1989, he chose to speak on the "Physician as Novelist." His subtitle has interested us in relation to our own fanciful metaphor of him as an Odysseus. In "Physician as Novelist" he bears tales of his journey to this particular late court appearance. That subtitle: "Or, Why the Best Training for a Novelist in These Last Years of the Twentieth Century is an Internship at Bellevue or Cook County Hospital, and How This Training Best Prepares Him for diagnosing T. S. Eliot's *The Waste Land*." The experiences of internship were of course his own, including that "piece of luck or Divine Providence" which brought him to his calling as physician novelist. That was a period of his own descent to the borders of the underworld, followed by an escape therefrom through Divine Providence, in an increasingly mysterious way. The piece of bad luck or good Divine Providence was his having contracted "a serious, disabling, but nonfatal illness," tuberculosis. What witness to bear in consequence? What to do? After or while reading (among others) Thomas Aquinas and Kierkegaard, he turns home, back to the South where "after much casting about and considerable depression if not despair . . . by luck or by providence," he strikes out anew on his intellectual journey.

If in his youth he had been more interested in science and in the fiction of H. G. Wells than in Revelation as presumably articulated at Sunday School, he has by the time he comes home from New York begun to become concerned with the difference between science and scientism as affecting community. He had pursued science in those intervening years. But at the time of *The Moviegoer,* approximately, he must admit a great chasm "between scientism as an all-pervading ideology and the scientific method as a valid means of investigating the mechanisms of phenomena." Percy is speaking, in this presentation of himself on receiving the Ingersoll Award, in the third person, in an imitation (in respect to his rhetorical stance) of that Yankee Stoic, Henry Adams, whose autobiography pretends by its rhetoric to be a biography. (We recall once more that Adams himself has specifically in mind as literary analogue to his work St. Augustine's *Confessions*.) And so Percy, incipient diagnostic novelist returned home, remembers having been threatened by despair, even as Eliot had been at the time of his *Waste Land,* though Eliot stayed in London to engage despair rather than returning to his boyhood St. Louis. For this pilgrim Percy, by luck or providence, but whether one or the other, "as the very consequence of his despair – it occurs to him that a search is possible, a search altogether different from the scientific explorations mounted by scientists or by the most perceptive of psychoanalysts." These, by implication, are legitimate "scientific" quests, but his quest must be different.

And so he comes to write *The Moviegoer* "almost by accident." That "accident" in retrospect now seems rather a providential consent of grace, a grace at work and leading him into but also through his "self" to a something larger than the self. For in making his *Moviegoer,* he subsequently discovers, he "landed squarely in the oldest tradition of Western letters: the pilgrim's search outside himself, rather than the guru's search within." We have heard him declare that "All this happened to the novelist and his characters without the slightest consciousness [in the novelist and hence in his protagonist] of a debt to St. Augustine or Dante." How extraordinary, then, and beyond mere accident or luck as a sufficient explanation, that the character Binx "creates within himself and within the confines of a single weekend in new Orleans a microcosm of the spiritual history of the West, from the Roman patrician reading his Greek philosophers [Aurelius] to the 13th-century pilgrim who leaves home and takes to the road." In retrospect, then, it appears that Odysseus becomes transformed by Augustine-Dante.

That wanderer, now beginning to settle in Louisiana for the duration of his journey, addresses his peculiar history as intellectual soul incarnate, as *homo viator*, insofar as cumulative history may further the journey. He is by earlier academic training a "diagnostician," that is "a person who stands toward another person in the relation of one who knows that something has gone wrong with the other." He, the physician-novelist, has "a nose for pathology." To this characterization of himself as physician-novelist he adds that other circumstance to his journeying: his having become something of a demographic oddity, a Southern Catholic. And so, having become a "pilgrim-searcher," he "is able to take note of other kinds of sentences that he had ignored before," such sentences no doubt as some of those to be recorded later in "How to Be an American Novelist in Spite of Being Southern and Catholic" (1984) and especially at last those concluding statements to his journey, "Holiness of the Ordinary" (1989) and "Why Are You a Catholic?" (1990).

His recognition of himself has become of a "self" as journeyman, discovering his own repetition of an ancient journey and so sharing in a commonality with the living and the dead. For the dead are discovered by memory, through signs left in the desert of the mutual journeying, to be a continuing presence, a body of which he is member. These recognitions come relatively late, Percy suggests. Or perhaps better put, they are more fully understood late, as they had been also by Eliot or Dante or St. Augustine. One famous and somewhat ancient sign signifying this common experience: "in the middle of my life I came to myself in a dark wood." Or that other famous cry, "late have I loved thee!" Such recognition opens the self to the Cosmos (see Percy's "Holiness of the Ordinary"), but it must always appear to the journeyman to have been discoverer as not simply *relatively* late as it may to us in retrospective reflection, but *very* late. The convert gaining a rescuing vision through grace, whether at twenty or forty years, sees his rescue as a death-bed conversion in his suspension between nothingness and a transcendent rescue. From such late discoveries there will follow, given a sufficient opening to grace, a reordering of those remembered earlier discoveries which, because now better understood, are better accommodated. Thus, while the earlier Percy will associate his *Moviegoer* with ideas out of Existential philosophy, and very specifically with an episode in Sartre's *Nausea*, he will also acknowledge Eliot and St. Augustine and Dante as having been companionable presences to him as an almost-despairing novelist in a desert. Without his reflective awareness of their supporting presence to him in overcoming the threat of despair, they prove to have been presences. They, too, are poets-novelists, considering (as we may) the *Confessions* as a novel about the "self" in the desert and as such our first "Modern" novel about alienated man. In a parallel recognition by Eliot, it was a long and "cold coming" Percy has "had of it," with "the ways deep" and at times (for both Percy and Eliot) the wayfarer threatened by despair out of the intellectual weathers of Cartesian dislocations. Percy might well have become an actual suicide, as he sometimes hints.

It was one of those deep ways that – or so our explorations suggest – almost put Percy off a final reconciliation with the Cosmos because of his early fascination with Sartre. At least by retrospection we may see it as a contingent moment to a self lost in the Cosmos. It was this self-endangerment, made initially through a philosophy mistaken for science and therefore both scientifically and philosophically confusing. That is the confusion with which he is still wrestling in his thought at his mid-journey. And that midpoint is signaled by *Lost in the Cosmos.* For Percy is not yet fully reconciled to the burdensome journeying in his *Lost in the Cosmos.* That continuing struggle is residually present, even in his late essay, "The Fateful Rift: The San Andreas Fault in the Modern Mind" (1989). The mystery he addresses with the deportment of the scientist is to the sign itself, and the question he puts to semiotic science for an answer (in "The Fateful Rift") is, "How does an organism get to be a person?" From very early, Percy has supposed that Charles Peirce supplies a persuasive answer, though it requires his own explication. From that anticipation of intellectual rescue he seldom wavers. Hence he intends after *Thanatos Syndrome* (as he wrote Jan Gretlund) an exploration of Peirce toward fuller understanding.

We to the contrary summon Aquinas to the question, through whose arguments an endangerment to intellectual actions based in Peirce may be the better revealed. Thomas would reject at once the implication of a *substantial* progress attributed to man as deduced from man's history in nature, a progress Percy assumes and posits in seeing man an *organism* first and subsequently *becoming* a *person* through the mystery of sign. That is a change he (and Peirce) talk about as a transformation from a dyadic to a triadic transmogrification. Thomas to the contrary would declare that the "organism" by its created nature is already a "person." That is the foundational doctrine of Thomistic belief, seen as proper to

Thomistic metaphysics and to the Christianity which Percy seems sometimes to set to one side when he engages in semiotic argument. Whether as strategy or through his conditioning as scientist, he seems to do so. But for whatever reason, it thereby becomes an ambiguously philosophical-scientific strategy of thought endangering the signs he uses. Instead of a Thomistic conclusion, which involves an address of intellect to *givenness* and especially to its *own givenness* as created in the image of God (in which gift resides the mystery of sign), Percy becomes concerned with an evolutionary transformation of the *organism* to *person*, though he is dependent less upon scientific than upon poetic persuasiveness in his argument. That is to say, Percy through this interest in Peirce's "coupler" as Percy names it – Peirce's *interpreter, interpretant, asserter, mind, "I," ego, soul* – Percy through that interest would engage a point of "conception" in which is melded organism and person as a "natural phenomenon," in an evolutionary process effected by the sign. Here *conception* bears analogy to the biological *conception* of organism in the womb, the joining of sperm-egg. The point of this event – and compare Pierre Teilard de Chardin's *Phenomenon of Man* – occurs at the threshold of that dyadic-triadic transformation, occasioning the "Delta" effect. There occurs a Teilhardian "leap in being," a concept we borrow here from Teilhard's *Phenomenon of Man* as parallel, remembering in doing so that Teilhard is one of the philosophical sons of Bergson.

What is ambiguous is Percy's employing a rational resolution of empirical evidence to assert a magical transformation of organism to person, in an attempt to set aside (as he does in the last sentence of this piece, to which sentence we shall presently advert) that mystery engulfing his intellectual dilemma. To a rational engagement of the materiality of the *given,* an empirical science presumes to resolve the mystery of givenness analytically. (There has been a huge library of scientifically speculative engagements of the relation of *mind* to the human organ the *brain* this past half- y.) The mystery of sign serves a transformation of organism to person, but in a scientific difference to man as organism. It is not such a transformation as that St. Thomas sees in relation to the Incarnation, in God become man. It is rather as if Percy feels as the over-riding necessity that he deal with a profound evolution of *essence* itself in order to persuade the "scientist" among us and the larger popular body devoted to the scientist as philosopher. The transformation is effected by man's having crossed a threshold from being merely an "organism" to being a "person," then. From *dyadic chrysalis* the organism emerges as *triadic butterfly* – as *person* or *soul* or *ego* or *I*. Hence concerning this mystery, Percy advises that we be not too troubled by the difficulty of naming it: "Don't name it, for the present, but talk about it. . . ."

It is (again) as if the necessity to Percy is to prove *rationally,* in the manner of the empirical scientist, a profound transformation occurring in man's history within the cosmos in order to make it acceptable to the Modernist "scientific" mind. It would seem to "fit" somewhat the theory of evolution. But Percy is now handicapped as scientist by his Christian perspective on his condition, that of a *fallen scientist* now become novelist. (He makes self-deprecating allusions to himself as *novelist* along this early way, in contrast to Flannery O'Connor who, when asked why she writes stories, answers "Because I am good at it.") Put another way, it is as if Percy feels compelled to demonstrate as acceptable to the physicist (or the biophysicist) an *evolved meta*physics, matching at key points the Darwinian myth and measured as a metaphysics by that scientific myth. He must make a persuasive argument of a transformation of the agent organism from being a dyadic biological creature into the triadic person. Hence the importance of person as thus "newly" conceived at a point of mankind's unfolding nature, but (as if in deference to Modernist commitment to intellectual autonomy) it must be seen as accomplished through an intellect transmogrified by its own actions as the transforming agency. It acts androgynously as it were – itself as "coupler" through conjured sign. Thus it becomes almost the *transubstantiating* agent of its own progress from organism to person. As for this "coupler" (Percy's term) Peirce names this "linking entity" (Percy's term) variously. Whatever we name it, it is a "third element" (*word* and *thing* are the other two. It is here that we must submit to an embarrassment, if we are the Modernist audience Percy assumes to be his primary one. The embarrassment to this audience (and in some degree to Percy himself) is that this "third element," which appears an undeniable reality, is also undeniably *immaterial*. Shall we call this "soul"? That term "carries too much furniture from the religious attic," he says. And the Freudian "ego" won't serve, because "smelling . . . of the Cartesian split."

And so Percy must call this embarrassing reality a "natural phenomenon." Though it is not an *entity*, he says, it is an *act*. Philosophers since Plato (including Augustine and Aquinas) have engaged this embarrassing mystery, a natural reality *in* man which seems an evidence that man by "nature" already carries a supernatural dimension as a given *before* intellectual act, even when the *given* seems empirically problematic to the skeptical rational intellect. But Plato and Augustine and Thomas do not argue from empirical *premises* as Percy attempts. They must nevertheless argue (as Plato might say) from within the "shadow" of empirical realities as empirically encountered by man as an incarnate soul. What troubles their argument again and again, since Plato at least, is a concern to avoid a dualism. Percy, too, would avoid dualism, but at last he rather builds it into his argument at a crucial point: the duality between *organism* and *person* within *homo sapiens* as *now* recognized out of the mists of an evolutionary history. What we encounter at this point is a "nonmaterial, non-measurable entity" whose undeniable reality may lie in some trans-natural arena, a transportation to which requires the sign. The sign allows at once both the transportation and a transposition into a unity – a singularity – of man himself. This, as Plato or Augustine or Aquinas would comfortably assert, is the arena of personhood called *soul,* in which arena the power of self-agency as both transformer and transporter becomes highly questionable.

Such an undeniable *thing* (soul?) is undeniable because it is "personally" experienced, however difficult to name. To the Modernist mind it nevertheless must be assigned to the province of biochemistry. To the more cautious philosopher, it rather seems to require, not biochemistry but metaphysics. For only by metaphysics may this self-evident but ambiguous agent – this "coupler" – be reconciled to man's given nature, whereby man participates in the cosmos in a becoming as an active agent, as the joiner of thing and sign. But that (Augustine or Thomas would argue) is an aspect of its *precedent* given nature, its unified nature, since it is a *created intellectual soul incarnate* – diverse differentia attempting to name a simple unity. Upon that precedent *gift,* its being turns and returns to consciousness and to an awareness of responsibility to its *givenness* – to its *being* as created. Thus follows its responsibility as steward of *beings* in the adjacent cosmos, in the context of the *beingness* of creation itself. It is here that the mystery of an already existing triadic relation, by virtue of *givenness,* may reconcile person to limit. The "organism" man as dyadic does not *become* triadic. It is precedently so, and only by a falling away from that triadic nature out of its givenness does it become dyadic. A fulfillment of givenness becomes therefore a responsibility to stewardship of its own givenness: a fulfilling of inherent potential nature through intellectual and spiritual acts.

Man as Percy's *homo symbolificus* is Marcel's *homo viator* as "judgmental" agent (and Percy touches upon judgment as central to naming). By this aspect of his givenness, he participates triadically as steward, responsible to *givenness,* then. For, created in the "image" of his Creator, he is by participation enabled to "couple" givens: creation and Creator. Most especially crucial to his judgmental action is a recognition of his own *limited* givenness, reflectively known through experiences of his limits as knower, as a peculiarly active creature within the cosmos. But this is experience already, antecedently already experienced before the point of a *self-recognition* by any intellectual "coupling" action. That seems the point at which Percy would have a radically different event, the triadic *transformation*. It is antecedent because at the point at which the person recognizes himself, he recognizes that self as already possessed of some knowledge out of precedent experience. He is long since beyond that theoretical dyadic-triadic threshold theorized by Peirce. Indeed, his nature, a given, exists in a continuous act whereby he is *this* limited, *this* discrete being. That continuous act is the sustaining act of Love, whereby he *is*. As such a being, if we attempt to locate him in the context of creation, there has occurred already a crossing of that threshold by the very act of his creation. It is at that point which the Church calls conception. The person is deposited here (so to speak) by an initial and continuous act of Love, which act has as its discrete intentional effect the actual but limited existence of *this* person. So John Paul II would insist – as would Augustine or Thomas – as they would argue that in this initiating point called conception lies a larger mystery than what is for us a very limited understanding of biological conception. Here our own figure suggests that the Act of Love posits the person in the context of creation, its limited nature a *peculiar given* which is both actual and potential.

This person is therefore necessarily a limited nature, since as created *person* he is not his own Cause as agent. We speak here of a mystery of knowing reserved to the term *comprehensive* – a containing conception of a limited creature by the act of that creature's creation by Love. For the person as a discrete effect of Creating Love (whereby he is *this* person) can be so only as contained, as limited. As *this* thing, man is only *comprehended* absolutely by that undifferentiated Love, his Creating Cause. That, one hazards, is the position taken by Percy's Church. Thus it is the philosopher, not the scientist – or perhaps possibly the scientist truly become philosopher – who may reconcile himself as *homo symbolificus viator* to the given, in pursuit of reconciliation to mystery through metaphysics. A witness of importance to us on this point we have repeatedly introduced, that self-record of Augustine of Hippo, called by us *The Confessions*. Percy, however, is reluctant to allow his argument that reconciliation. And so, as if here were an extreme suggestion going afield from Heidegger and phenomenology in pursuit of man's "thrownness," he engages the Peircean Triadic. One might as a corrective therefore explore this creature as *person,* recovering to the concern the traditional Judeo-Christian notions of man, who in falling prey to the worldliness of the world (see especially St. Paul) becomes pilgrim seeking his "salvation," seeking an exit from his own making of a "dyadic" entrapment. But that would involve some adjustment of semiotics as a science, requiring much more to our understanding than can be given by rational science, whose faith rests in our day in the myth of evolution. Admitting as much, Percy says as his final paragraph of five words: "But that's a different story." It is a story which the Modern reader is not comfortable in hearing, since the signs necessary to the telling lie dusty in the attic. Its telling is best deferred.

A most coy conclusion, if one take Thomas or John Paul II or Flannery O'Connor seriously. It is their *same* story, though a story embarrassing to tell in the mixed Modernist company which Percy recognizes as his audience. We need only imagine Flannery O'Connor's deportment to such a company. Or Thomas's or St. Augustine's for that matter, given their address to the immaterial immortal soul. That is the climate of an old thought, an old orthodoxy involving certain signs which Percy (as does Eric Voegelin) finds unpersuasive to any mixed audience of believers and unbelievers – mostly unbelievers – in our moment of history. Such words as *soul* or *essence* or *substance* in the old scholastic sense have become opaque, serving only the skeptic in satiric references. (Percy in several asides seems to scoff at "scholastic" attempts.) Because they are terms opaque (the skeptic insists), they but mirror subjective illusions, nostalgically summoned by our rummaging in memory. This is a consequence of the triumph of science which Percy both acknowledges and early praises, while also recognizing the inherent skeptical burden to such a position. He will himself resolve this personal dilemma by embracing Pascal's wager as logically persuasive.

Increasingly, after this point, he becomes severe in judging the abuse of science by "scientism." At first he tends to exempt the scientist from that tendency.

It is the scientist's laity, addicted to consumerism, who become tempting to the scientist perhaps in his concern for their consent of support to his science, until alas even the most careful scientist may incline to assume the role of philosopher – as if justified in that assumption because he is as a scientist looked up to by the laity. If so, he certainly endangers the limited purity of his science. As scientist, he may assume the role of philosopher by popular consent, philosophy having become a fall-back intellectual position made subordinate to science. That science determines the limits of philosophy might be suggested by the trickle-down erosion of the terms, as when we hear the sports commentator between batters reflect on a pitcher's "philosophy" as pitcher in relation to the physics engaged in his act of throwing a sphere in the proximity of a batter. At a more serious level of concern, consider our repeated parable of the celebrated geneticist Richard Dawkins, who from his intimate knowledge of the gene will declare man but "lumbering robot" whose genes have created him "body and mind." (Quoted by another geneticist we shall remember in rebuke, R. C. Lewontin, in *Biology as Ideology: The Doctrine of DNA*, 1992.) With such presences in his audience as a Dawkins and his kinsmen, Percy might well be reluctant to invoke the Trinity to his concerns. Percy, of course, goes in some fear of what scientific presences like Dawkins may *do* to us, forewarned of the dangers of Modern gnosticism by such arguments as those of Eric Voegelin in *Science, Politics, and Gnosticism*. That is the thematic fear humorously developed in *Thanatos Syndrome.* He has been persuasively forewarned by the destructive violence of the 20th century to which he calls attention, the most destructive century of history which destroyed so many *persons.* From the scientific certainties now informing abortion law and conjuring euthanasia as a political "right," to the terrors of the Bomb on small yellow people a hemisphere away, with millions and millions of persons obliterated in between. From World War I to our uneasy, nervous, and uncertain hopes for a new millennium, we might put the question of whether, through signs reduced to science and then exercised as magic upon being, we have not advanced the abolition of man beyond even C. S. Lewis's fears at the end of World War II.

XVIII

Percy does not invoke the Trinity as analogy in his pursuit of man as maker, man created in the image of that Triune God. One might have expected it in his attempt to rationalize the relation of "Naming and Being" in that early (1960) essay. He recognizes nevertheless that, in attempting to deal with sign as related to person, he is dealing with a mystery buried in the antecedent. Hence "trying to penetrate the act of naming is like trying to see a mirror." We contend the act of naming to be more an art in relation to Thomistic epistemology than a science, an inclination out of intuitive knowing. Our present attempt, then, is to take sign as more than mirror, since as mirror it can but reflect the self to the self. That is the tendency out of Nominalism which reaches its dead-end in Sartre. Instead, we suggest that naming follows from communal act between the discrete person and the thing he experiences. It is made communal through that person's openness, his consent to the independent reality of the thing itself by the act of his seeing it – his knowing the thing in a limited (as opposed to a comprehensive) knowing. By that *manner* of address to the thing, the temptation to a Nominalistic assertion of the thing's existence through logicism is lessened. Naming thus becomes a continuing act of refining of an always limited knowing, according to discursive rational limits to knowing. It is continuing (though not continuous) insofar as there is in it an explicit or implicit consent to the independent reality of the thing. It is this understanding of signs that leads Eliot to conclude the poet's responsibility to be "the purification of the dialect of the tribe." Such a purification would order community's (multiple) experience in relation to the thing commonly seen, but only as governed by the truth of the thing. In this office, the poet serves an ordering of community itself to existential reality by his signs, insofar as his signs engage both discrete and multiple experiences as susceptible to a common consent to the complexities of existential reality. That consent is vested in signs held in common. Thus Eliot will declare the poet's responsibility of purifying the dialect (not the language) of the tribe. *Dialect,* to signify the close relation of person to community in the context of local place.

Percy, at an early point of his pursuit of the mystery of sign – his essay on the relation of naming to being – declares that "an affirmation requires two persons, the namer and the hearer." We are arguing that instead there occurs an immediacy of affirmation by the person as he experiences the thing, an affirmation independent of a hearer. That is, the affirmative act of consent to the being of the thing in itself is the mode of an initial experience of that thing. Sign, as sign, may occasion a turning of the knower from the known thing to a hearer, and sign therefore may become a means of pursuing a *common* consent of affirmation through an ordering of common but diverse recognitions of truth about the thing. Hence that truth requires the purification of the dialect of signs. But in that purification, in the interest of a common consent to *a* reality, the consent continues to be dependent upon the independent actuality of experience of the thing *in itself* – according to its *essence.* Otherwise, the common consent would become a closed arena of sign Nominalistically governed – as it has so largely become to an intelligentsia separated from community. It was in response to this gradual alienation of intellects, at first singularly and collectively confident of sign as the source of power, that occasioned an internal revolt, giving rise to the phenomenological revolution of the 19th century whose banner became Husserl's "back to the thing itself." (That he tended to concentrate upon the experience as if it were the thing proved a complication, taken advantage of in part by Heidegger but brought to a totalitarian closing of intellect by Jean-Paul Sartre.)

And so we would affirm that an initiating affirmation is a communal act of consent by the discrete intellect to the thing itself as initially experienced. But in Percy's borrowings from Charles Peirce, this is a level of our experience of things either denied or obscured in the interest of the triadic (the Delta) metaphor relating sign to experience by consigning such experience to the organic, the dyadic, relation of person and thing. By positing the person as initially isolated to the dyadic – the biological – level in his antecedent relation to a thing before the advent of sign the argument moves to an evolutionary epistemology. Percy concludes he must posit "two persons" as necessary to sign itself. (We need only remember our own experience of "body language," as an utterance of awe and wonder in response to beauty, to know that language may be independent of any necessity of a second person.) Peirce's argument, as explored by Percy, suggests the sign effecting a transformation of the person himself by the turning and uttering of the sign to a second person, a hearer. Thus occurs (the argument holds) a transformation from the dyadic to the triadic dimension of the intellectual creature. The orientation is no longer merely biological; it has *become* "ontological," and apparently made so by the act of a sharing in the sign.

To the contrary, our position holds that the specific person responds to the specific thing initially in an ontological way, through an actual experience precedent to any *erected* sign. It is an experience intuitively, as opposed to rationally, effected in an encounter of the specific thing. This is to speak of experience as enveloping the person in that most fundamental community of all: that of the *connaturality* of things in being, of the person and that discrete other which the person encounters on the confluent plane inhabited by things and persons as intellectual souls incarnate in their several particularities. He has already experienced a "triadic" relation whereby in his being *this* particular being – intellectual soul incarnate – he discovers his own nature as to be fulfilled in a stewardship to the encountered thing, *this* creature. The "third" dimension involved in such an experience is *being* itself, the ground of connaturality. By his given nature, in an accord to the responsibility attendant upon his having been created "in the image of God," he knows the thing. It is here that he uncovers or discovers, then, his own peculiar nature as distinct among the orders of nature, while at the same time discovering the specific responsibility of stewardship attendant upon his being *this* person. That is, in response to experience, according to the limits of his *specifically* given limits as *this* person, he is called to the limits of that given nature through a specific stewardship of things along his wayfaring way. He is called to accord himself in his "calling." That is an interior ground, in which his travels as *homo viator,* enlarging his recognition of his own specific gifts as *this* person. Out of that growing recognition will be derived his understanding – more or less rationally tenable – of himself as *this* person. Here then the temporal and spatial circumstances to Percy's "self" in which that "self" intuitively recognizes its ontological orientation to the "cosmos." What is known at that fundamental level is the connaturality governed by *being,* through which recognition the person matures in his "calling" to a perfection as *this* person.

If this be a tenable position in respect to a triadic dimension to the person's action in nature, it will follow that Percy's judgment of the self, namely that "oneself is the only being that cannot be symbolized," becomes increasingly problematic. One might say instead that the person cannot *comprehend* himself as a self, as he may believe himself perfectly comprehended by God. That act of faith is another matter. Thus to say, as Percy proceeds to do in his early essay, that "I myself escape every such attempt at formulation," so that the "being of the namer slips through the fingers of naming" is to mistake the nature of *being* in relation to the "self." It must be said as well, we add, that the being of any thing slips through any attempt to name. The difficulty lies in our capacity to name *comprehensively,* whether we would name this already actively naming self or any thing. For the act of naming, as a rational action of finite intellect, necessarily falls short always of a comprehension of the thing as the ground of the naming action. This is a limit of human knowing in respect both to the finitude of intellectual knowing itself and to intentional naming by any gnostic attempt at power over being. That limit lies in the given nature of the namer, though out of that very nature, his *givenness,* man is tempted to be restless with limit, his restlessness a continuing symptom of his being fallen. It is by the fallenness of given nature that he is tempted to an absolute freedom, desiring himself to be his own cause.

In response to limit, along his limited way, *homo viator* comes upon that tempting formulation against limit, conjuring magical power by the will: *non serviam.* (The formula exists in diverse signs.) That is the false idol deployed by Nominalistic autonomy whereby the person may in the end come to serve Nothingness primarily, a Nothingness hidden from him by his intentional self-blinding and appearing to him as an illusion of Somethingness as he bows to that idol. The illusion of having gained an absolute freedom through rejecting *being* tempts him to dream he has "created" his own being as he may dream it reflected in his own sign. This is a progress toward suicide, the escape from which makes one Percy's "ex-suicide." What Percy seems to have discovered to his own security is that a prospect of a literal suicide is the absolutist position one inevitably comes to out of the *non serviam.* We are here speaking of the extremities of willful revolt, intending to include the progressive steps along that way, the multitude of possible actions of self-love, lesser and greater ones.

This progress toward suicide, already begun in degree by a turning of will to willfulness under the banner of *non serviam,* allows as well, we quickly note, a turning from that deadly way. Hence an escape from that way makes one, in Percy's term, an "ex-suicide." That is the turning he sees as possible to be made away from Modernist dislocations of the self that are all but consuming of the self. And so, in respect to this mystery of naming, in relation to the dangerous progress to the edge of the abyss of Nothingness, we may well remember – again and again, because it continues to us – the deceptive guide we have inherited in a variety of modifications in our intellectual history, that late Medieval doctrine proposed as solution to the mystery of sign: Nominalism. By its logical persuasiveness, Nominalism becomes a principle precipitating the Modernist illusions of the self which Percy treats playfully in *Lost in the Cosmos* at a Nominalistic dead end. The illusion of absolute power derived by "naming" rises in the self when it assumes itself autonomous and therefore believes itself absolutely sovereign in its relation to creation. It is in an uneasy waking from this illusion that the person may find himself suspended over Percy's "San Andreas Fault in the Modern Mind."

If by that discovery the self on coming to itself chooses a comic and satiric address to its own suspension through art's indirection, such a self might well name with an artful indirection, even perhaps with an excess like that of those animated cartoons in which the protagonist creature runs off a cliff and hangs suspended, legs "windmilling," suspended in a "place" which is noplace – before plummeting into reality when it recognizes the absurdity of its willed circumstances. That is a moment of suspense in which mere motion yet resists the plummeting, which suggests a dawning of panic that anticipates as an end despair, though it be made comic by cartoon animations of signs. The comic spectacle cannot prevent the gravity of despair. But then, this is the moment also in which may occur a miraculous rescue, not made by the flailing figure himself in flying by an angelism, but a rescue through grace. Such, then, the circumstances to a comic rendering of the spiritual and intellectual history of an "ex-suicide," for whom the terror of despair has been "personally" anything but comic.

How difficult to *name* as particulars the elements of such dramatic actions *upon* and *from within* the intellectual soul incarnate. No wonder that one might dream that some science may prove agent to a rescue from despair, if that agent can be reduced to the biochemical aspect of man as mechanism. Or if despair itself can be reckoned but an effect of psychological flux out of biochemistry, with no relation to the so-called "spiritual," and so treatable by the latest medications. One might well then seek a certainty of the empirically known, formulated in signs as if thereby effecting the dream as a virtual reality made actual, a rescue of the self through "science." Perhaps semiotics resolves the mystery of sign. But only in a very *limited* way may it serve. Thus Etienne Gilson argues persuasively in his *Linguistics and Philosophy* from his Thomistic commitment to metaphysics. In respect to Percy and his concern for the sign, our physician as novelist approaches an impasse regarding the mystery of sign, at which point he turns to science rather than to metaphysics. It is by that turning that he comes to a disquieting conclusion, at least disquieting for the Thomist, about the relation of being to naming. If the namer, attempting to name himself, "tries to construe himself in the same mode by which he construes the rest of the world, he must necessarily construe himself as nothing, as Sartre's characters do." It is a moment of impasse, in which the relation of knowing to "construing" – naming – becomes confused. And it will be nearly thirty years later that Percy will remark that this line of thought, while dependent upon the scholastic concept of *being* as borrowed and inverted by Sartre, will be discovered as itself to have borrowed the signs for its *process* of thought from traditional Christian "anthropology" concerning the nature of man. Reduced to mere anthropology, the process executed by signs may then be perverted by a borrowing from Revelation in an act of intellectual arrogance. The consequence of that attempt (Sartre's Existentialism) is the Existentialist's "upside-down pilgrimage . . . into absurdity."

In this "mirror" image of the self reflected from the power of naming assumed by subversion of being, the sign becomes opaque. But the self reflected in such names is a mirroring made not upside down but rather crosswise, we might say. If it were upside down, unacceptable absurdity might be a more conspicuous warning of an intellectual violation of being. Instead, in the mirrored image of the self through opaque sign the left becomes the right, the right the left. (Compare our own "vision" of our bodily self in an actual mirror.) The illusion of reversal proves encouraging to the self turned magician of its own being. For by the very presumption that by the power of naming an intellect *creates* substantial being leaves the self fascinated (in a literal sense) by its own image. Mirror, mirror on the wall! In the root meaning of that "name" (*fascinate* and its cognates) the image becomes acceptable as an idol to be worshipped. The self becomes mesmerized, though at first it does not recognize its idol (its "self") as suspended like the cartoon figure, oblivious of the intellectual flailing necessary to keep suspended – at least for the moment in which self-love seems sufficient. A Thomist, detached from this comedy of intellectual error, may be considerately moved. Or he may, as diagnostic novelist, engage that situation in its comic evidences of Modernist man, his looniness.

Not, of course, that the person in trying to name himself is not frustrated. But the cause of the frustration lies in knowing that the *something* he does in fact know (himself) can only with some wavering of precision be named. He is always more than his knowing, and so more than his naming. That is the intellectual circumstance to the self leading the true mystic (as opposed to intellectual magician) to contemplation. What may become disturbing, then, is the recognition that the naming is always partial, not comprehensive, insofar as pride treasures the dream of absolute freedom. Yeats has touched on the matter in a playful poem, declaring that only God can love the beautiful girl for "her self alone," while mere mortals seem doomed to love her for her "yellow hair." A sympathy for Jean-Paul Sartre as himself a dramatic specimen of man caught in the "Modern Malaise," wrestling to command signs to his own absolute intentionality, draws Percy to *Nausea*, which he will judge as less than a successful novel though fascinating in its diagnostic implications, especially its presentation of man in his penchant for "roles." (One might be tempted to describe Percy's early attraction as that of a rational sentimentality.) Similarly his sympathy is engaged by Heidegger, as it is still so engaged (we discover) in that serious footnote to his playful handbook on semiotic engagements of the cosmos. Contending with the problem of naming, he turns that difficulty to satiric play, caricaturing failed attempts at a variety of transcendences of emptiness by a variety of "selves," man in his multiplicity of "roles." (Remember our cartoon figure, legs blurred in running, suspended over the abyss.)

One wants very much to bring a different account to this attempt to reconcile the act of naming to the realities of being, suspecting an inadequate sense of the concept of *being* as underlying Percy's difficulty. Thus we appeal to Etienne Gilson. In his *The Spirit of Thomism*, Gilson gives us a point of departure, a formulation of *being* based in a passage from Thomas's *Questiones disputandem de potentia*, remarking in doing so that "if we want to philosophize," this is really "*the* problem of problems." There follows his formulation based in the cited text: "In Thomas' technical language, actual existence, which he calls *esse*, is that by virtue of which a thing, which he calls *res*, is a being, an *ens*. It is the being-hood or beingness of being. It is *be* in being. It is *to be* that makes a certain thing to be a being." It is, to our concern, *being* as the ground common to our intellectual consent to the existence of any peculiar thing, including that thing we engage as our own "self." By engagement we know (though only *partially* know) a thing in itself. And that knowing initiates recognition of a community with the particular thing, encountered through an intellectual consent of openness to the thing as actual in itself. That is: in such an experience, we recognize intellectually a *connaturality*, out of which recognition reason may begin to engage supportively what intellect already knows intuitively.

Gilson might suggest of this condition to our knowing that it is shared commonly, in an accord of persons and things, through man's given nature, whereby we may participate in community. It is "common" sense shared, the point of knowing out of which philosophy grows. And it is also in this point of knowing that we recognize our "self" as actual, having recovered our common "connaturality" in being. For through existing at all we thus actively share in that ontological ground. That is the reality of our knowing by "common sense" which is set aside by Descartes, to our subsequent confusions. (Again, see Gilson's incisive exposition of Cartesian error in *Methodical Realism.*) The sharing is consequently recognized as a commonality of *existing* as *created.* It is the most fundamental intellectual ground in which love – openness to things – dissolves the "self" from its possibly inordinate concern for itself. And it is here that as created image of God, as intellectual soul incarnate, the person intuitively responds within a "Trinitarian" context to its knowing, whereby *truth* is the bonding effect indwelling intellect through the communal union of intellect and thing. And here *truth* is understood in its relation to intellect as an effect of grace, in the light of Christ's speaking of "the Spirit of truth" as one of the names of the Lord and Giver of Life, truth being sustenance to the life of finite intellect itself as well as to the spectrum of created things. Such is that action of intellect which St. Augustine recovers on his long journey. And when he at last recognizes that recovery, he cries out those once famous signs: "Late have I loved thee!"

This passage in Augustine's *Confessions* we may revisit to our point. The words are set down near the beginning of Book 10, his "Philosophy of Memory." There he records having first commanded testimony from the things of creation, a certification by things of the unwavering Creator. Those commanded things, "all the things that stand around the doors of my flesh," he says, of one accord cry out together, "We are not God! . . . He made us!" "The inner man [the intellectual soul] knows such things through the ministry of the outer man," St. Augustine declares. "I, I, the mind, by means of my bodily senses, I asked the whole fabric of the world about my God, and it answered me, 'I am not he, but he made me!'" Thus Augustine's recovery to the ground of connaturality beyond both pagan and Manichaean reductions of "nature." It is the ground intuitively sought and now ontologically believed, but it is believed before any naming. This, we are suggesting, is an act at a *communal* point with things, before that subsequent action whereby Peirce and Percy would have us transformed in our creaturely nature by the act of signs – their movement from the biological dimension (the dyadic) to becoming a person in a triadic dimension. St. Augustine will subsequently, in this same book of the *Confessions,* argue that all along his failure has been not to look deeply enough into his own heart through memory – there to discover as always present to him his Cause, the presence of the Lord of truth.

It is through the grace of that presence to intellect that intellect is enabled to respond "to all the things that stand around the doors of [his] flesh" – the things he must then riddle with rational intellect in pursuit of an understanding of his own anterior being, whereby he becomes oriented to his potential being as person here and now but bound for eternity. That is, the grace of his givenness may at last be sought in its perfection as the limited potentiality to him as *this* person. Thus his initial loss has been the "ontological" ground of connaturality, that commonness in being of each thing as created, and it has been lost to Augustine through the willfulness of his Manichaean intent on the one hand and by a submergence of his "inner man" to the appetitive nature of the worldly desires of the "outer man" on the other. The loss is an effect of turning love into self-love, whatever higher "transcendental" name it may be given by the clever rhetor. Now as Dante makes dramatically evident in his *Divine Comedy,* self-love as a turning inward of the self is thereby a perverted love. St. Augustine discovers a quite different mode of turning inward in his "Philosophy of Memory," through which turning he discovers a Light waiting the self, interior to and pervasive of truth as held in memory.

The discovery is that "Truly, you [God] dwell in my memory, since I have remembered you from the time I learned of you, and I find you there when I call you to mind." Now, the truth of things abiding in memory speaks a higher truth than the appetitive desire alone when it is tempted to make an ultimate end of a desire to consume things according to its sensual nature. (*Pace* Epictetus.) For those things loved and yet remembered, the truths sustained in memory of past experiences of the contingent world: "They kept me from you, those fair things which, if they were not in you, would not exist at all." And so the recovery to Augustine of an *ordinate* love of creation in relation to its Cause. It is through such an ordering of a love of things that the person maintains a sacramental relation to creation – most especially in a remembrance through such "things" as bread and wine. And so out of that recovery occurs the joyful lament, that celebrated cry in the *Confessions:* "Too late have I loved you, O Beauty so ancient and so new . . . ! Behold, you were within me, while I was outside." While he was outside and rushing "headlong upon these things of beauty which you have made." And so St. Augustine, through the courage of a recovered openness to creation, is at once rebuffed in his Manichaean reduction of creation and in his tendency to an excessive worldly appetite. He recovers his orientation of will to creation. He recovers a unity of his "inner" and "outer" man. It is, Aquinas might add, a recovery of the providential gift to the intellectual soul called the "natural law," in recognition of which the intellect riddles the orders of being without violating being itself. The Modern scientist if given to a rigid mindset (such as Percy will at the end judge him to be possessed by) seems incapable of avoiding that violation. The necessary turning inward to a presence of the Abiding Beauty becomes arrested by a partial turning which rests faith in intellectual autonomy, failing to pursue the depths of intellect's givenness. What is thus lost is the mystery of our being created in the image of God, in a false expectation of the self as Godhead.

Here, we turn to Aquinas once more, who cautions the poet, perhaps especially the diagnostic physician-novelist, that art is indeed a making through reason. But it is a making according to peculiar limits to this creature man – peculiarly limited and blessed at once in being created in God's image. At the very end of his life Thomas returns to the place from which he had set out, to Naples, and there in the Neapolitan dialect delivers homilies to his hometown folks on the creed which they hold in common. In that series of talks he remarks the difference between man as image of God and God Himself. In respect to action the one *makes*, the other *creates*. Human beings are not able to make anything without preexistent material, and "that is because they are makers of the particular and are not able to draw forth this form [necessary to the act of any making of a particular thing] without material determined and presupposed from another [from the Creator God]. . . . [T]heir own virtuosity is limited to form alone, and therefore can be the cause only of this form." And, we continue, insofar as naming is itself a species of making, that form (the sign) depends upon the given, upon the preexisting. It depends as well, and necessarily so, upon actuals as *known* antecedently to the imposition of form (the name). If this is a truth consistent with our experiences as intellectual soul incarnate, experiences as inhabitants of creation within the connaturality of givenness, then we may object that there occurs a severe complication to the primacy Percy would assign to the "triadic." For he holds as a necessity to that leap in being a "co-celebrant," another person, before there can be celebration of openness to creation itself by the discrete, unique intellectual soul incarnate.

For Percy the "triadic" requires this "co-celebrant," whereby two persons transcend the biologically "dyadic" in a mutuality of intellectual action. That is an address to intellectual community within which lies the dangers of angelism, we fear. Because we take this to be potentially a very dangerous conclusion, counter to experience, we may turn for some support in an opposition to it, to recover from our alarm, to a small work by Josef Pieper, his *Happiness & Contemplation*. It is a work first translated into English in 1958 at about the time Percy begins to engage the mystery of signs in relation to being from a position which emphasizes the science of semiotics. Consider *contemplation* as Pieper develops it, and especially as it is relevant to the poet's concern for sign in witness to such special experience within creation as those which Wordsworth calls a "spot of time" or Eliot calls a "still point" of visionary experience. Not these poets, however, but Gerard Manley Hopkins is the witness Pieper summons as apt to his philosophical explorations of the nature of *contemplation.* Further, Pieper argues contemplation to be the central theme in both St. Augustine and St. Thomas Aquinas. *Contemplation* is the name of a reflective action appropriate to any person's specific experience of the world. Pieper turns and returns in exposition of the term, appealing to our own experiences and encouraging us in them by summoning the witness of poets and philosophers. Thus "Contemplation is a loving attainment of awareness. It is intuition of the beloved object" – the object become beloved through the act of openness toward it by consciousness – by an "I." It is "a form of knowing arrived at not by thinking, but by seeing, intuition." Thus, as we might put it as poet, memory is "peopled" as it were by discrete almost creaturely truths about things in themselves, as experienced. Perhaps more precisely, we are sustained through memory by a recognition of the actual creatureliness of things as consequent to their existing because created.

Pieper is exploring with his signs, by a redaction of signs from St. Augustine and especially from Aquinas. His arguments out of Aquinas may prove surprising, given our popular understanding of Aquinas as the rationalist philosopher or theologian *par excellence*. That is a position requiring adjustment, of course, in the light of St. Thomas's epistemology, which devolves from his understanding of the simple unity of intellect, whereby intellect acts modally out of that simplicity – being both intuitive and rational. For him the *ratio* is an *extension* of the *intellectus*, of the intuitive. In his formulations in pursuit of the reality of contemplation, Pieper depends often upon the *Summa Theologica*, especially upon II, II, 49, 5 ad 1, and upon the *Summa Contra Gentiles*, especially 1, 57 (8). Those texts argue that the "necessity for thinking is due to a failure of intuition." It is to be observed as well that "Reason is an imperfect form of *intellectus*," of the intuitive. For Thomas, the end of knowing is the simple perfection of the person through the perfection of the *intellectus* (the intuitive). (That is to arrive at a perfect state anticipated by hope as Beatitude.) One discovers that the *reason* is a necessary but ultimately a secondary gift to the person in respect to his pursuit of his *perfect* knowledge of reality. What reason leads toward, let us say, is an intellectual transparency of the self in its knowing which is beyond rational knowing, in that experience of a visionary still point. And it is in a memory of such fleeting visionary moments in this world that the mystic anticipates Beatitude in the next.

Contemplation, then, is the habit of openness to creation through love. It is an act which does not necessarily depend upon *duration* – as if we should mistakenly suppose that only a withdrawal into ascetic suspension in some desert, into a concentrated meditation, is capable of effecting the fullness of the contemplative moment as furthering us toward Beatitude. The habit of contemplation may serve to remove obstacles to a moment graced by vision. But even so, habit does not determine vision. Put directly, one cannot conjure vision. Always mysteriously, vision touches consciousness with what to consciousness seems a randomness, like that of the wind which bloweth as it listeth. For, as limited in existing as is the intellectual soul incarnate, there is that chasm of disproportionality between the person and that only Absolute Freedom, that Absolute Love. By the disproportionality there is obscured to, but not obliterated in, intellect any comprehension of the order of Providence Itself. Hence that slow and prolonged labor whereby, through the weakness of analogy, the orders of nature speak of, hint toward, Divine Order. (It is in this complication of disproportion between God and his image man that there lies the uncertainty of our naming by a science of names.)

The moment's vision speaks in support of our responsible but uncertain labor as stewards of order in creation. And if it is to the poet that such vision comes, his calling obligates him to the purifying of sign so that he may witness to the tribe. That is the labor of a purification seeking proportionality in relation to the limits of the poet's (or the philosopher's or the scientist's) own knowing. And it is this recognition that dawns on St. Augustine at a crucial moment to him when the orders of nature declare that they are not his God but that God made them. Augustine's responsibility becomes that of now purifying the pagan dialect that he possesses by virtue of his cultural and intellectual history. That is a witness St. Augustine especially bears to T. S. Eliot centuries later, supporting Eliot in his gradually clarified witness to his own experiences of creation, out of his own still points of this turning world which has so pervasively been clouded by Modernist impositions upon it. Thus it will be to Carthage that Eliot comes, "burning, burning, burning" in an echo from *The Confessions* in his *Waste Land.*

A considerable challenge, such witness, most especially to the confident skeptic fallen (seemingly most suddenly – "*late* have I loved thee") upon visionary ways. Visionary moments seem random to his journeying, no less than sudden and unsought. Indeed they have been actively rejected by skeptical reason as violations of the orderliness of time and place as reckoned by the progressive sciences evolved by autonomous intellect. That moment in a neglected garden at Burnt Norton for Eliot, however, proves beyond reason's explication. It is a reality undeniable in his experience, but inexplicable by skeptical reason. The neglected roses have the look of roses that are looked at. How *still* old uncertainty becomes. For such moments are not subject to *determinations* by time or place as when the cosmos is taken as uncaused machine. Nor by intentional intellect in its insistent rational pursuits in this time and in this place that it might resolve the newly encountered uncertainty by a resolute skepticism. As a shocking rebuff to intellectual Positivism, which has been made energetic by skepticism, it may well lead that shocked consciousness to a "nervous breakdown." It will appear a malfunction of man as mere integer in a world of thought governed by skepticism. But it may in truth prove rather a trauma of spirit, resisting its own death in rejecting an arbitrary skeptical willfulness.

How then find one's place as an acceptable novelist or poet with such disadvantages as discovered in the cultural accoutrements of signs, selectively bequeathed him by Modernist erosions? Those signs, to a dawning recovery, seem already subversive, indirect. How become an "American" novelist, if one is not only "Southern" but "Catholic" as well – in a discarded fundamentalist sense (a strictly orthodox sense) of designation by such names? By a counter subversion, through terms used in indirection? Tit for tat? Otherwise, one may have to be content with self-spoofing, as does Eliot in one of his "finger exercises" as poet, his puppeting response to his Modernist peers who are condescendingly skeptical of his "conversion." "How unpleasant to meet Mr. Eliot!" For, given his "features of clerical cut" and brow grim, his mouth prim, his conversation proves now hardly so lively as in those old days of sharp ironic skepticism in his signs. Now his conversation is nicely restricted to "What Precisely/ And If and Perhaps and But." Tedious intent to truth, and so inevitably boring.

Difficult as such experiences of roses in a neglected garden may be to celebrate in an intellectual climate largely devoid of sacramental inclinations, those experiences to the specific person himself are, Josef Pieper says, "transfiguring" moments. In them occurs an "experience of divine satiation." And to a world increasingly demanding sensational violence as the only spectacle releasing us from boredom – from our celebrated intellectual *ennui* – how absurd to speak a divine dimension in "the most trivial of stimuli," as Pieper insists is the avenue of grace to the intellectual soul incarnate. So attuned, in setting aside violent spectacles of intellectual arrest, one is transfigured on occasion by the most ordinary of experiences. Hence Pieper will summon Hopkins in witness, as we have summoned Eliot by remembering his experience in that deserted garden at Burnt Norton. Hopkins, responding to such experience of small things, declares God's grandeur flaming out in those things "like shining from shook foil," or gathered to greatness "like the ooze of oil/ Crushed," as from pressed olives.

In activity, but also in moments of rest, one may become attuned to beauty imperfect in "dappled" things and discover it a witness to a Beauty Perfect: the "rose-moles all in stipple upon trout that swim" or in "skies of couple-color as a brindled cow." It is this dappledness, the limited and imperfect thing speaking the Unlimited Perfect, through which we come to meet that Perfect Love. At a still point of the turning world we hear small things, though at first they may have confounded our celebrated "intellectual" poet T. S. Eliot. After a recovery, how unpleasant to meet Mr. Eliot. But he has reached a spiritual collapse that proves a grace to him. We see correspondence here to Percy's contracting tuberculosis as an act of grace. Eliot celebrates his recovery from skeptical autonomy in "Ash-Wednesday," the high point of his rejoicing focusing upon small things as his "lost heart stiffens and rejoices." The "heart" (the intuitive intellect) recovers the "lost lilac" and the "bent golden-rod," the "cry of quail" and "the whirling plover," and to the good health of the soul in its dark moment. Dappled things speak to that soul in an anticipation of undappledness, of perfection beyond this world's "fickle, freckled . . . swift, slow . . . sweet, sour; . . . adazzle, dim," as Hopkins has it. And what these small dappled things speak, to the inner fallen man, is what they spoke to St. Augustine. In Hopkins's words, "He fathers-forth whose beauty is past change." From such reflections, then, we may understand the better why Walker Percy on his long journey back to the place from which he set out turns more and more often to Hopkins as witness to discoveries he increasingly makes through small things experienced along that way – a hitching post slowly engulfed by an oak, a sunfish flapping in a flat boat in a swamp. But first a beginning, an exploring of the sign scientifically, and the making of *Moviegoer*. Reflecting on the effect of Southern "Stoicism" upon his own circumstances in a dark Southern wood increasingly shadowed by Modernist illusions, he will come upon "the oldest tradition of Western letters: the pilgrim's search outside himself, rather than the guru's search within."

Walker Percy by the time of his *Thanatos Syndrome* has more fully come to recognize the possibility that ordinary experience bears a true visionary nature no less than may some more spectacular encounter of truth. Such an ordinary experience is represented emblematically, we have said, in that last novel, through Tom More's response (Hopkins-like in Percy's signs) to that sunfish flapping in sunlight on the floor of his boat in the Louisiana swamp. But it has been a long journey to that more confident recognition. From his late perspective upon the ordinary, and remembering his own progress to such a moment in the role of the "Physician as Novelist" (1989), Percy will declare that journey, by his subtitle, to have been well begun in the "Best Training for a Novelist in These Last Years of the Twentieth Century[,] an Internship at Bellevue or Cook County Hospital," a submergence in the world which "Best Prepares Him for Diagnosing T. S. Eliot's *The Waste Land*."

The moment which the poet (Eliot, Percy, Hopkins) memorializes is, in its actuality, a moment reflecting a *simplicity* of person in his response to reality, occasioned by but not determined by his openness of love. It is an experience beyond the power of sign to fully witness, no less because of the terrors to the witnessing person than of his ensuing joy. Thus the person experiences a "perfection" of his nature for a moment. Or more accurately, by grace there is foreshadowed as possible to him an ultimate abiding perfection, yielded in that moment in which there is admixed terror and joy in his return to the "ordinary" world. It is an experience which is beyond the seemingly divisive uses of sign, as when we would define person as *intellectual/soul/incarnate* – as if a three in one, though by the multiple namings we are rather struggling to name a simple unity. The visionary moment dissolves person into a simple unity, foreshadowing that anticipated mystery of Beatitude, in a fleeting moment of self-forgetfulness. Pieper in his exploration of the relation of human happiness to contemplation dwells on the authority to this reality as witnessed by the poet, especially citing instances from Gerard Manley Hopkins's notebooks. He observes of these notations that they evidence visionary moments now *past*. If such moments as are celebrated by Wordsworth, calling them "spots of time," or by Eliot as "still points," it was such a moment that proved only baffling to Keats as he falls away from that transport of spirit in his communal moment of the nightingale song. He falls back to a despair as a "sole self." Hopkins sees, experiences, what he calls the "instress" of the thing as conjoined to person in such a moment. But he knows that the moment cannot be commanded not to fade through any word of his own. Nevertheless there has been effected a truth in intellect, *known* truth. His signs attempt to witness the experience by an "inscape" of signs. The independent reality he makes a celebratory thing, in an ordinately responsive memory of the moment's vision. That is the gift allowed to him as poet. Thus by witness of the known he may point *toward* by his signs.

Those moments remembered, however difficult to articulate, nevertheless prove (says Pieper) "how little contemplation need bypass or blur reality of the visible world by . . . premature 'symbolization.'" These are moments in which the intellectual soul incarnate becomes a *simple person* (*simple* in a philosophical sense of undivided) in communion with a thing beheld in its own simple reality. That is a triadic union of person, thing, and the Cause of both thing and person – God – though that Presence as a third (a Presence "looking" at Eliot's roses) is only to be reflectively named. In this light, the contemplative moment – the visionary moment – is not determined by the degree of intellectual or spiritual gift to this person, since the moment is a gift through grace. Pieper's concern in his argument is therefore to emphasize that such moments are not to be supposed reserved to the poet or philosopher or theologian, nor to the ascetic withdrawn into the desert, though these may well and properly be engaging such moments with a higher sense of the responsibility of their acts of naming. These are moments common in that they are possible to "ordinary" persons responding to ordinary things by an openness of love, no less than to the extraordinarily gifted. They occur in our "everyday" participation within created reality, sustained in a "triadic" ambiance of love – though that reality may be seldom recognized and even more seldom witnessed by poems or songs in signs.

That is the understanding Percy comes to and insists upon in his brief affirmation of "The Holiness of the Ordinary" the year before he dies. It is "the sacraments, especially the Eucharist, which, whatever else they do, confer the highest significance upon the ordinary things of this world, bread, wine, water, touch, breath, words, talking, listening. . . ." If man finds himself "in a predicament" he also finds himself "on the move in a real world of real things," action which refutes without the necessity of argument the Cartesian escape into a consciousness supposed isolated. Into that isolated self, the self may of course peer as if Narcissus seeking its own arrested self-image as final end. That was an attempt which proved attractive through Jungian psychology as an acceptable "metaphysics" to the mystery of the self, and so Jung (more than Freud) became the attractive metaphysician to the poet – up to the 1960s. In this inversion from the world, variously manifest in our turning inward, there develops a more subtle and seemingly sophisticated entrapment by history, whereby the cosmos serves Narcissism as mirror, so long as history is seen as a continuum of uncaused causes. It is thus through a theory of intellect's pursuit of an ancient, pre-consciousness state, supposed once a relation between *man becoming* a consciousness and the *cosmos* as confrontational cause to that becoming, that we advance a theory of the Peircian Dyadic as modifying somewhat the merely biochemical formulations of man. That is a first step toward a theory of the Triadic as immanent. Almost inevitably the present theorist must assume authoritatively a transcendent point to declare his theoretical pyramid. But neither the biochemical reduction of man to machine nor the mystically magical theory of Jungian "memory" can diagnose or effectively prescribe to the malady of alienation.

What is to be recovered through the holiness of the ordinary? Percy says "a world which is a sacrament and a mystery." Percy affirms this at the end of his journey. Within this world *homo viator* discovers himself "a pilgrim whose life is a searching and a finding." The sense of *world* in this late statement by Percy is in affirmation of reality as independent of psychological impositions of a "world" upon the "cosmos," the requirement in Percy's earlier position. That is, *world* is a term changed from that earlier use of the same term in his fascination with "science" as offering a possible solution to an intellectual reconciliation with the sign through a resolute self in its quest for self-certification. That may be still the burden in our impoverished TV fare, he now suggests, as for instance in an "educational" series explicating the thought of Joseph Campbell out of Jung, hosted by Bill Moyers with a solemn piety, on public supported "educational" TV. But, Percy says in the voice of the novelist engaged in a comic mischief (on behalf of the truth about the human condition) "In the end, ten boring Hail Marys are worth more to the novelist than ten hours of Joseph Campbell on TV." And, come to think of it, he concludes, "the notion of saying one's beads while watching Joseph Campbell is funny enough as it is." To those with ears to hear, the small voice of reality is omnipresent witness to the holiness of that sustaining Love to the "ordinary" person, not even excluded from whatever attempted distortions by technology. That is why the world itself, as opposed to any "world" imposed upon the circumstantial here and now, must be rediscovered by Modernist man as "a sacrament and a mystery," in Percy's words. That rediscovery will reveal, in Gerard Manley Hopkins's words, that "There lives the dearest freshness deep down things." Another respondent to the Modernist dead-end, the French novelist Bernanos (well known to both Percy and especially to O'Connor) puts it: "All is grace."

For all of these summoned witnesses, each has discovered variously, through varying gifts and circumstances, a ground zero of the self. The "self" makes its start from there, only to discover through the journeying a return to that point of departure, seeing it "for the first time" as Eliot has it. That beginning which is also an end becomes understood as the ontological ground in which the self exists, in which alone it may exist. The point is always the *here and now* when accepted as a sacramental moment in which the person (no longer a "self") is conjoined with things in a mutual (varying by *degree*) connaturality, attributable to the creating act of Love. It is the moment in which the self most deeply knows itself a participant in a sacramental moment. In this recognition, St. Augustine speaks, anticipating and rejecting Cartesian Idealism prophetically. In his *Against the Academics,* bidding farewell to the clever fantasies of the intellectual manipulations of sign by the professional rhetor such as he has been, he says that in questioning man's very existence, the learned academicians have "disputed long and much with very great copiousness and vehemence concerning the errors of unlearned men, a thing . . . most easy for any moderately educated man." On the same point, in *On the Trinity*: "The knowledge by which we know that we live is the most inward of all knowledge of which even the Academic cannot insinuate. . . . [H]e who says 'I know I am alive' says he knows that he knows a single thing. Further, if he says, 'I know that I know I am alive,' now there are two; but that he knows these two is a third thing to know."

St. Augustine would make emphatic the validity of such knowing, though in the Modernist world that seeming regression of the self in its knowing itself seems infinite, leading Descartes to his isolation of the self in an ideology. It is, then, a most ancient and modern gambit of the sophist as rhetor which St.

Augustine engages. He does so once more in *The City of God*: "Without any delusive representation of images or phantasms, I am most certain that I am, that I know, and that I delight in this. On none of these points do I fear the arguments of the skeptics of the Academy who say: What if you are deceived? For if I am deceived, I am." Here speaks St. Augustine as an "ex-suicide." It is a recovery leading him to sacramental moments with things. As Percy has it, "Reality is the prize solely of the highest form of cognition, and that is: seeing, intuition, contemplation," Percy insists. In this same concern, Pieper reminds us that "knowing [as a term] originally derives from a word meaning presence," in the sense of "immediate togetherness, intimate presence." Thus one may say of contemplation that it "is a knowing which is inspired by love," a "silent perception of reality" such as the poet may witness, but which any person may experience, despite his own willful "self." It is this perspective upon contemplation to which Eliot attempts that witness of roses in a neglected garden at Burnt Norton with their "look of roses that are looked at" despite the neglect of stewardship. All these – Hopkins and Bernanos and Marcel and David Jones and Eliot and O'Connor, and in the end Walker Percy – witness to a triadic moment, knowing that though no sign bears sufficient (*comprehensive*) witness, such are their gifts even so that their responsibility becomes to attempt that witness. For they are peculiarly gifted in purifying the dialect of that tribe called community, that temporal body to which poets bear witness, whether in its support or in opposition to it.

If this nature of the visionary moment frees the "self" of the impingements of time upon the moment (though but for a moment, a "spot of time") it is freed as well of the intrusion of thought upon the moment, as St. Thomas and Pieper argue. That inevitability of "thought's" intrusive return disturbed John Keats, in that it calls attention to the self in its act of thinking. In a return to the here and now, to the "world's" time and place, thought disturbs any false expectation in the self that the visionary moment – the "still point" out of the turning world – might be arrested by imaginative action. Desire when disoriented from reality might wish such a moment permanently occupied by the sole self. But that is only a waking dream. The visionary moment in hope's anticipation is rebuked when that hope would settle upon a moment of grace already past. Nostalgia is insufficient sustenance to hope. What the poet discovers by his reflective concern, perhaps a condition of intellect itself allowing "recollection in tranquility" (Wordsworth's famous phrase), is that a witness may be undertaken through signs ordinately related to the experience itself, but only after a return from the experience, not by a science of automatic writing nor through a wishful "thinking," turned backward. That is the point spoken to by St. Thomas in arguing that art is "reason in making." The poet always finds himself seemingly dissolved from the visionary moment into *a* time in *a* place – *here* and *now* – from his intuitive vision.

We have already engaged Pound's and Hulme's attempt through sign to exercise Hulme's "fancy" in an attempted arrest of the communal moment of the self and a thing, the literary movement called Imagism and renamed Vorticism. We may as well recall a concurrent "movement" which is a more radical attempt of fancy to circumvent the reality of communal moments, already alluded to, the brief moment of "automatic writing," a movement which becomes an instrument of Freudian "associationism" as a diagnostic tool retuning the mechanism we call person. Automatic writing was a brief fad at the time of World War I and a bit later, a fad attempting a willful disregard of time and place, seeking a self-induced transcendence by *exorcising* reason from making. It was a strategy in the event which proved to be a rational attempt at self-forgetfulness by theory, by conjuring an instinctive – as opposed to intuitive – articulation. Its rationale is scientifically posited in the new science of psychology and presumes will's absolute power to vacate thought so that intellect itself is made neutral. Given an "other worldly" dimension to such an experiment, a self-forgetfulness willed beyond any rational exposition possible of the pending witness, we might suspect that, in a rational retrospection upon the event of "automatic writing," the rationalizer easily mistakes the nature of the actuality. The attempt is not a mystical one, but a ploy of magic, a sacrifice in conjuring Nothingness as the condition of intellect as the emptied agency of the self, presumed random accident. That is a polar version of the self from that mystery of its recovery to reality in a still point whereby, as Pieper suggests, the self is "transfigured" by the "experience of divine satiation." The antithesis is that between conjured emptiness and a consent through love to Love. The difference is that between an exorcising of the self as a given by such magic flirtations with Nothingness and a sacramental openness in surrender to the holiness of small things. And our latest version of that same attempt at "automatic" being? The latest fad, more pervasive and dissolving of prospects for sacramental devotion to created reality? Virtual reality.

XIX

We are at this point of our exploration of that initial arrest of Percy at the Tupperware party, a party pitched by the Modernist theorist, engaging a concern as ancient as any poet. As well, we discover that Modernism itself is as old as Adam and Eve's temptations. But we wish to discover something more about the relation of the poet to his poetry in respect to his strategy of indirection, as that strategy may carry hidden danger to the poet as person – since Adam. To begin, the poet's address by indirection complicates his sense of a direct responsibility both to the good of the thing he makes through signs and to himself as person. For primarily, from his "personal" perspective, his gift relates to his own fundamental givenness as an intellectual soul incarnate, and therefore to his proper end beyond his journeyman calling. This is the complex of responsibility out of which rises his desire to discover proper ends, involving his *personal* relation to creation as the origin of his most direct "temporal" concerns for the *possible* or *probable* as poet. That possible or probable, discovered *here* and *now,* provides the matter to his signs as he attempts to dramatize something of the human condition in relation to what he knows of himself as a "self."

We have along our way engaged this complex reality to the poet in respect to his "role" as maker. Thus our juxtaposition for purposes of contrast of Dostoevsky to Turgenev and Henry James, with differences too ambiguous if we merely categorize Dostoevsky as "Romantic" in contrast to Turgenev and James as "Realists." We are attempting all along to riddle the conundrum of the personal in poetry, as Percy attempted to do, observing that it becomes a haunting terror to some poets. It seems to do so for James Joyce and Eliot, though Eliot makes (in his poetry) a turning out of that terror in the final section of his *Waste Land.* Neither seems so indifferent to the problem as Dostoevsky accuses Turgenev of being of course, so that it is a concern, then, with which Walker Percy struggles at the outset. Our concern for his struggle, while we concentrate upon Dostoevsky's reading of Turgenev from his own pilgrim interests, requires that we understand another reading of Turgenev as possible, though perhaps from our own perspective not probable. We must engage "Romanticism" and "Realism" not in their surface phenomena of a literature peculiar to the history of letters in the late 19th and throughout the 20th centuries. That has been a primary critical concern, in a vast library devoted to the relation of these two aspects of "Modern Literature," at least as that concern has been addressed by the academic mind. But we are attempting to uncover a more fundamental concern implicit in these terms: the dilemma the poet must engage by his very dependence upon signs. It is an abiding dilemma encountered in consequence of man's given nature, so that it is timeless, however variously manifest in literature – in the things *made* with *signs* that we discover in that desert called history. It is in those monuments to unaging intellect (as Yeats calls them) which we have inherited by discovery, beginning with the *Psalms* and the *Odyssey* down to us.

There is a certain purchase upon that dilemma possible if we broaden our context toward the long history of letters while attending to recent letters without turning all the way back to the mystery of Adam's naming. Thus we may, in looking more closely at recent letters (signs) left us by poets more or less familiar to us, discover the dilemma an abiding one to man as intellectual soul incarnate. We remember that the distinctions we seek require a focus in man's gift as sign-maker in relation to the grace of "divine satiation" which he may gather from momentary experiences here and now, to use Josef Pieper's pregnant phrase for the communal dimension of any person's encounter with a discrete thing. That is the encounter made first through St. Augustine's "outer man," the body, which is why St. Thomas reminds us that our first movement toward God is through the senses. We receive a spiritual manna which is ever present from our setting out, if cherished less and less in habit become routine as we engage diverse species of created bodily things. It is appropriate, then, to summon St. Augustine as pilgrim into a presence, recalling again and again his witness of encounter of that continuous manna that feeds the spiritual "inner man." In this respect our attention is independent of the historical "life" of that saint, by which he is relegated to the 4th century – buried in strata of history. But as Percy discovers in retrospect, we may hear St. Augustine still here and now, a present pilgrim witnessing to us of his "search outside himself, rather than the guru's search within," in Percy's words about St. Augustine as an unrecognized presence to him in his making his *Moviegoer*. It is St. Augustine's signs that mediate his always current presence to us if we recognize that presence, whether as a presence to the experiencing poet in his encounter of things offering him "divine satiation," or to that poet's possible rejection of the proffered spiritual food and of the Saint as witness. Such understanding recovered recovers us as well to that community of the living and the dead. If we accept that manna, we are likely to make a mediating response through signs to our current "tribe." To do so gains the encouragement of a companionable presence of St. Augustine. But it also gains more fully a sense of Percy's presence.

With such a concern at hand, a concern for sign as binding community, we look first to the "Vision at Ostia" in the *Confessions.* It is an account of a still point which St. Augustine shared with his mother, St. Monica, after their exhausting travels, a moment of vision experienced at Ostia as they lean out a window looking down into a garden on the Tiber. This "Vision at Ostia" (Chapter 10 of Book 9) is echoed by counterpoint as well in Eliot's "Ash-Wednesday," in Section

III, a visionary moment from a height looking down upon a garden and seeing – past the moss-greened statue of Priapus – a lady going in "Mary's colors." And so Eliot becomes a presence to us through his signs. Then, there is also a very similar perspective played at a more dramatic length in Percy's fire tower of *Thanatos Syndrome,* from which remove Father Smith looks down upon Louisiana swampland. How large a company of companionable presences we share! If Percy discovers in retrospect a parallel in his imagined experiences of Binx in *The Moviegoer,* seeing his own kinship to St. Augustine commonly sharing the circumstances of *homo viator,* he carries with him that recognition in his maturing visionary recovery, more deliberately witnessed through Fr. Smith than by Binx. It is as if Percy in that last novel has returned to the place from which he set out enabled to see that place for the first time.

And so St. Augustine's witness to us out of memory of a very personal moment. He reports himself as having been caught up by a colloquy with St. Monica, through shared signs. Their conversation, ordered by reason, intends a recovery to "the fountain of life." St. Augustine remembers that when their discourse had brought them "to the point [of] the highest delight of fleshly senses, in the brightest corporeal light," they are poised in an anticipation of a transcendent moment, a still point. They are stirred by "a more ardent love." Out of that stirring, they "proceeded step by step through all bodily things up to the heavens whence shine the sun and the moon and the stars down upon the earth." We may observe this progress as a reverse of that earlier engagement by St. Augustine, he standing alone – that earlier progress in which he demands witness of his God from the sun, moon, and stars, turning at last down to the small things that stand "about the doors" of his body. The answer to his insistent demand in that earlier still point had been answered by a loud cry from those things: "We are not he" but "he made us." We emphasize, then, that both these passages evidence St. Augustine's rejection of Manichaeanism, reflecting his warm acceptance of creation itself as good, making possible to him "the highest delight of fleshly senses, in the brightest corporeal light," because that incorporeal Light emanates *through* the corporeal, a Light greater than the things thus enlightened in their very being.

And so, looking down upon that garden, Augustine and Monica have "proceeded step by step" in their discourse, marveling at the beauty of creation itself in all its particularities and thereby transcending them in attaining a state in which "to have been and to be in the future do not belong, . . . but only to be." That is the threshold of an entry upon the visionary moment to which no signs are adequate. Yet because they are as persons still existing in the world's dimensions, from that moment they are "turned back again to the noise of our mouths, where a word both begins and ends," words that bear disproportionate contrast to that "Word . . . remaining in himself without growing old, and yet renewing all things." This moment's fleeting perfection is an anticipation he shared with Monica. It is one which Pieper would speak of as an "experience of divine satiation." It is a moment which, by his retrospection, is made poignant to Augustine, remembering as he does that very shortly after this vision St. Monica dies.

We are attempting here to characterize an aspect of our knowing as "personally" remembered through signs ordered by memory and to memory, in distinction from the immediacy of our actual experiences of existential reality. It is an experience recovered, challenging our authority to name such a known mystery. For it is a knowing wherein the intuitive dimension of intellect has responded to a thing earlier, in a *here* and *now* which is now past. That was a response toward a communal perfection which is beyond any *comprehensive* accommodation of the *ratio,* the rational dimension of intellectual act. The rational is not for that reason to be deprecated, though one must recognize it at last as incapable of a *full* articulation through signs of the experience itself. There may be a "Romantic" inclination of the poet to reject the mysteriously known by becoming primarily devoted to rational intellect in a Positivistic authority over experience. Thus occurs reason's elevation at the expense of the intuitive in pursuit of autonomy. That is a "Romanticism" we find increasingly operative in post-Renaissance science, attributed by cliché of intellectual history to the "Enlightenment" of the 18th century, the Age of Rationalism. That was an age in prelude to political and social history categorized as the French Revolution. That such might well be termed a "Romantic" inclination, *Romantic* an honorific term usually reserved to the alternate emphatic faith in the intuitively known – at the expense of the rational – lies in its rejection of the intuitively known.

In attempting to "name" this experience of a still point, a moment transcendent of finite will or power, as remembered by St. Augustine, we say that it is at last beyond either the capacity of or the necessity of sign itself to certify it as actual, as if by our naming truth itself is certified. The pilgrim person (St. Augustine) nevertheless bears a responsibility in relation to his specific gifts to bear witness to such experience, especially as a responsibility to his gifts as philosopher and poet, St. Augustine being both. In the light of this reality of our experience, the Peircian "dyadic" supposition that human intellectual nature is evolutionary, posed theoretically as if initiated out of a biological and non-reflective limit to actual biological existence, proves contrary to the reality of our given nature. Or so we contend out of the witness of poets and philosophers – Hopkins, Eliot; Augustine, Thomas, Pieper. For by our given nature, including a simple singularity of intellect itself (as argued by St. Thomas in his *On the Unity of the Intellect Against the Averroist*), the "triadic" experience is that of a sacramental communion of intellect and thing. Intellect possesses antecedent to this evolutionary theory of the sign – the Peircian "Delta" factor – a potential to an encounter of a thing in a "still point," a visionary encounter which as event is precedent to any rational discursiveness. That is the experience of finite intellect, which must then struggle to witness such a moment as actual. It struggles to do so in relation to a dimension of a reality to it which is beyond the mere spectacle of encounter. It is actual, this is to say, in a sacramental dimension which concerns Pieper in his little book on contemplation, whereby the person experiences as an effect what Pieper calls "divine satiation," though hunger for that spiritual manner returns to the person when he returns to the here and now. Not to recognize this actuality of experience, through reflection and contemplation within the here and now, whether through that intellectual mode as philosopher or as poet, will leave the person's signs haunted by pathos rather than resonant of hope. In reaction to pathos, of course, there may follow a fierce intentionality, pathos disguised as if determined to limits by arrogant certitude. That is the mode of Positivistic authority.

Perhaps we may, in the interest of revealing the difficulty of an intellectual response to creation which allows a feeding of intellect to a "divine satiation," introduce once more that poet who cannot at last remain sufficiently open to hope beyond despair. He is our counterpoint to Hopkins, the witness of despairing pathos as opposed to joyful hope. We have summoned John Keats before, but now we wish to explore his witness to us with a sympathetic intensity. Keats, we have argued, agonizes over his sense of a failure with his signs, summoned by a "negative capability," an openness to things. But he finds the sum of his surrender leaving him as a "sole self." He is left, not simply as poet or philosopher (as might be said of Eliot up to *The Waste Land*). His pain is personal, as *homo viator,* lost in the cosmos, though he struggle to find Dante's "true way." He recognizes the necessity of an openness to creation. He is both too honest a pilgrim and too much moved by a desire for rescue to take the sophist's out, to say with Socrates' antagonist Gorgias that "nothing is," though that seems a threatening shadow of his sole self. He attempts that openness, yet finds himself at the end an ambiguous and poignant witness to illusion taken as vision, and on the brink of nothingness. In this respect, by contrast, Hopkins may be seen as if he is a Keats graced through his own risk of openness to creation through love, through his "negative capability." He witnesses from beyond the Keatsian agony in his response to *pied* beauty. For Hopkins, the imperfection of things, things thus "pied" and not perfect, speak a loss of good affecting the eye of the beholder of beauty. For Hopkins loss itself speaks even more of a Beauty past change.

Hopkins poses in his "negative capability," composes himself in a contentment of surrender of the self to the small things that impinge upon him, things recognized as particular through his sensual experiences of them in the adjacent world. He is not burdened by "thought" as is Keats in Keats's "sorrow/ And leaden-eyed despairs." Hopkins, like St. Augustine, experiences things "in the brightest corporeal light," revealing that those things though "pied" – though imperfect in relation to their Cause – are yet sustained from collapse into nothingness. The very imperfection (limit) is made a celebratory cause turning him to the Perfect. In contrast, Joyce's portrait of the poet as arrogantly intentional (Stephen) becomes a portrait of a "Romantic" like Keats, but one who rejects the celebratory in setting forth upon a self-rescue through his presumed authority of signs. And

Faulkner's young Ike McCaslin, walking across the bear skin rugs, hears Keats as a failed transcendentalist (in Faulkner's "The Bear") though his response is not Stephen Dedalus's arrogant rejection of any dilemma in sign, in intellect's attempt to solve the mystery of experience. Ike knows it a dilemma always local, as the poet knows – whether he be Keats or Joyce or Faulkner. Or Hopkins. But it is not a universal problem determined by existence as accidental or mechanistic. It rather is universal circumstance to *homo viator* inherent to his given nature.

We summon Keats as touchstone, a presence to us somewhat widely remembered for his signposts in the desert. In his "Ode to a Nightingale" he laments that the sign is incapable of either witnessing to or conjuring up a still-point. In *this* moment and in *this* place for Keats, he knows only at last his "sole self." That failure, reflected through signs attempting witness to the visionary moment, he charges to his own imaginative attempt to command his imaginative gift, only to be betrayed by that "deceiving elf," fancy. One might argue that the failure attending his aborted attempt lies in his anticipation that sign is sufficient to a purchase upon the moment of grace. If St. Thomas might be summoned to the point, the effect is itself a sign of a failure to remove obstacles to grace through a presumption, perhaps naïve intellectually, that he may through sign regain the transcendent moment, self-justified by desire. We could as well use his "Ode on a Grecian Urn" or his Odes "On Melancholy" or "To Autumn" to the same point. And we suspect that, such has been Keats's experience of still-points, he begins to suppose in advance an inevitable defeat of any attempt to command signs to the witness of a vision that is true, supposing sign capable of certifying the reality of the experience. But signs seem to refuse irrefutable witness to any tranquil knowledge sustaining poet or seer, such a knowledge as Percy in his late essay speaks of as sacramental deportment to creation itself. (Hence that tendency to impatience as a response to mystical witness.) Poetry seems thus helpless to Keats, so that he concludes that fancy cannot "cheat so well as she is famed to do."

Fancy's "indirection" to Keats only leads to his inevitable collapse into the self, fancy's signs serving only to intensify the desperateness of alienation. The self is taken, therefore, to be hopelessly entrapped in the body, and the body in turn entrapped by a nature always in decay. That decay is proximately evident in this present body. Nor can one deny that any pilgrim self decays, for "palsey shakes a few, sad, last gray hairs" or "youth grows pale, and spectre-thin, and dies." How ominous then, any bald-spot in the middle of one's hair, prompting a panic of follicle transplant. How disturbing the dappled gray in one's hair or beard, to be resisted by chemical restoratives of "vibrant" but "natural" color. These are responses quite opposite those of St. Augustine or Hopkins, who celebrate the pied beauty inevitable to created things as a continuous prophetic evidence of a Beauty past change. Keats serves us then as exemplum of the self in its dilemma of the sign's inadequacy to the truth of things. Out of that failure of understanding may come a "Romantic" submission to oblivion through despair, an obverse of that activist despair whereby that other "Romantic," the Positivist, would defy reality by autonomous dissociation from it, an aggressive *non serviam*. (That is a response, incidentally, encouraging the "pragmatic" signs of denial such as quick color or follicle transplant.)

Truth is acquired perhaps through an agony of intellect, but it proves again and again for a Keats to be only a dark truth. Its sum may seem only a "self" hopelessly entrapped, unrescued by that subversive aberration in intellect itself called fancy, a luring contingency to action perverse in its devotion to destructions spawned by wishful thinking. He will conclude in uncertainty: "Do I wake or sleep?" Such a "truth" leads Keats, for instance, to remark a failure of Wordsworth in a poem called "Gypsy." He remarks, in a letter to his friend Bailey (in 1817), that Wordsworth must have written that poem "in one of the most comfortable moods of his life." Consequently, the poem proves only "a kind of sketchy intellectual landscape, not a search for truth." If we consider in contrast Keats's "Ode to a Nightingale," we may observe with regret that Keats could not be lessoned as it were by St. Augustine's "Vision at Ostia" in respect to landscapes and gardens. At risk here, of course, in our current concern, is Keats as person and not any question of the aesthetic virtue of his "Ode," a "good" of the thing he has made which by his very making leaves him on the edge of despair. That is a concern, but of a separate order. Certainly his "Ode to a Nightingale" is a better poem than Wordsworth's "Gypsy," not the least reason for which is that he risks himself in the making. It is, in fact, almost universally praised as a very great Ode, arresting us with an immediacy to us of a distressed person within formal signs, which at that dramatic level does not require that we identify the poem's voice with John Keats. It captures by a reason in form that sense of a spontaneous overflow of powerful feeling that Wordsworth speaks of as evidencing poetry in distinction from prose. (Keats's objection to Wordsworth's "Gypsy" might have declared it closer to prose than to poetry, in Wordsworth's sense of those terms.) In the Ode, the possible or probable nature of despair in an agent "person" is caught as it were in the superbly made thing. And it survives to us consequently as one of the great signposts in the desert we each must journey because it is superbly made. But it does so in part at least as a warning to us of our possible or probable failure in the contingencies of this here and now.

Keats can believe his own actual experience to have been illusional, unable to discover any divinity in the small things of gardens as they might be ordered by a stewardship of love. In his Ode, he attempts to command truth's permanence out of a moment of extreme intellectual discomfort, an actual state imaginatively addressed in his making. We see his signs dramatically accelerating in his poem, even as he begins to recognize fancy's betrayal. That is the center of the dramatic tension in the poem. In this respect it is made a great Ode because of the struggle to resist a surrender to despair through "negative capability." And so if this is indeed one of our great Odes, it may be said to be so because it captures the possible and (in our Modernist climate affecting intellect) probable scenarios of our actual, our "personal," self besieged, lost in the cosmos. It reveals a self attempting a transcendence through imaginative action, but failing through its very intentionality to an imaginative transcendence. The poem's persona is unrescued from an inherent presumption that no other possibility than by the imagination is rescue open to him. That illusion rebuffed by reality, that self turns in despair. The poem stirs pain in us, then, not only because it is a well-made thing. We also recognize that the suffering personae is not only Keats himself, but our own self in its possible contingencies.

There is an obverse "Romantic" poem suitably juxtaposed, one in which this other poet is bent on making a poem by an alternate strategy of imagination from Keats's. The attempt is made by this poem's protagonist to subvert signs, recognizing an advantage in their very insufficiency. He would use signs, then, in an attempt to dissolve consciousness through *ennui,* a suicide of consciousness. I mean here Eliot's "Love Song of J. Alfred Prufrock." What is to be noted in our comparison, as Eliot can recognize after "Ash-Wednesday," is that Keats as person risks his own "self" in his Ode. (It is after "Ash-Wednesday" that Eliot praises Keats as he could not earlier.) To the contrary, Eliot posits a persona as "voice," by a self-protective ventriloquism in his "Love Song." For Keats, as evidenced by this Ode (and by others), the intrusion of the rational intellect (thought) puts to flight the intuitive intellect through which he has known a moment's transport. In Pieper's phrase he has experienced a "divine satiation," but is unable to accommodate to the truth that it cannot last. Keats's experience has been actual, but his rational attempt to accommodate that experience leaves him forlorn. The fancy for a moment seems almost to have recovered him beyond the dark world, but by perversity, yet without a perverse agent to blame, it has instead dropped him into a hopelessness in the sensual world, leaving him in that world's "embalmed darkness." It is important to our reading to emphasize that the Ode is not made by John Keats in a *pose* as poet, as if the speaking voice were a mask such as Eliot chooses to project in his agent Prufrock. How deeply personal the poem strikes us as being! And how disappointed Keats seems to have been to discover his gifts as poet prove only destructive to his person. They occasion illusions of art's rescue, which he cannot transform or make substantial as a vision recovered to himself as person.

We have explored this dilemma which we may see the better by contrast to another later version of Keats, to Wallace Stevens, who unlike Keats delights in the game between himself and impinging reality as an intentional poet using fancy. Stevens is acutely, and playfully, aware of fancy's putative treachery, commanding fancy nevertheless as his "necessary angel" to a making of a momentary stay against the intrusive world, making a "blue" world (by fancy) in manipulating the "green" world (of reality). Stevens argues the point in "The Idea of Order at Key West," a poem which bears playful analogies to Keats's Odes, and especially to his "Ode on [not *to*] a Nightingale." In his poem Stevens justifies fancy's deceptions, so long as the intentional intellect does not mistake fancy's ordered illusions for reality. For by appropriating fancy, the poet may sing the green and decaying world into a transcendent blue – for the duration of the singing. Stevens's is a witty species of Nominalism, upon which he trades. And he enjoys a hedonistic delight in such sensual play of signs, where Keats in his seduction by fancy out of his sensual experience ends in melancholy, on the edge of despair. Neither poet acknowledges any validity to St. Augustine's version of imagination's engagement of the green (and decaying, pied) world. The "words" St. Augustine hears spoken by things to his "outer man" and through that outer man, recovers Augustine's "inner man" within Steven's green world, within what is for Keats the dark world of nature in decay.

We must especially notice, if we are to understand the Keatsian melancholy to which we are susceptible, that the poem is in response to a past experience, a response made in a moment of waking from it. The seeming transport is over. By a present reflection on that experience, the poet recognizes it as having been initiated by his actual sensual responses to the contingent world. There *had been* a movement of consciousness in response to a bird's song, in which the person Keats experienced a moment's self-forgetfulness, whose analogy we have suggested as articulated by St. Augustine's "Vision at Ostia." But now he finds himself fallen back, first into an isolating sense of his own bodily presence in a world in which that body decays. The nadir and conclusion of that experience for the person Keats is that the reality for him is that even any pleasing sensual perceptions in temporal moments speak the inevitability of age's palsey or youth's spectre-grayness. For those perceptions can speak only a decay toward oblivion. The voice of the poem is left at last wondering whether consciousness as a presence in the cosmos is but a dream within a dream, as Poe has put it. Keats's final words: "Do I wake or sleep?" Even happy moments are happy for him only so long as illusion holds back reality.

Keats's Odes dramatize the journey of a consciousness which is inevitably returned by fancy to the place from which it set out, but only to find it a dead end. Keats as person, at first encouraged by a prospect of relief through a willful use of the imagination to recover any "moment past," concludes each attempt only illusional rescue, betrayed by his very articulation. Surely that was an event of experiential immediacy to the *person* Keats, as opposed to the "poet" Keats, waking in him a melancholy speaking despair. As poet, Keats summons signs as the means to a rejourneying, but they prove signs which do not distinguish (in his act of making a poem) between his nature as person and action as poet. It is therefore a very personal and arresting discovery that he makes. By that desperate willfulness in a deployment of signs, in the end he finds himself only the more deeply fallen into the abyss of the self. The word *forlorn* proves a "*very* word," and as such a "bell/ To toll me back from [the nightingale] to my sole self!" The word *toll* carries that sense of death of the self, since bells *toll* to announce an actual death. This new, present event as inscribed by words laments the falling away as a death.

From the perspective of faith held by St. Augustine or Hopkins, such a word might rather speak a reality beyond fear, a moment of self-forgetfulness such as one may call the openness of love if read aright. Certainly both Hopkins and St. Augustine – and Pieper – would urge that conclusion as inevitable to an ordered contemplation. It is a recovery beyond an initial relief for Hopkins in the death of Felix Randal, the farrier, Felix's priest not relieved though his "duty all ended." That duty had required his attending a slow dissolution of Felix from his "boisterous years" at the forge, through a slow attrition of the body and a growing rage against death, to that state near the end when a "sweet reprieve and ransom/ Tendered to him" by his priest allows Felix to recover from the terrors of his lone self. For Keats as minister of the word as poet, his own past experience summoned to a self-consciousness only confines the present attempt in a closed spatial and temporal isolation. Past moments can be regretted and mourned in words that serve only to suggest that the remembered experiences of transport was an illusion.

Keats's Ode is a moving capture of a moment of despair, a poem holding such a moment out of time and place insofar as art may do so. For we as readers are caught up in an immediacy, a *now* of our being as we are drawn into the poem. It is experienced as an immediacy despite the mundane truth that the poem is more than a century old and its maker long since mouldered in his grave. Now, reading it yet again, we find it a present memory of a possible experience now past, which reflection suggests that it is a moment actual to its maker in that making now long ago. The moment of transport yet fades as the "plaintive anthem" of the nightingale's song fades, "Past the near meadows, over the still stream,/ Up the hill-side," to become "buried deep/ In the next valley-glades." A sequence of imaging of the actual in its possible service to Keats's own plaintive anthem for his dead moment. As such it is an obverse of the attempt through cheating fancy to escape whatever "Fatal four disorders, fleshed" in a Felix Randal, who is seemingly fading before the priest's eyes into a more distant valley. The actual nightingale speaks to the actual fading poet (who is not only poet but physician and as both aware that he as person grows daily spectre-thin). And in that equally famous Ode on the Grecian urn, there is another attempt by fancy, this time to fade into the art, to meld into a youth arrested by that beauty of the sensual which is, though in arrest, arrested from nature's decay forever. But that, too, proves but an attempt that leaves the sojourning poet "desolate," the term itself ringing as if from outside his thought and calling him back to his sole self as had *forlorn* in that other "faery land" he seemed to have entered through bird song. What we recognize here is that Keats as person, in the role of his calling as poet, is not *posing* as poet, as Wallace Stevens very deliberately does. Keats would be baffled by such an indirection as that of Stevens's playful assumption of the role of the clown as poet, as in "The Comedian as the Letter C." He cannot, as Stevens seems intent upon doing, stall beauty through indirection. And so, if this be true of Keats – if his attempt at recovering a personal accommodation to reality out of his disquieting sense of dislocation from it, and if that attempt be flawed by some misunderstanding of the nature of his experiences obfuscated to his understanding by his own signs as cheating him in his attempt – how are we to value the thing made of signs, his poem? If it is founded in illusion, is it nevertheless true in itself – even as may be said of a poem by Wallace Stevens in his very deliberate intent to make illusion the game which imagination plays with reality?

In respect to the virtues of art, virtues which depend upon the good of the thing made (the poem in itself), we might remember St. Thomas's admonition that art's responsibility is not that it be pragmatic, salvific of either the artist or of the respondent to that art thing. It is this delicate concern that he addresses in the *Summa* (Q. 57, Art 4, Pt I-II), to which we have alluded before, and it is a concern founded in the distinction between man as maker and God as Creator. Thomas distinguishes *prudence* from *art* in a distinction from each other among the virtues to intellect itself. "Rectitude of the will is essential to prudence, but not to art," he argues, in distinguishing *making* (art) from *doing* (prudential action toward the person's ultimate end). Art is *right reason of the things to be made,* and the primary end of that making is the good of the thing itself. Thus "the good of things made by art is not the good of man's appetite [in its "consumer" aspect], but the good of those things themselves: wherefore art does not presuppose rectitude of the appetite." It is therefore a "Romantic" use of art to appetitive ends when presumed salvific in the artist's primary concern for the "good," whether so presumed by the poet in an attempt at his own self-rescue by art or art commandeered to political or social ends (such as those accelerated out of Marxist doctrines in our last century). Not that a prudential act in response to art is therefore exonerated as a responsibility of the will to a virtue of intellectual action in regard to prudence at last. For a right will in this respect requires a judgmental engagement of *any* thing engaged, including a poem. But such an engagement must not deny the good of the thing in respect to its made nature. Here the question turns on the ultimate end proper to the person responding to the thing itself. Art acted upon as pornography is a failure of prudence. Indeed, this failure of distinction between the virtues of art and prudence complicates our current difficulty in determining a difference between pornography and art.

In the light of these concerns, we may the more appreciate Keats's Ode as a dramatic making. But it is one in which the dramatic center, in respect to the good of the thing made, is to be at first distinguished from the maker, the voice of the poem distinguished from John Keats's voice as person. That the poet in his making distorts reality does not belie truth itself as represented in the poem, since such distortion is a possible, even probable, condition to the poet's given nature as intellectual soul incarnate engaged in making. Actual fallibility in the person may prove a ground to the possible as appropriate to the good of the dramatic thing made, yielding a certain truth of fallen human nature. In this respect, art's perfection is to be valued for the very truth of a possible or probable distortion of truth itself. That is a distinction implicit, for instance, in Greek tragedy in respect to hubris, a distinction no doubt which perhaps set Aristotle on his concern for the truth of poetry as differing from the truth of any actual history feeding poetry, that distinction between the possible or probable and the actual.

It is in recognizing this as a significant distinction that St. Thomas will argue the delicate concern for distinguishing the virtues proper to prudence from the virtues proper to art. In our present argument, we are thus urging distinction as helping us better recognize the virtue peculiar to the art thing, to Keats's Ode, or a play or a novel. For truth in this aspect involves the work's correspondence as a thing made good in itself to human possibilities of failure. That is a relation that yields at last the aesthetic dimension of a "good," so long as we do not reject out of hand, by a strict aesthetic concern, an eventual necessity to prudential concern. It is in relation to prudential concern for our actual "self" that we contemplate the urn and its poem as a part of our memory. And so we may prudentially reflect upon the poet as actual person, a John Keats registered by history between 1795 and 1821, who has left signs suggestive of his failure as person, as *homo viator,* in his sojourning as intellectual soul incarnate. This is a concern then, not with the biography of a Keats – a history of the facts of his life – but a concern for his continuing presence to our concern for prudential virtue in the light of eternity.

That prudential virtue and aesthetic virtue are at last inseparable was a lesson most difficult to Eliot at his outset, he listening to great poems and great philosophical arguments as Keats listened to his nightingale. Thus Eliot's fascinating essay on Shakespeare's *Hamlet* becomes lively text to the academic mind as Percy is setting out as diagnostic poet, though "Hamlet and His Problems" appears at the end of World War I, after Eliot's Prufrock volume and before those sardonic and self-lacerating *Poems* in 1920. In the essay as byproduct of the poet's own workshop (as Eliot calls his criticism), and still uncertain of whether he is poet or philosopher or both, he knows rather more certainly that he struggles to maintain a detached skeptic distancing of himself from the impinging world. Eliot nevertheless is forced to engage the dilemma of the personal as affecting his art's possible or probable.

This is the essay, then, in which he makes that famous (and to the later Eliot notorious) argument about the "objective correlative," arguing that the good of Shakespeare's play is flawed through the poet's unwittingly confusing himself as person with his agent Hamlet, a confusion suggested as out of grief over the loss of a son. When Eliot comes to his late poems – his "Journey of the Magi" or "Ash-Wednesday" or the *Quartets* – he will have become more comfortable in dealing with the inescapable complication to the poet in his making of the personal, beyond reason's attempts to exorcise the personal from art. For he must come to recognize that, if the center to a dramatic making (and even the lyric is dramatic in this respect) is the possible or probable as derived from the actualities of a person's responses to existential reality itself, then willy-nilly the personal touches any "theoretical" drama about the personal as common to us, as effecting an aesthetic communion as it were through whatever "objective correlatives" prove suited to a commonly personal condition to each person as *homo viator.*

The poet makes, in response to an existential reality as intellectually engaged (in some degree) by each person. Insofar as the poet acts in his making through a Keatsian "negative capability," with a regard for "objective correlatives" as a "tribal" virtue in signs, his making engages the personal as partaking of the common as possible or probable to each. His responsibility as maker to the good of the thing he makes, his making according to the virtues of art, therefore cannot deny the elementary condition to his act of making: he makes out of himself as a given, as a created person in the midst of a given reality impinging upon his givenness in this present moment of his making. He shares therefore in a "tribal" connaturality. That is the recognition Eliot comes to, leading him to affirm his responsibility as poet to "purify the dialect of the tribe." By this metaphysical deepening of his initial concern for aesthetic virtue as dependent upon suitable "objective correlatives," he will discover a quite different view of his "Romantic" antecedents, especially Wordsworth and Keats, from what he held before his *Waste Land.*

In Keats's Ode, the dramatic tensional center is a failure of prudential action in the persona of the poem, the *voice* ordering through signs a response to an event. That the voice corresponds so closely to the actual prudential (or unprudential) action of its projector Keats, is a second, not the first, concern to us in valuing the Ode as a great Ode. This distinction as peculiar to the virtues of art requires exploration, some of it already undertaken in our past attention to the relation of Percy as maker to his fictional agents, to Binx in *The Moviegoer* for instance. In responding to the good of the thing made, the Ode or *The Moviegoer,* we may value as a good in the thing made the persuasiveness of the very failure in the personae, insofar as that failure has been dramatically rendered as true to the possible or probable as dependent in human nature itself. At this point of an ordering of aesthetic response to that good, the question whether the voice of a persona in the dramatic thing is the poet's becomes a secondary though subsequent question and therefore not an irrelevant one. Not irrelevant, since our own aesthetic response requires at last our own return to a prudential governance of limit to our aesthetic response. It is by this failure to reestablish prudential concern, for instance, that we may become victim to self-induced pornographic intellectual actions, perhaps consumed by similarly unprudential violence of intellectual deportment, occasioned by the possible or probable to human nature as persuasively rendered by art but not prudentially ordered beyond aesthetic virtues. Dante touches upon this in the pathos attending his encounter of Paolo and Francesca, who blame their adultery on having read together that work of art to which they attribute their lust-full fall.

We may see that Eliot's critical address to *Hamlet,* then, turns on such a distinction. His faulting of the play as play – its lacking (in his critical judgment) a certain good in itself as a made thing. Eliot attributes this to Shakespeare's failure as poet to concentrate upon the good of the thing he is making, the play itself. The argument holds this weakness in the play to be out of Shakespeare's personal failure to distinguish between himself as *this* actual person, bearing actual memories of "personal" experiences in his past, and the projected character Hamlet. There becomes an entanglement of the possible or probable, in a making underway, with the actual in Shakespeare's experience, the ungoverned confusion detrimental to the good of the thing he is making. That is, directly put, Shakespeare (by Eliot's argument) allows a confusion of his autobiographical "feelings," residual in his memory, with a proper reason in making, a flaw leading to insufficient "objective correlatives" to the detriment of the thing he is making.

We are not here concerned for the persuasiveness of Eliot's argument, but with his implicit recognition of the abiding dilemma to the poet, remembering again that he speaks of his criticism in these early days as a byproduct of the poet's workshop. We recognize it as a critical theme, as it is a poetic theme, in Eliot's early work, touching upon the conundrum which is very personal to Eliot himself: the relation of his own *personal nature* (called T. S. Eliot) to himself as *maker* in the actions of poems and critical essays. Here we do not ourselves intend to suggest an inevitable dualism at work, but rather of an insufficient self-forgetfulness in the maker, a failure of love toward the good of the thing he makes. That is an experience any person may recall from his memory by reflection as having been actual to him, even if rare, whether in relation to a flower arrangement made in preparation for a party (even a Tupperware party) or the experience of making and tending a garden or laying a brick wall or walk – or even ordering business accounts in some instances – such examples sufficient to possible or probable credentials in ourselves to the point of our argument.

Since art must deal with truth *actual,* there is a grounding of the made thing in the truth of things in themselves, therefore, constituting a complex of limit in making. In respect to the made thing as dramatic – Keats's Ode, Shakespeare's *Hamlet,* Percy's *Moviegoer* – the distinction between the actual and the possible or probable will mean that the personae (the voice or voices) of a dramatic thing may be judged good even though his possible or probable actions as enacted through signs themselves are evil actions. It is here that we encounter the poet's attempt to engage evil at its extremity, evil at its verging with the inexplicable as a mystery when we attempt to relate it to fallen human nature. Considerable ink has been spent in attempting to riddle Shakespeare's Iago, for instance, though we feel more confident in dealing with Shylock. Iago seems alien to humanity, as that "black" Moor Othello does not, more than Shylock appears alien in his pursuit of his pound of flesh. On either hand, of course, Shakespeare engages in pursuit of suitable "objective correlatives," the more easily come by in relation to Shylock, given the cultural relation of the Jew to Western civilization at that point when the Christian perspective Percy would rescue is in a gradual but accelerating decay. (Remember Percy's affirmation of the Jew in his "Why Are You a Catholic?" as one of the only two dependable, "significant" signs available: "One is oneself and the other is the Jews.")

Dostoevsky, we have seen, has a difficulty analogous to Shakespeare's in attempting to make a persuasive "incarnation" of evil and of good in his art. By intention, he would dramatize a good person, the work itself called *The Idiot,* unfolding Prince Myshkin to us. The work itself rebukes his intention to dramatize a perfectly good man, since all are fallen. Dostoevsky then turns to the obverse, to an attempt to "incarnate" evil, a contradictory possibility since evil depends as a negation of good. The work made from that intentional perspective is called *The Demons.* The titles themselves suggest the tendency intended to an extreme, though art proves in the issue to require a relation of the possible or probable extremity as inescapably dependent upon that actual human nature as a given from a Perfect Love. Reality itself thwarts the poet's intent to an extremity in pursuit of the mystery of good or evil as absolutes which he may wish to make dramatically incarnate by the poet's signs.

To make such an argument as ours is to be reminded of Eliot's early concern, then, not only with the indecisive Hamlet of Shakespeare's play in his essay on that problem, but of Eliot's own drama of the indecisive but subtly skeptical intellect, J. Alfred Prufrock. We are well reminded also of a relation between Walker Percy in an arrest, combating personal despair, and his Binx Bolling as corresponding the one to the other in a similar arrest. For the possible or probable drama of Binx bears a relation to the actuality of Walker Percy as *homo viator* in his act of making Binx. Always, reason in making must deal with art as dependent *from* the reality of human nature, in the context of limit to the making implying the maker's responsibility to the good of the thing he makes within the limited context. And the most insistent limit to that making, preventing a creation ex nihilo by art, is the givenness of the artist himself. The failures of virtues in possible or probable circumstances in a drama lies in relation to the truth of human nature itself. The making will thus require a truth in the made thing in its projecting the possible or probable, in some the correspondence to the poet's actualities as *this* person.

We must in valuing the good of the thing made, therefore, admit as good even a representation of evil itself. That is a realization governing Dostoevsky's or O'Connor's fictions conspicuously. It governs the immediacy to us of Shakespeare's Iago in *Othello.* It is in this light that we may speak of Oedipus's lack of prudence as King of Thebes. And so we may speak as well of the lack of prudence in the voice speaking Keats's Ode. This does not mean, then, that in valuing the Ode (or *Oedipus Rex*) as a made thing we deny any relation of the poet's intellectual action of making (out of the reality of his being *this* person) as involving him as responsible to prudential virtues in relation to "*the right reason about certain works to be made*" (*Summa,* Pt. I-II, Q 57, Art 3). It means rather that the made thing is to be understood in the limited context of the thing itself, as made by an actual limited person. Thus we may conclude that the artfully made thing is at last *of this world*, though implicitly implying a transcendent world proper to the person as *homo viator.* To lose this relation is to be tempted to faith in art as ultimate rescue of the self.

If we engage the question of the poet's prudential uses of a right will toward making (whether the uses are made by a Keats or Sophocles, a Wallace Stevens or Walker Percy), we must make distinctions among questions about the good of what the poet has made, on the one hand, and the relation of the poet's own prudence as orienting him to the limits possible to him in his making or of his reader's response beyond an aesthetic response on the other. To do so will make clearer to us, for instance, the importance of our distinction between *making* and *creating,* recognizing thereby the impossibility to the poet of any absolute severance of himself as person from his act of making. It is this attempt by Joyce's Stephen Dedalus that motivates his *non serviam,* his rejecting of his dependence in being as a limit upon any absolute freedom of *creating* a "world." It is a distinction which will make clearer to us perhaps St. Thomas's concern when he says, emphatically, that "the good of things made by art is not the good of man's appetite, but the good of those things themselves: wherefore art does not presuppose rectitude of the appetite" (*Summa*, Pt I-II, Q 57, Art 4). Does not *presuppose,* but does not thereby obviate a responsibility, consequent to aesthetic experience, to a rectitude of the "self."

XX

In the light of such considerations, we must at last (or so we seem obligated to do) "judge," acknowledge, Keats's Ode as superbly capturing the *possible,* even the *probable,* failure of prudential intellect itself to respond to the reality of its own limits, in relation to the mystery of being itself. In doing so, beyond aesthetic pleasure in response to this well-made thing, we may discover a resonance of the possible or even probable as echoing the potentiality of our own prudential actions toward the mystery of being in what is sometimes called our "real life." Nor need we, by the sort of purified aesthetics advocated by Gorgias against Socrates, remove from our understanding of the Ode the presence of Keats himself, the dejected person making a cry as person from within his seemingly dark world. If for Keats himself (and so transferred by the act of his making to his Ode) there is his personal interest in a prudential rescue through making, there is also a personal dimension inescapable to our own prudential address beyond aesthetic response to that great Ode. It will not follow that by this involvement of our own prudential person there must necessarily follow as well a rejection of the made thing as if it were flawed by the lack of a prudential action reflected in the poem's voice, and so perhaps responsible as a seduction of our own prudential responsibility.

That has been a recurring fear, accelerating in importance from the advent of the so-called "Romanticism" in our art, down to the murky political and social agitations over pornography. Out of that fear we may attribute the poet's failure or triumph in respect to prudence as determined by the poem he makes. And indeed that has sometimes been a fear to the poet which evolves in the 20th century to a prominence of "technique" as if technique were solvent of fear in the dilemma unresolved between art and prudence. One technique requires a special attention – the subtle and ever more subtle uses of the "mask" of personae, as if the strategy of the mask removed and rescued the poet himself. Sometimes that technique proves a detriment to the poem, through a loss of a "reason in making" which fails to recognize the poem as necessarily grounded by limit in the realities of human nature that are most proximate to the making in the poet as person. It is, for an Ezra Pound, a deportment he takes as out of a cowardice protecting the poet as person from the risks of art. Thus Pound makes a relation of himself to the poem in an act of "possession" of his mask, a willed transubstantiation whereby he is confident that the mask is himself, Ezra Pound. Hence that poignant remark when he is arrested in Italy and charged with treason at the end of World War II is more complex in relation to his sense of honor than may be credited: "If a man will not stand by his word, either he is no good or his word is no good."

Keats's Ode, then, occasions a rather complex response in us, affected by the proximity to intellectual action of the virtues of art and the virtues of prudence as at once both diverse and most personal to us in our aesthetic response. It is complicated in that, because of the virtues of such a work as the Ode, we have stirred in us by our response (if but faintly for some) a memory of our own experiences of illusions, a truth about our "self" residually held in our memory out of actual experiences which we may have "masked" from our self. That is why there is an advantage to us, in sorting these related virtues (prudence and art as modes of intellectual *action*), to refer to the passage in St. Augustine's *Confessions* which celebrates his vision at Ostia, a telling counterpoint to our specimen of "Romanticism," Keats's Ode. To juxtapose the two witnesses through signs will perhaps further enlighten our understanding of a response to the Ode which we call *pathos*. Our argument, here, implies that pathos is an effect of "Romanticism" as the "role" assumed by the person in response to reality. This we have suggested already sees pathos as an effect in us of our aesthetic response. It is a distinction we may critically invoke to distinguish "Romantic" literature from "Classical" tragedy, or in turn Classical tragedy from Dante's sense of comedy in his great *Divine Comedy*. In St. Augustine's recovery of a vision through signs, his witness of the vision at Ostia, he concentrates not upon an inevitable falling away from a moment of vision (which he and St. Monica experience). Instead, by reason in support of a reflection on actual experience, he explicates a progress toward that moment of transport as remembered. Reason in recovering that progress finds it both valid and supportive of hope, though he too is fallen away from that moment into the ordinary experiences of everyday existence.

The temptation out of such experiences of a still point is to attempt to seize a premature Beatitude, and though such a concept is not one Keats engages, his attempt to arrest a "still point" of his turning world is very much out of that buried desire. But *homo viator* by the gift of his peculiar nature (as intellectual soul incarnate) must endure the journey among the ordinary things of the cosmos, and he must do so most often through ordinary experiences of them, though mysteriously on occasion such experience turns extraordinary, whether occasioned by a nightingale or the flapping sunfish for Percy's Tom More. With will righted, accepting an enduring – i.e., become given to ordered habits of life in a duration proper to an ordinated nature as person – the person may be strengthened in his journey. He may become enabled to hear, as St. Augustine says in his account, the Word deeper than signs and biding in ordinary things no less than radiantly present in a moment's vision. All along that enduring way, things cry out, "We did not make ourselves, but he who endures forever made us." That is a deportment to the created world which is to be participated in sacramentally, by habit. Percy affirms this as his belief unhesitatingly at last, declaring that the "World is a sacrament and a mystery." Such a recognition does not preclude the comic speculations of the novelist, as he contemplates what might be made by a projection of the possible or probable through his art, in response to the spectacle of our refusals to hear. Not hearing, we become apt to exhibit ourselves through such spectacle as but loony, as lunatic rather than sun-struck as St. Augustine might have it. Perhaps a person sitting before a television set watching a public educational series on that Jungian, Joseph Campbell, while telling beads (at least through "ten boring Hail Marys" undertaken as well) might even be stirred to hear. Or perhaps sitting on a verandah in Louisiana, sailing paper airplanes out into the winds of an opening morning, he may see a light restored to the flat brightness of the usual day. Even a swamp becomes fecund of life beyond the merely phosphorescent reflections of life so easily explained by physics or biology, focused in a still point which (as Eliot might have it) is still and still moving, centering in the flapping sunfish.

Let us for a moment, then, reflect discursively – more widely – on the nature of contemplation, considering St. Augustine's account of his vision at Ostia in relation to Keats's account of his vision as fading into illusion, dissolving in a lament that the nightingale's ease at its full-throated song escapes the burden of thought as the poet cannot. If St. Augustine and St. Monica rose to the level of their own minds, through words first focused upon the things of creation before them in a garden, Keats seems rather bent upon discovering his moment of transport independent of intellect's rational engagement of such a world as that impinging upon his "natural" body. Was it a moment of grace in a self-forgetfulness unlabored by thought? It seems to him at first to have been such, and he responds to it just as the moment already begins to fade, experiencing as the moment's after effect a state of emotional languor disturbed by thought. It is as if for that moment he had drunk "hemlock" or "some dull opiate," and "Lethewards had sunk." His words, attempting to witness that experience now one moment past, prove already burdened with allusive implications he hardly recognizes, summoned out of an intentional "poetic" diction by a habit of dependence upon traditional poetics unexamined. How secretly subversive to know Socrates' toast to truth with hemlock! Later Keats recognizes as much on Margate sands, having withdrawn from London. Thought needs a reckoning, and so he writes a friend to send him three or four books, since he feels the need of gaining some metaphysical understanding.

There is that faint echo in his sign of Socrates and the old pagan speculations about death as Socrates drinks the hemlock in the *Phaedo*. So pleasant-seeming to Keats's languor the possible oblivion called death, felt in his very carnate being and almost stilling intellect. Its most present reality, his memory of that "one moment past." And so he would recapture it, only to be rebuffed by more intrusive thoughts of death as decay, bourne in the very words he uses. He will not submit easily to that escape of *ennui* which has proved so attractive to subsequent poets in their self glorification of alienation. Nevertheless, he must deal with a closing world and attempt to force fancy to a defense against that closure. Thus such forced imagery as "haply the Queen-Moon is on her throne,/ Clustered around by all her starry fays." A false, illusional transcendence through signs. For he must acknowledge the reality of his continuing entrapment under the trees in a dark, amid "verdurous glooms and winding mossy ways." In these circumstances, those proximate things to his "outer man" cry out to him their pied nature, which he hears increasingly as rather a withdrawing of things into nothingness. Lost in a dark world which Dante might recognize, but a world too intrusively real to Keats, he cannot recognize or summon such a companionable presence as Dante as kindred *homo viator,* let alone summon St. Augustine. He turns to the small ordinary things about the doors of his senses, but they only speak his entrapment in an "embalmed darkness." Those things – the musk-rose just coming into bloom, the violets already fading and presently to be covered up in leaves – such pied things for Keats, unlike for Hopkins, can speak only of death as oblivion, making him "half in love with easeful death," in the prospect of becoming but a "sod" to the nightingale's "high requiem."

Indeed, "fancy" cannot cheat him out of such dark thought. But we might ourselves turn from his melancholy response to his visionary moment to Wallace Stevens, who (up almost to his own death) knows but rejects St. Augustine's perspective. He will as well scoff at the Keatsian failure. To do so, he assumes Keats's position in his own version of our famous Ode, in his "The Idea of Order at Key West." Fancy for Stevens is used as instrument by intellect, suited to an aesthetic pleasure, regardless of the implications of oblivion to the self that haunt Keats. The analogue to Keats's nightingale in Stevens's "Idea of Order," executed arbitrarily as if "at Key West," is a woman singing, suspended in a full-throated ease by her singing. One suspects (out of broader readings of Stevens's poetry) that, whereas Keats's nightingale was actual, Stevens's singing woman is but an imaginary projection. By fancy he deploys signs *beyond* such intrusive reality. One may imagine a woman as walking on a beach and singing "beyond the genius of the sea," as if oblivious to the sterile, imaginatively neutralized sands. Stevens imbues her with the poet's own authority as poet: she is "the maker of the song she sang." If a poet (like Keats) should be tempted to read *place* itself as subversive of the song (an actual Key West) in the visionary moment, anticipating the transcendent as but an illusion conjured out of the immanent through wishful thinking, Stephen responds yes, yes. Very well, let us pretend it so! He then embraces the fancifully supposed. For the "ever-hooded, tragic-gestured sea/ Was merely a place by which she walked to sing." By this process of an indifferent appropriation of the actual place to a song (it is merely a "setting" suited to fancy's uses) he may conclude that "there never was a world for her/ Except the one she sang and, singing, made." Hers is a "Blessed rage for order" accomplished by sounds "keener" than the actual sound of the sea, the higher keenness emanating from her. Her aesthetic "philosophy," we might say, is borrowed from Joyce's Stephen, and ultimately (by the poet's implications) from Socrates' Gorgias.

In considering this imaging in Stevens's poem, we may again recall the moment of escape for Keats through fancy, but in an instance more closely analogous in imagery to what Stevens projects by signs, we recall from another of Keats's Odes the figure of the flutist on the Grecian urn, who is arrested as if made immortal by art and so is forever "piping songs for ever new." Bravely arrogant praise of fancy by Stevens then, as if in response to Keats's melancholy born of Keats's disjunction as mortal poet from the arrested (and so immortal) figure on the urn. But Stevens too must willy-nilly fall from such high moments. Unlike his arrest of an imagined woman at song in his made poem (she arrested by his poem as for Keats the flutist arrested on the urn), there comes the inevitable falling away into thought out of the imagining intellect freed of the actual. By that falling, the haunting question about art's transport rises again and again. Stevens's answer is to sing yet another song. For Keats, however, such a moment remembered in signs out of actual experience gnaws any possible content with escape by fancy. Was that transcendent moment with the nightingale "a vision or a waking-dream"? Nor can Keats turn toward Pieper's habits of contemplation as Hopkins does. But as well, unlike Stevens, he cannot turn endlessly to the making of yet another song by an indirection avoiding the green world of reality, in a subversion by denial of the haunting question.

In the interest of pursuing the question beyond the reaches of either art or philosophy, Keats might have turned to St. Francis of Assisi, if not to St. Augustine. St. Francis's comfort, too, is in the ordinary things adjacent to his own senses but with less concern to pursue the meaning of his contentment through metaphysical philosophy or theology. Things speak with a continuous immediacy to him of their Cause. That simple presence to us of St. Francis, borne to us through remembering signs, has proved encouraging because he speaks in a more elemental way to the manner of our possible participation in being through ordinary things. After all, St. Augustine's pursuit of metaphysics is most complex, requiring even more than three or four books to lead to a metaphysical understanding of it. And so, alas, the difficulty to singing high songs or to pondering high questions about the self seems fraught with a possible danger out of despair to some of us, unwilling to continue melancholy or to turn to an arrogant fancy as a weapon. Indeed, neither Keats's fancy nor Stevens's witty logic can cheat so well as poets (or even philosophers) may dream they may. (Stevens, at the very end of his life seems to concede the point, entering the Church on his death-bed.)

Poet or philosopher, we may discover ourselves as *homo viator* longing for high plains suited to high comedy such as we find in the *Divine Comedy,* or for the persuasiveness of logic such as that of St. Thomas's *Summa Theologica.* What we may discover as poet or philosopher in a less intense attempt, however, is what St. Francis knew: the validity of any truth, in whatever high sentences or songs attempted, rests at last in the depths of the holiness to be recognized with an immediacy in our experiences of the ordinary. Such thoughts may come, more healing than those to Keats, as we contemplate perhaps even some cast concrete statue of St. Francis in some garden nook beside a prefabricated house. Or so let us imagine. Perhaps this house is what the English might call a cottage, surrounded by flowers, by plantings revealing no aesthetic sense in the planting. Perhaps only a trailer in a compact trailer park. Such possible (though not probable) encounter seems scarcely promising of artful, aesthetic, dimensions. The statue itself? Cast in lowly commercial concrete, not made of marble. Evidence of a mass production by some entrepreneur trading on our sentimentality? But, through contemplation, we may come to see sentiment itself as deeper than the spectacle that speaks sentimentality at the level of either commerce or aesthetics. For we may be reminded still – dislocated Modernists struggling for sophisticated art and science – of something of St. Francis's mystical vision as he experienced small things through an openness to those things called love.

We might in such a moment even discover that in such a lowly and unartful garden the small things have the look of things looked at, though lacking such cultural resonances as Eliot encounters at Burnt Norton. And to approach such a recognition, we may be approaching as well a recovery beyond that melancholy which consumes Keats, a recovery beyond the more Promethean uses of the imagination by a Wallace Stevens also. Beyond the pragmatism of spewed and molded cement statues of St. Francis in a housing project, that *place* spawned by a pragmatism justified ultimately by logical Positivism which unleashes will upon nature itself in programs purporting to be in the name of the general good.

With such a possibility in mind, we turn to a more substantially effective dramatization of this recovery in Flannery O'Connor's "The Artificial Nigger," in which her protagonist, Mr. Head, is shown as a deeply prejudiced, unlettered old man, charged (to his irritation) with the keep of his grandson Nelson. The boy is a boy on the verge of adolescence and so suspicious of the world in general, but particularly suspicious of his grandfather's good intentions for him. The cultural milieu is that emanating from what has been called "white trash." But the analogue echoed most subtlely in the story is Dante's *Hell,* Miss O'Connor's mischief lying in her using Atlanta as its geographical location (her "Taulkingham" of *Wise Blood*). Mr. Head is an arrogant Virgil who attempts to guide Nelson, a rebellious Dante as pilgrim. The moment of epiphany occurs when by accident (or is it by grace?) they encounter "the plaster figure of a Negro sitting bent over on a low yellow brick fence," in a pseudo-affluent suburb. The two have become hopelessly lost in the city of man, both actually and figuratively – the figurative aspect highlighted by Mr. Head's Judas-like denial of Nelson at a crucial moment. Nelson in his panic over being lost has knocked an old woman down and there are loud cries for a policeman against this "juve-nile delinquent." Mr. Head, catching up with the fleeing boy later, after having denied him, follows after Nelson. Together again, the crisis past, they enter each other's company, both changed but still lost. It is then that they encounter that eroding plaster statue in a suburb. It mimics the hitching post replicas of "artificial niggers" that were popular as kitsch décor on lawns in the 1950s, speaking a culture quite dislocated from St.

Francis, not to say from horses. In this "epiphany," the old man and child find themselves arrested before the crumbling figure. "Mr. Head looked like an ancient child and Nelson like a miniature old man," both frozen in an awe inexplicable. But out of that moment, Mr. Head, a stickler for justice as governed by the letter of the law as sanctioned by custom, comes to understand for the first time the mystery of mercy. For the first time in his long life he feels futile as father to the boy. Nelson's eyes implore him "to explain once and for all the mystery of existence," a mystery out of their encounter with that decaying and corrupted image of man.

There has been recent criticism of O'Connor as a "racist" – citing this story in evidence – by those who cannot see that she uses the Negro here in much the same sense that Percy uses the Jew as a rescuing sign. In "Why Are You a Catholic?" Percy insists we have seen that there are only "two signs" that are of significance in a world "where all theoretical cats are gray." The one is the "self," the other the "Jews," a sign of "the worldwide ecclesia instituted by one of them," God-become-man, a Jew. In a cultural milieu where few Jews abound – for a Mr. Head, for instance – the Negro fills that role, in an agency of grace to O'Connor's characters, and in this story most centrally so. If Dante at Hell's pit encounters the terror of Satan made palpable, Mr. Head (though he could not say it, because the experience is beyond words he could recognize, let alone understand) has encountered Christ mediated through a "racist" piece of pseudo-art.

Back home, back in the "country," at last having escaped the city, Mr. Head is attempting to digest his encounter. He knows that "there were no words in the world that could name" the action of grace that has touched him in his epiphany, consuming his pride slowly, mercy itself proving terrible as if it were a cancer to his pride. That is the effect he continues to experience from the encounter with that eroding "artificial nigger." In the story's concluding paragraphs occur Hopkins-like images of the country place now holding Mr. Head and Nelson. Not that they are yet able to respond to that "freshness deep down things," even things seemingly depressing if "unseen." But even the railroad "clinkers under their feet glittered with a fresh black light" and the treetops, "fencing the railroad junction like the protecting walls of a garden," accentuate the clouds overhead that hang like lanterns. Their dreary world wants their seeing it transformed, though these yet lost souls are not sufficiently recovered from their being lost in the cosmos to do so yet. Because they are by gift and circumstance *very* limited in the nature of their gifts responding to circumstance (they are both irritatingly willful), they have till now imposed a "world" of their own upon their small corner of the cosmos. They have done so through a pride differing in power but not in nature from such impositions as Percy sees apparent in the sophisticated Modernist's distortions of reality through a science freed from ordinate stewardship.

There is a pride long fostered by Mr. Head, but just a-borning in Nelson. Thus O'Connor's resolution of her fictional version of this descent into Hell by her wayward heroes, both of them unprepossessing in either gift or circumstance.

Their possible rescue, already underway in Mr. Head particularly, has been effected through pseudo-art, that decorative "hitching post" made in the image of a Negro – an "artificial nigger." And here one is well reminded of Percy's similar scene, affecting a more cultured and sophisticated protagonist, Will Barrett, in *The Last Gentleman.* Will fingers the bark consuming the iron hitching post, he standing in the dark outside his ancestral home. The difference is that Will turns from his moment which has been unresolved by an epiphany. Miss O'Connor, in treating "white trash" as protagonists, rather shockingly reminds us of that Biblical admonition that the lame, the crippled, the wounded may enter Heaven first. Compare Mrs. Turpin's "vision" in "Revelation," or Julian's comeuppance in that story with a phrase from Teilhard, ironically used, "Everything that Rises Must Converge." How shocking such revelations, but most particularly shocking to the sophisticated Modernist intellect. That intellect (like those the Misfit encounters on his way) are likely to hold that a Mr. Head may be rescued only by "social rehabilitation," rather than by a Love invading a prideful moment as Mercy, requiring an answering act of love in that moment's arrest before the "artificial nigger."

All these small things, a multitude of things singing to those with ears to hear, cry out: "We did not make ourselves, but he who endures forever made us." For even the avaricious entrepreneurs "make" only out of that givenness – though both cement and their own selves may be perverted by the avaricious. But by the grace of givenness, poorly made or deceptively made "art" may speak beyond art's or nature's perversion. Always there is a foundation, an ontological ground in small "pied" things or in large ones as well, since all is sustained in being: from Julian of Norwich's hazel-nut to cement statues of St. Francis; from random songs on a deserted beach by Stevens's imagined singer to *The Divine Comedy.* And that is the argument which has been made endearingly in relation to the virtues of both imagination and fancy by G. K. Chesterton in his "Ethics of Elfland" (*Orthodoxy*). "A child of seven is excited by being told that Tommy opened a door and saw a dragon. But a child of three is excited by being told that Tommy opened a door." A return from fancy to the immediate holiness of small things. The realistic tale fascinates before we come to reach toward "Romantic" tales. In the same paragraph, as conclusion, Chesterton laments that "we have all forgotten our names," recovering them if but partially in blessed moments: "All that we call spirit and art and ecstasy only means that for one awful instant we remember that we forget." We may observe the truth of Chesterton's observation by watching a child wake to the marvels of existential reality. Thereby we might even, at last, discover a closer witness in the child to such moments of our own fleeting moments of happiness in response to things. It is here, deeper than perhaps Wordsworth could understand, that the child proves to be father of the man. And that continues a haunting spiritual ambiance to us through those signs O'Connor uses to show Mr. Head and Nelson for a moment arrested before that "artificial nigger."

XXI

Concerning this visionary moment to us, young or old, Pieper remarks them available to all, lest our address to such experiences be either reduced to the merely mystical (and supposed therefore to be reserved to mystics), or to the explications of the theologian, or to the concentrated fusion of signs by a poet such as Hopkins. Says Pieper, it is "meaningless to distinguish between religious and non-religious contemplation." For our careful thought about this reality of our experiences of a still point proves – tests – the weak necessities of our dependences upon reason. This does not mean that we are absolved of using reason to explore the reality of these moments of grace, notwithstanding Wordsworth's early complaint against the necessity of "thought." Reason itself must nevertheless concede them "simultaneously poetic and philosophical." But most fundamentally they are *religious*, regardless of the particular person or of the degree of his sophistications as intellectual in his response to the experience of a moment. A still point violates the even tenor of a person's ordinary ways at a moment out of time and place, revealed to reflective understanding as a moment in which the person experiences a visionary participation in the fullness of reality *here* and *now*. Therefore the place and time, containing and occasioning encounter with divine things, is known as sacred. Such an event may be taken by the ordinary person who thinks himself submerged by seemingly ordinary things, not as St. Augustine or St. Thomas would take it, but as a "strange" event, occurring even to the doggedly secular mind. If so, it may also prove frightening. One has a dramatic representation of just such a terror in the ordinary, made by Flannery O'Connor in her *The Violent Bear It Away*.

In that novel, O'Connor's agent Rayber, a rationalist behaviorist, experiences a series of still points as inescapable, though they make sense to him only as symptoms of an encroaching madness within his own independent and autonomous mind. He feels himself "overwhelmed by the horrifying love. Anything he looked at too long could bring it on. . . . It could be a stick or a stone, the line of a shadow, the absurd old man's walk of a starling crossing the sidewalk. . . . [H]e would feel suddenly a morbid surge of the love that terrified him – powerful enough to throw him to the ground in an act of idiot praise. It was completely irrational and abnormal." It is, as Pieper would have it, a moment of a true seeing, a moment in which grace melds intellect's intuitive action, the seer with the seen. in a communion encompassed by Love Itself. That is the moment, we are arguing, as truly a triadic moment – a transfiguration accomplished *through* the "ordinary."

In the light of this Thomistic "triadic" dimension to our experiences of a still point – experiences not limited to poet or philosopher or saint we must emphasize – we may better understand as problematic Percy's pursuit of the mystery of sign in a science of signs derived from Peirce's version of epistemology. (We remember that Peirce, in his quest for a psychological epistemology, in fact takes his point of departure in Medieval scholasticism, particularly interested in Duns Scotus, though Peirce does not make the Christian dimension emphatic in his philosophical-scientific concerns. I have explored Peirce's position in relation to Percy at length in "*Walker Percy and Charles S. Peirce: Sign Posts at Divergent Paths,*" in manuscript.) It is an undertaking Percy makes very early, we have observed, as he begins to wrestle with the despair descending upon him at his homecoming – a wrestling with local realities which is seemingly exacerbated by his now professing himself a Christian by conversion. The uneasiness seems at first related to his also being a Southerner come home. We suggest, then, a complication to his thought consequent upon his reading of Peirce which affects his intellectual inclinations, from which influence he is never fully freed in his rational address to the mystery of signs through a pursuit of a science of signs. He comes near that freedom, certainly, in what amounts to a break with science itself as arrogantly dominant of our world. That is the essay, published in the year of his death, which we have already introduced, "Why Are You a Catholic?" In it he observes that the "great paradox of the Western world is that even though it was in the Judeo-Christian West that modern science arose and flourished, it is Judeo-Christianity which the present-day scientific set of mind finds the most offensive among the world's religions." Not Eastern religions, not those New Age inclinations drawing the girl friend of the nuclear scientist to the Corn Dance in *Lost in the Cosmos*. These latter-day neopagans (or so St. Augustine would consider them) turn inward, in a Cartesian removal of the "self" from creation, as if thereby accomplishing a "transcendence" suited to a scientific creationism of the self. And, as Percy observes early, such a turning may well turn the person also to the "guru," rather than to an anointed priest.

This new and rigid mindset of science, Percy says, finds "Judaism . . . offensive because it claims that God entered into a covenant with a single tribe, with it and no other." But "Christianity is doubly offensive because it claims not only this but also that God became man, He and no other." Hence one "cannot imagine any statement more offensive to the present-day scientific mind set." It is a mind set Percy much earlier would have termed *scientism*, though he does not in this late essay make such a distinction, trying nevertheless to rescue science back to its proper limits. For "the scientific method is correct as far as it goes, but the theoretical mind-set which assigns significance to single things and events only insofar as they are exemplars of theory or items of consumption, is in fact an inflation of a method of knowing and is unwarranted." Indeed warrant is denied, from the

Thomistic perspective, since the presumption is that *form,* abstracted and reduced to exemplar, may then be reimposed by formula, by the will, in that Voegelinian gnostic action: an intent to reconstitute being itself in service to system. It is an upside-down intellectual action, a perverse scientific trinitarianism in which form as the operative "Son" and matter as receptive sustainer of form (its "Holy Ghost" turned upside down) conspire with the gnostic intellect as "Father" to create an illusion that the "Father" creates *ex nihilo*. Thus *being* will then *be* as it should have been if there were a God. The gnostic actor in this science of the absurd thus supersedes God in an art of the absurd. The scientist now becomes God the Creator.

Perhaps it is still possible to recover something of the Christian mystery of the Trinity as proportionately relevant to man as maker. That is the direction in which Percy is tending when he comes to affirm at last the holiness of the ordinary. The ordinary is holy because created, and it is to be held as holy through sacramental dedications to the ordinary by *homo viator.* The sacramental surrender is that intellectual action of a returning offer of things created, to the Creator. It is the action of stewardship of nature nurtured by art. The Christian mystery of the Trinity is formulated out of a faith resting in Revelation – lately and anciently rationalized as an article of that faith by such conspicuous intellects who are still *present* to us: St. Augustine and St. Thomas Aquinas notably. For they are continuing presences to us, we have insisted, as defended recently and resolutely by John Paul II. The Trinity, in a part of that anciently consenting formulation, is declared to be of "one substance," though three "persons." But the Modernist mind whose faith rests exclusively in science must exclude this mystery as but superstition. After all, the *substantive* nature of the Trinity is not submissive to DNA tests of measure by which the Modernist intellect could rest its uncertain faith in its own autonomous power. Thus it has come to attempt more and more a resolution in support of its own magic of the gene, often with emotional excitement with quasi-religious emotionalism. The Modernist scholastic in science's clothing holds, heretically in the Thomistic scholastic's view, only with *hard* evidence as established by the measure of the cleverest (i.e., the latest) machine devised to measure. Not a measure of the truth of things, but a presumed measure by an abstraction turned theory, derived from coincident accidents of things as the only absolute and so the only full measure of any truth, to be decreed by the authority of theory. Gabriel Marcel remarks of this scientific mind-set, especially as encountered in the sociologist, that such a person is a "producer" bent on "employing the methods of an engineer." What we in turn remark is that, with the perfections of the machines, with the latest technology, of measure, that which is thus measured becomes exponentially removed from reality by abstractionism, requiring analogy – metaphors – of signs to suggest a Modernist's version of visionary depths of things. That mind-set, then, supplants not only the philosopher, but in the necessity of the moment, the poet as well.

The heretic turned skeptic to such Modernist magic as orthodoxy must withhold his full consent to the confident faith in an intellectual *comprehension* as asserted by the dogmatic faith of Modernism, the dominant religion of our moment. For such a dogmatic intellect's supposed comprehension must be believed to be divine in itself and beyond question, lest we become heretics to system. Things thus controlled by intellect make intellect itself divine. *Comprehension* here once more names a presumption by finite intellect of its absolute rendering of a thing through *knowledge held*, overtly or tacitly intending thereby to use that knowledge in reconstituting being. But even a Modernist as scientific "scholastic" seems to present as his hard evidence only "pictures" of the measure made by the machine, with the machine derived from theory. The "picture" is then presented as if evidence of a full measure. But such a dogmatist as here described proves vulnerable as much as the poet has ever been charged with vulnerability. He is made so through the indirections of the "figurative" reduced to theory, an action pretending to make the abstraction itself substantive by intentionality.

Currently, in a secret certainty of reason as authority, the Positivistic dogmatist in his role as scientist heavily rationalizes his faith in the gene, through mathematical certainties as a mode of metaphor subsuming in the end all differentia. What proves absent at last from such pictures as thus rationalized, however, is the mystery of life itself. Thus pictures of DNA as the "Son" of a recessive "Father" (governing mysteriously a genetic Providence) are more and more evident in a variety of our actual social and political trials, civil and criminal – the charts of evidence panned for us by the TV camera – charts set before juries of a prisoner's "peers." Those members are required to ponder graph pictures, evidenced responsibly by wrinkled foreheads. It is difficult to value the caricature of a person in graphs as if graphs gave a full dimensional portrait of the living person. Not that one may not accept such measure as bearing increasingly a *limited* accuracy to a necessary judgment of the *measurable*, on the limited authority of the ever-improved machines of measure. Indeed, that is a welcomed prospect, but a prospect which bears only a subordinate relevance to our moral judgment at last in respect to the *life* of a *person*. For the moral burden of responsibility to creation, to the world in a sacramental response, must be fundamental to such judgment. That is a principle increasingly obscured in our world by the overwhelming mechanics of measure in weighing verdicts in matters civil or criminal – in judgments beyond the restrictions of judicial purview.

What is discarded, or obscured by reduction to measure (as if measure were the absolute comprehension of existential reality), is *life itself*. That is, life in the sense formulated as person, as *intellectual soul incarnate*. Such *life* is to be abolished, since it is incompatible to measure. But still, despite the most intricate measure, life proves more complex than if it were spectacle of a machine, the absurdity of which reduction becomes apparent when we contemplate *life* measuring *life* as if a machine measuring a machine. Additionally, of course, intellect when presuming autonomy must deny as well *conscience*, since conscience speaks a dependence beyond the self – beyond the intellectual autonomy. Conscience implicates the self in its moral responsibility of judgments of reality. When Percy is scathing about Modernist argument for life's extinction through abortion, then, his irony skewers the pretensions of Modernist pretensions to a moral authority, since the rational ground of morality has already been denied despite the pseudo-rationality of the denial. Thus, as the irony reveals, in a disregard for the mystery of life through legalized abortion there yet echoes, if but faintly, a residual presence of conscience itself, whose proper ground is the holiness of such small things of creation as the living cell, a holiness incipient to being through connaturality. What wonder that we should hear also, if but faintly, that ancient warning: "Vengeance is mine, saith the Lord." To which we might add that classical adage: the mills of the gods grind slow, but exceedingly fine. It is under the steady presence of these warnings, faintly heard, that the Modernist mind-set in its overbearing scholasticism yet rationalizes its own autonomy, oblivious to such warnings. So our heretic against Modernism warns. That unknowing in action is most manifest in the spectacles of destruction in our last century, and the spectacle conjures a vengeance by its transgressions against being itself. That becomes the threatening shadow falling across so much of the current experimental manipulations of life with the magical machines devised toward reconstituting DNA.

The heretic against Modernist orthodoxy, then, must sort as best he may the limits of – and so the significance to – finite intellect of any *hard* evidence concerning the mystery of life. It is a concern affecting always and immediately his own personal responsibility to the dilemma of his suspension of action between justice and mercy in relation to prudence. This heretic to Modernist orthodoxy, here speaking, finds himself increasingly skeptical and, as well, increasingly fearful of the eventual consequences of genetic speculation as deployed in laboratory actions which are pursued in an attempt to support the Modernist faith. Such a heretic to Modernism, then, may in his reaction turn speculative in defense of the mystery of life, through common sense. In doing so, he may long for the support of the philosopher – long for some wise man elevating common sense to viable philosophy through a love of the truth of things. For we sorely need (such is the pain of *life's* oppressions by gnostic intentionality) a persuasive rational defense against these Modernist distortions of reality. The heretic's common sense, then, suggests that Modernist actions out of a confident illusion of autonomy very likely are but naive intrusions upon the unknown, made by those professing a full knowledge. The heretic might put it, with a Percy-like serious playfulness, in the manner of analogy. We may grant that the "pictures" of DNA presented to our judgment with such confident authority, enhanced by graphings or by mechanical artistry (as in that famous portrait of the double helix): those are pictures sometimes arresting. Yet they *are* pictures, though only of an ultimately ineffable thing. We find ourselves thereby still in Plato's cave. But it is Plato's cave with a difference: the projected images we are bound to engage (lest declared heretical to science) are shadows cast not by the Light of the Sun, but by intentional autonomous intellect itself. Similarly arresting are those pictures at the other end of the speculative spectrum, which perhaps once a month we encounter in the pseudo-serious advocacy of internet or television: pictures of UFOs, believed both actual and measurable by highly rational, specialized intellectuals – some of them no mean "scientists" themselves.

On either hand, the context of the unknown (being independent of the finite rational intellect bent on knowing – and sometimes so bent as to distort itself) obscures the possibility of the unseen as a part of a reality it would reduce to intellectual control. There is always something yet beyond any measure by finite intellect and its machines. That is why the heretic to Modernism is ridiculed as a heretic, in that he denies the Modernist faith in its comprehension as ultimate: a faith which holds that, if not today then tomorrow, all *will* be known. It is just a matter of the progress of time, even as the grinding of the mills of the gods is. But our heretic to Modernism is inclined to reject those dogmas which assert that the limits of reality are established by whatever is measurable, requiring of us an act of faith in scientifically pure reason as finite intellect's inevitable *comprehension* of things. For this gnostic intellect to the contrary, such a faith speaks an irresistible magic: its own power of self-transmogrification into becoming a current Lord of Power over being itself, another grindstone reducing an accidental cosmos to control. It is a power devoted by intention to the absolute freedom of a transcendence of being, thus to become self-elevated and empowered over being. Against such a spectacle of person as a Modernist tending to a transcendence through "virtual" reality as superior to actual reality, Percy poses a simple mind at its rosary before an educational TV series, watching the thought of Joseph Campbell unfolded by a famous voyeur of ideas. Which is the more comic? Which, this may be to ask as well, is most mediate as a cause to the spectacle of the members of that California cult who committed suicide in order to be "beamed up" to a space ship comet. Enough to make more insistent to us the difference between choosing Lost Cove, Tennessee (in circumstances hopeful to a recovery perhaps along "Agrarian" lines). Or choosing a projected Europa beyond our galaxy as the means to a recovery from a consciousness imploded by Modernist thought. These are the possible alternatives which Percy playfully and most disturbingly presents to our final checking, on the lists he provides in his last self-help book. So that the machine may render an accurate measure, we no doubt must use a number two lead pencil to fill in the answer, to be fed into the computer and yielding public opinion polls about the truth of things as the final certification of the truth of things.

Walker Percy in his sojourn of the cosmos is in quest of the path leading to his own proper end. Along that way he is increasingly concerned for a recovery of the ontological ground to himself as *homo viator*. He says, in defending

Heidegger against the positivist Fromm, that indeed our Modernist dilemma lies in "modern man's loss . . . of being, . . . a homelessness from being" which Fromm would reject as a "metaphysical" notion long since "superseded by cultural evolution." Here Percy adds (in countering Fromm), "One can't help thinking of what Marcel, in describing the spirit of the age, calls 'ontophobia,' the dislike of being." And it is to counter that modern phobia that Percy sets himself to engage the mystery of the sign, as if by sign (as Heidegger might have it) being could be summoned back into our world. But, as St. Thomas would have it, being has never been absent, only rejected or ignored by the intensity of the modern self's attempt at transcendence on its sole authority of intellectual autonomy. And so here, in drawing toward our own parting from Percy in these pages, we make a brief revisiting of the ontological ground in which, willy-nilly (conceding or not), even the pretentious autonomous intellect has origin – as St. Thomas would have it.

In approaching this ontological concern, we may see it involving a crucial argument for one of those rescuers of Percy. At a time when Percy is threatened by intellectual arrest through having accidentally contracted tuberculosis – thus threatened by despair – he begins to read recent philosophers, as well as reading St. Thomas and Kierkegaard. Among the recent are descendents of Kierkegaard, more popular in the academy than Kierkegaard. Especially there were Camus and Sartre. How ironic, especially from Percy's later perspective, that the actual sickness unto death for so many 19th-century writers (Keats among them), tuberculosis, should have arrested him, a medical doctor (as was Keats), in our advanced century, turning him at last toward becoming novelist rather than physician. In his reading of those French intellectuals while recovering, intellectuals grown out of Kierkegaard and out of 19th-century Phenomenology, it was inevitable that he would come upon Gabriel Marcel. He will recall a sequence of discovery (in an interview in 1971), remembering with some uncertainty the specific order of his encounter. He had come to Existentialism out of Kierkegaard he says "probably through Sartre first, probably through reading *Nausea*." After that he turns back to Kierkegaard, and then there is a "coming forward to Heidegger and Marcel." In that coming forward, he will have encountered Marcel's commentary on Sartre, an extended engagement of Sartre's *Being and Nothingness*. That essay is included in the collection of lectures to which Percy alludes often, Marcel's *Homo Viator*. An excited discovery for Percy no doubt, this battle over spiritual life or death, with terms – with signs – believed decisive to survival. For Sartre, there is the primacy of intellect over all. For Marcel, the soul is at risk in such a primacy. And in this clashing of signs, Percy becomes spectator to an intellectual-spiritual drama which he will conclude to be decisive to his own survival, to his own escape from the deadly despair which is threatening him. He owes a debt to these heroes who wield their signs like swords or daggers, a debt that makes him reluctant to reject Sartre, for instance, even after concluding that Sartrean Existentialism is unacceptable. For in a wayward intellectual world Sartre raised fundamental questions largely ignored in the euphoria following World War II. Even so, Percy must conclude that Sartre, his intellectual hero, enlisted on the wrong side of truth itself.

In interviews, Percy speaks often of a trio of French philosophers and writers who were important to him: Sartre, Camus, Marcel. They were important at the outset because they took their ideas about the nature of man in the world seriously, devoting their lives to a concern for words as unfolding ideas, seeking truth about human nature. "I use the fiction form as a vehicle for incarnating ideas, as did Jean Paul Sartre and Gabriel Marcel," he says to Don L. Keith in 1966. Sartre "has been of value to me," he says in another interview in 1971, "not because of his philosophy, because I think his philosophy is self-contradictory." He has been influenced irreversibly by *Nausea* "because the idea of having a certain belief and then trying to communicate it through a novel . . . was very exciting." Again, "Sartre's various descriptions of bad faith in role-playing [*vide. Being and Nothingness*] are marvelous phenomenological renderings of this quest of the self for some, any kind of habiliment" (interview in 1986).

In another interview in 1986, Percy declares that Sartre continues important, "because like Sartre my ideas have very much to do with the concrete predicament of a self, a consciousness, placed down in the world." (In a Heideggerian mode he might have said "thrown.") Percy finds himself "much more congenial with the style and the method of people like Jean-Paul Sartre and Albert Camus" than with most American writers. And, given repeated questions by interviewers about his French connections, he responds with a hint of irritation to the question whether Existentialism has "offered any solutions as regards the human condition." His answer: "Yes, it has . . . done so. Sartre did it," adding quickly a mannerly demurer, "However, I don't quite agree with Sartre." There is in the extended answer which then follows no reference to Marcel. This is an interview in 1984, but the year before he was more careful in response to a question about "significant transitions" in his commitments to literary and philosophical "influences." He has moved "from Tolstoy to Dostoevsky. From Sartre to Marcel. From Plato to Aristotle. From Wolfe to Faulkner." To which he adds: "Though in no case did I lose admiration for the former performance. It was a matter of further discovery."

In considering the history of intellectual influence on Percy, we must dwell especially on Marcel. We do so to suggest that Marcel's influence is deeper and more lasting than Percy himself may have at first supposed, especially given Percy's early excitement over Sartre as a philosophical novelist, encountered just as he is turning to art in his analytical manner of indirection to engage what he calls the "modern malaise." In November of 1943, Gabriel Marcel writes a delicately precise philosophical analysis of Jean-Paul Sartre's essay on ontology, Sartre's position is born out of a Husserlian phenomenological perspective, the intellectual midwife to which was Heidegger. Sartre is a Heideggerian activist who appropriates Phenomenology to his own authority, with a Positivistic intellectual demeanor one might add. Marcel, in a close analysis of Sartre's terminology of *Being and Nothingness*, reveals its intention to an intellectual autonomy over being. At first Marcel seems generously complementary. But what gradually emerges from his acute examination is an indictment of Sartre as a philosopher playing shell games with terms, in Marcel's judgment.

Sartre provides nevertheless an ironic value by this work: he calls attention to the bankruptcy of philosophy in our century, a bankruptcy out of and developed from what Marcel calls earlier (in "The Ego and Its Relation to Others") the "illusion" of a "moral ego-centricity" bent on proselytizing intellect with a pseudo-morality of the self as autonomous. Given the intricate play of signs by Sartre in his work (as we see it revealed in Marcel's critique), we might characterize Sartre's pose as that of the Modernist as scholastic. Indeed, Sartre is more subtle in his play of terms than even that vague popular judgment of Thomistic metaphysics in our century holds, a judgment which usually begins by condescending to Medieval scholasticism as primarily concerned with the problem of how many angels might dance on the head of a pin. Even Percy uses this deprecatory anti-scholastic shibboleth, without observing the Thomistic struggle underway with Nominalism in such arguments. (And how arresting, given the inclination to take Thomas as benighted intellectual to hear him on the current astronomical theories of the mid-thirteenth century, as Pieper points out in his *Guide to Thomas Aquinas*. Thomas observes that "The fact that the phenomena can be explained in this way is no proof of the truth of the theories, for possibly the same phenomena might be explained in a wholly different way, as yet unknown to men." That is an observation made before Galileo.) For Marcel, this Sartrean subtlety is dangerous. It is Luciferian, not Promethean as usually taken in elevating Sartre as hero. For it is intentionally subversive of ontological reality. Marcel's indictment, then, is worth remembering, given Walker Percy's admiring allusions to Sartre, though Percy's interest centers largely upon Sartre as novelist – as in his recalling the relation of *Nausea* to his own *Moviegoer*.

It is at the level of Sartre's game with terms that Marcel explodes the Sartrean position, exposing it as deadly to intellectual openness, although an argument taken seriously and with high regard by Western intellectuals. As his analysis unfolds, Marcel comes to remark that in it there appears what "it is difficult not to call [a] crudely materialistic foundation of the doctrine" as Sartre advances it. What bothers Marcel is that the work starts "from premises which in another age would have been called idealistic," but arrives "at conclusions which a materialist would not disclaim." The Existentialist's "absurdity," which rapidly becomes an intellectual fad as idea in the Western academy after World War II, is merely absurdity to Marcel, since Sartre by his argument condemns himself "of his own free will" to a self-imprisonment as intellectual. It is such an entrapment from which he can be rescued "not by the mere powers of [his] own being," but only through "a help or inflowing which is nothing else but grace." Thus Sartre as philosopher "shuts himself within the narrow circle of immanence, denying any other world or afterlife."

Marcel's devastating conclusion from reading *Being and Nothingness*: the work "appears in the last analysis much less as the expression of reason made wise by experience and ever ready to learn from it, [than] as the Luciferian refusal with which a rebellious individuality, intoxicated with itself, spurs the signs and calls to which Love alone could make it sensitive. . . ." And so "it turns back on itself" through phantasms which reduce its chances (save through intervening grace) of attaining any fulfillment. As argument, Dante would say, Sartre's is a Modernist philosophy justifying perverted love. In terms we have used, Sartre's motto is *non serviam.* Marcel's argument here, we observe in passing, is reflected in that denouement to O'Connor's "Good Country People." In that confrontation by the Sartrean Existentialist Hulga with the Bible-salesman, he having left her devastated to discover him no "good country" person, he leaves her, taking as trophy her wooden leg. "Hulga," he says at parting, "you ain't so smart. I been believing in nothing ever since I was born!" He needed no encouragement from the Sorbonne, by way of the imitative American academy.

XXII

In a concern for ontological recovery, Percy is closely allied with Gabriel Marcel despite his fascination with Sartre's word games, then. Both of them are attuned to our general loss of any assuring confidence in *being* as the ground of our existential reality *here* and *now*. It is a concern Percy could but encounter in his early reading of Marcel's *Homo Viator*, so that we may properly credit Marcel for encouraging Percy to an intellectual openness. That dislocated Southerner, Percy, returning home from Up East and very uncomfortable in the new tension between recognizing his "self" as inescapably Southern on the one hand but complicated by his having become Catholic on the other, needed all the help he could get. How avoid that circumstance to his homecoming which leaves him wondering whether as *Southerner* he is at best an intellectual scalawag? Marcel's insights into these confusions to this particular *homo viator* Percy were important from the outset, though one might argue that the depths of Marcel's insights into the human situation became available to Percy the more fully only late in life, as "a matter of further discovery." For on first encounter, Marcel might be taken only as one of those fascinating French "Existentialists" whom Percy turned to, leading him to Kierkegaard and then back to the volatile arena of the French intellectuals.

Here, the tendency of our concern is toward seeing Marcel as more Thomistic than might have seemed at first apparent to Percy, who at this early point of his journey was also reading St. Thomas, a point to be made since our "standard" epithet for Marcel has him a "Christian Existentialist." That epithet tends to isolate him to our past century, when he himself is very deliberately in that continuum of metaphysical thought out of St. Augustine and Thomas Aquinas. We may discover Marcel, for instance, taking a point of departure very like that of Thomas, who reminds us that, since we are by the simple unity of our nature as *person* an intellectual soul incarnate, the senses are therefore our natural point of departure as intellect toward understanding the ontological mystery of being which we must come to understand, lest we become lost in the cosmos. Our first movement toward God, toward our recovery of a dependence "upon a superior order" as Marcel has it, is through our carnate nature, through which we turn outward from the self to creation itself, *here* and *now*. For this is the arena to both an initial and continuing proximate experience of the ordinary as holy. Our experience is necessarily of proximate *things* through our dimension as soul *incarnate*. The present place, therefore, governs and initially limits our prudentially ordered speculative attempts to understand current experience, increasingly reflected upon in relation to past experience. If we put it as the poet might, the infant's hunger for its mother's milk initiates a journey toward understanding the milk of human kindness.

Thus for Marcel, as for Thomas, we begin our journeying as *homo viator* through sensual responses *here* and *now*, experiencing ontological certainties intuitively, which certainty most probably will be removed erratically from our confident knowledge of the truth of things by an emerging will. Our will, because fallen, is prone to a willfulness dominating reason. That initially confident dependence upon "common sense" suffers changes by thought's reflective intrusion. Reason, engaging actual experience remembered properly, should lead us to attempt to order those experiences. But, given a fallen nature, we are likely rather to accrue an excessive credit to our understanding through pride in our own reason as authority, encouraging us in our self-dislocation from the present place as the immediate and proper context governing speculative reason. There may likely follow a growing uncertainty, exacerbating will itself in a response to a growing sense of dislocation in the *here* and *now*. Thus the adolescent anticipating adulthood is likely to "lite out" for an ambiguous "West" as Huck Finn anticipates doing, signaling a Modernist literary theme pervasive of 20th-century Western literature.

That was the concern we dealt with earlier in exploring the nature of contemplation as adumbrated by Pieper, in which a recovery of reason *ordinately* related to the gifts of intuitive knowledge becomes intellect's responsibility to its own simple unity – that unity insisted upon by Thomas. In a recovery of unity as person, person gains perspective upon *place.* As for Marcel, he will speak toward a centering, toward a simplifying relevance to intellectual certainty of our intuitive knowledge. Through that recovery, intellect is anchored in an ontological confidence that *things exist in themselves* here and now, not by virtue of speculative rationalism. They are things anterior to and other than the laboring rational intellectual self. It is this loss in Descartes's thought which makes him as a person burdened by pathos, though in his stance as philosopher he becomes increasingly arrogant. Indeed, given Gilson's account of Descartes in his William James lectures, *Unity of Philosophical Experience,* Descartes conducts himself as person with such an intensity that he could only appear to his philosophical contemporaries (however much they might be fascinated by his ideas) as egocentric. For Gilson is more kindly in his unfolding of Descartes, an irascible person, than warranted either by Descartes's arguments or his deportment. One might, from the evidence of his deportment to his current philosophical peers, be tempted to declare his conduct as philosopher that of a whining intellectual bully. (We are saved somewhat from that exacerbating lack of both charity and attendant manners by time's distancing us from Descartes's actual presence perhaps.)

Marcel's concern is, then, Thomistic – a concern for a recovery of community of the self and things in *being,* through that Thomistic principle of *connaturality*, though that is a term Marcel would not likely use. Indeed, he is reluctant to use that "much abused term intuition," he says, preferring a "little used" term, "synopsis, the act by which a group is held together under the mind's comprehensive gaze." Thus "Person – engagement – community – reality: there we have a sort of chain of notions which . . . do not really follow from each other by rational deduction . . . but of which the union can be grasped by an act of mind." For, he remarks parenthetically, "there is nothing more fallacious than a belief in the value of deduction." What we discover in Marcel's lectures, delivered in France during the Nazi occupation and collected with other essays as *Homo Viator: Introduction to a Metaphysics of Hope* after World War II, is that this turning to *things* in themselves, *here* and *now*, is precisely Marcel's own movement. The signs he deploys, however (if not carefully read), may seem to reflect too much of the Modernist intellectual milieu, and especially that wavering sense of our intellectual loss developing out of Phenomenology as Nominalistically appropriated to gnostic intentionality. His philosophical language, indeed, takes that recent thought as its point of departure. But he is acutely concerned, not with phenomenology in its Modernist dress, but for a recovery of ontological reality deeper than the arguments of Husserl or Heidegger or Sartre can provide. That is the recovery upon which is dependent a recovery of personhood, toward hope of an ultimate fulfillment called Beatitude.

Marcel in this concern recognizes the Modernist dangers to recovery, represented for Percy (as Percy says near his life's end) in that scientific "mind-set which assigns significance to single things and events only insofar as they are examples of theory or items of consumption." Taken as "examples" they are thus severed from the immediacy of here and now. To restrict mind to that level of material reality as but sensually known is to dwell at the level of spectacle, a spectacle fed by phenomenology itself in its aspect as pseudo-science, which becomes a philosophy devoted to appetitive existence as its end (as Marcel reveals in showing Sartre to be a materialist). Mind itself so appetitively restricted in its desire becomes reduced to appetitive nature, devoted as consumer of things through theory executed against reality. Or mind becomes ascetic as theorist in relation to the material world, justifying consumption as a byproduct of scientific asceticism. (There is a "scholarly" phenomenon of cannibalism among these theorists, theory devouring theory, with an illusion of a progress toward a "unified" theory dreamed capable of overpowering being itself.) In this pursuit of "theory-consumption" (Percy's term) we have come to dwell increasingly upon the magic of "technics" (Marcel's term), those technics exercised by mind upon "nature" in pursuit of a dominant theory, whose effect however proves counter to the truth of the things of nature, especially those things called persons. It is the exercise of tuning things as if things were machines, the most crucial thing of all requiring such a tuning of the *person*.

Marcel argues in *Homo Viator* that indeed it is *person* reduced to *machine* that removes the actual person from his recognition of dependence upon Creating

Love, a Love discovered through ontological recognitions of that Love in the immediacy of our experiential communion with things. The effect of that turning away from the ontological ground is a self-love whose end is a self-consumption, characterized by Marcel as an evil disposition in the *person* called *despair*. Marcel's *Homo Viator* appears in 1945, its English translation in 1951. And in 1951 he follows this theme with his *Man Against Mass Society*, which enlarges upon the single *person*'s destruction by despair as exacerbated by our larger social confusions. It is in this respect that we know his concerns to be larger in *Homo Viator* than with the traumatic destructions at the level of spectacle known as World War II. His is a prophetic concern for the loss of soul before, during, and in the aftermath of that war, the growing endangerment of soul by what is taken superficially as "peace," given the euphoric relief after that war. Our suggestion, in the light of his concern, is that Percy in his growing appreciation of Marcel will come at last to a fuller understanding of him. Hence his growing concern for an ontological recovery from the Modernist dislocations of the isolated "self." It leads Percy to "The Holiness of the Ordinary" in speaking to this point, as we have observed. We are suggesting further that Percy himself becomes more "Thomistic" in his deportment to the "ordinary" than we find him to be at the time of *The Moviegoer*, Thomas seemingly inhabiting his explicit thought in the later essays and interviews more than in the earlier. And so we must recognize the Thomistic aspects of Marcel's *Homo Viator* – in order to recover "existentialism" from its reductions in that philosophical movement which is usually taken as a very "Modern" contribution, that celebrated intellectual fad Existentialism. In such recognition, we return to the influence of Thomas and St. Augustine as corrective.

St. Augustine would consider the scientific "mind-set" Percy finds dangerous to be rather far removed from a potentially healthy paganism with which he first became familiar as a teacher of literature. And so, insofar as we reflect on both Augustine and Percy as poets, we recall St. Augustine's affinity for that old pagan literature, especially for that of the Greeks. His confidence is that, since it was at least concerned beyond mere self-reflection, it recognized something of the holiness of the ordinary, though attributing that holiness to a variety of gods and goddesses. He might as Christian rescue that literature to a service of the true Lord of Holy things. Thus there is a distinction to be made here between the early paganism which St. Augustine addresses and his address to Neopaganism at the time of *The City of God* as embraced by a remnant of intellectuals. It is a difference as well from that Neopaganism adrift in the 20th-century mind which Percy addresses. Our latest version, engaged satirically by Percy, has been nurtured out of our Cartesian turning inward whereby (as Percy might put it) the self becomes its own guru, with the larger world but a reflection of the self to the self.

Concerning this difference, we might observe that in the old pagan world memorialized in Hesiod and Homer, philosophy subsequently grows out of literature. But that literature itself had grown out of common experiences of creation by community and celebrated in religious ceremonies, served by the poet as priest. Our new paganism to the contrary reveals that, since Descartes, literature seems rather to have grown out of philosophy in decay, the effect upon community thus accomplishing an increasing alienation of the self from common experience. St. Augustine, in his turning from the dangers of Manichaeanism, discovered his soul in need of becoming "enlightened from outside itself, so that it can participate in truth," since "it is not itself the nature of truth," as he observes in Book IV of his *Confessions*. The soul is an insufficient guru, then. In his turning from a devotion to the Manichee Elect as his "guru" – himself but a lowly "Hearer" – he discovers something both deeper than and other than the self. He discovers it within his own memory, a "Something" sustaining even that earlier turning from it when he first became a Manichaean. If through his later turning to Christ St. Augustine discovers himself (aided by Plotinus) a wayfarer, he discovers as well his own Manichee entrapment. It is, similarly, as aided by Gabriel Marcel that Percy finds a beginning of his own recovery from the dangers of Modernist gnosticism, including that temptation to a rigid scientific "mind-set."

The opening lecture of Marcel's *Homo Viator: Introduction to a Metaphysics of Hope* finds support for hope over despair, which support he adumbrates in his second lecture, turning toward establishing a suitable "metaphysics" of hope. That first lecture, "The Ego and Its Relation to Others," had appeared some two years after France's capitulation to Nazi Germany, by which time the foreign presence had begun to reveal Frenchmen to themselves in ways difficult for them to accommodate – certainly difficult for Marcel and like-minded Frenchmen to reconcile in themselves. And so his concern becomes for a rescue of the self. His participation as a "resistance fighter" is to be discovered in these essays, then, rather than in activist underground operations against the occupying Nazis such as that credited to Jean-Paul Sartre. It is not the "self" in resistance to the Nazi Lords of power represented by Vichy Frenchmen that most concerns Marcel, but an official betrayal of France by intellectual Frenchmen. For the rescue he envisages is not that of an absolute freedom of autonomous intellect, as it is for Sartre. Vichy authorities did, in response to his words, forbid publication of one of the eleven pieces he chooses for his *Homo Viator* at war's end – his reflections on "Obedience and Fidelity." But for Marcel that is symptomatic of the deeper malady of soul in the French intelligentsia, Left and Right, than accounted for by the spectacles of betrayal by Vichy traitors.

It is the self as person toward which Marcel directs his concerns, but he sees that self also as its own worst enemy. His lectures must have seemed at first to address a rather esoteric concern, and so hardly threatening to the triumphant Vichy regime in that moment. Since only one piece of his was denied publication, he must have appeared to the authorities as hardly a dangerous subversive. What is the danger in his speaking as he did about the "ego" or "phenomenology" in relation to a quest for his "metaphysics of hope"? We might remember in comparison the political consequences visited upon a contemporary and companionable resistance fighter against Modernism, one who as a German citizen began to raise parallel political questions to those raised by Marcel and at the philosophical level. He, too, puts such questions directly and in doing so becomes a threat to immediate social and political triumphs of the Nazi lords. We recall Eric Voegelin, who found himself *persona non grata*, having to flee into exile. But one might (with our retrospective advantage) wonder whether Marcel in his lectures such as his extraordinary "Mystery of the Family," given publicly to L'Ecole des Hautes Etudes Familiales at Lyons and at Toulouse in 1942, is not even more subversive than Voegelin, in that his resistance to Modernist doctrine is at a ground zero in its inception – focused upon the *family* in *place*. Rather certainly the subversion touches not only false French intellectuals or Nazi lords, but the decay already underway in England and America. Indeed, his works continue deeply subversive of Modernist doctrine to this very moment, both in America and in Europe.

We should properly remember as well, in relation to Voegelin, the career of his fellow German, Heinrich A. Rommen. When Rommen published his *The Natural Law: A Study in Legal and Social History and Philosophy* in 1936, his first reward was imprisonment by the Nazis. After that experience he came to Virginia in exile, as Voegelin came to Percy's Alabama. Rommen's *Natural Law,* which is not widely known, is a direct engagement of Modernist ideology as it grew out of a rejection of Classical and Christian natural law, that emerging new ideology fermenting in one of its species as Nazism. And we discover that Rommen's book is very centrally relevant to Marcel's concerns for the dissolution of the family and community. It is a work crucially relevant to the rapid social decay in his adopted country in the last half of the 20th century.

Voegelin is more conspicuous in his opposition to the looming "new order" of the Nazis, while Marcel's subversion is more indirect, as is Rommen's as well. Alarm bells must have gone off in Nazi minds, of course, when the "legal" history of natural law seemed a fact, established as governing fact, established by the mind-set of science. Close attention to that aspect of the history of the idea of "natural law" could but underline the subversion of natural law underway since the Renaissance – a subversion aiding and abetting Nazi power. Centering upon a spiritual rescue of person in the light of eternity, then, Marcel proves to have had the same concern as that very orthodox German, Rommen. Marcel, however, uses a vocabulary ambiguous in that it seems to share in a dependence upon Modernist philosophy itself, Marcel one of those far-out "Existentialists." Therefore there is seemingly little cause for concern within the enveloping chaos of a catastrophic World War II. That war was scattering civilization everywhere into fragments through contentions over order, but order understood on both sides of that destructive war as to be determined in an accord with the technological Power of the moment. How peripheral Marcel must have seemed in the midst of spectacular and subtle subversions of family.

After all, Marcel is only talking of the *soul*, in the midst of massive air raids and invasions and threats of invasion that are more commanding of immediate attention. Such a term as *soul* had already been long since relegated to the philosophical attic of discarded terms. There was before his eyes an accelerating blitzkrieg against being as Marcel saw it nevertheless, with Berlin and Paris and London and Washington as orienting places – places in that moment of a general war to consolidate Power in contention, command posts of Modernist ideologies within a desert land rubble created daily by the shifting forces of Power. There were also more local, "interpersonal," destructions of both places and families underway, of course, through the mobility of tanks and planes – human bodies strewn among scattered trees and bricks. And so how quaint, and unthreatening, then, Marcel's concerns for our spiritual deracination – his talk about the "mystery" of the "family" or of a "metaphysics" of "hope." How "out of it" he must have seemed in lamenting the family's dissolution as the darkest consequence of a Modernist doctrine rooted in the Enlightenment, for him more terrible in consequences than the physical destructions underway. He spoke in the midst of social and political and military chaos which was displacing millions of persons from "home." But talking about the soul? How mild a concern compared to those handy spectacles of violence between the forces of "destiny" and the defenses of "democracy." His concern for the family in dissolution, and especially his concern for the child in such a family, seemed far removed from current "reality," the "big picture" of the moment. The family, become deracinated geographically by a mobility dictated by the gradually advancing technology of the machine, could only leave the child disoriented through his being denied any comforting sense of place in Marcel's concern. And that was a more subtle war against humanity, one accelerating for four or five hundred years, in intentional subversion now evident (to a Marcel or Rommen) in the bombs and tanks and planes destroying the here and now. It is the consequences, after the silence of those guns and bombs, to which Marcel turns in his *Man Against Mass Society,* in his continuing concern for the soul.

In this interval of lectures and air raids, what a disparity: Firebombs on London, where Eliot walked the streets as fire warden, and Dresden turned into Hell's furnaces, while the philosopher talks of the child in the family, the family in a place. This is the moment, in England, when Eliot raises his agonizing question in *Little Gidding*: "Who then devised the torment" of this wild moment in the history of the West, in which "the only hope, or else despair/ Lies in the choice of pyre or pyre – / To be redeemed from fire by fire"? Eliot's answer (and Marcel's): "Love is the unfamiliar Name/ Behind the hands that wove/ The intolerable shirt of flame" made by Modernist hands in rejecting that Love. We may see, as Percy came to see, that our distractions, in moments of such seeming disparity between love and the spectacle of war, lie more deeply in our violations of persons and family than political ideologies can account for in history's ledgers of accountancy. There is a reminder floating mutely in that loud moment, in the pale smoke above Auschwitz and Buchenwald. Here begins, then, as Marcel is prophetic in seeing, the age of the Displaced Person, the phrase Flannery O'Connor will use in a telling story. And it is such a displaced person whom Percy will introduce as agent, his Fr. Smith, in his last novel, *The Thanatos Syndrome*.

And so in the Spring of 1942, concerned for "The Mystery of the Family," Marcel was exploring the spiritual burden upon a child when that child is denied membership in family through disruptions of *family from place*. For "we must recognize that all which tends to destroy the sense of a habitation and of permanence in the surroundings of a being in process of formation will contribute directly to the weakening of his consciousness of the family itself." Family consciousness disappears "where nomadic life, not of the tent and caravan, but of lodgings and furnished rooms, is the order of the day." And so "the disappearance of the settled habitation, or rather of the home, is inseparable from the fading away of traditions." For "these traditions are to the inner man what the family setting is to the visible one." Marcel, talking in such terms, might as well have been one of those strange fellows out of Vanderbilt, one of those Fugitive-Agrarians, opposing FDR's new programs which they saw submerging family to the interests of Centralized Power, local towns dissolved under waters backed up for generating "power" in Tennessee valleys. Centralized Power in two guises (as J. R. R. Tolkien argued at the time) were embattled through technologies of mobility, taking terrible toll on families and places in the "European Theatre of Operations" – that is, within those confines where Marcel wrote and lectured. The flow of collective power in contention for dominance through the machine is diametric to the spiritual journeying that is Marcel's concern and which will become Eric Voegelin's after his actual travelings. It will be in an Eliotic mode that Voegelin returns to the place from which he set out in the 1930s, back to his Germany (though he dies on a remove, in California).

Marcel will declare in his "Preface" to the gathered lectures and essays of *Homo Viator* that it is "precisely the soul that is the traveler," hardly an acceptable declaration to that more famous "Existentialist," Jean-Paul Sartre, who figures as a considerable presence to Percy at his own most tenuous point of turning toward spiritual recovery in relation to place – when he comes back to that strange home, the South. The point is notable, since Percy will allude to those three French writers in tandem as we have said: to Sartre, Camus, and Marcel, seldom distinguishing them. And there is a strong suggestion that he addresses them at least in part from the perspective of what we (and perhaps he as well) might call the stance of that American "Semiotic Existentialist," Charles Peirce, who seems to anticipate them in some respects a half-century earlier. There may have been for Percy the added comfort that Peirce approaches the phenomenon of signs from a more deliberately "scientific" position, especially given that the new psychology at Harvard (William James its principle founder there) has become by our mid-century generally accepted as a dependable science.

Marcel's second lecture as collected, his "Sketch of a Phenomenology and a Metaphysics of Hope," we notice, was given in February of 1942, nearly a year before that first one in his collection, his "The Ego and Its Relation to Others." It may be that Percy, having been engaged by the Peircian themes of the first which concern the "ego," read this quest for hope in the light of his readings of Peirce. At any rate, he must have engaged Marcel's phenomenological signs of the quest for hope against a tensional "psychological" pole of despair then rising in himself. Despair seems to have been a present threat very much burdening Percy at the time, as he will subsequently tell us. But it is a burden especially in relation to any concern for the mystery of the family as Percy must deal with that mystery out of his personal experiences. He would surely be acutely attentive to what Marcel has to say of *despair* as polar to *hope,* in the general context of Marcel's concern for family and place.

And so Marcel must have been both alarming and supportive to Percy in his unsettled state of soul as he turns South toward "home" in quest of a supportive "place," after his New York venture. We might see the likelihood in a sentence or two from the second of Marcel's lectures. As we summon words from that lecture, we need to note as well a kindred relevance of Marcel's third lecture, which concentrates so heavily upon the relation of family to place. In it he has much to say about *tradition* in support of spiritual concerns. That is of course a theme central to the "Southern" concerns of most of the poets and essayists and fiction writers associated with the "Southern Renaissance" in our letters, including Percy, for whom Eudora Welty will emerge as a "Virgilian" figure in regard to the relevance of place to the writer. Those themes of *tradition* as related to *place* had already been emphatic in the work of the Fugitive-Agrarians with whom Percy is nevertheless uncomfortable. We may wonder, given this common concern between the Agrarians earlier and Marcel in the midst of World War II, why Percy was uncomfortable with the Agrarians. One possible answer is that he, as Eliot had been at the time of his *After Strange Gods* (1933), was fearful that the Agrarian concern for *tradition* lacked a sufficient strengthening of that position by a sound and commonly recognized concern for *orthodoxy.* Marcel's position in recovering tradition to a support of family in place proves thoroughly orthodox. And so the more orthodox concern for place in Marcel, a concentration upon the spiritual implications of family in a place in relation to the soul, sheds an additional light upon Percy's struggle with despair toward becoming at last an "ex-suicide," seeing "place" for the first time, and becoming comfortable with his "Southernness."

Marcel observes that "the truth is that there can strictly speaking be no hope except when the temptation to despair exists." Reassuring, then, at least to one conscious of his own despair? As for despair itself, it "appears as an enchantment, or more exactly as a kind of witchcraft, whose evil action has a bearing on all which goes to form the very substance of a person's life." It feeds upon and stifles the flame which is life, destroying "the personal *becoming* which it is its function to consume." Hope, then, in relation to despair, will be revealed somewhat in Percy's amused delight in life itself as possible to him only as an "ex-suicide." And we should remember that Eliot, as an "ex-suicide" two decades earlier, leaves us a memorial of his own struggle and escape in "Ash-Wednesday." As his *Waste Land* sets out from an Augustinian theme, in an "April" cruelty in which there is a "mixing [of]/ Memory and desire," a tensional suspension in the desert called London, the later poem engages a dark ascent (Section III) in escaping the "deceitful face of hope and of despair," the tensional suspensions which seem threatening to the soul.

Marcel is pursuing the "phenomenology" of hope in a lecture delivered under that dark cloud of the Nazi occupation of his beloved France. He gives that lecture however in the interest of the rescue of the discrete soul, not as a program to rescue France. It is not a call to underground military action as such words would be for Camus or Sartre, a concern for rescue of a subdued nation. At issue, not a *Frenchman* but *man*, *homo viator* – for Marcel. His centering concerns are in the immediate circumstances to *a* soul struggling to survive its always dark time, whatever that time or place. He will, incidentally, also make a remark about the inadequacy of Scholasticism to the circumstances of the frantic soul coming to itself in the 1940s. Medieval scholasticism seems hardly appropriate he suggests, a sentiment we have remarked as echoed by Percy, who alludes to those dancing angels. This distancing, even though Marcel and Percy profess indebtedness to Thomas Aquinas. But we may demur from a too hasty conclusion of an inadequacy of Medieval scholasticism to those pressing concerns with Modernist deracination of family and the loss of place, if we realize that ancient concern as raised for us along with the rising of Nominalism as subversive of Thomistic scholastic thought in the late Middle Ages. That Nominalism is destined toward a secular rationalism, to be used as gnostic instrument against being. And so once more we summon a contemporary of Marcel to a defense, he too a Thomistic metaphysician, but more openly dependent on Thomas than Marcel (or Percy). We may observe as well an irony: at the time of Marcel's lecture, this witness we are now summoning was a soldier serving in the German army. Joseph Pieper was a contemporary not only of Marcel but of Tolkien and C. S. Lewis and T. S. Eliot in England, to Allen Tate and Donald Davidson and Cleanth Brooks in America. Meanwhile, Eric Voegelin had turned in his exile to Percy's Alabama and Louisiana, where he becomes a close friend of Cleanth Brooks and comes to know and to know about the Agrarians. And, as Cleanth Brooks has pointed out, Voegelin becomes important witness to Percy along his way.

Pieper, himself more isolated at the time as German citizen, is a companionable presence in this Christian intellectual community. He will emerge as a Christian Thomist, with such gifts of a simple direct incisiveness on Modernist spiritual failures that he reminds one of C. S. Lewis as an effective Christian apologist. Soon after World War II, Pieper gives lectures on *Hope and History,* in that intellectually riotous decade of the 1960s at Salzburg, on the border of France and Germany. That is a place which seems always the local ground for political and military contentions erupting in violent destructions. In those lectures (*Hope and History,* August 1966), Pieper turns almost equally to Marcel, on the one hand, and to Aquinas, on the other, for confirmation of a point he is arguing. His concern is in part a reconciliation of the two, so that we may recover an abiding significance of Thomistic metaphysics to our Modernist difficulties. Pieper concludes the series of lectures by special reference to Marcel's "profound insight" concerning hope in his essays of *Homo Viator*.

It is this relation of the two "metaphysics," Marcel's and Thomas's, that has prompted our reference to them in relation to Walker Percy's deepening understanding of himself as *homo viator*. In doing so, we signaled particularly Marcel's initial lecture (December 1942), which announces a concern for the state of the soul, here and now, as conflicted by the Modernist world – a concern as prelude to any quest for hope, let alone any attempt to articulate for others a settled metaphysics of hope. If Marcel were Dante in these circumstances, he might begin by observing himself as at the middle of his life, coming to himself in the dark wood of the Modernist's intellectual morass. The war itself which he endures is rich in its "objective correlatives" appropriate to a Dantesian Inferno. There is an actual undeniable physical war all about him. It is not a war so local as that between Dante's Guelphs and Ghibellines, but between an "Axis" of powers and "Allies" in power. Whether either of these two globally-warring factions was truly on the side of the soul was a question raised by Solzhenitsyn at Harvard years later, to the consternation of the Western intelligentsia. It was not in question during that war for J. R. R. Tolkien. He found both sides committed to the machine as instrument to science, used in a devotion to a magic exorcising the soul – a theme Marcel himself will develop in his *Man and Mass Society*.

In this first lecture, as it is set in *Homo Viator* (on the *ego* in response to the *other*) Marcel is less concerned with the invading Nazi lords than with the betrayal of the soul by the French intelligentsia, as St. Augustine was less concerned with the invasion of Rome by Alaric the Goth than with native intellectual scalawags as Neopagans when he came to write his *City of God*. Marcel's antipathy to that intellectual establishment is such that he marks as extreme the distance between his own "existentialism" and Jean-Paul Sartre's. He says in his "Preface," at war's end when he comes to collect these pieces, that he intends to "awaken an echo in this time of universal sacrilege when some of the most vigorous minds which have been known in France for the last twenty years really seem to imagine that blasphemy . . . can become the corner-stone of philosophy and politics." (Shades of Flannery O'Connor's Haze Motes!) In the first printed lecture, he finds the dominant intellectual position in France to be that of an "ill-starred" philosophy of "moral ego-centricity" precipitating "mankind into chaos" because it has deconstructed the reality of *person*.

If not Dante, then St. Augustine provides apt parallel to Marcel's position. We have remembered that, in his *City of God*, at the point of the seeming collapse of a tenuously Christianized Roman civilization, St. Augustine is at pains to warn that the true enemy endangering a Western collapse is not the external barbarians, but that subversive and growing internal intellectual betrayal, lying at the heart of Roman culture itself. He underlines the point in retrospect in his *Retractions*.

"When Rome was devastated as a result of the invasion of the Goths under the leadership of Alaric, the worshippers of the many false gods, whom we are accustomed to call pagan, began, in their attempt to blame the devastation on the Christian religion, to blaspheme the true God with more bitterness and sharpness than usual." That is the thorn thrust into Christian intellect which had occasioned his writing the *City of God*. A very similar cause, as Marcel sees it, then, and the recognition prompts him to the lectures of *Homo Viator*, with his concluding words of his "Preface," a retrospection, announcing as loudly as he may that his own time has been one of a "universal sacrilege" in which the best minds of France have been content to "imagine that blasphemy, conceived . . . rather as a statement than invective, can become the corner-stone of philosophy and politics."

Marcel prepares for this judgment against the French intellectuals in his activist resistance, the lectures and essays he collects at war's end which suggest that the crucial intellectual wars long underway continue ominously. He counters Rilke to Proust in an extended argument on this concern. Proust is of the Modernist enclave, now become dominant. Proust's destructive moral ego-centricity is reflected in his work, which "develops between two very different planes: that of Platonism on the one hand, and of an empiricism inspired by nihilism on the other." Here is a foretelling of that analysis Marcel will make, not of Proust, but of Sartre: that incisive analysis of Sartre's *Being and Nothingness*. In contrast, Rilke, in *Sonnets to Orpheus,* is "like a breath of air from another world," for that poetry's principle is a "reverence for souls and things of which the secret has to be recovered to-day." It is a discovery which must begin with a reverence of things here and now, recovered toward the soul's hope. For (as Marcel will presently say) "the self is *here, now*," though *now* and *here* be especially burdened by the wound of the *ego,* a Modernist term of indirection avoiding the issue of "self-love" as destructive of the soul. The argument developed in that first lecture, then, is concerned that we deal with the here and now as preliminary to any hope of an acceptable metaphysics of hope. The "self" must come to terms with the wound now popularly called the ego, the festering of which in intellect tempts us to aspire "to possess, to annex, or still more absurd, to monopolize." Deep in the soul itself has been planted a seed, a gathering darkness in "self" consciousness: "after all I am nothing but an empty void." An empty void, insofar as the "I" is disoriented from the cause upon which even its sense of emptiness depends – a sense which if stirred might set the recovering "I" upon a quest for fullness beyond possessive desire.

In resolutely pursuing this "existential" situation of the self as it has become emptily self-aware, Marcel remarks the initial movement toward recovery, and in such a way that Percy might well have recognized analogy to Peirce's arguments for the relation of the dyadic and triadic states of the human creature as involving a leap in being to a triadic level of consciousness through the agency of the sign. One must move with caution here, as perhaps Percy was not sufficiently cautious.

Thus Marcel: "Very early in the development of a human being this consciousness of existing . . . is linked up with the urge to make ourselves *recognized* by some other person, some witness, helper, rival or adversary who . . . is needed to integrate the self, but whose place in the field of consciousness can vary almost indefinitely." That might seem to echo the turning of the self from the dyadic to the triadic. But Marcel sees it in an interestingly ironic way, especially if we keep in mind Percy's concerns for his own role-playing as diagnostic novelist. This is the point for Marcel where consciousness is at its most tempted: the "self" as *poseur*, who though he seems "only to be occupied with others in reality [is] entirely taken up with himself." That other "person" only interests him insofar as that "other" may "form a favourable picture" of the *poseur*, reflecting himself to himself. One might suggest that at this point of turning of the self – toward a self-justification – may occur a projection of a role upon the "other." By sign is imagined a "witness, helper, rival or adversary," often personified as *Nature* in a collective "otherness." Thus a "play-acting which degrades and betrays" the self. Such posing is self-flattery, and beneath the posing "we invariably find self-love and . . . pretension." Marcel, knowing Sartre's argument for that "role playing" which so interested Percy in Sartre as adaptable to fiction, seems to have Sartre very much in mind.

What we begin to discover in Marcel's concern for our tendency to play-acting is perhaps the "phenomenology" of a transition of *person*, not from dyadic to triadic, but from an empty "I" desirous of fulfillment to a gnostic but arrogant "I" presuming self fulfillment by willed autonomy. Concerning this posing, then: "From the very fact that I treat the other person merely as a means of resonance or an amplifier, I tend to consider him as a sort of apparatus which I can, or think I can, manipulate, or of which I can dispose at will." Eliot, we remember, was at first captivated by the poetry of the French Symbolists, but he will come to much the same conclusion as Marcel when his concerns as poet and literary critic are enlarged in response to the spiritual implications of image itself. He will see this manner of the French Symbolists as a reduction of Dante's sense of symbol deployed in *The Divine Comedy.* In his essay "From Poe to Valléry" (1948), he will chart these poets as leading themselves into an intellectual cul-de-sac. In our metaphorical description, they engage in a role-playing whereby the imagery they project glazes over reality, so that in a self-amplification, in a tyranny over image, the role-playing self becomes the poet as Narcissus, increasingly lost in the cosmos which can be perceived only as a hall of mirrors. This, philosophically, is the Sartrean address to the other, a position which Sartre as philosopher thus translates by his aggressive arguments into an advocacy of direct action in the social and political arena. In this respect, Sartre's fiction serves a larger intentionality, though why he should be concerned beyond a self-entertainment in his private hall of mirrors becomes a question.

Marcel sees this contradiction early, before the popularity of Sartre in the Western intellectual community. And he anticipates for it a troubling end, for it can only lead to a more oppressive cul-de-sac to intellect than that experienced by the poets of the French Symbolist movement. What must rise in us in consequence of the Sartrean projection of the self against the cosmos (in a phrase from Marcel's "Preface") is a "religion of technics," the most destructive species of that tectonic manipulation to community being that of the sign's reduction and deployment in a service to self-love. It gives rise to "individualism in its most harmful form," exemplified among other ways by our intellectual fixation upon "examinations and competition in which our young people are struggling," whose rubric becomes "I must win, not you!" That is a "technic" – a process – which is "depersonalizing," insofar as through it one distorts that intuition whereby the person properly turns to another in that openness of love proper to his responsibility as steward. For that turning, if properly made, is toward an embodiment in community. Our principal presences through these pages – Augustine, Aquinas, O'Connor, Pieper, Marcel, and especially Percy in struggling for it – have spoken our desire for membership in that body, whose head for them is Christ, against the inevitable despair of alienation through self-love.

The openness of love to the other will lead, when *homo viator* is set aright in the here and now in quest of a perfection of unique gifts, to a recognition of the self not as a *void* such as posited by Jean-Paul Sartre, but rather as a *person*. He will recognize as well that (in Marcel's words) the "best part of my personality does not belong to me, I am in no sense the owner, only the trustee." The "self" is thus a gift of being, whose inherent responsibility is the person's becoming. It is, in this course of self-discovery, a multitude of gifts to *person* to which the "I" as their guardian is responsible as steward – responsible for a fruitfulness of his gift which is possible here and now through art in making. (Again, this is the theme I develop at length in *Making: The Proper Habit of Our Being.*) For it "is pure fiction to imagine a pre-existent self on whom these gifts were bestowed in virtue of certain rights, or as a recompense for some former merit." Here Marcel sets himself directly against Sartrean Existentialism: "I must puncture the illusion, infinitely persistent it is true, that I am possessed of unquestionable privileges which make me the centre of my universe, while other people are either mere obstructions to be removed or circumvented, or else those echoing amplifiers, whose purpose is to foster my self-complacency."

Such is the illusion of a "moral ego-centricity" which is deeply rooted in our nature and fertilized and watered by abstractionism as it were, in consequence of the Modernist triumph of the ego over the soul. But it is not the Cartesian motto *sum,* says Marcel, but *sursum* which is proper to *person* as opposed to the Modernist *ego* as the self-apotheosis. Thus Descartes's famous *cogito ergo sum* reflects what Marcel calls a reductionist "moral ego-centricity." The motto *sum* expresses the position of the "cynic," the dominant *ego* which would reduce others "to little machines . . . to examine and regulate according to his fancy." In this light, intellect itself becomes a "little machine" to be fine-tuned with signs Nominalistically derived. (Again, see Gilson's narrative of Descartes's arrogant pursuit of this philosophical final solution to his own *cogito ergo sum,* in Gilson's "The Cartesian Experiment," *The Unity of Philosophical Experience.*) In respect to the subsequent dominance of the Modernist sociologist as prophet in the public arena, for instance, he becomes a producer "employing the methods of an engineer." Even so, the person as person proves more resonant than if he were in actuality a machine. "How can we help seeing that the personality is not to be conceived of apart from the act by which it creates itself, yet at the same time this creation depends in some way upon a superior order?" In opposition to this reality stands the Modernist *autonomous intellect*, the term we have developed through these pages to characterize a self-declaration in an arbitrary *sum,* arbitrary in that it denies any "superior order" to its own. That we have discovered, has implicitly in it *non serviam* as the chosen opposition to any *other* than the self by intellectual actions. On the other hand there is our heretic to Modernist doctrine, the fallen *person*, whose fullness may yet be recovered by his turning to the immediate here and now in an openness of consensual love of that "other" as actual in itself because existing in consequence of a higher order. That is a turning toward a hope of joy, signaled by that motto for such a person: *sursum*. As person, "responsible for my own acts," rather than as "an anonymous unit of that anonymous entity 'one,'" the person may always turn in that openness to creation, recovering thereby the truth of what we have called his *connaturality* as seen in Thomistic metaphysics. And, we have also argued, it is a turning to the responsibility of "making," whether one be poet or philosopher, shepherd or tiller of the soil.

As Marcel summarizes his point: "What I have been trying to say is that the personality is only realized in the act by which it tends to become incarnate [in a book, for instance, or an action or in a complete life]." Thus it participates "in the inexhaustible fullness of the being from which it emanates," in order that it may approach to a "supra-personal reality" in that Eminent Perfection, its sustaining Cause. It does so through a deportment we have called the *openness* of love toward creation as holy, but not itself its own cause. Thus the *other* stands with the *self* in what Marcel calls "availability (*disponibilité*)." That is a response to a "call" – this deportment of openness – which "comes both from me and from outside me at one and the same time." And here we hear an echo of St. Augustine's discovery about the "self" in his *Confessions.* It is a call to a "knowledge of an individual being who cannot be separated from the act of love and charity by which this being is accepted in all which makes him a unique creature or . . . the image of God."

Marcel, then, is intent to recover us to life, acutely aware of his Modernist world's commitment to the "thanatos syndrome" so spectacularly displayed in the horrors of World War II. "What is the sign by which we can discover whether the personality [i.e., our "self" as *person*] is indeed surpassing and transcending itself or whether, to the contrary, it is falling back in some degree and sinking below its true level?" That is the "tragically acute" question to our moment, given the "fascinated and fanatical multitudes who . . . rush singing to their death." It is as if Marcel alludes here, not to some lines by Rilke, but to the note Eliot appends to those lines of the *Waste Land* beginning "Who are those hooded hordes swarming/ Over endless plains, stumbling in cracked earth/ Ringed by the flat horizon only." Eliot's note quotes Hesse from *A Glimpse into Chaos:* "Already half of Europe, already at least half of Eastern Europe, on the way to Chaos, drives drunkenly in spiritual frenzy along the edge of the abyss, sings drunkenly, as though singing hymns, as Dmitri Karamazov sang. The offended bourgeois laughs at the songs, the saint and the seer hear them with tears." The rushing to death has become the current "official gospel," dependent upon the "dismal and bare rationalism" whose effect can but be a "retrogression."

Against this rush to death, Marcel poses a quote from Gustave Thibon as guide, Thibon having recently preceded him in lecturing to the "Institut Supérieur de Pédagogie" at Lyons. Thibon, Marcel says, "admirably expressed the need for incarnation from which the personality cannot escape without betraying its true mission, without losing itself among the mirage of abstraction, without paradoxically reducing itself to one impoverished indigent form of the very *ego* it falsely claimed to surpass in every way." The remedy so aptly expressed by Thibon resists the increasingly dominant tendency of the theorist-consumer age, as Percy will call it at the end of his life when he seems more fully appreciative of Marcel's argument that he had first read so long before. The proper turning is toward the sacredness of the ordinary, he will then argue. And so had St. Augustine and St. Thomas argued. Gustave Thibon's words: "you feel you are hedged in; you dream of escape; but beware of mirages. Do not run or fly away in order to get free: rather dig in the narrow place which has been given you; you will find God there and everything. God does not float on your horizon, he sleeps in your substance. Vanity runs, love digs. If you flee away from yourself, your prison will run with you and will close in because of the wind of your flight; if you go deep down into yourself it will disappear in paradise."

And so this course of *homo viator* here and now, in this given time and place. A *becoming* to be distinguished from the randomness of deracinated man rushing headlong into death. *Here, now* – not *there* or *tomorrow*. For Percy the running away and the coming to rest, mischievously put, is from that corn-dance in a New Mexico desert to his perhaps sitting before the "idiot tube" listening to the Jungian blather about Joseph Campbell as philosopher, but in the end valuing as of infinitely more worth "ten boring Hail Marys" through which may be restored the holiness of the ordinary. It is in recognition of that holiness of the ordinary thing that we may at last recover ontological grounding in being, here and now. But it is a recovery necessarily made in the immediacy of "personal" experience of things. It is a recovery possible no doubt to the disoriented young woman and to her physicist man even on the fringes of a Corn Dance sponsored by the Chamber of Commerce or by the National Endowment for the Arts. How interesting that we should have arrived at correspondences between the prophetic philosopher, Marcel in *Homo Viator,* and the prophetic poet, Percy in his last novel *Thanatos Syndrome.* Both attempt to recall us from our headlong and even passionate embrace of what Pope John Paul – after them – calls in a now-famous phrase, the "culture of death."

From this imagined immediacy of Hail Marys in the proximity of the Modernist argument for a paganism represented by Joseph Campbell, projected to us out of what Marcel calls a "religion of techniques" so widely worshipped by a sacrilegious age as a virtual reality intent upon making incarnate by will a global village, let us turn to the rational metaphysics of St. Thomas, with the aid of recent and avowed Thomists, in order to reach a pause at least to our present attempt to "go deep down" into our "self" in a quest like Lancelot's, though ours be without the spectacle of heroism suitable to the art of that knight's quest. We shall perhaps thereby be better prepared not only to endure whatever Tupperware party or Prufrockian Tea party at which we may find ourselves guest, but even to celebrate within such circumstances, recovering a sacramental deportment that rescues us through grace beyond "technic" circumstance itself.

Afterword

In a fascination with the semiotic conundrum as spoken to by Peirce's dyadic-triadic theory, one may become too much entangled in theory, we have suggested, though Percy himself is also concerned to measure theory by experience. For most of us, experience confusingly tends to be based in having heard witness of such experience unself-tested, with the result that we may overemphasize theory as the measure of experience. That is the concern of St. Thomas which he wishes us not to forget: "The purpose of philosophy is not to learn what others have thought, but to learn how the truth of things stands," and a part of that learning requires bringing philosophy or science to the test of reality itself. The very desire not only to know but to understand is most tempting of excess. No wonder, then, Percy's fascination with Helen Keller's discovery of "water" from within her desert existence, in which exile she was at first denied signs. But what is to be recovered, in recovering an ontological orientation, is the elementary experiences in that desert. We have argued that this recovery is initiated through that immediacy to things in a communion through which the desert is to be discovered in flower. That experience of Helen Keller with actual water is effected through a mystery beyond the reach of science. For there is already a presence binding *homo viator* and *thing* in *being*, setting the person toward his ultimate helper, Being Itself, occasions (by grace) a movement, one consequence of which is the mystery of sign. Not hearing that resonant calling *through* things to which St. Augustine responds, man as wayfarer will continue to stumble lost in the desert, the reality of which desert is that it is a rich garden when seen in its transparency. Those words in the hymn "Amazing Grace" – "I once was blind but now I see" – are truer than metaphor when metaphor is taken only as fancy's tool. That is a witness Eliot makes in *Little Gidding,* in summary of his own desert journeying. As intellectual soul incarnate, he has discovered that the proximate end to the journeying is to truly see the place of an always present point of a new departure, to see that place "for the first time" in the light of eternity. That experience occasions an awakening, to which I recall witnesses, experienced by me in their signs. The first is that of the sophisticated poets, but the second witness to me is by my youngest grandson just as I am completing these pages. First, a resummoning of a poet already with us, one who is still critically taken as if primarily a "nature" poet. It was in mistaking him as such that the young skeptic T. S. Eliot found reason to reject him. Yet after Eliot's own fuller recovery of vision in the desert, whereby he sees *through* spectacle imposed upon it by Modernism, he catches fleetingly a transcendent vision. Then Eliot will come to praise this poet as a great "philosophical poet," William Wordsworth. We have observed along our way that Wordsworth testifies to having experienced "spots of time." A particular moment he leaves us as a signpost in our desert, his "Tintern Abbey." Consider the long, even dull, "historical" title he gives his poem. He does so to suggest the immediate context to his experience as actual and independent of signs till in contemplation he must use signs: "Lines Composed a Few Miles above Tintern Abbey on Revisiting the Banks of the Wye During a Tour, July 13, 1798."

This footnote to the poem's history reveals that the title is more deeply autobiographical than it at first appears as a history of our actual moment. The title is, for the poet, a personal historical marker, in relation to which as person he may subsequently measure his subsequent journey. (He had at first thought to call the poem an "Elegy.") Even so, the validity of any measure by signs so posted seems uncertain to him. And indeed after "Tintern Abbey" he falls away from that reassuring spot of time experienced on the banks of the Wye. He does not fall away as does Keats in minutes after his "one moment past." Wordsworth's is a more prolonged falling away, whose memorial of defeat is to be his "Ode on Intimations of Immortality from Recollections of Early Childhood." He will attempt to rescue a unity to that Ode, after writing the first four stanzas. After an interval of some two years, after having written the first four stanzas, he at last completes it, but he does so by depending upon fancy's forcing Platonic resolution upon the "glory and the dream" now fled from him.

Wordsworth up to his "Tintern Abbey" (like Hopkins or Eliot or Percy) is initially uncertain of the sign as it relates to experience, more confident of the experience than of any sign erected in relation to it. After all, there has been a general dislocation of sign from its ancient validity as certifying experience, an erosion of sign in the gradual devolution which separates sign from the immediacy of experience – out of the increasingly pervasive philosophical inheritance from Nominalism. The dislocation has been effected especially by a double scandal against reality: first, the Nominalistic dissociation of sign to the province of intellectual intent; second, a confounding of that disjuncture as experienced by Descartes's "doubt" as to whether the self exists at all. That was a doubt appropriated to the new authority of Enlightenment thought. Together, these dislocations gradually decay any confidence that the self is an actually existential thing, especially when thought centers centripetally upon the self by questioning any reality independent of thought. But, that fearful doubt aside, an appropriation of uncertainty may be used to encourage bolder and more radical selves to exacerbate the dislocation, to pursue under various mantras a radical *non serviam,* denying at last the givenness of *being*. Thus is prepared an interior ground to intellect in which it may cultivate autonomous power. To do so requires intellect to reject existential reality as independent of that doubting intellect, whereby intentionality jettisons as well the moral responsibility attendant upon thought. To accept moral responsibility is to accept as well a responsibility to sign, the responsible deportment calling in question the varieties of Nominalism abroad, each of which may be cultivated interiorly by an intellect to its own apotheosis of the "self." Hence, in rejecting that responsibility, the "self" also feels free to reject any reality as antecedent to its own actions as the cause of its own existence. And here, an ironical circumstance: in rejecting any outer reality, intellect proves in the end to have rejected itself as given. That Sartrean shell game with signs, designating by sign the self as initially a vacuum, is far more ancient than Sartre of course. What seems peculiarly "Modern" is the pervasive climate of such thought in social and political actions in our last century, against which we have attempted to summon oppositions in order to recover moral responsibility.

What if some late sojourner within this climate of the world as restricted to Modernist doctrine should stumble upon a desire for and the necessity of recovering to himself the sign as bonding *homo viator* in ontological ground? He may look about him, confused by the current state of social and political man, whom he observes wandering in aimless circles shouting his aimlessness to be a progress. Such loonies appear in this moment's arrest as circling lost in the cosmos. They themselves seem to have largely reduced all gardens to desert. Such a wanderer arrested by that spectacle, standing aside for a moment in contemplation, might well consider himself a questor like Lancelot, though discovering himself also a citizen and social integer at a Tupperware party sponsored by "Enlightenment" intellects. A large party, at which are gathered consumers to share fragments of the world, in preservative plastic containers out of the "technic" largesse of theorists who join (or seem to join) the festivities. But as confused as such a waking heretic to Modernism may be, he may also sense himself as having discovered a heady wine seemingly desert-sprung – a wine quite other than that proposed as rising only from within the self-feeding vineyards of intellect when the garden of being has been carefully walled from the world by gnostic visions. Thus *walling* is confused with *freedom* and pursued as the only absolute serving autonomous intentionality. That is the party milieu in which such a traveler, graced in his seeing as *homo viator,* must reclaim his common sense and re-educate it, refusing to be cowered by either a wishful Cartesian Idealism or a truculent Nominalism succored by dreams of power over being. He recognizes the Tupperware party for what it is in itself, which is not what the party-goers may suppose it to be.

In this conditioning, this re-awakening to reality, our traveler will find himself tensionally held nevertheless. On the one hand, there is the promise of his recovery, especially through bread and wine (St. Thomas or Marcel or Pieper would say). But on the other hand, recognizing the lost stumbling selves all about him, he might well suppose himself also alienated from them in this stumbling world, caught up in aimless currents of his own illusions. He may well, in such an Either/Or world, be tempted to despair. Even so, that is a despair which might, at an unrecognized depth, take its origin in the first stirrings of compassion in him

– a waking love. He may be more saddened than angered by recognition of lost selves all about him. That, Percy might agree, is a first movement of an ex-suicide. How may he speak *loss* to the lost? Perhaps by indirection, given as common and immediate with those lost others only inherited signs radically decayed, though they radically dislocated by neglect or by deliberate abuse. They may even have become opaque (as Voegelin says of them) and so for "self" convenience stored in the attic of memory. Such signs, dissociated from reality, were seen by Eliot as symptomatic of a "dissociation of sensibilities," a separation of "thought and feeling," affecting poetry adversely. He will subsequently discover the "dissociation of sensibility" as fundamentally not an aesthetic but a spiritual dislocation of the "self."

That is a response to the symptomatic level (Eliot will later conclude), made academically popular by Phenomenological Philosophy since the late 19th century. The root cause of the dissociation lies in a willful separation within intellect itself, a dissociation of the rational from the intuitive, as if these were antagonistic hemispheres, which divisions of the brain in pursuit of the mystery of thought and feeling have been so thoroughly explored in the bicameral physical organ. The imagined antagonism, the Thomist might suggest, prevents the wholeness of intellect as a simple "sphere," to translate metaphorically into current scientific terminology which labors to comprehend mind itself. What is missing from such mind-set as focused on the mechanics of the brain is any sense of a predilection to a spiritual recovery in that "mind," a reaction to the reductionism which declares as a principle of Modernist faith that thought is an *effect* of the *biological* brain. In relation to the full dimension of intellect itself to our understanding, the biochemical ground of speculative psychology is not irrelevant but it is a subordinate concern. For the question rises: can accidents of the symptomatic – signs out of dissociated sensibilities, in their sad accidental state as thus limited – serve toward signifying loss to the lost? What the heretic to Modernism will conclude is that the abiding sense of loss to the person can be explicated only superficially at the mechanistic level of dissociation.

Perhaps by an indirection (in which wit deploys signs satirically, while the deploying intellect itself assumes the role of the physician as novelist) the poet may pry open the closed speculative arena of Modernist reductionism and so allow ancient truths about our spiritual nature to once more participate in resolving mysteries of the "mind." By that "fiction" of signs, concerned in its depths for the health of the soul, there is allowed a reaching of thought itself beyond any simple dead-end concern for the *body* or for the ever popular *psyche*. Something might – must – be at least attempted. Not as a life-restoring "operation," but (in Percy's intent) at least an autopsy of the dying "self": that seems possible, or so it does to Percy. Perhaps one might even prompt a reflexive response, out of a recognition of the horror of man as pictured by distorted thought (separate from man *experienced* in all his looniness). More is involved than accidental spectacle. By such speculative recovery, one might come to suspect man a spiritual creature, drifting without a spiritual grounding in the holiness of things.

One might hope that by such a ruse he may aid lost selves to remove obstacles to the miracle of grace, first in oneself and perhaps then even in some other "self." That is, one might possibly escape despair through hope recovered. That, indeed, is the concern Percy must have discovered at least intuitively in Marcel's *Homo Viator: Introduction to a Metaphysics of Hope*. Of course Marcel proceeds directly, not indirectly, in his autopsy of the Modernist psyche, and with a most subtle scalpel. Especially relevant to his incisive judgment is that extended lecture we have introduced, his "Sketch of a Phenomenology and a Metaphysics of Hope," which explores intellect to depths which one finds metaphorically expressed in St. Augustine's "Philosophy of Memory" in the *Confessions*. Marcel eschews the satiric, as Percy embraces it, though both share a genuine concern for revealing the lost to themselves. It is in this common concern as approached differently through signs (each according to his peculiar gifts, St. Paul would remind us) that one may see Marcel as important to Walker Percy, who is on his first encounter of Marcel a wanderer suspended between hope and despair.

With this likeness in unlike artists, revealed in their signs as a continuing guide we inherit, both prove devoted to the truth of things. We may quote a passage from Marcel's argument that a *metaphysics* of hope lies beyond any reasoned *science* of hope to see them companionable, his words suggesting how closely the two are in accord on the point. Both see that empiricism disregards limit, contributing thereby to the gradual separation of the self from reality through the presumption of a freedom from limit justified by autonomy. Thus Marcel: "A systematised empiricism, crystallised into impersonal and permanent formulae, could confer upon what is in truth only a movement of the soul, a retraction, an inward disloyalty, the theoretical (and fallacious) justification which such a step needs in order to establish itself in its own eyes." Thus the truth of things already known may be dislocated by formulation, by an absolutist empiricism, leading finite intellect to its presumptuous conclusion: it *determines* truth itself. Marcel adds that, "Against this combination of temptations there is only one remedy, and it has two aspects: it is the remedy of communion [with things, out of which rises] the remedy of hope."

If Percy turns increasingly to Hopkins as poet – a poet we have argued as himself acutely attuned to reality through his communion with things – it is the German poet Rilke to whom Marcel himself turns, as we observed. *Homo Viator* concludes with those two long explorations of Rilke as a "Witness to the Spiritual." In the concluding pages of the concluding lecture, Marcel praises Rilke, especially those *Sonnets to Orpheus*, as revealing a remedy possible to a world already rapidly disintegrating all about Marcel, even though the great war is over. As World War II was drawing to its close, Europeans, and especially Frenchmen, have seemed held by the "image of a disintegrated God," which image proves only a projection of the disintegrating self imposed upon that world, for it is the self which has gained a false apotheosis. All about him is "the spectacle of a disjointed world where it does not even seem to be given to most of us to discern all the scattered currents of confidence which are ever issuing from the very heart of real things," those things speaking to us (as they did to St. Augustine) and so inviting us "to a reintegration of the human and of the divine." It is in responding to this holiness of small things, fragmented as they seemed even to Rilke, that Rilke bears his anxious witness to our loss of the spiritual as Marcel argues. In his poems, then, lies evidence to us that the heaviness in us is not a heaviness of the world, for that heaviness is "not in things but in us." And that recognition is the beginning of hope.

In a considerable portion of his *Homo Viator* Marcel explores Rilke's waking from that heaviness, finding in him

> the reverential love for the created which men of my generation have seen drying up before their eyes in so many souls doomed to aridity in the most miserable desert of self-adulation. The mechanised world thus becomes also the world of pure consciousness [the world of the theorist-consumer], that which burns without giving any light and gives light without any warmth. Thus we see a gulf widening between the masses who are literally *denatured* [as mere appetitive consumers] by a more and more inhuman way of life, and a very small company of super-naturalised elect [the theorists] whose life's foundations are more and more fragile and unsteady and who for this reason are in danger of falling a prey in the end to the most fatal mental disorders, and the worst collapse.

This is a passage one might use in explication of Percy's summary term, his name for our age as the Age of the Theory-Consumer. Each (the theorist and the consumer) makes the other burn down without light or warmth to the detriment of the mystical body of mankind – that body in which they are properly ordered by discrete intellect itself as each a person, a divine "thing" because created. Each intellect therefore is rightly employed by stewardship of things – especially to be recovered the "self" to that body of a community in being whose head is Christ.

What does common sense as opposed to philosophy or science serve? It begins to recover to the wanderer in this Modernist desert, through reflection complemented by contemplation as we have adumbrated *contemplation*, the old sad history of the radical exploitations of created beings through "systematised empiricism, crystallised into impersonal and permanent formulae." That empirical action is to be – not abandoned but recovered to an accord. Recovered from the now dominant philosophical theory of self-justification which rises out of Enlightenment authority whose principle is self autonomy as the only absolute. (Gilson comes to this conclusion as well in his *Unity of Philosophical Experience,* remarking Bertrand Russell as an end, where Marcel sees it in Sartre.) From the poet's situation at the close of the 18th century (Wordsworth our exemplum), Enlightenment rationalism seems to have succeeded in calling into question metaphor itself and so making sign suspect to the poet. Likeness in unlike things, once made a dependable aid to a metaphysics oriented by the concept of connaturality, provided confidence in an ontological ground: that is the telling loss to philosophy. Metaphor, says the triumphant rationalism, is only a species of fancy, a decayed version of an old outmoded Nominalistic authority whereby man created God anthropomorphically. It is in Modernist terms only a wishful thinking by intellect and so unrelated to the prime (though accidental) *matter* of the cosmos upon which rationalistic Nominalism practices its latest magic art: the art of a transformation of being itself through Logical Positivism as the ultimate authority. Poor John Keats, then! What wonder that he will declare that the "fancy" cannot cheat so well as she had been famed to do in those olden, pre-Shakespearean and pre-Chaucerian days.

Keats makes his own failed attempt to recover reality through metaphor, despairing of his failure to do so despite his initial intimations of connaturality through his experience of the nightingale's song. That "dreamed" moment seemed somehow to echo mysteriously a likeness between himself and that bird. He is left destitute, void of any likeness experienced through communion with the bird through its song as sign, or with anything that seems to exist outside his isolated self. That illusional experience he can credit at last only as his own interior and isolated "fancy" out of desperation. We have remembered that some years before this nightingale encounter, Wordsworth too had found himself uncertain about sign in relation to his desire for a recovery of accord with creation. Then came his own arresting experience, one which Josef Pieper would describe (on the evidence of Pieper's *Happiness and Contemplation*) as a contemplative moment of reunion with created things as bearing a hidden manna. Wordsworth's witness is "Tintern Abbey." In the reflective aftermath of his experience on the banks of the Wye, the haunting problem of metaphor's authority intrudes upon his thought, though he would prefer not to have to think about it. Indeed, he laments having lost that old circumstance to him of his "thoughtless youth," which in Thomistic terms we might call the experiences of intuitive communion with things in sacramental moments. But now questions rise in the signs of "Tintern Abbey." Do signs bear a relation to the world, a relation which – when properly recognized by thought – is independent of intentionality, though "fancy's" intentionality may attempt to force a "world" upon the cosmos (as Wordsworth will himself attempt to do in his later "Intimations Ode")? By allusion here, we bring to bear Percy's semiotic concern for signs as imposing a "world" upon the "cosmos," to recall his earlier concern for self-dislocation attendant upon an address to sign. There, in Percy's early engagement, the address is counter to the implications of responsibility to the "cosmos" born out of a recognition of and a growing understanding of existential reality – the complex of creation calling *homo viator* to a stewardship, and through an ordinate stewardship (made ordinate by thought's educating common sense) to Beatitude. That is a recognition of having already been fed by grace antecedent to the waking particular consciousness as it falls away in sensing a separation in thinking, the thorn in intellect we may call inherited as "Original Sin." But in so recognizing the conditions to him as created, he may with hope journey creation as *homo viator*.

In this experience of a contemplative moment and its aftermath, what Wordsworth calls a "spot of time," there is for us each a context to reflection upon St. Augustine's memory rationalized in *The Confessions*. It is limited to the responding consciousness by its willed relation to the thing it engages. There is no necessity of a party to be gathered about this triadic experience such as Peirce (and Percy at first) proposes. For that experience is both actual and already beyond any merely dyadic reductionism of human nature. There is no necessity of another, a third listener, to the colloquy of *this* person and *this* thing. Wordsworth in his response to his own particular present experience (in "Tintern Abbey") is at first moved by a nostalgia for a state which *might* appear a dyadic one: a state in which as "thoughtless youth" he now remembers himself to have been "like a roe" bounding over mountains and beside rivers, led by "impulse" and freed of the necessity of thought and so of sign. Or so it seems *now* to *have been*. But now, thought intrudes to engage that youthful state in nature, to riddle memory toward understanding. In retrospect, those were actions "more like a man/ Flying from something that he dreads, than one/ Who sought the thing he loved." We have suggested another "reading" of this remembered experience: an active "contemplation" in the sense of *contemplation* as developed by Josef Pieper.

"Tintern Abbey," then, records a reflective moment in which the consciousness speaking the poem juxtaposes a present experience to a memory of past experiences – all gathered within a common context of place at a specific time, on the banks of the Wye at noon. That is itself a species of metaphor in thought. These are early and late encounters of a self with things in creation. In this moment of contemplation, there appears no necessity to thought of signs shared with some other, even at this late date – in 1798 when Wordsworth is in the middle of his way. Not that any *other* is intentionally excluded, as Marcel suggests to be the subversive intention in our role-playing. Indeed, in the literal circumstances to the experience, Wordsworth is accompanied by his beloved sister Dorothy. But it is only at the end of that contemplative poem that the poet's words rather abruptly acknowledge her presence, as if only at that point he *remembers* her actual *present* presence. That is in a moment of doubt, the visionary "spot of time" itself thus endangered by a newly intrusive speculative thought about the future, again recognized through metaphor.

The metaphor involves a middleness which implies an end, a thought of death. For the Wye River empties into the sea. He stands, removed from the ocean into which these present flowing waters will empty, despite any backward effect of the actual tide on the River Wye. Those once "deep" and "lonely" streams – upstream from this present place as it were and remembered from youth – had spoken even then of more than water, rushing as they did to some terminus. At the end of the poem, Dorothy proves reassuring by her presence as read by the poet. She is an external certification of the validity of his thought on his own past experiences. Wordsworth addresses her directly in thanksgiving for the witness of her own response to this place at this time. It is evident to him through his sensual perception that she (five years younger than he) now responds to this present experience as did he five years ago when he first visited this place. It is as if by this return he has seen this place for the first time. Dorothy's eyes sparkle in evidence of her communion with these things of nature, in such a way that he concludes her present response his five years ago. He is on the verge of a mystery about time, perhaps, which Eliot will engage in those openings of *Burnt Norton*.

Likeness and unlikeness in experiences of unlike yet like things suggests a reality beyond the merely speculative or wishful thought, such thought which may assume itself independently empowered by sign to a transcendence. Nominalistic intentionality, even an intentionality to a nostalgic arrest of the journey in creation itself, is insufficient. Wordsworth we remarked first considered calling this poem an elegy, a lament for the loss of that state of "thoughtless youth." But what has become necessary *now* and *here* is a reconciling through thought of the realities of those old past experiences to these present experiences of creation. There *had* been those past moments, *now* remembered, in which he had experienced being "laid asleep/ In body" to become "a living soul," thus granted through that harmony with things a vision. He had then been enabled to "see into the life of things," that old experience yet resonant to a present reflective thought. *Now* he is reassured of the reality *then*. Such experience was not an illusion born of wishful thinking. Now by thought he is once more attuned to creation in this present moment, in which he remembers the interval. And so now he is enabled "oftimes" to hear the "still, sad music of humanity,/ Nor harsh nor grating, though of ample power/ to chasten and subdue."

For the first time, Wordsworth can acknowledge having experienced a "presence" through those past experiences, a presence which enfolds him and the things he engages even now, despite the shadow of death falling on thought. It is a presence which "impels/ All thinking things, all objects of all thought." How like, this witness of Wordsworth by his signs, to that argument Pieper makes about the nature of *contemplation* as a triadic moment, a moment of sacramental communion of consciousness and thing requiring no second "party." In Wordsworth's reluctant acceptance of the necessity of thought, in order that he might reach an accord with experience, we have at least an echo of that epistemological argument from St. Thomas which holds intuitive intellect as preferred, as making possible a perfection of intellect through the complementing reason. For the most disturbing aspect of Eliot's "dissociation of sensibilities" as symptom of Modernist dislocation lies in the consequent discord within the person himself of the intuitive and rational modes of simple (i.e., unified) intellect itself, a diverse operation of intellect properly complementary. Wordsworth's "thought" as sign of the *ratio* complements his remembered intuitive experiences of actual things, things known with an immediacy through the *intellectus*, the intuitive, though sometimes problematic to the *ratio*. But under the burden of thought's necessity, Wordsworth now discovers that sign itself aids ratio in a recovery of accumulated experiences into a present. Sign bears witness to a reflective intellect as it summons the "dead" past to a living presence, an old past to the *now*. Thus may sign serve as valid signpost toward a recovery in creation, here and now, a recovery from radically decayed intellect which has been increasingly besieged by the seemingly empty desert and under that pressure susceptible to a "dissociation of sensibilities," a separation of thought and feeling. The very manipulation of signs consequent upon Nominalistic and Cartesian dislocations of the self from reality may thus be overcome.

This, then, proves not only a circumstance complicating thought about memory to Wordsworth as it will to Eliot, but also to that would-be diagnostic physician Percy, for whom the sign must be somehow a key, a compass needle in the cosmos guiding a gravity of spirit itself. Such distinctions as we have argued out of Wordsworth's attempt at an accommodation of his own "triadic" experience of consciousness and thing, conjoined by a "something deeply interfused," speaks a sublime "something" bonding the two. That is a recognition not to the fore in Percy's early speculation. For Percy's fascination with Peirce's version of the triadic turns him from such remembrance of things past. We are saying (once more) that Percy could but somewhat distort the mystery of sign by his concentration upon a science of signs, to which science the sign is at last unyielding of its mystery. Better the assurance of shared presence in a communion with things whereby for a moment we may even be laid asleep in body and become a living soul. The body itself may wake then into living, rescued from appetitive ends, from "consumer" reductionism as ultimate.

We may take Wordsworth's subsequent account of the circumstances to his poem in relation to its actual composition as accurate. These words, he says, he composed as he walked away from a noonday pause under the shade of a sycamore, he and his sister Dorothy at last finding lodging for the evening. That evening he set down the already composed words. What may interest us here is a pattern of metaphor in that dull title he gives the poem. His thought about a moment under a sycamore at noon summons signs to his musing contemplation as he walks the English countryside toward evening shelter. It is a reflective revisiting in which the actual experience of a moment just past, under that sycamore tree, was quite independent of the signs now articulating it. Though a moment past, in remembering he seems less falling away from the visionary moment than does Keats's as he stands in embalmed darkness, increasingly falling away from a seeming transport by the nightingale's song. Thought moves over memory as the eye had moved over the landscape lying before Wordsworth at high noon, he in *shadow* under the tree in his still-point. When Wordsworth sets down his title to the now recorded poem, he could not have escaped a coincidences of *middleness* to his experience. In the middle of the day, in the middle of a year, which by calendar measure is in the middle of his own life (given three-score and ten), in the middle of a stream which he recognizes as only slightly affected this far upstream from the ocean by the tides: all this middleness speaks both a beginning and an end. It is a moment of vision, a coming to himself under that shading tree, in a recognition that signs, however one may account for them, are not to be arbitrarily imposed as Nominalism would have it. Nor can they be rejected arbitrarily as related to that reality called givenness. The meaning in full of his moment's arrest he has not riddled to its end, but it has been an experience reassuring on his journey. Even the signs seem proffered in relation to something larger than thought's uses of sign. There will follow in Wordsworth's subsequent "history," we have anticipated, a radical falling away from this moment's reassurances, a growing doubt about his own reality as a consciousness – as what Percy would call a "self." It is then that he will turn to a forced impositions of sign in an attempt to recover the old vision he once had on the banks of the Wye. That is the poem we yet value, his "Intimations Ode," though intimating (intuition) and reason make it tonally an elegy.

Remembering Wordsworth's Ode on "recollections" from "Early Childhood": that is the circumstance to experience which I summon in my second witness to the danger in our intellectual entanglements by semiotic theories. Indeed, my witness is here at hand as I write these last signs: my infant grandson who, an hour ago, came up our walk in his mother's arms, excited to recognize me and to show he can almost say "bird," as one flies up. A comic tangent, inescapable to me but one I cannot *now* share with this infant, though I trust I shall. I can now, nevertheless, recall with amused pleasure, if but to my "self," the poignant and satiric play Flannery O'Connor makes with this same sign *bird,* learned by the retarded child-woman in her story "The Life You Save May Be Your Own." (One might, indeed, play this fictional scene against Helen Keller's joyful learning of the sign *water.*) In the O'Connor story, the diabolic theorist Mr. Shiftlet manipulates that "angelic" creature (trapped as it were in intuitive "life") through teaching her to say "bird." Her mother wants Shiftlet to teach her quite another word: "Teach her to say 'sugarpie,'" she urges. For the mother is anxious to be rid of the burden of this grown woman who, retarded, is a child in mind. Uneasily, if also amused, I remember both Helen Keller and O'Connor's Lucenell Crater as my grandson stutters his word. I know myself to be possibly my grandson's "Shiftlet" so to speak, though with no diabolic intent to a manipulation on my part.

He and I have already shared a recognition of the creature bird before this struggle to say a name. Months ago I saw him see and become fascinated by a brown-thrasher wallowing in dust in the driveway. In that moment, he was quite oblivious to my own presence, though when the bird flew away, he turned to share his experience – for which he had no sign save what his eyes said. (The drama here is an echo by analogy of Wordsworth's experience caught in "Tintern Abbey.") This morning, making plosive sounds recognizable as an attempt to say "bird," he turns to look in the trees around us. And, moments later, encountering our friendly cat come out to greet him, the same excited sound in witness of an experience itself quite independent of sound, a recognition of a *particular* creature *alive* in his encounter of it. It is in this recognition of a *thingness* alive that excites wonder in him. First awe, then wonder stirring him toward signs. He turns to a prospect of words, to share his exciting experience of some other. But his is already a triadic experience, this is to say – one anterior to any sharing with me by stuttered sign. He would share it with his mother and with me, standing on our front porch now. But the witness he would bear, as we have contended, is of a triadic experience already intuitively known as triadic, though he cannot *say* its cause as already lying deeply within his own created, given, nature.

It was a triadic experience antecedent to his turning back now to a remembered dependence on us, attempting sign as witness to an experience independent of our presence. His, save for a poverty of sign in him, I believe was a triadic experience not unlike that which has been witnessed in signs by that consummate user of signs, Gerard Manley Hopkins: a witness to *consummate* moments, actual experience precedent to the sign; experience recovering to Hopkins a "something" both larger and deeper than the principals involved: himself and any discrete thing. The experience he now witnesses by sign was of the holiness of the thing triadically known, implying his knowing already the Cause of its holiness. If we would name my grandson's experience of the brown-thrasher in relation, it might be called one of those moments of *contemplation* as explicated by Pieper out of St. Thomas, though more simple and direct than such moments may come to be for him in his growing sophistication – his recognition of creation as multitudinous of things, and so commanding his reason to a sorting of the orders of beings according to whatever gift latent to his intellect, a sorting in the light of natural law. It is such a moment that Wordsworth attempts to recover, though he tends to a forcing of signs. It is a communal moment at last in this time at this place, but not *determined* by such specific circumstance. For that reason, the "differential" between my relatively inexperienced grandson at one-year-old and my own relatively experienced endurance at seventy-plus years – past all my days in this dark world and wide by Milton's reckoning – is not relevant to our own determining the validity of his or of my moment of love – our present communion with each other out of communion with things precedently, with cats and birds, here and now. Such are thoughts without words yet, as he comes into my old arms with joy.

From a Thomistic perspective upon this journey of the physician-novelist Walker Percy (or of my grandson's coming up our front steps, for that matter) we see *homo viator* devoting himself to diagnosing his own speculations on the nature of nature as it were, especially concerned to register speculation in signs along that way. We may, then, feel a certain relief when we listen to Percy at the end of his life pay tribute to "The Holiness of the Ordinary" (1989). He begins by observing that it is "hard to think of a great writer more Catholic than Dante or Chaucer and less self-consciously 'Catholic.'" Then once more his old admonition: "Novelists are a devious lot, Catholic novelists more than most." But then he remarks that the Catholic faith is of a "particularly felicitous use to the novelist."

Indeed, one could do no better if he set out "to design a religion for novelists." That is so because, unlike other "world religions," its emphasis is on "the value of the individual person."

This is the Christian view of man, "a creature in trouble, seeking to get out of it, and accordingly on the move" as journeyman toward the infinite. But no longer is that journey for Percy so simply expedited by that creature man's proficiency of self-rescue through the sign. It is rather the *sacraments* that become the telling resolution. Man – Western man as Modernist – has gotten into trouble (we have argued) precisely through a flirtation with autonomy, a faith in the power of signs over nature to impose a world on the cosmos. That is the intellectual gambit subversive of a sacramental deportment to the holiness of things. For thus man reduces himself from a sacramental deportment to things as Divine by electing the illusion of his own absolute freedom. At this late point, then, Percy speaks of the sacraments, not of Peirce or of the dyadic-triadic – the "Delta" – solution to man's being lost in the cosmos. The "sacraments, especially the Eucharist, . . . confer the highest significance upon the ordinary things of this world, bread, wine, water, touch, breath, words, talking, listening. . . ." It is through the sacraments that man discovers his predicament and his dependence. He "is on the move in a real world of real things, a world which is a sacrament and a mystery." He moves through the created "world" not through an ambiguous "cosmos." He is a "pilgrim whose life is a searching and a finding." As a Lancelot, we might adduce, he is capable of discovering the holiness of the ordinary, even at a Tupperware party. Even in watching a brown-thrasher dust-bathing, or a cat coyly pretending indifference to the presence of persons.

The vision thus recovered is the "recipe for the best novel-writing from Dante to Dostoevsky," and even that "excellent atheist novelist . . . Sartre borrows from this traditional anthropology for the upside-down pilgrimage of his characters into absurdity." And so in the end, "ten boring Hail Marys are worth more to the novelist than ten hours of Joseph Campbell on TV." To borrow from Eliot once more, Percy like Eliot's Magus in his journeying arrives at evening, "Finding" his "place." "It was (you may say) satisfactory" – that stable-cave in that old, but also even back then "Modernist," world at Bethlehem. The place is an enfolding holy world, not an amorphous "cosmos" with the self a random center. The spiritual macrocosm writ small in the microcosm of a stable-cave in Bethlehem, an enclosing parenthesis so small and yet holding the cosmos. A world not made by man through his signs, which signs prove always contingent in all places. And even man's own words themselves prove always to bear a Presence, an Incarnate Presence, through Whom the holiness of the ordinary may be certified to the created intellectual soul incarnate – the wayfaring person in a moment of a truly triadic communion. Even by denial, that certification proves implicit – as reason itself at last discovers.

Its most celebrated celebration, the Mass, is through bread and wine, the most local of the local to the intellectual soul incarnate. In those creatures occurs a drawing of all creation into a reality, on the tongue or on the open palm. That is a moment, a still point, at the center of creation, a presence *here* and *now* which is paradoxically (to finite intellect) to be granted as also comprehensive of creation in a mystery beyond all signs. Certainly that must be granted by the Christian. Georges Bernanos sums our own tentative recognition of that revelation to finite person in his own visionary moment: "All is grace." In the light of our explorations in pages past, then, we ponder a formulation of signs: As Jean-Paul Sartre's *Nausea* affected Percy and his fiction, setting him on a painful way toward Bernanos's conclusion, Georges Bernanos's *Diary of a Country Priest* assured Flannery O'Connor from the outset. The spiritual contest, involving good and evil, must be engaged. Not that she, like Percy, does not provide loony spectacle along her own way. Both at last, or so we pray, were sustained by that good news to the wanderer: All is grace. So too, we must pray as well that these others whose company we have kept in these pages, at the imagined Tupperware party thrown by Modernist ideology at this way-station to *homo viator,* may be transported by grace, by mercy. Even a Will Barrett or so unsavory a character perhaps as Mr. Head or Hulga or any Misfit.